D1082930

Democracy and
Its Discontents
in Latin America

Democracy and Its Discontents in Latin America

edited by
Joe Foweraker
Dolores Trevizo

LYNNE
RIENNER
PUBLISHERS

BOULDER
LONDON

Published in the United States of America in 2016 by
Lynne Rienner Publishers, Inc.
1800 30th Street, Boulder, Colorado 80301
www.rienner.com

and in the United Kingdom by
Lynne Rienner Publishers, Inc.
3 Henrietta Street, Covent Garden, London WC2E 8LU

Library of Congress Cataloging-in-Publication Data
A Cataloging-in-Publication record for this book
is available from the Library of Congress.
ISBN: 978-1-62637-276-4

British Cataloguing in Publication Data
A Cataloguing in Publication record for this book
is available from the British Library.

Printed and bound in the United States of America

The paper used in this publication meets the requirements
of the American National Standard for Permanence of
Paper for Printed Library Materials Z39.48-1992.

5 4 3 2 1

Contents

Tables and Figures

Tables

Figures

Acknowledgments

All of the key steps leading to the creation of this book depended on the generous support of Occidental College, first and foremost through Dean Jorge González and the Marie Young Fund, and later also through the college's Latina/Latino and Latin American Studies program. The college supported Joe Foweraker's first talk on "Democracy and Its Discontents in Latin America" in February 2012, a one-day workshop that followed in February 2014, and finally his most recent visit to Occidental College in February 2015, when he spoke on human rights and worked with Dolores Trevizo on the book. We are grateful to Occidental and to all of the colleagues at the college who helped us put the project together and deliver it in good order.

Many of the chapter authors participated in the 2014 workshop, endorsed the project as it emerged, and remained committed throughout the subsequent planning and editing stages. Others were recruited later to achieve a more complete and balanced collection. But they all engaged openly and responsively with the editorial process and were equally professional in approach. So we wish to record our thanks to the authors, not just for doing their job, but for doing it in such style. We also thank Min Yoo for her help in formatting the manuscript and putting together the unified bibliography.

For us, it has been an exciting and fruitful project that has continued to generate fresh ideas and open up new horizons. The conversation between us—hundreds of e-mails and hours of Skype—has been a happy one.

Joe also wishes to thank the Center for Latin American Studies at the University of Florida at Gainesville, where he was the Bacardi Family Distinguished Visiting Scholar in 2012 and first began to ponder the discontents.

Dolores would like to thank Warren Montag for his support over many years.

1

Democracy and Its Discontents in Latin America

Joe Foweraker

In a broad comparative view, Latin America is the great success story of the third wave of democracy. All the countries of the region, with the exception of Cuba, have now enjoyed relatively stable democratic government for at least twenty-five years and, over that period, the rhythm of their political life has been set by regular schedules of competitive and reasonably free and fair elections. Yet this democratic revolution seems to have brought scant satisfaction, either to professional observers of Latin American politics—academics, survey specialists, nongovernmental organizations (NGOs)—or, more importantly, to the increasingly mobilized peoples of the region. Indeed, the progress of democracy in Latin America has been closely accompanied by increasing discontent with the cumulative outcomes or record of its democratic governments. While the motives for this discontent may vary over time and across countries, it appears that there is a palpable dissonance between the democratic aspirations of the demos and its experience of democratic governance, a discontent with the content of democratic government itself.

This pervasive sense of discontent is distinct from the many and diverse political struggles of the 1990s and early 2000s that expressed a certain confidence in the capacity of mobilized civil society to improve the quality of democratic government, and still more so from the optimistic era of democratic transition that preceded them. Moreover, the discontent persists despite some notable achievements over the years in procedural democracy and in its policy outcomes—indicating that the earlier optimism was not entirely groundless. On the one hand, the vote has been extended, contested elections have continued, and the military has been removed from politics almost completely. On the other, poverty has been alleviated and even economic inequality reduced in some instances. But in large degree, these achievements have recently been outweighed by three major problems that together explain the pervasive and persistent discontent: first, executive overreach; second, corruption and lack of accountability; and, last but

1

nowhere least, citizen insecurity. Possibly only the first of these requires some elucidation here.

It is clear that incumbency confers an increasing advantage in electoral competition across the region, an advantage that can be damaging to democracy when combined with an extended or even indefinite mandate for the executive. In times past this problem was thought of as peculiar to sub-Saharan Africa, if not exclusively so, rather than Latin America—with the scandalous exception of Alberto Fujimori in Peru. But times change. In Argentina, the Kirchners first tried to finesse term limits by passing the presidency between them and then, following the death of her husband, Néstor Kirchner, Cristina Fernández de Kirchner tried unsuccessfully to extend her mandate against the ruling of the judiciary. In Bolivia, Evo Morales persuaded the Constitutional Court not to count his first partial term on the grounds that the rules had changed in the interim, and few are convinced that he willingly will step down at the end of his current (second but, in fact, third) term. In Colombia, Álvaro Uribe Vélez tried for a third term, but was blocked by the independence of the Supreme Court. In Ecuador, Rafael Correa has easily persuaded a compliant Constitutional Court to wave through the abolition of term limits to allow him to run for office again in 2017 when his current term expires. Although the opposition is mobilizing around a referendum to stop him, the final decision will rest with the equally compliant National Electoral Commission. In Nicaragua, the opposition was complicit in Daniel Ortega's power grab and the abolition of term limits in January 2014, just so long as its major figures could continue to pursue their business interests without interference. And notoriously, in Venezuela Hugo Chávez succeeded in extending the executive mandate indefinitely in 2009, a prerogative now enjoyed by his successor. All of this suggests that the continuity of the electoral cycle does not everywhere contribute to spreading democratic norms across the political system but, on the contrary, may lead to political polarization and a loss of system legitimacy. Indeed, the strength of the tendency has led to rather bizarre calls for democratic transitions to return government to a more procedurally constrained and openly competitive form of democracy.

The problems of endemic corruption and radical and widespread citizen insecurity tend to go hand in hand, largely because both of them derive in large part from a lack of accountability in the democratic regimes of the region, and especially in their criminal justice systems. The evidence in support of this proposition is now overwhelming, and it finds further and ample confirmation in the chapters assembled here, demonstrating beyond doubt that these problems are ubiquitous, however much they may vary in degree and scope across national boundaries. Naturally, attention tends to be drawn to the most recent or notorious cases, whether in Argentina, Brazil,

Mexico, Venezuela—or even Chile. But subliminal corruption and insecurity of the kind that is present throughout the subnational governments of Peru, for example, may be just as serious in their effects as high-profile national failings. One lesson to be drawn from this is that a Manichean view that demonizes some governments while extolling others makes little sense, in that all these governments suffer from similar symptoms and face analogous challenges. Thus, there seems to be little doubt about the lack of accountability, political polarization, widespread criminality, and citizen insecurity in Venezuela, but it must be recognized that the Mexican regime suffers from all of these in equal or greater measure while the degree and reach of political violence and insecurity were greater still in the Colombia of Uribe, albeit in circumstances of armed insurgency against the regime.

Accordingly, there is more than enough evidence of the failings of these democratic governments—both occasional and pathological—to provide good reason for the discontent, though it should be recognized that this picture may be overdrawn or distorted in some degree by the predominant academic preoccupation of recent years with the quality of democracy in Latin America. Since the premises of this body of research—and the universal measures that derive from them—are drawn either from a descriptive and ideal-typical version of the established democracies of the West (or less frequently from a normative model of a classically liberal democracy), they tend to reach largely unfavorable judgments on democratic governance in Latin America. Indeed, the judgmental tenor of the enterprise tends to focus first on the failings and only later, if at all, on the successes of these governments in meeting considerable challenges, both political and economic, despite the institutional and cultural constraints inherited from the past. More importantly the deployment of speciously objective criteria for judging the quality of democracy can justify the ignorance of these constraints—the exclusion of any sense of historical and cultural context—and, consequently, any consideration of the distinct nature of democracy in Latin America.

The Nature of Latin American Democracy

Taken together, the chapters assembled here provide a balanced account of the democratic record to date that encompasses both failings and achievements, both the bad news and the good news. But the chapters aspire—each in its own way—to move beyond this descriptive tour d'horizon to analyze and explain the variations in the record by reference to the nature of democracy in Latin America. Unsurprisingly this notion of a distinctive nature is interpreted differently by our different authors, with consequences for their subsequent analysis, but these interpretations tend to fall into three distinct approaches. The first approach adheres quite closely to the received notion of the quality of democracy and focuses on the breadth or fullness of the contents of democratic government and its effectiveness in delivering its policies and securing its goals; the second sees the nature of democracy in terms of the specific model of democracy adopted by different countries of the region and the political aspirations and practices that follow from it; the third understands the nature of democracy to be shaped by deep historical patterns of state formation and development. It is clear that these different approaches are not mutually exclusive and may intermingle in the analysis and argument of each chapter, but it is useful to look at them separately before bringing them together.

The core question that informs the first approach is, Just how much democracy are we getting? Although democracy now appears to be securely embedded as the default form of government in Latin America, recent developments in some countries of the region have led some scholars to doubt the fulfillment of the basic requirements for democracy that comprise the institutional machinery of electoral politics, a differentiated political party regime, and reasonably free and fair elections that can make a plausible claim to be able to change the composition of the government. These features represent the minimum measure of democracy imagined at the time of the democratic transitions but are now seen as under threat in some countries, notably Venezuela and Nicaragua, and—as emphasized above—in many more countries if an extended mandate, even an indefinite mandate for the executive, is seen as a significant retreat from the minimum measure. Beyond this minimum, the concern is with the breadth of the democratic remit, whether it promises social rights and basic welfare in addition to individual and minority rights and protections; and whether policy is concerted to address problems of poverty, inequality, and uneven educational opportunity. Last but possibly most pertinent is whether democratic government is delivering on its commitments, however narrowly or broadly defined, and here the outcomes are often counterintuitive—or at least contrary to what might reasonably have been predicted at the time of the transitions. While the reach and impact of social policy of different kinds have greatly improved overall in the past couple of decades, the regime of civil rights and protections has drastically eroded over the same period, with insecurity the dominant public issue nearly everywhere in the region.

The second approach is mainly concerned with what kind of democracy is emerging across the countries of the region and what kind should be preferred, for this is a question that is hotly debated by the intellectuals, politicians, and political publics of Latin America. In many instances, the question is stereotyped into a simple choice between two divergent models. On the one hand is a more or less traditional model of liberal and procedural democracy, where political parties do their usual job of translating the preferences of an amorphous political public into policy platforms that eventually become government policy and programs after being subject to the discussion and deliberation enshrined in the legislative process. On the other is a more participatory and possibly less pluralist model that maintains electoral politics, but favors forms of more direct representation combined with a stronger and often more enduring executive with increased powers and greater legislative initiative and capacity. In the context of the so-called pink tide, which ushered in an era of speciously left-wing government in Latin America, these two models are often distinguished by a greater or lesser concern with poverty and inequality, an emphasis on either group and minority rights or individual rights, and the delivery of social welfare packages either to mobilized political constituencies or to individual families through Conditional Cash Transfers (CCTs). In fact most countries of the region have maintained a fairly stable and centrist economic and social policy mix for many years now, combining fiscal discipline with moderately progressive goals of redistribution. The key difference is in the model of government itself, pluralist and subject to institutional checks and balances versus plebiscitary and mobilizing, with legitimacy derived either from democratic procedure or from charismatic appeal and popular acclaim.

For the third approach it is the historical context, both political and cultural, that is all important for the nature of democracy and, in particular, a patrimonial pattern of state formation—to use Max Weber's language—where the state is shaped by oligarchic and eventually corporate interests in a way that blurs the divisions between things public and things private, so preventing the establishment of a legal-rational authority that can regulate these divisions and defend the republic, or res publica. As a consequence, the democratic regime can only ever be one part of the political system (not coterminous with it) and only one source of political power, and will always be constrained in its policy reach and capacity to tax by the structured inequality that derives from the direct insertion of oligarchic interests into the structure of state. There is no claim here that this circumstance is static or immune to political protest and struggle. Indeed, it is the emergence of civil societies and the mobilization of political publics that have underpinned the democratic revolution of our times. But there is no doubt that these variegated or combined and uneven political systems strongly influence the scope and modus operandi of current democratic regimes, not least the multiple combinations of formal and informal rules that are so often required to make democracy work and that, in the realm of high politics and especially executive-legislative relationships, tend to create trade-offs that privilege governability over the democratic principles of representation and accountability.

The analytical premise of this latter approach assumes an explicit distinction between the state on the one hand and the democratic regime on the other, thereby suggesting that the apparent failings of the democratic regime may—in some instances at least—be attributed to state incapacity or state constraint. This complicates the application of the accepted normative model of liberal democracy to the democratic governments of Latin America because core democratic values tend to resonate differently in the context of combined and uneven political systems, and often have different empirical references. Thus, autonomy is a fundamental principle of the normative model, expressing the belief that each individual citizen must be presumed to be the best judge of their own best interests. But autonomy in the Latin American context tends to be either a negative reference to the collective autonomy of the military or the police (often vested in the democratic constitution) and the political license that flows from it or a more positive reference to the collective autonomy implicit in minority rights and prerogatives, and especially in recent decades to the autonomy of indigenous communities. Similarly, accountability (and representation to the degree that it is a sine qua non of accountability) sits at the center of the normative model because the primary purpose of democracy is to make government accountable to the people. But in Latin America, it is the lack of accountability that is central because the oligarchic and corporate interests inserted into the carapace of the state resist accountability wherever possible while their presence at the apex of clientelist networks of different kinds tends to vitiate the working of accountability within the democratic regime. One notorious if clichéd reflection of this systemic failing is the lack of any word for "accountability" in the Spanish or Portuguese vernacular.

These three approaches to the nature of democracy have been treated separately for the purposes of exposition but, in the chapters that follow, they tend to be mixed and matched or layered according to the topic and the objectives of the inquiry. This has the virtue of bringing together and, in some instances, connecting things that are often kept apart such as the normal politics of procedural democracy and populist politics, or the low politics of social mobilization and the high politics of legislative coalition building. It also has the virtue of not just recognizing but often highlighting the malleable and dynamic qualities of democracy in Latin America, with democratic institutions, practices, and values all evolving in sometimes different directions (in addition to sometimes advancing, sometimes retreating), at different rhythms, and differently too at national and regional levels. As a result of this dynamism, there is considerable variation in the institutional composition and quality profile of these democratic governments that creates a rich resource for comparative inquiry across both time and space.

The chapters in this book deploy these analytical perspectives in different ways and degrees, and use their own particular methods to explore the nature and current condition of democracy in the region. But they are all consistently comparative in approach and they all tend to address the same broad set of core issues—in response to our editorial brief!—and, hence, share a common thematic content (as I illustrate below). These common themes allow the chapters to be divided into two broad descriptive categories that comprise, first, a section on state and regime that encompasses institutions, policymaking, and accountability; and, second, a section on citizenship that focuses on rights and representation. Inevitably, there is some degree of overlapping if only because the chapters tend to bring together things usually kept apart on the understanding that analytical insights are often achieved at the orthogonal and tangential intersections of the political system overall. By way of illustration, much of the pressure for change (as well as resistance to it) in these political systems and in the composition of their democratic governments has come from a rising tide of social mobilization and protest across the region over the past two decades, a process of mobilization that has expressed not only economic and social demands but, increasingly, legal and constitutional struggles for increased representation and accountability. It may appear remarkable, therefore, that no chapter is exclusively dedicated to the topic of social mobilization, but only because many of the chapters do address the topic as an important element of their overall analysis.

The Thematic Content of the Chapters

State and Regime

The first section of the book opens with my own chapter, where I state the reasons for my belief that the quality of democracy in Latin America cannot be properly understood without a clear sense of the nature of this democracy. In my view, what determines the quality of democracy in Latin America above all else is accountability—or the lack thereof. The deficit of accountability so often observed in the governments of the region can be best explained not merely by the mode of democratic transition, but especially by the process of state formation in Latin America as well as by the structured inequality that expresses the consistent but variable influence of oligarchic and corporate interests in this process and their tendency to resist accountability wherever possible.

Yet the political systems formed in this way are not fixed or static, but rather beset by a rising tide of social mobilization that pushes for change and has some degree of success in increasing access to the political arena of institutional representation, and even in changing democratic institutions—

as the democratic governments of the region seek to respond to an autochthonous perception of a crisis of representation. But unsurprisingly, attempts at reform are often captured in the legislatures by the same oligarchic and corporate interests, thus leaving the root problems of representation and accountability unresolved. In some cases, this may lead to populist insurgencies that inveigh not only against the parties in government, but against the *partidocracia* in general. Whether this happens or not, it is noteworthy that political crises in contemporary Latin America do tend to exhibit a systemic dimension with extraordinary, but often constitutional, measures required for their resolution. Consequently, both party and popular leaders often come to see the constitution as the key to a more democratic politics and defend their reform projects in these terms, especially insofar as they concern rights and representation.

In Chapter 3, David Doyle takes up and explores the question of accountability by looking at its variation across the region as viewed through the prism of public policy making and asking why some governments are effective agents of the citizenry, providing effective public policy through channels of accountability and representation, while others remain predatory, producing policy that is ineffective and sometimes harmful. He argues that the causal link between citizens' preferences and aspirations on the one hand and effective policy on the other is state capacity, as reflected in a consistent and uniform defense of the rule of law, the provision of public goods, and an ability to gather enough tax revenue to fund these attributes. Consistent with my own arguments above, the variation in state capacity is then explained by different trajectories of state formation and the subsequent stickiness of state institutions; however, Doyle also suggests that the colonization of state institutions by oligarchic and corporate powers is expressed in Latin America today through political parties that are personalist, clientelist, and largely unconcerned with policy effectiveness.

In Chapter 4, Melissa Ziegler Rogers looks at the same issues through the lens of modern political economy, beginning with the question of inequality—which is germane to both Doyle's argument and my own. In a groundbreaking analysis, she divides this question into interpersonal and interregional inequality before looking at the effect of both on democratic institutions. Her first important finding is that interpersonal inequality drives government spending up (presumably to address the social consequences) while interregional inequality drives it down. This represents a difficult disconnect between regional demand for distribution and its eventual supply. Rogers then goes on to explore the impact on democratic institutions, especially electoral systems, some of which are more attuned to interpersonal inequality (strong centralized party systems with broad social constituencies) while others are more regional in orientation, with more particularistic connections between voters and local representatives. The latter systems reflect the presence of strong regional oligarchies with regionally bound ambitions and preferences—an analysis that connects directly to Doyle's investigation of the variation in state capacity and policy effectiveness. Add legislative malapportionment and what Rogers calls "enclaves of subnational autocracy" and distributional policies are rendered ineffective because regional autocrats capture a large share of any interregional transfers that then fail to reduce overall inequality. As suggested, her argument dovetails at several points with that of Doyle, and reminds us that the quality of subnational democracy varies far more across Latin America than that of national democracy.

In all of these chapters, there is an implicit recognition of the importance of institutional reform for effective policymaking and accountable government, and of the political and cultural constraints that make reform so difficult. In Chapter 5, David Pion-Berlin addresses these concerns directly by shifting the focus from vertical to horizontal accountability and seeking to answer the central question of how to make the military more accountable to freely elected democratic governments. The question is central because—given the long history of military intervention in the region and the recent experiences of the four countries under scrutiny, namely, Argentina, Brazil, Chile, and Uruguay—the survival, development and quality of democratic government depend on it. For Pion-Berlin, the answer to the question lies in institutional development and design and, specifically, in the reform of the Defense Ministries in these countries and beyond, with the Ministry of Defense being the "key link in the chain" of accountability. He demonstrates notable improvements in design in all four cases and this is good news for democracy, but Brazil and Uruguay tend to lag behind Chile and Argentina because of the delegation of vital tasks to military agencies and personnel, so attenuating and clouding accountability. In his account, there is no single overarching explanation for the variation across cases that rather depends on country-specific institutional histories and features.

In Chapter 6, Gerardo L. Munck pursues a similar line of inquiry to those of Doyle and Rogers insofar as he addresses the variation in the form and degree of representation, accountability, and the effectiveness of public policy—but now as refracted through distinct models of democracy. For Munck, the democratic transitions of the 1980s and 1990s did not settle the question of democracy but, on the contrary, made it yet more salient. The concern for a minimal standard of democracy that had motivated the transitions remained but, in addition, a new concern with the development and deepening of this democracy arose—and transformed democratic politics. In particular, the divide between those who supported and those who opposed neoliberalism—the key axis of ideological conflict—spurred the emergence of different and in some respects opposed models of democracy, with implications for how democracy developed and, in extremis, whether it would endure. After first describing the main models to emerge, Munck goes on to examine the record of four political and ideological actors—right, center-right, center-left, and left, both in government and out—to assess their impact on the basic rules of electoral democracy as well as on the core institutions of democratic government. Coinciding with the analysis of both Doyle and Rogers, he argues that the main points of contention between the models tend to turn on the questions of inequality and, by extension, of what to do about the oligarchy; he returns to my own core concerns when pointing up the implications for constitutional reform and reformation and the defense of accountability. Munck's detailed and differentiated account leads him to conclude that the central issue is not the presence of opposing models so much as the way in which some political actors—regardless of the model of democracy they favor—accentuate a top-down form of governing that suppresses the roles of parliament and the extraparliamentary opposition. This raises the contentious question of whether the democratic governments of Latin America have in fact governed democratically; he refers, in particular, to those cases of left government where efforts to build an alternative to liberal democracy have gone furthest because this is where the conflicts between government and opposition are most bitter.

In Chapter 7, Javier Corrales picks up the inquiry at this point by examining the experimental alternatives to liberal democracy in Venezuela, Bolivia, Ecuador, and Nicaragua—in particular, their radical projects of participatory democracy. These are understood as a response to the popular rejection of the partidocracia and the public perception of a crisis of representation, whereby democratic governments are made unaccountable to the demos. Early in the life of these projects constitutional reformation extends rights to previously excluded groups, so promising stronger vertical accountability, but at the same time vitiating horizontal accountability by constraining institutional checks and balances and hobbling those autonomous actors in civil society with some capacity for contestation. The growing strength and invulnerability of the executive leads to increased state intervention and regulation, a more autocratic style of policymaking, and a retreat to social conservatism. In consequence, where some measure of participatory democracy subsists, it tends to be partisan and polarizing (seeking not to include, but exclude opposition elements of all kinds) while representation overall is further curtailed—with accountability more apparent than real. In an interesting tangential argument, Corrales notes the increasing dependence of these speciously national regimes on international finance capital with their governments obliged to put the interests of foreign capital above those of domestic social actors through reconstructing conservative ruling coalitions comprising foreign capital, domestic banks, large landowners, mining corporations, and the military. In this way, he assimilates these specific cases to the more general analyses that precede his chapter; paradoxically, the effort to reconstitute the nation in the name of the people eventually invites the return of an even less accountable oligarchy.

Citizenship

In Chapter 8, Todd Landman sets the scene for the section on rights and representation by putting together the big picture of human rights across the region over the entire period of democratization from the 1980s to the present. Democracy is one story. The other begins with the Inter-American Commission on Human Rights and the Inter-American Court of Human Rights, which together constitute the second most developed regional system for the promotion and protection of human rights in the world. Landman first sets out to compare measures of both democracy and human rights, carefully distinguishing the institutional from the rights dimensions of democracy, to discover that there is a strong association between the two in Latin America, if a far from perfect fit. He then explores a series of explanations for the patterns emerging from his statistical description and analysis, emphasizing political and contingent influences over structural explanations deriving from trajectories of socioeconomic development. Clearly, there remain obvious and often depressing gaps between rights in principle and rights in practice, disparities between legal protections and the lived experience of the citizenry, and a long way to go politically before most countries approach anything like a secure rights regime. But there are also significant improvements in the record over recent decades and greater availability of legal redress for public wrongs. In sum, despite the pessimism of the intelligence required for any informed reading of human rights, Landman concurs with the conclusion to my own chapter in choosing to emphasize the optimism of the will that drives the continuing political struggle to make rights a democratic reality in Latin America.

The chapters that follow all flesh out the bones of the big picture in different ways, beginning with Jennifer M. Piscopo's investigation in Chapter 9 of the state's role in promoting quota and more recently parity laws for women's representation in national legislatures. Impressive progress in this direction has been made almost everywhere, the most glaring exceptions being Venezuela and Guatemala; and Piscopo makes effective use of the analytical distinction between negative protections from discrimination and positive rights enshrined in law through constitutional amendment to counter the skeptical view that this is all just lip service, *para inglês ver*—a view that is anyway belied in large degree by the evidence of quota diffusion. In this regard, the state ties its own hands (the point of all constitution making in some degree) and commits governments to a proactive enforcement of legal provisions—which simultaneously provide pathways to legal redress. For this reason, the proportion of female legislators in Latin America rose by 15 percent between 1990 and 2015; this successful push for greater gender balance in political decisionmaking clearly improves the quality of Latin American democracy and stands as an unalloyed good news story. In one instance, Piscopo looks forward to Jane S. Jaquette's discussion of complementarity versus equality (see below) when noting that in Mexico the push for quotas and eventually parity supersedes the restrictive and often oppressive practices implicit in *usos y costumbres*.

In Chapter 10, Jaquette poses the difficult question of whether a plurinational democracy that encompasses local autonomy for indigenous communities can address a crisis of representation while protecting human rights and fostering social cohesion. Her answer focuses on the conflict between indigenous identity politics and women's claims to equal rights and the end of gender discrimination. The indigenous view contends that gender complementarity protects and values women as women while Western notions of equality violate important cultural norms, and that outside interference, whether by the state or NGOs, has created a problem that was never part of native culture. Most feminists retort that the blatant discrimination and violence against women within indigenous communities leave them marginalized and vulnerable, and conflict with core liberal values of individual rights and protections. These positions appear hard to reconcile and any solution hard to come by, especially if indigeneity is understood as a moral and holistic stance that enshrines the sui generis nature of the community against the feminist and liberal projection of universal values. Jaquette sees real autonomy as a bad outcome for indigenous women while simply waiting for cultural change to occur through enhanced communication and mobility offers no affirmation of liberal values. But if gender oppression can achieve equal salience with those of class and race, then perhaps it may be alleviated in some degree with a more effective and inclusive rule of law.

In Chapter 11, Neil Harvey adopts a very different perspective on indigenous communities and peoples by beginning with the novel indigenous mobilization of the 1980s and 1990s. Although the focus here is usually on the emergence and impact of new ethnic parties and organizations, Harvey sets out to redress the balance by examining the internal practices that sustain or erode them. He understands the initial electoral mobilization as a response both to neoliberalism broadly writ and to the political manipulation of the traditional parties while the variable success of indigenous parties in achieving constitutional reform depended—inter alia—on a willingness to broaden their political agenda and engage in political coalitions beyond their indigenous heartland. A primary dilemma of electoral participation—even if successful in winning reform—is the potential loss of autonomy and corporate protections, yet there was no guarantee that refusing participation would offer any better prospect. In this regard, the Zapatista insistence on autonomy was—at least in some degree—a frustrated response to the lack of constitutional reform, but Harvey's examination of the internal organization and governance of the Zapatistas' liberated areas shows impressive democratic advances that in his view offer important lessons for democratic governance more generally. For example—recalling the conflicts central to Jaquette's chapter—Harvey invokes the Zapatistas' concerted efforts to resolve gender disparity and discrimination so as to counter perceptions that women's rights and indigenous cultures are incompatible. But possibly the lesson of his story is that the compatibility is a consequence of the Zapatistas' transformative project—a combination of Jaquette's cultural change and affirmation of liberal values.

Many of these chapters refer to the changing nature of party systems in Latin America (Doyle, Chapter 3; Rogers, Chapter 4; Munck, Chapter 6; Corrales, Chapter 7), but in Chapter 12 Will Barndt addresses the issue directly by switching the analytical focus to the question of party building; whereas Harvey is concerned with building indigenous parties through social mobilization from below, Barndt looks at how corporate interests build them from above. The majority of parties across the region have converged on an electoralist or campaign-oriented model with campaigns their predominant raison d'être but, since campaigns are expensive and traditional resources scarce and dwindling, the process of party building is increasingly driven by the need to maximize private sources of financial support. This has led to a proliferation of classic conservative parties with broad core constituencies in the business sector but, in some instances, individual business leaders or their conglomerates have built their own parties that draw directly on the assets and infrastructure of the business, so spawning the emergence of what Barndt calls "corporation-based parties." For Barndt, the rise of this electoral conservatism has a range of potentially negative consequences as policy choices are narrowed and nonprivatized parties are forced to seek shadowy and possibly corrupt sources of funding, so destabilizing and delegitimizing the system overall. In this way, electoral conservatism may precipitate a more populist politics—as Corrales would agree—as party systems are increasingly shaped by a reversion to forms of competitive oligarchy; and Barndt's self-conscious use of this phrase from Robert A. Dahl's *Polyarchy* connects his chapter directly to the dominant themes of the first section of the book.

The ultimate two chapters of this section are both Mexico centered—though still maintaining a fully comparative perspective—and concerned with the question of legitimacy, one of the more slippery concepts in the study of politics. Roderic Ai Camp's point of departure in Chapter 13 is the ambitious reform agenda of the current Institutional Revolutionary Party (PRI) administration in Mexico and, more important for his purposes, the pragmatic strategy that has sought to garner broad political party and legislative support for this agenda. This unprecedented degree of cooperation among the elite actors of Mexico's high politics has the potential to deliver a far-reaching package of political reforms that could transform Mexico's economy and society. But the endemic violence within Mexican society and the pervasive corruption of its legal and political systems may yet place the effects of the reform in check as well as continuing to erode the quality of Mexican democracy. In this view, the greater degree of trust among the country's political party elites that leads to greater governability sits in stark contrast to a marked deterioration of trust in the core institutions of democratic government and in their capacity to solve the public's most pressing problems. Support for democracy in Mexico is now at an all-time low. So the paradox is the declining legitimacy of the system even as it begins to deliver what Doyle might call "effective public policy." This is an important finding for our understanding of democratic quality in general, for it demonstrates that the aspects or dimensions or values that comprise democratic quality do not necessarily move in the same direction to create a uniform improvement or deterioration in quality but, on the contrary, some may improve while others deteriorate, so changing the quality profile or mix.

In Chapter 14, Dolores Trevizo begins to unpack this paradox by developing an original approach to the question of legitimacy that focuses in the first instance on one of Mexico's most trusted institutions, its armed forces. Her rigorous comparative analysis demonstrates that there is significant variation in that trust across space and over time. Furthermore, comparisons of two time periods (the first following the dirty war of the 1970s and the second following the beginning of the war against the drug cartels in 2006) across different states of the federation reveal how past experiences of military abuses serve to construct a collective memory that continues to impair the legitimacy of the system in the present. It is also true that current and recent rights violations tend to reduce the previously high levels of trust in the armed forces, but the legacy of the past remains strong. At the same time—paradoxically once again—there are continuing calls for repressive action to restore law and order, but the benefits of such action are a lot less apparent to those suffering the violations or close enough to witness them. These effects are specific in the sense that the public is clearly capable of distinguishing poor system performance owing to a lack of resources from institutional incompetence and abuse that degrade the quality of citizenship. The consequences include significant legitimacy deficits at the local level and the emergence of fragmented loyalties that leach legitimacy from the system overall.

In conclusion, it may be helpful to recall that the thematic content of the chapters in this book derives first and foremost from their empirical focus on democracy and its discontents. Thus, while all the chapters certainly address the nature and current condition of the democracies of Latin America, their primary concern—clearly manifest in the chapters by Camp and Trevizo—is with the lived experience of the citizens of these democracies as measured by the fulfillment of their aspirations as well as by their wish to be rid of tangible evils. Hence, the chapters in the first section on state and regime seek to assess the degree to which the inner workings of government and, in particular, the process and outcomes of policymaking succeed in attaining the primary goal of democracy, which is to make government accountable to the people. Then, the chapters in the second section on citizenship examine the practical progress of the rights enjoyed by the citizens in principle; the degree to which their views and preferences are effectively represented within the political system overall; and, last but not least, the consequent impact of all this on the political legitimacy of the region's democratic governments.

It was Dankwart Rustow who referred to "the wish to be rid of tangible evils" as the main motor of the "prolonged and inconclusive political struggles" that nearly always pave the way for democratic transitions (1970: 352). In his seminal essay, Rustow argued that the achievement of democracy did not depend on "functional requisites" so much as on strategic agency, a proper sense of the autonomy of politics, and purposive action over at least one generation and often more (361). These insights were largely vindicated by the ensuing third wave of democratization, yet today the lessons of the third wave make it quite clear that the moment of transition is not the end but only the beginning of the process of democratization, not least because transitions cannot provide complete or enduring solutions to tangible evils. Hence, insofar as the governments of Latin America remain unaccountable, the progress of rights partial and imperfect, the views of the citizens undervalued or ignored, and democratic legitimacy diminished by corruption, insecurity, and poverty, democracy will continue to be assailed by its discontents. One generation on from the third wave, the prolonged and inconclusive struggles continue—and will continue into the foreseeable future.

2

The Characteristic Contradictions of Democracy

Joe Foweraker

Over the years, my approach to the quality of democratic government has reflected a clear operational decision to choose liberal democracy as
the yardstick, rather than participatory or social democracy, let alone democracy tout court, and has also sought to distinguish the question of quality from
that of government efficacy in general. So rather than assessing government
performance in providing national security or social welfare, or seeking
measures of legitimacy and system support, it has focused on the values that
are intrinsic to liberal democracy such as participation, representation, and
accountability. In other words, it sees democratic quality as a clearly normative question concerning the degree to which liberal democracies achieve in
practice the values to which they subscribe in principle (Foweraker and
Krznaric 2000).

This approach assumes that democracy requires liberal constitutionalism, so encompassing both the procedures for electing governments and the
goals of elected governments. By extension, a poor quality democracy may
sometimes be attributed to failings of liberal constitutionalism rather than
any imperfection in strictly democratic procedure.[1] This assumption is not
unproblematic. The confluence of liberal thought and democratic discovery
(or rediscovery) reflected a unique set of historical circumstances that
resulted in the very particular historical product that is liberal democracy. It
may be unrealistic to expect democracy to be reproduced in this form across
time and space (even supposing different genealogies are at work) so the a
priori inclusion of liberal constitutionalism may be alleged to prejudge the
question of democratic quality. In other words it may represent nothing
more than an Aristotelian assertion of what constitutes "good government"
with the notion of the "good life" it supports heavily circumscribed by history and culture.[2]

Methodologically, these are problems of commensurability—of providing any kind of comparative yardstick—rather than problems of a normative
approach per se. But this approach was rejected by Joseph Schumpeter as

"so patently contrary to fact" (1943) and subsequently by Robert A. Dahl's *Polyarchy* (1971) in favor of a descriptive approach that derived an ideal type of democracy from the main features of established democracies, principally the United States and the United Kingdom. Thus, these governments set the standards against which all others would be judged, with the unfortunate if unforeseen consequence that their own quality was deemed good or worthy by definition. Hence, it transpired that the scales of democratic quality constructed first in *Polyarchy* and then by Freedom House throughout its life have tended to measure the quality of such established democracies as both relatively uniform and superior to that of democracies elsewhere.[3]

Practically speaking, neither a normative approach nor its emphasis on liberal constitutionalism poses any particular problem for the comparative study of democratic quality in Latin America. Although the norms are rooted in the tradition of natural philosophy that recognizes rights as inherent to us in our condition as human beings (an understanding that informs contemporary notions of human rights and the international human rights agenda), the approach can easily encompass the regional variation in civil and political rights that corresponds to culturally specific legal and rhetorical traditions that are configured by particular processes of political struggle. However, here as elsewhere, the substance of rights depends on their cultural anchors and the shared cultural understandings that inform them (Habermas 1985).[4]

But there are objections to the parsimony of a normative model that precludes any consideration of social and economic inequality, or indeed poverty or welfare or any other concern that is exogenous to the model. In its defense, it is argued that the relationship between democratic government and inequality has always been indeterminate with no government, democratic or not, ever able to shift inequality curves in any perceptible degree (Pareto's law), while questions of social justice in general are always fiscally contingent. The familiar riposte in communitarian political philosophy is that democratic values like political equality are difficult or impossible to achieve in conditions of extreme social inequality because the poor are not only poor in income but in health, dignity, political knowledge, and, hence, any sense of political efficacy (Almond and Verba 1965).[5]

In large part, this methodological debate turns on a view of inequality as an external fact of political life susceptible to objective measurement on single uniform scales such as the Gini index whereas in reality it is structured socially and politically by different forms of corporate and oligarchic power. And in Latin America as elsewhere, it is political oligarchies that do the most to constrain the public sphere of democratic politics,[6] which is consequently cross-cut by clientelism, cronyism, and corruption[7] in ways that impact directly and indirectly on the quality of democratic government.

It will be seen below how the political structure of inequality in Latin America has been shaped by its particular pattern of state formation, with predictable effects on democratic representation and accountability in particular.

This structured inequality is supported and reproduced by property rights, so creating a conundrum for a normative approach to democratic quality. That is because liberal democratic theory always views the right to property as an important civil right,[8] and for good reason insofar as it promotes the plurality of power (Dahl 1998, 2001) and serves to constrain the scope and mode of state action. As such, it is included in most measures of democratic quality. But civil rights are in general universal and inclusive whereas property rights are exclusive, and often violently so. Indeed, it is often the defense of property rights (whether in land by traditional oligarchies or in more opaque instruments of financial value by modern corporations) that leads to the direct infringement or outright violation of other civil rights.[9] But the more pervasive and indirect impact of such inequality can be traced through its structural support for clientelism and the subsequent dissolution—at least in part—of the separation of the public and private spheres (and with it, the possibility of a political and cultural defense of the res publica), so slicing through the horizontal and universal claims of democratic rights with vertical and particular claims of patronage, fealty, and power.[10] The conundrum therefore remains and reflects the ambiguities and contradictions of democratic politics in Latin America—which I now proceed to explore. The general lesson—here and throughout—is that no consideration of the quality of democracy can advance far without investigating the nature of that democracy.

Constitutionalism and Accountability in Latin America

Arguably, the primary political purpose of liberal democracy is to make government accountable to the people. Accountable government was scarcely to be seen in Latin America in the 1970s, when just three of its twenty or so republics were democracies. By the late 1980s, all these republics were democratic—with the exception of Cuba and Mexico—but it was the democratic deficiencies of these governments that attracted most academic attention and, in particular, there was little conviction that they were truly accountable. Furthermore, it was widely accepted that the deficiencies did not derive from imperfections of democratic procedure so much as from failings of liberal constitutionalism, and that it was often too much democracy—in the form of unbridled majoritarianism—that did most damage to accountability. These concerns were encapsulated in Guillermo

O'Donnell's seminal statement on "delegative democracy," which meant little or no accountability between national elections (O'Donnell 1994).[11] O'Donnell went on to address the problem of an overweening executive—the main manifestation of delegative democracy—through the distinction between vertical and horizontal accountability, with the former kept largely intact through the ring-fencing of elections but the latter impaired by executives who subverted the constraints of liberal constitutionalism (O'Donnell 1999c).[12] Without effective checks and balances, there are no institutional means to hold government to account between elections.

O'Donnell's original analytical insights continue to inform current concerns about the extensive use of decree powers in some countries, with the judiciary sometimes subordinated to the executive, often through the packing of Supreme Courts (Argentina, Nicaragua). Even the redress of past abuses by authoritarian governments through processes of transitional justice—or, indeed, for current abuses committed in combatting armed insurgencies or drug barons or any other threats to national security, real or imagined—has proved uncertain and partial.[13] And delegative democracy has emerged full-blown in the "competitive authoritarianism" (Levitsky and Way 2010) or plebiscitary democracies of Venezuela, Ecuador, Nicaragua, and—in a more mediated and contested context—Bolivia. So it is worth pondering why it continues to prove so difficult to hold governments to account in Latin America, before proceeding to examine the consequences of this accountability deficit.[14] The four main explanations that follow should not be seen as mutually exclusive, but rather as overlapping and mutually reinforcing.

The Original Sins of Democratic Transition

By any measure, the process of democratic transition in Latin America represented a massive political challenge. For by definition, these are not the slow accretion of the attributes of polyarchy over decades or even centuries but, on the contrary, a rapid assumption of the full polyarchy package, no cherry-picking allowed. And it really matters not whether the package is seen (often from the left) as too permissive (lacking essential communitarian components) or too exigent (making it unlikely that any political system will ever fully embody it), it was simply a lot to take on all at once.[15] For this reason, but not only for this reason, these were elite-constricted and pacted transitions, and most accounts acknowledge that the pacts and settlements that underpin them were intended primarily to protect oligarchic interests and so bind oligarchic actors to the democratic outcome (Karl and Schmitter 1991). Consequently, the transitions tended to squeeze the ideological and policy spectrum, and did so more from the left than from the right in conditions of major economic and social inequalities combined with economic downturn, a politics of austerity, and neoliberal policy prescriptions that worked to deepen the inequalities as well as dismantling or at least diminishing state institutions and agencies, so reducing an already partial and often fragile state capacity to achieve civil order and implement social and welfare policies.

State Formation

Democratic transitions are a matter of regime change, but these original sins must be interpreted within the larger historical process of state formation. The mainstream political science of recent years has tended to focus exclusively on the regime rather than on the political system of which it is a part, so ignoring the state, as if the matter of the democratic regime exhausts the matter of politics writ large. In this way, democratic theory has come to colonize a bigger political world, now masquerading as political theory tout court. The problem, to put it simply, is that this theory will then assume that normal politics—and the democratic policy process in particular—is manifest and accountable within a pristine and uncluttered public sphere that is ensconced within a homogeneous democratic system. This world of opinion surveys, political platforms, party competition, ideological debate, civil contestation, and lively lobbying and maneuvering by pressure groups, NGOs, and civic associations is an imagined Habermasian sphere of communicative action (Habermas 1985) that is the context of pluralist theory's definition of democratic politics, uncontaminated by corporate power and ignorant of the presence of the state.

But the process of state formation in Latin America makes this portrait of the public sphere empirically dubious—or possibly just plain wrong—because it leads in typical fashion to the construction—in Max Weber's language—of a patrimonial state where the dividing line between public and private is consistently blurred and often porous. Hence, the state is not constructed and defined as a legal-bureaucratic and neutral arbiter and enforcer of rules but, to the contrary, is so far shaped by particular powers that it is incapable of policing the division between private and public.[16] It follows that the modern political systems of the region encompass and combine a public realm of often lively and highly contentious democratic politics with a private and patrimonial realm of oligarchic powers. This involves a democratic politics that is in principle public, responsive to public opinion, and committed to political equality through universal individual rights (so requiring that political power be made accountable) combined with an oligarchic politics that is private, protected from political representation, and rooted in the particular ties of clientelism and nepotism (so seeking immunity from accountability).

In this context, corruption occurs where public offices or public resources come to serve private purposes so appropriating the commonweal for private use; this is one reason why republicanism or the achievement of a res publica has proved as elusive as the establishment of a liberal polity in Latin America.[17] In these circumstances, the rule of law too is placed in check (*la ley se acata pero no se cumple*) as in time-honored fashion the powerful seek to protect themselves—and the devil take the hindmost. The most visible consequence is the decline of civil and political order (the principal plank of the reason of state), which has routinely and increasingly succumbed to crime and violence from uncivil and sometimes state actors. Unsurprisingly, the Latin American Public Opinion Project (LAPOP) and other surveys of the past several years have seen insecurity rise to become the chief preoccupation of the Latin American publics, relegating even unemployment to second place.

State Capacity

Although not unrelated to the process of state formation, the question of state capacity is distinct in its concern with the (in)ability of the democratic government to implement its policy decisions effectively. State capacity is curtailed if there are areas of the country or sectors of the economy where the writ of law does not run—O'Donnell was once again prescient in his description of these "brown areas" (1999b, 1999d). And it is enfeebled if the application of law or the implementation of policy has to be negotiated with or is otherwise refracted through oligarchic powers, corporations, and other local powerholders, elected or not. This is worthy of mention if only because the inadequate reach or consistency of the state is sometimes wrongly read as a failing of the democratic regime.

Structured Inequality

The radical economic and social inequality of the Latin American republics do not simply describe a continuum from very poor to very rich; this inequality has been structured over time by the process of patrimonial state formation. The primary consequence is a consistent, but variable, pattern of entrenched oligarchic interests that have proved highly resistant to democratic control and accountability. This is commonplace. In the neoclassical theory of liberal democracy, the main threat appeared to come from majoritarian abuse rather than oligarchic caprice. But once the successful Madisonian defense of private property ensured the permanence of the oligarchy, the principal challenge for liberal democracy is to control it. Hence, the Whig reading of England's modern political history enshrines the constraints of liberal institutions, but recognizes the crucial role of oligarchy in its expanding democracy; and Schumpeter's idea of protected democracy seeks to preserve a traditional way of life—the "good life"—from oligarchic ambition and caprice by defending a "democratic method" that promotes popular sovereignty as a recurrent constraint on oligarchic interests (Schumpeter 1943). In fact, in the relatively short history of the modern form of representative democracy, all successful democracies have had to find effective ways of accommodating their oligarchies. It has long been assumed that such constitutionally balanced solutions are not viable in Latin America because of its patrimonial politics and the much-lamented weakness of its liberal institutions.[18] And within Latin America, there is a widespread and culturally embedded view of the oligarchy as always everywhere the enemy of democracy. But it is too easily forgotten that in several countries limited democratic rule and oligarchic power have served as mutual constraints over not inconsiderable periods, mediated to a greater or lesser extent by liberal institutions.[19] Though these past experiences can be seen as a matter of historical contingency, they are sufficient to reject a counsel of despair that governments in Latin America can never be made accountable. Whether they can or not will depend on the effectiveness of such mutual constraints in the contemporary context and, subsequently, it will be argued that this in turn depends on the ways they are framed constitutionally. But the first requirement is to explore the characteristic contradictions of Latin America's democratic politics so that the constitution will be understood as the political outcome of complex processes of struggle and compromise, mobilization, and negotiation; and constitutional reform as incremental, piecemeal, and contingent on finding solutions to systemic political crises.[20]

Diminished Representation and Demands for Rights

An exclusive focus on the democratic regime will tend to assume that power operates in a predictably formal fashion whereas a flurry of recent research has revealed the prevalence of informal rules governing political interactions in fields as diverse as law enforcement, political party systems, and executive-legislative relations (Helmke and Levitsky 2006). In this political context, the formal reflects—however imperfectly—the tenets of liberal constitutionalism while the informal is imbued with clientelist relations and corruption. But the operation of the informal rules is complicated because their effect cannot be construed simply as parasitic on or destructive of formal procedures. On the contrary, it is the combination of the two that may be required to make democracy work.

This is seen in the sphere of executive-legislative relations, where the informal rules of executive patronage, pork, and logrolling frequently combine with the procedural rules and committee structure of the legislatures to provide legislative support for executive initiatives and so contribute to governability.[21] In this account, party indiscipline in voting and switching and the opportunistic attitude of individual legislators are not only common, but necessary to the predominant style of coalitional presidentialism in Latin America. In this ambivalent world, George Tsebelis's (formal) "veto points" can be seen—conversely—as (informal) opportunities for bargaining and exchange (2002). Yet this emerging but generalized pattern of successful collusion may render legislators and their parties increasingly less responsive to constituency claims and popular preferences, so revealing a stark trade-off between increased governability and democratic representation (Foweraker 1998).[22] It was a historical coincidence that political representation began to fail at the same time as the human rights agenda made the question of individual rights more salient. And if demands for individual rights did not provide sufficient points of political dissatisfaction and contention, there were new claims for regional, community, ethnic, and, in general, minority rights making themselves heard in often cacophonous fashion as both rights and rights agendas came into conflict (Foweraker 2005). Emblematic of these claims were the politically unprecedented demands for indigenous rights that emerged from the 1980s and 1990s to provoke radical upheaval in the traditional politics of some countries of the region. This was a reversal of the expectation on the return to democracy that such demands would lose relevance as citizenship rights were enshrined in new constitutions. Social movements in particular—those specialists in demand making under authoritarian regimes—would lose their reason for being and quietly fade away as political parties took center stage (Jaquette 1989). In fact, and quite to the contrary, there has been a rising rhythm of social mobilization across the region over the past two decades (almost without exception), and this rhythm has continued to accelerate in recent years.

Social Mobilization and Constitutional Struggles

After a sharp rise in the late 1980s, social mobilization receded regionwide in the early 1990s before beginning to increase again especially after 1997. This mobilization was focused on the realization of formally encoded citizenship rights as well as cultural, regional, environmental, and gender rights; it continued to increase across the region in the decade after 2000, peaking at its highest point for thirty years in 2009. Over most of these years labor mobilization followed a different trajectory,[23] only becoming strongly correlated with social mobilization broadly writ in the years after 2005 (with the exceptions of Venezuela, Colombia, and Ecuador). Some argue that it was the economics of liberalization and the ensuing economic grievances allied with a democratic politics that raised expectations of redistribution that drove this social mobilization. But the evidence suggests that it was the legal and constitutional reforms promising more effective citizenship rights (especially more permissive electoral rules offering enhanced political representation) that precipitated the high rates of mobilization after 1997 and opened up the political party arena, encouraging social movements to ally with opposition parties or eventually to become parties themselves.[24] In fact, there were sixty-seven electoral reforms in Latin America from 1978 to 2009, twenty-nine to the rules governing the election of executives and thirty-eight to those of legislatures.[25]

There is no doubt that this was a sea change in social mobilization, beginning in the 1990s but continuing thereafter, often coinciding with the emergence of left-wing governments, and creating the appearance of greater political inclusion. Unlike under the preceding authoritarian regimes, it is no longer the labor movement but a diverse collection of other social movements that now take the lead, with the rhythm of mobilization no longer driven by economic fluctuations of different kinds but rather by the electoral cycle and, more importantly, by the incidence of institutional and especially electoral and political party reforms designed to increase the representative capacity of the political system. In sum, on one reading, the democratic governments of Latin America have been recurrently engaged in a complex process of institutional reform and constitutional amendment intended to correct their failings and especially to counter and resolve their autochthonous perception of a systemic crisis of representation.[26]

But this is not the whole story, for mobilization that presses for or responds to constitutional amendments has often been encouraged or provoked, sometimes by incumbents eager to protect their accumulated privileges and sometimes by elite contenders who want to win power and supplant them. In these instances—where social mobilization is conjoined with partisan politics—it proves crucial that the process of institutional reform tends to return to the cockpit of party politics in the legislatures, where it is recurrently captured by corporate interests, so failing to resolve the root problems of political exclusion and the ensuing illegitimacy. In other words, the inclusion of new actors in the political arena did not necessarily or often lead the party system to respond effectively to their political demands. So mobilization may be motivated in the first place by the aspirations of the socially and politically excluded for more representation. But it is motivated in greater degree by frustration at the subsequent incapacity or unwillingness of the government to satisfy citizens' demands for public goods, including jobs, education, clean government, and public security, thus further damaging the legitimacy of many governments across the region.[27]

All of this may appear uncomfortably redolent of Samuel Huntington's pessimistic view of democratic development where increasing mobilization is likely to outpace the system's capacity for institutional response, so leading ineluctably to new forms of mass praetorianism (Huntington 1968).[28] But the pessimism is justified only in those cases where the pressure for constitutional amendment has become clearly endogenous to oligarchic manipulation and struggles for political advantage within the legislature since this is the point where the process of constitutional reform elides into constitutional reformation of the kind that aspires to refound the nation through the medium of populist resurgence. It is but a short step from the frustration of stymied reforms or a recurrent lack of effective implementation to the politics of antipolitics and calls for *que se vayan todos,* so making it easy for aspiring populist leaders to inveigh not merely against the party in government but against the partidocracia in general.

Populism and Constitutionalism

Much academic ink has been spilled in debating the reasons for the populist resurgence in contemporary Latin America.[29] There is little doubt that the perception of a partidocracia that feeds from the public trough, but ignores both the public interest and constituents' concerns, can fuel popular discontent and, for the present purpose, it is important to note that this is ultimately a question of accountability. Once the process of constitutional reform becomes endogenous to the struggle for political power in the legislature, any show of accountability becomes merely perfunctory. And the radical constitutional promise of the new populism to refound the nation is a promise to restore accountability and return government to the people. The massive increase in social mobilization across the region—pressing for political representation and accountable government—is a measure of the political potency of the promise.

There are significant similarities and analogies between past and current populisms in the construction of a politics of difference or polar antagonism between the people (both as a general claim and a specific category of the excluded) and the oligarchy (most often in a specific cultural and political form). While the rhetorical tropes can look more radical today (not least constitutional reformation and the refounding of nations), analogous populist tropes have always looked radical to contemporary observers. But it is important to look beyond the appearance of things to note an enduring feature of populist politics in Latin America: namely, its tendency to reproduce that which it consistently aspires to chastise and suppress—the presence of oligarchic power. This is familiar ground in the study of politics, recalling the democratic pessimism of not only Vilfredo Pareto (1991) but also Gaetano Mosca (1939), and especially Robert Michels's "iron law of oligarchy" in political party organization (1959).

It is noteworthy that political crises in Latin America today do recurrently exhibit a systemic dimension with extraordinary and often extraconstitutional measures required for their resolution. And it is clear that the crises do not express a linear process of democratic advance, but a more complex and ambiguous process of readjustment that may eventually reproduce the same or similar politics in different guise. But this does not mean that nothing happens. On the contrary, the systemic crises of Latin American democracy can and do impel a "circulation of elites"—in Pareto's language—that can and often does lead to a (usually partial) recomposition of the ruling coalition.[30] Yet if this is a process of reproducing and reshaping oligarchic politics, in the more radical populist cases it is now an oligarchic politics more or less untrammeled by liberal constitutional constraints, depending on how far these are suppressed by a plebiscitary and polarizing politics that bypasses established forums of representation and deliberation that require negotiation and compromise. In these cases, therefore, the promise of greater accountability through radical constitutional engineering turns out to be false. The promised accountability is crude, uncertain, and ineffective.

Populism looms large over the landscape of democracy in Latin America and it has a visible impact on the composition of ruling coalitions. But the populist cases comprise a minority set in the democratic universe of the region—they are not the whole democratic story by any means—and their political outcomes vary widely. Thus, in some cases, populist antagonism is narrowly focused on the political elite and the political party system (Fernando Collor de Mello in Brazil, Alberto Fujimori in Peru, Carlos Menem in Argentina) while in others it encompasses both political and economic elites, including export agribusiness and multinational energy companies (Hugo Chávez in Venezuela, Evo Morales in Bolivia, Rafael Correa in Ecuador). These different definitions of the oligarchy, one narrow and one broad, correspond, albeit imperfectly, to a division between populisms of the right and populisms of the left, and the differences do contribute in some degree to distinguish political outcomes, with some populist insurgencies having a far more enduring impact than others.[31]

Yet although the number of populist cases is relatively small, they do not represent a deviation of any kind in the democratic life of Latin America. On the contrary, they are expressive of the normal politics of the region in at least two significant ways. First, they express the tensions that are everywhere evident between a public sphere of democratic politics that requires political accountability and a private patrimonial realm of oligarchic powers that seeks immunity from the same. For most periods, in most places these tensions are managed through political party competition, democratic procedure, and the mix of formal and informal rules that characterizes high politics. But when the tensions become acute in conditions of low institutional capacity or moments of institutional inflexibility and rising popular demands, they can find expression in a populist insurgence that may alleviate the tensions in the short term, but never—or never yet—resolve them. Second, they seek—as do most democratic governments in Latin America from time to time—to respond to and indeed resolve the tensions through constitutional means, even if their chosen means are more radical and less liberal than those adopted elsewhere.

Much of the social mobilization across Latin America represents struggles that are not strictly democratic so much as political-legal struggles for elements of liberal constitutionalism that lead, at best, to a process of constitutional reform that is incremental, piecemeal, and—yes—frequently contradictory and sometimes counterproductive. But this reform process sticks, however imperfectly, to established democratic procedures and so is clearly very different from the recent projects of constitutional reformation and national refounding, especially in their millenarian but illusory aspiration to purge the polity of the oligarchy and return the nation to the people. In my view, these projects are susceptible to Michael Oakeshott's critique of political rationalism (1977), whereby the bright designs of the present may be no better, and may indeed be worse, than the contingent products of the past and new oligarchies no better, possibly worse than old, since it requires political learning over the generations to give oligarchies a chance of being good. Indeed, they may spawn, at worst, a noxious combination of majoritarianism and oligarchic caprice. This suggests that both the means and the ends of constitutional reform are important to political outcomes to a degree that is unprecedented in Latin America as political leaders and popular classes come to see the constitution as the key to a more democratic politics—and defend it as such. For these reasons, the shaping of the constitution is likely to remain a privileged terrain of democratic struggles for many years to come.

The Current Condition of Democracy in Latin America: A Glass Half Full or Half Empty?

From the beginning of the current democratic era, the quality of Latin American democracy has been placed in doubt by the endless repetition of its deficiencies, whether occasional failings or pathological disturbances, so that the best these adjectivally laden (D. Collier and Levitsky 1997) "electoral," "illiberal," or "defective" democracies (Merkel 1999) can aspire to live is some form of low-intensity citizenship. In short, the glass was seen as half empty from the outset. But this negative view severely underestimates what is—in the perspective of the longue durée—an extraordinary political achievement. It is also analytically inadequate on two principal counts. First, it leads to an analytical cul-de-sac where Latin America's democracies are recurrently characterized by what they fail to be rather than by what they are in fact (an analytically undemanding and therefore rather soft option). Second, the negative view is also a remarkably static view that does not recognize or address the dynamic elements of these regimes or their capacity for change, not least through diverse forms of democratic and legal struggle.

It may be the case that the democratic failings are judged against received notions of accountable government in a pristine public sphere, possibly leavened by a dose of cultural bias. But irrespective of the cherished illusions of some political scientists, this is not and may never be the normal politics of Latin American democracy (O'Donnell 1999a). And the judgment is further complicated by the fact that it is so often the failings (in the form of the combination of informal and formal rules) that serve—if only in part—to make these democracies work. Furthermore, the static view of these hapless governments is belied by their dynamic engagement in complex projects of institutional reform and constitutional amendment. The easy objection is that constitutional formality may do nothing to change political practice, as it may not in the short term.[32] But as Fareed Zakaria (1997) suggests, it is precisely the insistence on liberal constitutionalism that can do most to correct for so-called democratic failings. In this perspective, the conflicted process of constitutional reform can and often does express a public enactment of political struggles for a more democratic regime. To the degree that this is true, the quality of democracy in Latin America is likely to continue to improve, so making the democratic glass now emphatically half full rather than unhappily half empty.

Notes

1. Zakaria begins his article on the rise of illiberal democracy by asserting that "democratically elected regimes, often ones that have been re-elected or reaffirmed through referenda, are routinely ignoring constitutional limits on their power and depriving their citizens of basic rights and freedoms" (Zakaria 1997: 22).

2. For Aristotle "good government" was defined as that government that best promoted the "good life," which was the whole point of the polis. He admitted the possibility of bad democracy as well as the likelihood of bad oligarchic rule—both democracy and oligarchy being debased forms of government incapable of support-

ing the "good life." Analogous concerns about the constraints of history and culture informed Huntington's discussion of "Asian values."

3. In an earlier article, I sought to demonstrate that the quality of some established democracies (specifically the United States, the United Kingdom, and Australia) was not always uniform or indeed superior, especially with regard to civil and minority rights. For this purpose, I employed a normative approach across a broad range of values, departing from the premise that the question of quality is not one- but multidimensional, so that measurement should not seek to produce single scales but rather quality profiles. This implies that not all aspects of quality may move in the same direction over the same period not least because different values may trade off against each other in some circumstances, though there was no formal model to require that they should always do so (Foweraker and Krznaric 2003).

4. The problems of commensurability do not arise with these variations within the broad ambit of liberal constitutionalism, but in the encounter with long-established legal and rights traditions that offend the liberal ethos such as sharia law. These may be deemed incompatible with liberal democracy—unless its values are diluted by some form of moral relativism.

5. Such material inequality can also constrain and distort access to the law, leaving one law for the rich and another for the poor, while the lack of both legal protection and political efficacy reduces effective political participation and fosters supplicants in place of citizens, so creating what Habermas called the "clientelization of citizenship" (1991). In this way, material inequality can affect democratic rights by undermining the universalism implicit in these rights.

6. Throughout his long career, this has been Dahl's overriding concern regarding the quality of democracy in the United States (1961, 1989).

7. As was also characteristic of Japanese and Italian democracy throughout the post–World War II era.

8. The right to property is also included in the 1948 Declaration of Universal Human Rights.

9. Elsewhere, I have argued that it is precisely this oligarchic defense of private property combined with partially unaccountable military, police, and paramilitary security services that leads to the patchy and highly imperfect rule of law in many democracies of Latin America and to the feebleness of their rights regimes (Foweraker and Krznaric 2002).

10. It is widely acknowledged that the unequal relationships that characterize clientelism are an expression of informal power, but it tends to remain power without a subject, so that clientelism appears to float free like some cultural epiphenomenon that is unconnected to social structure, or to private property in particular. However, it remains largely unremarked that the particularistic claims of clientelism are—ipso facto—inimical to the universal claims of individual rights vested in democratic norms of political equality. In the present perspective, it is clear that the political subject of clientelism is the oligarchy in all its many political and cultural expressions. Yet there are no comparative measures of clientelism or any plausible proxies for the same.

11. Recalling Voltaire's pithy observation that the English of the eighteenth century were "free every seven years."

12. There was subsequently some debate about whether the checks and balances of liberal constitutionalism are not so much a matter of accountability as of executive constraint (Moreno, Crisp, and Shugart 2003). In my view, the constraint is required to achieve some measure of accountability.

13. Although the process of transitional justice has proceeded slowly but surely in Chile, it has flip-flopped over the years in Argentina, while Brazil resisted any

accounting until last year and Uruguay simply agreed to forget in most instances. Oddly, there have been some recent advances in Guatemala, though these may not withstand subsequent legal challenges.

14. As Levine and Molina conclude,

> The most notable democratic deficit across the region is clearly on the dimension of accountability. . . . Without exception in each country considered individually, the dimension with the lowest scores is precisely that of accountability . . . [and] by far the lowest average score for the seventeen countries included in our index comes on the dimension of accountability. (2011: 255–256)

15. This is not to deny the long history of (often constrained and curtailed) democratic experiences in Latin America. But that history had suffered a brutal interruption prior to the contemporary era.

16. It may be objected that this is universally true in some degree (and this is so), but rarely to the same degree as in Latin America. Studies by Rauch and Evans (less well known than they should be) suggest that the state in Latin America is only marginally more legally bureaucratic and, hence, neutral than the state in sub-Saharan Africa (Evans and Rauch 1999; Rauch and Evans 2000).

17. There is certainly a liberal tradition in Latin America, especially in the narrow sense of its rhetorical and legal tropes, but it is etiolated and often feeble in its support for the individual rights of citizenship. If anything, this often became more apparent with the transitions to democracy when, following the excesses of the military-authoritarian regimes and the international spread of the human rights agenda, the question of rights was increasingly salient. There are exceptions to prove the rule. Chile has a relatively strong legal tradition in defense of individual rights and its *auditoria general* has had considerable success in monitoring and regulating state agencies, while successive democratic governments have gradually purged the legislature and judiciary of their *pinochetista* residues. Colombia has a strong legal culture and a highly independent judiciary that has recurrently proved capable of holding the executive to account and providing true checks and balances.

18. Yet it must be recognized that the resilience of liberal institutions varies widely from country to country, and there are some few cases—Chile, Uruguay, Costa Rica—where normal politics has been maintained by constitutional checks and balances, the horizontal accountability implicit in competitive party politics, the legislative process, and legal and rhetorical traditions that require some respect for the rights of the citizenry.

19. These cases may include Argentina 1916 to 1930, Brazil 1945 to 1961 (in some regions), Chile 1932 to 1973, Colombia 1957 to present, Costa Rica 1948 to present, Uruguay 1911 to 1973, and Venezuela 1958 to 1988, but would certainly exclude Argentina 1955 to present, Central America apart from Costa Rica, and Mexico and Peru for most of their modern history.

20. One recent discussion of interrupted presidencies in Latin America has suggested that such solutions often involve paraconstitutional practices where de facto political fixes anticipate and possibly precipitate de jure reforms (Llanos and Marsteintredet 2010).

21. There is a contrary account that includes an increasing capacity of legislators to hold executives to account with instances of impeachment and—more frequently—interrupted presidencies (Marsteintredet and Berntzen 2008).

22. It is recognized that problems of representation often begin with electoral rules and especially permissive forms of proportional representation that allow open and unblocked lists, which lead to weak party identification and allegiance on the one hand and prevalent patterns of personal and clientelistic voting on the other. This can occur not only where most (Brazil), but also where least (Chile) expected. In Chile, it was the peculiarities of the electoral rules (binomial system) combined with the insider deals required to keep the different strands of the Concertación governments together that fomented the grassroots desertion of political parties and increasing support for known personalities (Luna and Altman 2011).

23. Labor mobilization did rise in the late 1980s, but fluctuated considerably in subsequent years before dropping back from 2000 to 2005.

24. In truth, it is never this easy to distinguish the economic from the political motives for mobilization if only because changes to electoral rules will also change the relative participation of particular interests in deciding the outcome of distributional conflicts.

25. Over these years, every election in Ecuador was run under different rules.

26. These reforms did work to improve the quality and expand the quantity of representation in these regimes, with the constitutional reforms often moving electoral democracies in the direction of liberal democracies. Literacy requirements for enfranchisement were removed (so empowering ethnic minorities); there was a decline of urban patronage and rural *caciquismo,* giving a political voice to previously excluded sectors.

27. The Luiz Inácio Lula da Silva government in Brazil and the early Concertación administrations in Chile provide partial exceptions to the rule. The reforms were intended to address the problems of political exclusion—and, hence, legitimacy and political instability—that were the likely longer-term effects of the trade-off between governability and representation. But at least in some instances, these ex post solutions tended to induce the political instability they were intended to avoid.

28. In Huntington's view, mass praetorianism was a leading cause of insurgencies and coups, weak and disorganized governments, or both.

29. These are by Weyland (1996, 2001), Roberts (1995, 2003), Levitsky (2003), Corrales (2010b, 2011), and others, and are examined at length in a recent book by Philip and Panizza (2011).

30. If this is correct, then it would appear to follow that political party competition in the electoral arena cannot usually achieve the same order of recomposition.

31. In yet other cases like that of Daniel Ortega in Nicaragua, the current object of populist animus may be entirely opportunistic.

32. Aristotle defended a particular form of government he called "politeia" (the polity), which was a constitutional balance of oligarchy and democracy. It has often been objected that Aristotle was talking of constitutional design, and not really existing political systems. But in the polis of the Athenian city-state (and in the other 122 constitutions he studied), sovereign authority had to be recurrently present and visible in a public enactment of the constitution that dissolved the distance between constitutional form and political system.

3

State Capacity
and Democratic Quality

David Doyle

In countries such as Chile, Costa Rica, and Uruguay, government policy is generally considered stable, effective, and of good quality. The provision of public goods penetrates society, and the rule of law is effective across different social strata and territorial districts. In contrast, in some of the small Central American republics and in Paraguay, Venezuela, and Bolivia, we frequently witness violent swings in government policy. The provision of public goods is unevenly distributed, and the rule of law often remains the purview of privileged groups in society. This begs the question as to why some Latin American states act as effective agents for their citizens, providing them with channels of accountability together with effective and representative public policy, while other states remain predatory and produce public policy that is largely ineffective.

This is a concern that extends beyond government effectiveness. It is fundamental to the overall quality of democracy: specifically, the degree to which contemporary Latin American states can uphold in practice the core liberal democratic values of representation, accountability, and participation (see Foweraker, Chapter 2, this volume). In (overly) simple terms, we can think of the relationship between citizens and the state as one akin to a principal-agent framework (similar to Strøm 2006), where the citizens of a given state are the principals and the state is the agent. At the very least, citizens can expect their state to have a monopoly on the legitimate use of physical force in the enforcement of order (Weber 1978: 54). But the principals can also reasonably expect their agent to provide and uphold a legal framework that is fairly applied across different issues, social classes, and territories within a given state (see O'Donnell 1998b). When this occurs, representative, efficient, and effective public policies will result. By effective policy, I refer to public policy that, regardless of the issue, reaches and penetrates all geographical regions and social strata (O'Donnell 1998b: 5). Effective policy is also efficient and lean policy, and effective policy should be primarily concerned with the public interest and the broad-based provision of public goods (O'Donnell 1998b; Kurtz 2013). When the state is unable to act as an effective agent for its citizens, we have agency loss (Strøm 2006). The observable implication of agency loss in this context is unrepresentative and ineffective public policy.

Unfortunately, in Latin America, we frequently observe this type of agency loss. The purpose of this chapter is to explore why this is so and why we observe such variation in policy effectiveness across the region. I suggest that the intervening causal link between the citizens and the quality of the observable policy produced within the framework of their state is the capacity of these states (see also Mainwaring and Scully 2008). By capacity, I am referring to state capacity as Marcus Kurtz understands it: *"institutional* power—the ability of the state to induce residents, firms and organizations to act in ways they would not in the absence of its regulatory and administrative presence" (2013: 3, emphasis in original). At the micro level, high levels of state capacity should result in citizens with confidence in their state. They should have some sense that the state is acting as their agent, and will be more likely to pay their taxes or serve in the military. At the macro level, Kurtz (2013: 3) suggests that high levels of state capacity should be reflected in the uniform imposition of the rule of law, the provision of public goods, and the capacity to generate taxation to fund these endeavors—in short, effective public policy.[1]

There are clear echoes here with the work of Guillermo O'Donnell (1993a). For O'Donnell, state capacity rests on three pillars: the capacity of state bureaucracies to discharge their duties with efficacy, the effectiveness of law, and the extent to which the decisions of state agencies promote the public good.[2] The combination of these three factors will affect the degree to which political decisions made at the center, and the orders issued by state organizations, "have similar effectiveness throughout the national territory and across the existing social stratification" (O'Donnell 1993a: 5–6). Similarly, Laurence Whitehead suggests that we can understand the modern Latin American state along three interrelated dimensions: territoriality, administration, and command over resources (1994: 11). For Whitehead, the direct consequence of variation along these dimensions will be the capacity of Latin American states "to elaborate more complex and sophisticated forms of public policy" (1994: 14).

In what follows in the first part of this chapter, I discuss the causal channel between state capacity and effective public policy, before considering some of the long-term explanations for variation in state capacity itself. Then, I take a cursory look at some data on state capacity and policy effectiveness for Latin America, and highlight some long-term trends and the correlation that exists between ineffective policy and weak states across the region. Finally, I consider some contemporary challenges and threats to state capacity and, by implication, policy effectiveness, before I conclude.

A last point about the claims I make here before I begin. In no way are they novel. Indeed, there is now an impressively large body of work linking state capacity to public goods provision (e.g., Geddes 1994; Mainwaring and Scully 2008), long-term economic performance (e.g., Acemoglu, Johnson, and Robinson 2001), democratic quality (e.g., Bäck and Hadenius 2008), and reductions in ethnic conflict (e.g., Horowitz 1971). My purpose in this chapter is to provide some synthesis to reasonably disparate debates concerned with state capacity in Latin America (e.g., Geddes 1994; Kurtz 2013; Soifer 2009) and the quality of public policies across the region (e.g., Scartascini, Stein, and Tommasi 2009; Pereira, Singh, and Mueller 2011; Tommasi 2011; Doyle 2014).

The Causal Link: State Capacity

To understand how state capacity can shape the effectiveness of policy, it is useful to return to O'Donnell's idea of brown areas (1993). O'Donnell proposed a conceptual map of Latin America, where areas with a high degree of state capacity would be represented in blue; green would represent a middling level of capacity; and brown would represent areas where the presence of the state, both in terms of effective bureaucracies and the penetration of law, is largely absent. In these brown areas, ineffective states and weak bureaucratic administrations have either created or reinforced "systems of local power" (O'Donnell 1993a: 8–9). There is a functional hole in the state if you will, and into that hole has stepped powerful and predatory individuals and local groups who have assumed many of the functions of the state.

In the democratic era, the power of these local sultans became embedded in political parties that are rife with personalism, nepotism, and clientelism—parties that continue to feed off local bureaucracies to sustain their own domination and survival (O'Donnell 1993a: 8–9). At the national level, legislators elected from the brown areas have little interest in the overall quality of public policy. Rather, they seek to channel resources back to their brown areas to bolster their local strongholds. So they act opportunistically and without regard for the public good.

This idea is actually central to our contemporary comparative understanding of executive-legislative relations in Latin America (Cox and McCubbins 2001). Let us consider an imaginary Latin American state. This state may have a strong (blue or green) center, but if the process of state formation (more of this anon) gave rise to one brown area, then in all likelihood there are numerous other brown areas within the state borders. This means the national congress will be filled with legislators seeking pork to channel back to their home districts with little regard for the overarching public good.[3] The president may wish to enact legislation that is more congruent with the wishes of the median voter, but this is often a difficult thing for Latin American executives to do. Many party systems in Latin America are highly fragmented (Amorim Neto and Cox 1997), so presidents across the region are frequently faced with the necessity of building multiparty coalitions (see Cheibub, Przeworski, and Saiegh 2004; Negretto 2006).

In this scenario, the president is forced to bargain, largely through material resources and government appointments, to get any legislation passed (Cox and Morgenstern 2001; Raile, Pereira, and Power 2011).[4] When the house is filled with legislators from brown areas, then favors, resources, and important appointments flow to these pivotal but rent-seeking legislators. The end result is that brown areas invade the central bureaucracy, and national resources are not distributed evenly, but are channeled to key brown territories and districts in return for legislative support (O'Donnell 1993a: 9). The effectiveness of public policy is undermined. It is no longer concerned with the public interest and the broad-based provision of public goods, but rather reflects the short-term interests of specific legislators and their geographic idiosyncrasies. Brazil is often held up as the prototypical example of this dynamic (see Samuels 2002; Ames 2002).

This may have implications for the rate of legislative output and the success of the executive's legislative agenda. It is plausible that brown legislators may hold the executive to ransom and stymie any legislative initiatives until their demands for targeted transfers or government appointments are met. For example, in early 2005, Brazilian president Luiz Inácio Lula da Silva saw his legislative agenda grind to a halt due to dissatisfaction among the "lower clerics" in the house, legislators who were unhappy with their access to government posts and federal funding for their local projects (Flynn 2005: 1225–1226).

These arguments also resonate with recent work on the stability and quality of policy across Latin America (see Crisp, Desposato, and Kanthak 2011; Scartascini, Stein, and Tommasi 2009; Pereira, Singh, and Mueller 2011; Tommasi 2011; Doyle 2014). The central thrust of this work is quite simple: when political institutions fail to encourage long-term time horizons and a concern for national policy, political actors will behave myopically, with a view toward maximizing their "own welfare without any intertemporal considerations for those holding power in the past or in the future" (Scartascini, Stein, and Tommasi 2009: 8). In all probability, these are the types of institutional structures that go hand in hand with weak state capacity, or when O'Donnell's (1993) brown areas dominate the state. In these cases, policy tends to be of poor quality, narrow, and ineffective and subject to serious volatility as it changes according to the whims and dynamics of political coalitions.

Alternatively, where the institutions of the state can generate the credibility and capacity to enforce political and policy agreements (i.e., when the map of the state is largely blue), political actors will be more likely to consider policy from the perspective of a longer time horizon (Tommasi 2011: 200; Scartascini, Stein, and Tommasi 2009: 6). In this scenario, policy tends to be of higher quality, be more stable, and have greater depth and penetration across all social strata and geographic territories within the state.

It is important to note, however, that the venal and opportunistic nature of brown legislators may not always be considered a bad thing. In fact, while brown legislators may undermine democratic representation and the effectiveness of public policy, in the context of Latin American presidential systems they may also facilitate political stability and governability. In this scenario, to some degree, there is a trade-off between democratic quality and the day-to-day functioning of the government.

Let me explain further. Juan Linz (1990) famously warned that the separate election and autonomous survival of the presidential office was more likely, relative to parliamentarism, to breed executives who were imperial, unwilling to compromise, and intolerant of opposition groups, thereby eliminating many of the incentives to build and maintain coalitions in presidential regimes. As a consequence, minority governments or minority coalitions would become commonplace, but these governments would be characterized by legislative ineffectiveness. This would produce deadlock between the house and the executive, and unlike parliamentary regimes there is no recourse to a vote of no confidence to alleviate the building tension, resulting in breakdown of governability.[5] Eventually, one of the institutional branches will turn to noninstitutional actors, such as the military, precipitating some form of democratic breakdown.

Linz (1990) was primarily trying to explain the debility of Latin American presidential governments. However, a revisionist literature, very much in the vein of the institutionalists above, began to challenge the core assumptions underlying the Linzian causal mechanism. First, they established empirically that coalitions are not actually that rare under presidential governments (see, for example, Cheibub, Przeworksi, and Saiegh 2004). Second, they began to highlight that Latin American presidents can make use of a number of "efficient secrets" to build and maintain governing coalitions (Abranches 1988). A central component of these arguments involved the distribution of pork and government appointments by the executive at key strategic moments to legislators and coalition partners.[6] The degree to which this strategy would work would be dependent on the extent to which the assembly was "parochial" or "venal" (see Cox and Morgenstern 2001: 178).

As such and somewhat paradoxically, low levels of state capacity may have actually facilitated the governability and political stability of some Latin American presidential systems in otherwise weak states. At different times, the venality and parochialism of legislators from brown areas have enabled executives to build governing coalitions, undermining the potential for interbranch conflict. So, on the one hand, poor state capacity in Latin America is more likely to generate ineffective and unrepresentative policies that undermine the overall quality of democracy. But at the same time, it may also facilitate coalition building and negotiation between the executive and legislative branches, aiding the governability, political stability, and, ultimately, the survival of democracy.

The upshot of this discussion is that where state capacity is weak and where there are numerous brown areas, this will affect the effectiveness of public policy. It may result in policy that is narrowly targeted toward powerful interests or small geographically based groups. That is, the policy lacks what Cox and McCubbins termed "public regardedness" (2001). In addition, the quality of this policy, with regard to its implementation, enforcement, and coherence, may be poor (see Scartascini, Stein, and Tommasi 2009). It may also result in significant swings in policy, thereby undermining the long-term development trajectories of these countries (Hausmann and Gavin 1996). In this regard, the quality of democracy has been undermined. Where we see big policy swings, particularly in light of a given mandate, or narrow targeted resource transfers as opposed to the more broad-based delivery of public goods, then clearly democratic representation has been undermined (Stokes 2001; G. Johnson and Crisp 2003). Agency loss has occurred in the principal-agent chain.

Explaining Variation in State Capacity

Of course, this naturally begs the question as to what explains the presence or absence of brown areas in the first place. Any discussion of the relationship between state capacity and policy effectiveness must at some point consider the process of state formation. We now know that variation in state capacity can be largely explained by different trajectories and experiences during the process of state formation. Once established, the stickiness of state institutions can have long-lasting and durable implications for regime type, state capacity, and, of course, policy effectiveness (e.g., Gerschenkron 1962; Tilly 1990).

The seminal explanation for state formation, developed largely for Western Europe, rests on the near-accidental by-products of interstate war (Tilly 1990).[7] However, given the lack of pervasive interstate war in the nineteenth century, and particularly the twentieth century, this explanation clearly has less traction in the context of Latin America (see Thies 2005; Kurtz 2013).[8] Of course, the lack of widespread interstate war could be interpreted as an explanation for the uniform and persistent weakness of Latin American states (e.g., Centeno 2002) but the reality, however, is demonstrable variation in state capacity across the region. War, or lack thereof, as the generative cause of Latin American state weakness struggles with this variation.[9]

Two excellent explanations have instead developed accounts of state formation in Latin America inspired by classic neoinstitutionalist work (e.g., North and Thomas 1973).[10] For Hillel Soifer (2006, 2009), the variation we observe in the strength or weakness of contemporary Latin American states can be traced to the institutions of local rule established during the early phases of state formation. Where central leaders relied on their own deployed agents to run local territories, then local institutions were more likely to develop in conjunction with, and with links to, the central administration. These deployed agents are loyal to the central state and their power is dependent on the reach and penetration of state infrastructure. In contrast, when central leaders relied on local elites, institutions tended to reflect the incentives and interests of these local elites. These local elites did not depend on the state for their power or wealth, but rather on their landholdings and position in the local community. They also had no great stake in the expansion of state infrastructure. In these areas we were most likely to see the development of brown areas and their concomitant powerful, but shortsighted and venal (at least from a national perspective) local powerbrokers. For Soifer (2006), this can help us to understand the weakness of the Peruvian state in comparison to the Chilean state.

Kurtz (2013) has developed a similar explanation, but one that is rooted in social relations and electoral incorporation. Kurtz's explanation is based on two key critical junctures. The first of these occurs immediately following independence. Where labor is free at this time and when "elites cooperate to form an exclusionary oligarchy," institutional building can occur (Kurtz 2013: 9). This is Chile, Uruguay after 1876, and Argentina after 1881. In contrast, where labor is not free and where elites are in conflict, national-level institutions will not develop properly (e.g., Peru). These different institutional trajectories will either be consolidated or derailed by a second critical juncture, the electoral incorporation of the middle and working classes. When electoral incorporation occurs after the Depression, then an alliance between the middle and working classes can form around a strategy of state industrialization, bolstering and reinforcing state institutions (e.g., Chile and Uruguay). When electoral incorporation occurs before industrialization, then such an alliance between the social classes becomes unlikely, and institutional development is either undermined (e.g., Argentina) or further weakened (e.g., Peru).[11]

Once established, these institutions, and the extent of their social and geographic reach, tended to prove sticky over time (see Kurtz 2013; Soifer 2006). So, brown areas that emerged during the period after independence, or the period of electoral incorporation nearly 100 years ago, have largely remained brown into the contemporary era. This was to have a profound effect on the ability of Latin American states to deliver effective and representative policies during the tumultuous period of the dual transition to democracy and to the market. During this period, enormous strain was placed on already feeble state institutions and agencies (see Foweraker, Chapter 2, this volume). Some states, such as Chile and Uruguay and Brazil to a lesser extent, were able to manage the transitions in a reasonably ordered way and to reorient the state to absorb some of the uncertainty and risks of market liberalization. In other countries, weak state institutions and ineffective policies saw more chaotic transitions, involving *autogolpes* (Peru) or dramatic policy switches (Argentina, Peru, and Venezuela), further undermining representation and the legitimacy of the state (see Stokes 2001).[12] It is no surprise that it is in many of these latter countries where policy in the contemporary era is least effective, in terms of societal and geographic penetration, enforcement, and stability. It is to these empirical trends that I turn next.

Observed Variation in State Capacity and Policy Effectiveness

The purpose of this section is to add some empirical flesh to the previous theoretical discussion. By no means is this a systematic analysis of the relationship between state capacity and policy effectiveness. Rather, I am aiming to highlight three things: first, the variation in state capacity that exists among Latin American countries; second, the long-term stickiness of these trends (see also Kurtz 2013); and, third, the variation in policy effectiveness across the region. I also suggest that there is a general correlation between the proxies for state capacity I employ here and the proxies for policy effectiveness. However, for the moment, it must remain a general correlation and I make no attempt to systematically test the causal mechanisms discussed above.

Measuring state capacity is not an easy task. I follow Kurtz (2013: 61) and use the ability of the state to tax its citizens as a simple metric of state strength. If we look at long-term trends in data on tax revenue across Latin America, for example, between 1900 and 2000, we can observe two things: first, there is significant variation in the capacity of Latin American states to extract revenue from their citizens and this relative capacity has remained largely unchanged, barring some fluctuations, over the course of the twentieth century.[13] Table 3.1 highlights this contemporary variation a little more forcefully. This table lists the mean revenue from taxes, as a percentage of gross domestic product (GDP), collected between 1990 and 2010 for eighteen Latin American countries. As the table clearly demonstrates, countries such as Chile and Uruguay collect significantly more taxes than Paraguay, Ecuador, El Salvador, or Nicaragua.

Over the past number of years, some countries, such as Mexico and Argentina for example, have notably improved their tax take. However, while part of this trend can be attributed to increased direct tax collection, in the form of income and capital taxes, a significant portion can be

Table 3.1 Mean Tax Revenue Across Latin America, 1990–2010

Country	Mean Tax Revenue as a Percentage of GDP
Argentina	9.8
Bolivia	14.5
Brazil	13.5
Chile	15.3
Colombia	10.2
Costa Rica	12.4
Dominican Republic	11.9
Ecuador	7.9
El Salvador	10.9
Guatemala	10.1
Honduras	13.9
Mexico	9.4
Nicaragua	11.1
Panama	10.1
Paraguay	9.6
Peru	13.2
Uruguay	15.5
Venezuela	13.7

Source: Based on data from the Economic Commission for Latin America and the Caribbean.
Note: GDP is gross domestic product.

explained by an increase in indirect taxation, mainly via consumption taxes (see Castañeda-Angarita and Doyle 2015). While indirect taxes may be far easier to collect than direct taxes, they also carry a redistributive cost. Poorer groups in society consume a higher proportion of their income relative to wealthier groups, and so the burden of taxation is not evenly distributed (e.g., Beramendi and Rueda 2007). Given this, increases in taxation may suggest higher state capacity, but it may also mask public policy that is not equally applied across all social strata.[14]

Additionally, as Kurtz (2013) has suggested, this variation in state capacity is also reflected in individual-level attitudes. In the 2010 wave of the Latinobarómetro survey, respondents were asked, on a scale of 1 to 10, how justifiable it is to avoid paying taxes. Table 3.2 reports, for ten Latin American countries, the percentage of respondents who believe it is justifiable to avoid paying taxes. Unsurprisingly, Chile has the lowest percentage of respondents who favor tax evasion, 6.8 percent, in contrast to Guatemala at 21.66 percent and Nicaragua at 21.29 percent.

This variation in state capacity is also reflected in the degree to which states are able to control or penetrate their national territories (e.g., Whitehead 1994) and the extent to which policies provide broad-based public goods. For example, if we consider the coverage of railways per square kilometer between 1900 and 2000 for two groups of countries, Argentina, Chile, and Mexico on one hand, and Nicaragua, Bolivia, and Colombia on the other, on average the former group has far greater rail coverage than the latter (a difference that is statistically significant at $p < 0.01$). That same pattern applies to illiteracy rates. The mean illiteracy rate for Argentina,

Table 3.2 Public Support for the Evasion of Taxes

Country	Percentage of Respondents Who Believe Evading Tax Is Justifiable
Argentina	8.3
Bolivia	10.4
Chile	6.8
Colombia	8.1
Guatemala	21.66
Honduras	9.5
Mexico	14.96
Nicaragua	21.29
El Salvador	8.36
Uruguay	9.47

Source: Latinobarómetro 2010.

Chile, and Mexico between 1900 and 2000 is 14 percent. In contrast, for Nicaragua, Bolivia, and Colombia, the mean illiteracy rate is 32 percent ($p < 0.01$).[15] What is more, this divergence between the two groups has remained remarkably consistent over the twentieth century, even as all six countries dramatically improved their literacy rates (see also Kurtz 2013).

Are these patterns reflected in the effectiveness and quality of public policy? Policy effectiveness is multifaceted and a hard thing to pin down, as discussed earlier. Nonetheless, Heather Berkman et al. (2009) have collected data on public policy across Latin America and used these data to construct an index of policy quality, which I report in Table 3.3 as a proxy for policy effectiveness. This index consists of six separate components that include the stability of policy; the adaptability of policy in response to crisis events; the coherence and coordination of policy across the administration and bureaucracy; the quality and depth of policy implementation and enforcement; efficiency or leanness; and, finally, the public regardedness of policy, or the degree to which policies "produced by a given system pro-

Table 3.3 Policy Effectiveness

Country	Berkman et al. (2009) Index of Public Policy
Argentina	1.85
Bolivia	2.06
Brazil	2.43
Chile	3.04
Colombia	2.30
Costa Rica	2.43
Dominican Republic	2.05
Ecuador	1.84
El Salvador	2.33
Guatemala	1.90
Honduras	2.14
Mexico	2.33
Nicaragua	1.89
Panama	1.86
Paraguay	1.73
Peru	2.08
Uruguay	2.33
Venezuela	1.66

Source: Data are from the Politics of Policies Dataset, www.iadb.org/en/research-and-data/publication-details,3169.html?pub_id=dba-008.

mote the general welfare and resemble public goods . . . or whether they tend to funnel private benefits to certain individuals, factions or regions" (Spiller, Stein, and Tommasi 2008: 12). Again, the general patterns are clear. Chile, Uruguay, and Costa Rica have high-quality and effective public policies that provide broad-based public goods, in contrast to Paraguay, Nicaragua, Guatemala, and Ecuador.

These patterns are also reflected in Table 3.4, which reports an attitudinal measure for the rule of law in society from the Worldwide Governance Indicators (Kaufmann, Kraay, and Mastruzzi 2010).[16] The degree to which the rule of law is effectively and equally deployed across all societal actors, social strata, and territories is one of the key components of any understanding of policy effectiveness (O'Donnell 1998b). This measure ranges from −2.5 (weak rule of law) to 2.5 (strong rule of law). Once again, Chile and Uruguay clearly stand out from the other countries. In fact, they are the only two countries in this group with positive scores for the rule of law, suggesting that there is a general perception in these countries that their judicial and legal systems are effective and proportionally and equally applied. In contrast, Honduras, Guatemala, and Bolivia all have scores below −1.0. In these countries, the general perception is one of weak and ineffective judiciaries, police forces, and contract enforcement.

This variation in policy effectiveness clearly echoes the cross-country variation we can observe in state capacity. In fact, the relationship between state capacity, as measured by the mean tax revenue collected between 1990 and 2010 and one component of the policy effectiveness index, public

Table 3.4 The Rule of Law

Country	Rule of Law (2010)
Argentina	−0.46
Bolivia	−1.07
Chile	1.34
Colombia	−0.45
Guatemala	−1.11
Honduras	−1.23
Mexico	−0.58
Nicaragua	−0.65
El Salvador	−0.68
Uruguay	0.50

Source: Data are taken from the Worldwide Governance Indicators (Kaufmann, Kraay, and Mastruzzi 2010).

regardedness, which captures the degree to which policies provide broad-based public goods, appears to be very strong. The correlation is remarkably high, at least for this simple cross-section (0.6, $p = 0.008$). Of course, it is impossible to elicit causation from this cursory examination, but it clearly shows the strength of the contemporary relationship between state capacity and policy effectiveness across Latin America.

One final point: this discussion has suggested that there appears to be clear clustering between two different groups—those countries with high capacity and effective public policy and those with low capacity and narrow rent-seeking policies. There is also a notable gap between these two groups. Can anything be done to bolster state capacity in the latter group and narrow this gap? It is to this topic that I briefly turn next.

What Is the Future for State Capacity and Policy Effectiveness?

So, what is the future for state capacity and policy effectiveness in Latin America? Social scientists are notoriously bad at prediction and I therefore will limit myself to a discussion of some important factors that may influence the future trajectory of Latin American states. This is not an exhaustive list, but here I consider migration, labor informality, the rise of the new middle class, and organized crime. I see these issues as largely posing a threat to the strengthening of state capacity and, by implication, policy effectiveness, across the region.

One of the weaknesses of the state-building literature is its determinism. The major explanations are all dependent on big critical junctures to inspire change and, once placed on a particular development trajectory, it requires another critical juncture to alter this path meaningfully. This means that in the absence of such a systemic shock, it is difficult to imagine, at least from the perspective of causation, state capacity dramatically improving across the region. State capacity, of course, can plausibly improve incrementally over time. The successful implementation of a broad-based public goods program can increase support and confidence in the institutions of the state, increasing citizen engagement and state legitimacy. This may have a knock-on effect on revenue and tax evasion, resulting in a self-reinforcing (and endogenous) cycle of policy effectiveness and state capacity. Bolsa Família in Brazil, given that it covers nearly a quarter of the population, is perhaps an example of this. Nonetheless, it is much easier to foresee the gradual erosion of state capacity. Like tiny spears slowly causing blood loss to Goliath, the issues I discuss here all pose long-term threats to state capacity and subsequent policy effectiveness across the region.

Let me begin with growing labor informality. Bar the Southern Cone, across Latin America and particularly since liberalization, the size of the informal labor market has been steadily growing (Loayza, Servén, and Sugawara 2009). In some countries, such as Guatemala, Nicaragua, and Bolivia, the informal labor market now comprises over 65 percent of the economically active population. This is placing dual strains on the capacity of Latin American states. First, while atomized, members of the informal labor market nonetheless appear to have fairly unified preferences when it comes to support for more broad-based and universal social programs such as education and health, in opposition to more traditional and yet often narrow and regressive social security and pension provision (see Berens 2015; Castañeda-Angarita and Doyle 2015). In this sense, the growth of informal labor is placing pressure on the state to deliver more effective and broad-based public policies. At the same time, the informal labor market is largely outside the purview of the state and so is a serious challenge to the state's capacity to raise revenue through contributory income tax, thereby further eroding state capacity. For many administrations, this has left them with little option but to revert to consumption taxation to raise revenue, a more regressive form of taxation and in the context of this discussion, a less effective public policy (see Castañeda-Angarita and Doyle 2015). In this sense, there is clearly a tension between informality, state capacity, and policy effectiveness.

At the same time, and again particularly since the period of liberalization, some Latin American states have experienced a rapid growth in outward migration.[17] In fact, over 5.2 percent of the region's population are migrants (World Bank 2011: 25). Even aside from the fact that many of those leaving tend to be young, thereby depriving these countries of some of the most important sectors of their labor force, some work has begun to suggest that outward migration may have a deleterious effect on the capacity of the state via remittances; that is, money remitted by migrants back to family members in their country of origin. In 2011 alone, $62 billion was remitted to Latin American households (Ratha and Silwal 2012) and for some of the small Central American states, such as El Salvador and Honduras, remittances now account for over 15 percent of their annual GDP. I have argued that, given the scale of these financial transfers, these capital flows are exerting an effect on the political behavior and attitudes of those that receive them (Doyle 2015). If you receive remittances on a regular basis, this means that due to both your increased income and reduced personal risk, and the increase in your overall consumption power, you will have less support for government taxation, of any type, to fund redistribution. In effect, you will have a private social security and redistributive mechanism, which allows you to step out of the shadow of the state. In Latin American countries that have large outflows of migrants and large inflows of remittances, the implication is that state capacity and the effectiveness and penetration of public policy will diminish. This means that the chasm between weak and strong states across the region may widen further.

But even when countries across the region have enjoyed economic success during the past decade, plausible threats to state capacity still have emerged. One of these may be from an unlikely source—the rise of the middle class. Between 1995 and 2010, at least 40 percent of the region's households have moved up in socioeconomic class. While this largely involved movement to a vulnerable position somewhere between the poor and the middle class, the middle class itself did expand from 100 million in 2000 to 150 million by 2010 (see Ferreira et al. 2013).[18] However, as Ferreira et al. (2013) have suggested, contrary to what we might expect, the rise of this educated urban middle class does not necessarily mean a strengthening of state capacity and the solidification of the region's social contract. Rather, the existing weakness of the state and the ineffectiveness of public policy to deliver broad-based public goods may interact with these emerging social groups, causing these middle-class groups to opt out of the social contract. This means that rather than engaging with the state and paying taxes to ensure delivery of state services in health, education, security, and so forth, these new middle-class groups may instead prefer, given their disillusionment with existing public policy, to avoid taxation and seek private medical care, private education for their children, and private security for their homes, thereby further weakening already feeble states and reinforcing the ineffectiveness of public policy.[19]

Finally, it would be difficult to discuss state capacity and policy effectiveness in Latin America without some reference to crime. Much has already been written about inequality before the law across Latin America (see, e.g., O'Donnell 1998b; Foweraker and Krznaric 2002) and the lack of "horizontal accountability" (O'Donnell 1998a). With liberalization, however, and the advent of mass consumer demand for narcotics from North America and Europe, the growth of an organized and violent drug trade across the Andes and Central America has served to seriously exacerbate this problem. Crime and public security are now the main issues of concern for Latin American electorates, regardless of their ideological orientation (Wiesehomeier and Doyle 2014). Nearly every day, news stories report on the violence of this commerce and in many regions—for example, in parts of northern Mexico, Honduras, and Guatemala—it seems evident that the state has lost even the most basic Weberian of capacities to monopolize the use of force within its borders. An already weak judiciary and police force (e.g., Davis 2006) has allowed the state, in some rural areas, to be supplanted by *narcotraficantes*. In parts of the region, it is these groups, in all their different guises, that now tax the population, provide employment, and regulate the use of force. In these circumstances, it is reasonable to suggest that both the territorial reach of the state and the rule of law across society have largely been dismantled. Chronic policy ineffectiveness has been the result, manifest in spiraling homicide rates[20] and criminal impunity.[21]

Conclusion

By no means do I wish to be overly pessimistic. There are institutionally sound and strong states across the region, producing effective broad-based public policies that cut across social and geographic divisions. As Joe Foweraker (Chapter 2, this volume) notes, support for democracy has increased across Latin America, and indeed a quick glance at public opinion data clearly shows that, regardless of the country, a strong normative commitment to democracy pervades the region. However, while there is a normative commitment to democracy as a system of governance among the majority of Latin American citizens, there is more marked variation in the satisfaction of these citizens with the day-to-day functioning of their democracies. And again, this variation tends to reflect the patterns of state capacity and policy effectiveness that I discussed earlier.

It is this division between stronger states producing effective public policy and those weaker states producing policy that remains narrow and rent seeking that should be of major concern to policymakers and social scientists alike. Public policy and state capacity are, to a degree, locked in a self-reinforcing endogenous cycle. As policies become less effective and representative, citizens will increasingly evade tax and refuse to engage with their states, weakening the capacity of these states, thereby further undermining the efficacy of public policy, and so on. Given the contemporary threats to state capacity that I have discussed, escaping from this cycle is of paramount importance. Otherwise, we will continue to witness a growing chasm between strong and weak states across the region.

Notes

1. A caveat: I realize that policy effectiveness can be a difficult thing to separate from state capacity. Indeed, the claim that state capacity results in more effective public policies sidles toward a tautology. Additionally, as Kurtz warns, we do not necessarily want to elide "strong states" with particular policy content (2013: 57). The content of policy is primarily a product of ideological and distributional political battles. Strong states often produce policy with notably different content. Rather, our concern is how effective public policy actually is at producing broad-based public goods in as efficient a manner as possible.

2. For O'Donnell, the state is far more than the aggregate of public bureaucracies: "The state is also, and no less primarily, a set of social relations that establishes a certain order, and ultimately backs it with a centralized coercive guarantee, over a given territory" (1993). Some of these relations are embedded in a formal legal system, but some are norms and expectations.

3. And this effect will be either magnified or impeded by the nature of the electoral system (see Foweraker 1998) and the value of the party brand (Carroll and Shugart 2007). Of course, the choice of electoral system does not emerge from the ether so it is reasonable to suggest that, in countries with a large amount of brown areas, then there is pressure to choose more candidate-based electoral systems.

4. A situation that again is exacerbated depending on the level of executive power to which the president has recourse (Shugart and Carey 1992).

5. A relatively new strand of the literature has begun to suggest that an informal norm has developed across Latin America, allowing for the early removal of presidents before the end of their term, either through impeachment or the threat of impeachment, thereby alleviating the tension between the branches of government and allowing democracy to survive (see Pérez-Liñán 2007; Hochstetler 2006; Marsteintredet and Berntzen 2008).

6. Other work highlighted the informal institutions that enabled presidents to secure legislative support among coalition partners in Chile (see Siavelis 2006) or Ecuador (see Mejía Acosta 2006).

7. For Tilly (1990), technological innovations in defense and attack, such as the emergence of gunpowder and cannon, saw the practice of war move from its feudal roots to a larger, more professional, and mass-based endeavor. This change gave birth to an incentive to centralize administration and resources, paving the way for long-term institutional development.

8. The majority of conflicts across the region were intrastate and there was only one significant interstate conflict, the Chaco War (1932–1935), during the whole of the twentieth century (Kurtz 2013: 35). Yet Centeno (2002) and López-Alves (2000) have each attempted to use the experiences of war to explain state formation and state building in Latin America. However, both explanations do acknowledge the lack of interstate conflict and attempt to overcome this missing link in the causal chain by drawing on unique regional experiences such as that of limited war.

9. Thies (2005) has attempted to overcome this obstacle by suggesting that we cannot understand the experience of state formation and the variation in state capacity across Latin America with reference to interstate war, but rather with reference to interstate rivalry.

10. Other popular accounts of state formation highlight the importance of resource rents in undermining the incentives to construct wide-ranging state structures and the legacy of extractive colonial practices in establishing weak and vulnerable long-term institutional structures (Acemoglu, Johnson, and Robinson 2001).

11. It is worth noting that there are many similarities between the explanations for state capacity and some of the seminal explanations for the development of Latin American party systems. For example, Coppedge (1998) suggests that we can understand the variation in party system institutionalization across the region with reference to the timing of mass enfranchisement and electoral incorporation. Where clear political cleavages existed before the franchise was extended to the middle and working classes, then this was reflected in more stable and representative party systems and vice versa. It is no surprise that there should be a relationship between the party system and state capacity, or that more institutionalized and stable party systems should develop in tandem with stronger states, given the

incentives that brown areas create for political behavior and representation. This just reinforces the link between state capacity, policy effectiveness, and democratic quality.

12. For Roberts (2013), the adoption of the market model, and the ability of the state and political parties to successfully manage this process, became a critical juncture that has either aligned or dealigned party politics across the region, with long-lasting implications for representation and the quality of democracy.

13. Based on data from the Montevideo-Oxford Data Project, http://moxlad.fcs.edu.uy/es/basededatos.html.

14. This is not a trend that is limited to Latin America. Similar developments have also been observed in Europe (see Beramendi and Rueda 2007).

15. Again, based on data from the Montevideo-Oxford Data Project, http://moxlad.fcs.edu.uy/es/basededatos.html.

16. This is based on a series of elite, business, and public surveys. The measure reflects perceptions of the extent to which agents have confidence in and abide by the rules of society, and in particular the quality of contract enforcement, property rights, the police, and the courts as well as the likelihood of crime and violence. Of course, this is a perception-based approach and these measures are subject to selection biases and often conflate policy with institutions (see Kurtz 2013: 59–60).

17. Of course, there is clearly a causal relationship between state capacity and the growth of informality and outward migration. Where states have more capacity to deal with liberalization and compensate and protect those affected by this process through redistributive strategies, then we probably witness lower levels of informality and outward migration, in contrast to states with low capacity that are unable to effectively manage market reform.

18. The middle class—that is, all those earning between $10 and $50 a day—comprise about 30 percent of the Latin American population (Ferreira et al. 2013: 2).

19. O'Donnell was once again prescient when he suggested that

> the sharp, and deepening, dualism of our countries severely hinders the emergence of broad and effective solidarity. Social distances have increased, and the rich tend to isolate themselves from the strange and disquieting world of the dispossessed. The fortified ghettos of the rich and the secluded schools of their children bear witness to their incorporation into the trans nationalized networks of modernity, as well as of the gulf that separates them from large segments of the national population. (1996: 7)

20. Honduras, for example, now has the highest homicide rate in the world at 90.4 per 100,000. In contrast, Singapore has a homicide rate of 0.2 per 100,000 (UNODC 2013).

21. This is characterized by the mass kidnapping of forty-three students in Iguala, Mexico, in September 2014 following a protest at a conference led by the local mayor's wife.

4

Inequality and Democratic Representation

Melissa Ziegler Rogers

Latin America has the highest inequality of any region in the world. Uneven distribution of income fundamentally threatens the continuance and quality of democracy in the region. Unequal democracies face threat from both the rich, who fear redistribution to the poor majority, and the poor, who see existing institutions as unresponsive to their demands (Acemoglu and Robinson 2006). Related to this, inequality may have distorting effects on the party system and encourage clientelism. The quality of democratic institutions, including voter turnout especially among the poor, is also known to be worse where income is more disparate. These dynamics are troubling in any nation, but are particularly so where nascent democratic institutions and young governments may not be able to manage these conflicts.

This chapter addresses the role of inequality in Latin America from a different approach than nearly all previous work. I focus on the threats to democratic quality that may come from interregional inequality—divergence in income level and economic productivity across geographic regions within a nation. I compare these effects to those expected from interpersonal inequality and examine how democratic political institutions structure attention on these distinct types of inequality. My modest goal in this chapter is to show a systematic difference between interpersonal inequality, the unequal distribution across individuals, and interregional inequality. Latin America has long been discussed as the region of the world with the highest interpersonal income inequality. The data below show that Latin America also has the highest level of interregional inequality of any global region.

Using a new dataset on interregional inequality, interpersonal inequality, and government spending in Latin America, I show that these types of inequality display different incidence and effects. Not only are these types of inequality conceptually distinct, they also drive divergent government behavior. I address the classic political economy concern with the effect

51

of inequality on government spending, applying the existing theoretical work to interregional as well as interpersonal inequality. I found that while interpersonal inequality tends to prompt higher government spending to address social ills in the region, interregional inequality has an opposite and robust effect to drive down government spending as regions become more lopsided. This finding alone has implications for the quality of democracy if indeed the regional demand for redistribution is disconnected from its supply.

In this study, I took a cautious further step to address whether certain political institutions may condition government responses to inequality. I suggest that electoral rules vary in their attentiveness and reactions to regional versus interpersonal concerns. Some nations have electoral systems more attuned to the challenges of interpersonal inequality: namely, centralized strong party systems with broad social constituencies. Other countries' national institutions are more clearly geographic in orientation, with decentralized political and administrative systems and strong personal vote connections to local zones. How and whether nations address these challenges of inequality will depend fundamentally on how political bargains are struck in nations and the incentives of politicians to represent constituents.

The chapter is structured as follows. First, I address the concept and incidence of interpersonal and interregional inequality within Latin America and in comparative perspective with the rest of the world. Second, I suggest theoretical reasons why interpersonal and interregional inequality may drive conflict in governments and different ways these conflicts are managed within democratic political institutions. Third, I show empirical results on the relationship between inequality and government spending and the interaction between inequality and political institutions on government spending. Finally, I link the findings in this chapter to the quality of representation for the less privileged in Latin America's democracies.

Background: Inequality and Democracy in Latin America

The historic focus of inequality and democracy in Latin America has been on the uneven distribution of income and resources (especially land) among individuals within a nation (Acemoglu and Robinson 2006; Boix 2003). Interpersonal inequality is the concept that motivates nearly all studies (and quantitative measures) of inequality in academic and policy research. This focus on distribution among individuals is appropriate and important, but does not paint a complete picture of politically relevant inequality. Most countries, especially in the developing world, have wide variance in administrative and political authority within their territory and weak mechanisms for government distribution across individuals and regions. Moreover, democratic politics in most nations of the world are organized spatially, around geographic jurisdictions, rather than individuals. Geography, and distribution across regions, is thus important to politics in many nations, and inequality of individuals and regions is irrevocably intertwined. To advance our understanding of distributive conflict in Latin America, we need to consider in more detail how inequality across regions influences political outcomes and thus democratic quality.

Latin America, like much of the developing (but also the developed) world, is characterized by uneven development and agglomeration around a central city. In most nations, the population of the largest city dwarfs the size of any other city. In Latin America, the examples of population concentration come easily to mind—the megacities of Mexico City, Buenos Aires, and São Paolo dominate the population and economic activity of their respective nations. Latin America is a highly urbanized region of the world, second only to the wealthiest Organisation for Economic Co-operation and Development (OECD) nations in urban population, and much of this population is concentrated in one city center. These cities in Latin America are modern, economically diverse, and reminiscent of their counterparts in the developed world. However, much of the area outside of the capitals of Latin American countries is set apart by economic stagnation and depressed development (Sawers 1996).

The history of any country is structured by distributive conflict not only between social groups (rich and poor classes), but also between regions and economic sectors. The wealthy in agricultural regions, for example, may have fundamentally different economic interests from the wealthy in industrial regions. Their attitudes toward redistribution, trade openness, and government investment may be more strictly opposed than those of rich and poor within the same sectors and regions (Cusack, Iversen, and Soskice 2007). National policies strongly affect interpersonal distributions of income, of course, through labor and social welfare policies. Central policies are perhaps even more critical, however, to adjudicating between regions and economic sectors through laws addressing trade policy, taxation and subsidization, and fiscal federalism. Import-substitution industrialization provides a cogent example of political adjudication of regional interests in Latin America.

Regional inequality is largely absent from politics research for both theoretical and empirical reasons. Historical accounts of inequality in most nations have typically centered on class interests, in narratives motivated by the experience of class conflict in Western European nations. Additionally, the measurement of inequality has focused nearly exclusively on individual or household distributions of income quintiles, through indicators such as the Gini coefficient and the ratio of low to high incomes (e.g., 90/10 quintiles, 50/10 quintiles). This chapter is meant to address both gaps in this literature, by raising theoretical reasons to focus on regional distributive conflict and its role in democratic quality, and by adding quantitative evidence to begin to explore these questions.

In Table 4.1, the incidence of interregional inequality is shown for available Latin American countries for the period 2000–2010. The measure listed is the population-weighted coefficient of variance in regional GDP per capita, discussed in more detail below. It is apparent in the table that the level of interregional inequality in the region varies quite widely, from the low in Bolivia to the high in Mexico. The large federations of Latin America have strikingly high levels of interregional inequality. Not surprisingly, differences in regional income are a pervasive political concern in Argentina, Brazil, and Mexico. Even the countries with relatively low levels in comparison to their neighbors, such as Bolivia or Colombia, are nonetheless on the upper side of the global scale.

Table 4.2 features average values of global regions to compare Latin America to other parts of the world, again in the period 2000–2010. Table 4.2 reveals that the Latin American region has very high levels of interregional inequality. This level is particularly striking in comparison with Western Europe. Each Latin American country has interregional inequality levels higher than each Western European nation. In fact, if you exclude Indonesia (the highest value in the world) from the Southeast Asian sample, Latin America has the highest inequality of any global region. These simple charts reveal the potential relevance of the question of interregional inequality to the political environment of Latin America today.

Table 4.1 Regional Inequality in Latin American Countries, 2000–2010

Country	Regional Inequality Score
Argentina	0.621
Brazil	0.485
Bolivia	0.306
Chile	0.421
Colombia	0.388
Ecuador	0.610
Mexico	0.719
Panama	0.483
Peru	0.495

Table 4.2 Regional Inequality in Global Perspective, 2000–2010

Global Region	Regional Inequality Score
Latin America	0.477
Western Europe, North America, Australia, and New Zealand	0.206
Eastern Europe and the former Soviet Union	0.373
East Asia	0.342
Southeast Asia	0.626
South Asia	0.402

The interregional measures of inequality shown above are calculations of coefficients of variance in regional GDP per capita. The regional unit used in this study is the state, province, or department as defined by the nation itself. The conceptual analog is to the US state, although the powers designated to those units clearly vary across nations. The coefficient of variance aggregates the values of regional GDP to one value for a nation that is comparable across nations. The interregional inequality measure shown above is weighted according to regional population, on the assumption that regional wealth or poverty is more politically meaningful when attributed to a large segment of the population. The calculation formula is shown in Figure 4.1 below and the summary statistics for nations in the sample can be found in Appendix 1.

A few examples provide some context for the regional gaps in Latin America that are apparent in these indicators. In Argentina, the city and province of Buenos Aires together produce nearly 70 percent of national GDP. Thus, two provinces out of twenty-four generate the vast majority of economic output, and nineteen of twenty-four produce less than 1 percent of GDP each. Of course, the measures use regional GDP per capita, rather than GDP, meaning certain provinces with high productivity relative to sparse population (e.g., Santa Cruz or Neuquén) dampen the statistical effect of what is highly lopsided economic output. Similarly, São Paolo in Brazil and the federal district of Mexico alone produce 33 percent and 16 percent of GDP, respectively. Bogotá produces 25 percent of GDP in Colombia. These figures indicate a geographic concentration of economic might within Latin American countries.

These simple summary statistics reveal a notable difference between inequality in Latin America and the rest of the world. In the sections below, I apply these new data to much-studied relationships between inequality and redistributive politics in the political economy literature. As the most common entry point into this literature, I examine the differences between the two types of inequality for their effect on total government spending. Next, I address the role that political institutions play in this distribution—what incentives do politicians under different systems of representation have to deliver goods to social groups or regions?

Inequality and Government Spending in Latin America

Inequality encourages political conflict as rich and poor groups articulate different preferences for government spending. In the most simplistic formulation of economic reasoning, rich groups should press for lower government spending under increasing inequality. In a progressive tax system, government spending is inherently redistributive—those who benefit from government spend less to consume it. Poor groups should have opposite preferences, pressing for more redistributive government spending as inequality grows. These dynamics have been almost exclusively attributed to rich and poor individuals, most famously through the Romer-Meltzer-Richard model (RMR model; Romer 1975; Meltzer and Richard 1981).[1] They can also be reasonably attributed to regional actors who face similar incentives to block or advocate redistribution. Rich regions, like rich individuals, should hope to limit government spending and, under certain institutional conditions, have the means to do it (Giuranno 2009; Rogers 2016).

Where politics is structured and resources are administered along geographic lines, politicians and voters are incentivized to evaluate distributional concerns in terms of their region (Beramendi 2012). Certain political institutions, notably geographic constituencies, federalism, personal vote elections, and, to some extent, presidentialism territorialize political competition (Rogers 2016). In contrast, parliamentarism, closed list proportional representation, and unitarism have centripetal effects—they encourage focus on national politics (Gerring, Thacker, and Moreno 2005).

Where resources are divided to provinces or districts, politicians push to maximize resources going to their district, regardless of whether they prefer fiscal constraint or expansion at the national level (Rehfeld 2005). Federalism, bicameralism, electoral rules, and even the presidential-parliamentary distinction not present in Latin America inform politicians and voters about whether they should think primarily in terms of their districts or their social group, or both. All political systems have some concept of both geography and social group representation, of course, but most systems fall closer to one or the other. Chile, for example, has very nationally oriented politics while Colombia is a strongly local political system. These institutional features shape the distributive debate in a nation to be either more concerned with local public goods or with broad social goods (Milesi-Ferretti, Perotti, and Rostagno 2002).

The primary reason politicians in geographically oriented systems focus on local allocation is that politicians' careers depend on pleasing their districts. This takes different forms depending on the structure of political institutions. For US politicians, this means bringing home pork to their districts to win reelection (Grimmer 2013). For Argentina and Brazil, federalized career paths incentivize attracting central transfers to the coffers of governors. In Chile, politicians' career paths depend more on national parties that aim to please social constituencies that span regions (Harbers 2009). Political institutions fundamentally shape whether politicians (and voters) evaluate the national distributive game in regional terms.

The examples above of the United States, Argentina, and Brazil provide clear examples of institutions that influence distributive structures in national politics. First, the US localized credit claiming is attributed primarily to the personal vote, which stems from single-member district simple plurality systems for members of Congress (Cain, Ferejohn, and Fiorina 1987). All legislators in the United States (and some in Latin America) are elected according to these rules, which motivate members to bring resources back home. In Argentina, there is not an equivalent personal vote because members are elected through closed list proportional representation. However, list access is determined by local party leaders, typically the governor. Accordingly, the nomination process for national legislators makes politicians think about national policy in provincial terms (Jones et al. 2002). Open list proportional representation in Brazil incentivizes credit claiming for politicians who must compete within their own party lists. Bringing resources to their home territory is one way to distinguish themselves, although the specific geographic pull is less clear than in single-member districts (Samuels 2002).

In this analysis, I focused on the effects of electoral rules, as opposed to the more obvious choice of federalism, on the territorialization of politics. Importantly for both the theoretical implications and the empirics, the design of electoral rules is not obviously endogenous to regional disparity. The case has been made that the design of federalism is endogenous to regional inequality (Bolton and Roland 1997; Beramendi 2012). The design of electoral rules has been argued to be endogenously driven by class conflict, but not regional inequality (Boix 1999; Cusack, Iversen, and Soskice 2007). Variation in electoral system design in Western Europe, for example, has been attributed to concerns with income redistribution and social insurance (Boix 1999; Iversen and Soskice 2006). Class conflict may have regional implications, of course, but the primary motivation for electoral rule design appears to be whether incumbent groups can win a majority, or will need to share power with rising socialist parties. In this regard, electoral rules that territorialize politics may be plausibly exogenous to concerns of regional inequality per se. Of course, this question remains for future research.

The dynamics of regional preferences are not as straightforward as those of individuals.[2] While rich regions may want to keep their resources within their borders, there is individual heterogeneity within those borders. More specifically, rich regions have both rich and poor individuals with different preferences for government spending. Under different institutional and economic conditions, poor or rich groups can form coalitions across regional borders to maximize their gains as social groups, rather than regional units (Beramendi, Rogers, and Diaz-Cayeros, forthcoming). Just as with regional interests, therefore, the institutional structure of national politics should be crucial to how and whether groups of individuals or regions are able to collectively act to attain their policy preferences.

This introductory empirical investigation of regional and interpersonal dynamics tested two primary questions: What is the effect of regional inequality on government spending? And how do political institutions condition the effect of inequality on government spending? These questions are complex and the empirical analysis is necessarily preliminary, so I keep the theoretical explanation short and concise, relying on existing theories with specific application to regional dynamics in the Latin American context in particular.

Theoretical Expectations

The RMR model of interpersonal inequality shows that increasing inequality should drive higher government spending. In this theory and its extensions, the decisive median voter will push for higher government spending as inequality grows. The median voter, who grows poorer relative to the mean voter with rising inequality, should advocate more government spending that is increasingly redistributive as incomes become more uneven in a progressive tax system. The simplified model of this theory has been largely dismissed for empirical and theoretical reasons in comparative political economy. The empirical predictions are not born out in the data; in fact, the opposite is often shown to be more accurate—inequality drives down government spending rather than increases it (cf. Alesina and Glaeser 2004; Benabou 2000; Gouveia and Masia 1998).

One reason for these weak empirical findings is the inadequate portrayal of the political process in the RMR model. That the median voter is decisive (or, more cogently, that the full spectrum of individuals votes) has been seriously refuted in formal and theoretical models (Benabou 2000; Gerber and Lewis 2004; Beramendi 2007). More importantly for the purposes here, RMR assumes a form of political representation—a single district with direct democracy—that is far removed from politics in any nation. Rather, nations divide their territory into voting districts, most often in geographic units, and establish a range of actors with veto authority able to halt the interests of the aggregate median voter. Regional inequality will press distributive conflict that discourages cooperation and coordination to boost government spending. For a large sample of countries, Rogers (2016) has shown that political institutions empower regions to constrain government spending through veto authority and enable poor individuals to increase government spending through majority power. As interregional inequality grows, therefore, rich regions should have greater incentive to block spending, leading to my expectation in Hypothesis 1.

Hypothesis 1: Higher interregional inequality drives lower government spending.

Electoral systems structure the bargaining dynamics of politicians, whether on the grounds of interpersonal or interregional inequality. By dividing nations into regional electoral units, the interests of regions are highlighted and voter incentives to express preferences on a regional basis become more likely. Electoral systems affect whether politicians think more in local or national terms, increasing or decreasing the relevance of the region-specific preferences. In this manner, incentives created by electoral systems interact with inequality to influence government distribution.

Hypothesis 2: Electoral institutions interact with regional inequality to shape government spending.

Research Design

The basic statistical model for Hypotheses 1 and 2 is

Total Government Spending/GDP =
βRegional Inequality + βInterpersonal Inequality +
βRegional Inequality * Personal Vote + βInterpersonal Inequality *
Personal Vote + βPersonal Vote + βPopulation(log) +
βTrade Openness + βCapital Openness + βGDP per capita (log) +

$\beta GDP\ Growth + \beta$Ethnic Fractionalization $+ \beta$Population over 65 $+$
βFederalism $+ \varepsilon$

Dependent Variables

The large literature on the effects of income inequality on government policy typically begins with an analysis of government spending overall and redistributive spending (typically, social transfers) in particular. This analysis is a comparison of interregional measures of inequality to interpersonal measures of inequality, so I employed this most common measure, government spending, as the primary dependent variable. Of course, other dependent variables are highly relevant and will be explored in the future. For this preliminary research, I preferred to evaluate the effects of inequality as they have been traditionally measured in the field so that scholars could have a direct apples-to-apples comparison.

Within the government spending categories, I used two common measures—general government and central government expenditures.[3] General government expenditure refers to spending at all levels of government (central, state, local). Central government expenditure is restricted to resources distributed by the national government. In theory, the central government variable may seem the most appropriate for evaluating the effects of regional inequality on national policymaking. The framework I have provided is one in which representatives of regions and social groups come to the national bargaining table to divide up the spoils of the central government. However, I think it is appropriate to consider general government expenditures for at least two reasons. First, one primary effect of fiscal federalism (which would be captured only in general government measures) is for subnational regions to tax and spend to their own preferences. Expenditures in jurisdictions below the national level could be strongly affected by regional inequality as rich territories spend at high levels to their preferences and tax bases, and poorer areas have fewer resources to distribute. Moreover, poor regions are subsidized with (somewhat) progressive national transfers that plump their spending.

Second, regional inequality may be endogenously related to the fiscal structure of a nation (Beramendi 2012). That is, rich regions may prefer to decentralize many government functions so that they can consume to their preferences without subsidizing poorer regions. Regional inequality in this case would not necessarily reduce government spending, but shift its geographic incidence. In that case, central government spending would still be the best theoretical indicator of the effect of regional inequality on shared resources, but the comparison with general government spending would provide a more complete picture of its overall impact.

Independent Variables

Regional development has long been a topic of interest in political geography and economics but not much explored in political science due, in large part, to a dearth of data and theoretical models devoid of geography. In this study, I utilized a large dataset of interregional inequality collected from fifty nations around the world for the period 1980–2010 (Rogers 2016).[4] The focus of this examination was the nine available Latin American countries (Argentina, Brazil, Bolivia, Chile, Colombia, Ecuador, Mexico, Panama, Peru), with comparison to results for the entire sample. Although not all Latin American countries have available data, those countries included account for the vast majority of citizens and economic productivity in the region.

    The interregional inequality measures used in this analysis are country-year observations synthesizing region-level GDP per capita data for each country. I employed the population-weighted coefficient of variance of regional GDP per capita.[5] The formula for this measure is shown in Figure 4.1, with y representing regional GDP per capita, n the number of regional units, and p the population. This indicator is calculated independent of the number of regions considered, is not sensitive to shifts in average GDP level, and satisfies the Pigou-Dalton principle.[6]

    Importantly, regional inequality is not fixed in Latin America. Several of the nations included have experienced significant changes in regional inequality in the period under examination. For example, in Bolivia, the regional inequality value fluctuated between .2 and .39, a nearly 100 percent difference between the minimum and maximum value between 1988 and 2011. Notable changes are also observable in regional inequality in Mexico and Chile, with fluctuations of 50 percent between the minimum and maximum observed value. Other countries' values, such as Peru and

Figure 4.1 Calculation of Regional Inequality Measure

$$\frac{1}{\bar{y}}\left[\sum_{i=1}^{n} p_i(\bar{y}-y_i)^2\right]^{1/2}$$

Note: y-bar represents the country's average GDP per capita, y_i is the GDP per capita of region i, n is the number of regional units, and p_i is the share of the country's total population in region i.

Panama, were relatively static. Appendix 3 and Appendix 4 show changes over time in the Latin American sample nations, and descriptive statistics by nation. Overall regional inequality fluctuated somewhat less in the Latin American (standard deviation = .14) than in the global sample (standard deviation = .20), but the changes are nonetheless notable. In comparison, the Gini coefficient of income inequality had a standard deviation of .04 in Latin America and .09 in the global sample. This variation over time makes the regional inequality data plausibly suitable for time series cross-sectional regression analysis.[7]

I compared the effects of interregional inequality to available measures of interpersonal inequality, namely, the Gini coefficient. The Gini coefficient is the most widely used measure of interpersonal inequality and it is based on a nationally aggregated concept of inequality between quintiles of income.[8] Of several available cross-national datasets of interpersonal inequality, I used Frederick Solt's data, the Standardized World Income Inequality Database (SWIID) (see Solt 2009). These data have advantages both in coverage (which tends to be spotty in Latin American countries) and in distinguishing income before (Gini market) and after (Gini net) government transfers. For theoretical reasons, I used the Gini market value in the regression analysis. I was looking for the effect of inequality on government spending, therefore the Gini market value provided a cleaner indicator because it excludes government taxation and spending in its calculations. Intraregional inequality is also a relevant distributive concern to national politics but data are sparse, even in OECD countries, and are not commonly collected by Latin American countries (see Beramendi, Rogers, and Diaz-Cayeros, forthcoming). Accordingly, I could not include these values in the analysis.

The theoretical focus of this chapter is on the interaction between inequality and political institutions. I focused in this preliminary research on the effect of electoral rules, although I recognize many other institutions can influence these dynamics (Rogers 2016). Accordingly, I measured political institutions to capture the incentives of politicians to deliver resources to social or geographic constituencies with a measure of the personal vote (Carey and Shugart 1995). The personal vote is not, by definition, a geographic concept but tends to relate highly to the spatial orientation of a country's political institutions.

The personal vote is the relative value of an individual politician's reputation to his or her party's reputation in the electoral fate of that politician. The personal vote is high when politicians must distinguish themselves on personal characteristics rather than party characteristics. This highlights the intraparty conflicts as well as the localized incentives that are the focus of my theoretical development. The personal vote measure is an additive index of ballot structure (takes a value of 2 if parties do not control access or ordering of candidates, 1 if parties control access or order, 0 if parties control both access and ordering), vote pooling (2 if votes are not pooled, 1 if votes pooled across some members in a district, 0 if votes pooled across all members), vote type (2 if voters cast a vote for one individual candidate, 1 if voters cast a vote for a party, 0 if voters cast one vote for a party), and district magnitude (Johnson and Wallack 2006).[9] For each component of the index except the district magnitude, a higher value implies a higher personal vote.[10]

For my purposes, I was concerned with the extent to which politicians must think about their local jurisdiction more than the nation as a whole. I argue the same electoral system structures that tend to cultivate personal reputations are also those most likely to encourage geographic-focused representation. Although this is not a perfect measure of the concept, it does provide a reasonable proxy for the geographic orientation of an electoral system. The average values of the personal vote scores, by Latin American country, are shown in Appendix 2.

Control Variables

When measuring government spending, several economic and demographic characteristics are necessary to isolate specific political effects. The first is level of development, measured with the log value of gross domestic product per capita (GDPPC) corrected for purchasing power parity. This variable helps to control for Wagner's law, which predicts higher government spending as countries grow richer. Second is population, again logged, because larger populations might offer returns to scale in delivery of public services (the numerator) or increase productive capacity (the denominator). The third is an age ratio, the percentage of the population aged sixty-five years and older. In developed countries, this is an important variable to capture the size of the population dependent on government health and income subsidies. This variable may not be quite as relevant in certain Latin American countries, but should play a role in places such as Argentina, Chile, or Mexico, with notable pension systems.

I included ethnic fractionalization because some studies have found social expenditure is lower where ethnic heterogeneity (and, presumably, ethnic tensions) is high (Alesina, Baqir, and Easterly 1999). This may be important, in particular, in the countries with considerable indigenous populations such as Bolivia and Peru, and racial diversity such as Brazil. Globalization, measured as trade openness and capital openness, also controls for the likelihood that countries with open borders are constrained from taxing at high levels to provide government services. With very open markets, this variable could be even more important in Latin American countries (Wibbels and Arce 2003).

Political institutions other than electoral rules may have similar effects on the territorial scope of national politics. Most importantly, federalism should orient budgets and politician behavior more toward the regions than unitary systems. Federalism is particularly important toward explaining central government expenditure, which should be low relative to unitary systems because significant fiscal activity occurs at the subnational level. I also controlled for institutions that may influence the speed and veto authority in the budget process, including the presidential budget authority (Alesina et al. 1999) and territorial bicameralism in alternative models. The budget authority was similar (and high) for the president in the included countries, with the possible (relative) exception of Peru. Bicameralism is frequently linked to territorial politics and was present in the bigger (and more decentralized) countries in the sample. Only Chile featured a unitary system and bicameralism in the sample. I excluded country fixed effects because I was concerned primarily with the variance across countries on regional inequality and political institutions. The political institutions were fixed in the sample, with the exception of Bolivia, prohibiting over time within country comparisons. Regional inequality did change over time in the sample, but it was a slow-moving variable. Accordingly, cross-country comparisons offered more theoretical and empirical value in this initial examination.

Estimation Techniques

Predicting government spending requires several adaptations to the standard ordinary least squares model to correct for violations of its assumptions. Throughout, I employed panel corrected standard errors (PCSE). I controlled for autoregression in spending with the lagged dependent variable, or alternative, an autoregressive (AR1) process, to reduce the considerable variance absorbed by the lagged dependent variable.[11] In the models presented in the body of the text, I focused on PCSE models with AR1 autocorrelation.

Results

Effects

Interregional inequality had a consistent effect of reducing government spending relative to GDP in a cross-national sample. This result, and its comparison with interpersonal inequality, is shown in Table 4.3. This effect

Table 4.3 Effect of Inequality on Government Spending (percentage of GDP)

	Latin American Countries		All Available Countries	
	General Government Expenditure, % of GDP	Central Government Expenditure, % of GDP	General Government Expenditure, % of GDP	Central Government Expenditure, % of GDP
Regional inequality	−6.266** (3.105)	−21.514*** (4.555)	−3.370*** (1.210)	−4.594** (2.281)
Gini coefficient	0.430*** (0.099)	0.658*** (0.116)	0.019 (0.028)	0.181** (0.077)
GDP growth	−0.100*** (0.039)	−0.098** (0.044)	−0.108*** (0.020)	−0.203*** (0.042)
Population over age 65	0.983* (0.588)	3.122*** (0.434)	0.525*** (0.101)	1.619*** (0.231)
GDP per capita (logged)	0.403 (2.317)	0.756 (2.563)	0.000 (0.539)	−2.754*** (0.996)
Population (logged)	0.411 (0.644)	0.645 (0.691)	−0.445* (0.247)	−1.958*** (0.457)
Capital openness	0.599* (0.326)	−0.124 (0.292)	0.119 (0.163)	−0.734*** (0.285)
Trade openness	−0.011 (0.017)	0.056*** (0.017)	−0.009 (0.008)	0.026 (0.017)
Personal vote rank	0.261** (0.119)	0.606*** (0.153)	0.044 (0.070)	0.1 (0.126)
Ethnic fractionalization	11.687** (5.509)	24.462*** (6.301)	−0.391 (1.089)	−4.185 (2.772)
Federalism	1.492** (0.650)	0.746 (0.602)		
Constant	−25.187 (22.126)	−49.890* (25.643)	13.918*** (5.060)	38.252*** (9.639)
R^2	0.518	0.842	0.586	0.614
Observations	127	83	875	725
Countries	9	8	45	42
Country fixed effects	No	No	No	No
χ^2, F [Prob > F]	58.773 (0.00)	200.935 (0.00)	269.423 (0.00)	332.485 (0.00)

Note: GDP is gross domestic product.
*p <0.1, **p<0.05, ***p<0.01, two-tailed test.

was thoroughly documented for the Latin American cases and held true for the larger sample of all available countries with regional inequality data on the right side of Tables 4.3 and 4.4 (Rogers 2016). Whether the dependent variable was general or central government spending, a rise in interregional inequality was associated with a reduction in government output.

Interpersonal inequality, measured with the Gini coefficient, appeared to have a strong positive effect on government spending in the Latin American sample. In the global sample, the effect was highly inconsistent and often negative.

The control variables performed largely as expected. The personal vote was associated with increased spending in the Latin American sample, but had no clear effect in the full sample. Importantly, the personal vote was not a proxy for regional conflict, but for territorialized political institutions.[12] Territorial orientation of politics may very well incentivize overspending on pork by districted politicians who have little regard for the national budget. However, nationalizing political institutions may also encourage overspending as politicians collude to extract rents (Persson, Roland, and Tabellini 1997). There are conflicting expectations for how the personal vote should impact government spending overall, but district-targeting incentives are likely to drive down social spending in the national budget (Milesi-Ferretti, Perotti, and Rostagno 2002).

The effect of trade on spending was negative, although capital openness had an ambiguous, and sometimes positive, effect on spending. There was no evidence of the Wagner effect—that higher GDP per capita drives increased spending—in the Latin American or general sample. Contrary to broad expectations, in the Latin American sample, ethnic fractionalization was associated with higher government spending relative to GDP. The association was negative in the full sample, but not significant. The effect of ethnic fractionalization may have been driven in the Latin American sample by the relatively high spending and high fractionalization in Brazil, Bolivia, and Colombia. GDP growth was associated with reduced spending, likely because the denominator grew and spending did not keep pace.

The effect of interregional inequality on spending in Latin America was the opposite of that on interpersonal inequality. While differences in income across individuals drove higher government spending, as regions became more unequal, the generosity of national expenditure declined. This is an important difference in the nature of inequality and its relation to government that has not been previously theorized or tested in Latin American countries. The important question becomes, Why, in Latin American countries, does distributive conflict manifest itself in two distinct ways? Why do the preferences of rich regions win out in Latin America while the desires of the poor individuals appear to shape changes in government spending? I discuss two of many possible answers here. First, it is possible that rich regions are also unequal regions (such Buenos Aires), so rich regions may align with poor regions for social spending that will benefit their poor individuals but dampen spending that will redistribute to other, poorer, regions. This is unlikely in Brazil and Mexico in which the rich regions are also

Table 4.4 Interactive Effect of Inequality and Electoral Institutions on Government Spending (percentage of GDP)

	Latin American Countries			
	General Government Expenditure	Central Government Expenditure	General Government Expenditure	Central Government Expenditure
Regional inequality	−12.457***	−5.883*	−27.505***	−18.187***
	(3.971)	(3.193)	(6.436)	(4.161)
Gini coefficient	0.509***	0.623***	0.647***	0.610***
	(0.090)	(0.166)	(0.106)	(0.210)
Regional inequality x personal vote rank	1.163*		1.379	
	(0.694)		(1.229)	
Gini coefficient x personal vote rank		−0.036		−0.004
		(0.028)		(0.045)
Personal vote rank	−0.124	2.086	0.166	0.85
	(0.241)	(1.451)	(0.437)	(2.340)
GDP growth	−0.099**	−0.095**	−0.097**	−0.099**
	(0.042)	(0.038)	(0.044)	(0.045)
Population over age 65	1.499***	1.093*	3.517***	3.052***
	(0.519)	(0.580)	(0.540)	(0.423)
GDP per capita (logged)	−0.568	−0.348	−0.466	0.006
	(2.041)	(2.459)	(2.592)	(3.028)
Population (logged)	0.47	0.346	0.587	0.97
	(0.584)	(0.628)	(0.678)	(0.695)
Capital openness	0.488	0.641**	0.035	−0.256
	(0.328)	(0.327)	(0.312)	(0.264)
Trade openness	−0.006	−0.014	0.053***	0.059***
	(0.016)	(0.017)	(0.017)	(0.017)
Ethnic fractionalization	12.666**	10.632*	24.463***	23.389***
	(5.123)	(5.555)	(6.209)	(6.755)
Federalism	1.505***	1.666**	0.968	
	(0.552)	(0.661)	(0.600)	
Constant	−22.371	−28.398	−39.195	−41.979*
	(20.120)	(21.023)	(25.675)	(25.398)
R^2	0.545	0.525	0.845	0.836
Observations	127	127	83	85
Countries	9	9	8	8
Country fixed effects	No	No	No	No
χ^2, F				
[Prob > F]	90.782 (0.00)	58.4 (0.00)	254.528 (0.00)	197.75 (0.00)

Note: GDP is gross domestic product.
*$p<0.1$, **$p<0.05$, ***$p<0.01$, two-tailed test.

more equal. It is plausible in Argentina, but unknown in the other countries in the sample (Beramendi, Rogers, and Diaz-Cayeros, forthcoming).

Another possibility that I could test more directly is how the electoral rules shape political winners and losers. Does the political system give incentives for politicians to cater to geographic regions or to social classes? If politicians are rewarded for representing the poor as a group, for example, we should expect interpersonal inequality to drive higher government spending. If, however, all politics is local, then politicians should advocate geographically based resources as interregional inequality increases. I examine this below with the electoral system variables from Latin America.

Conditional Effects:
Inequality Under Different Electoral Systems

The simple theory I offered above is that politicians should care about different constituencies depending on electoral rules. If electoral rules incentivize politicians to deliver goods to national social groups, regional concerns should be less important. If electoral rules motivate locally oriented thinking, politicians will debate geographically oriented spending with more fervency. What is unclear from this theory is what the general effect of inequality should be, given the electoral system. Does regional inequality drive more or less spending in regionally oriented political systems? Does interpersonal inequality drive a wedge between voters and politicians only in party systems oriented to social class? The interactive results of inequality based on electoral system help to sort these dynamics.

Figure 4.2 Marginal Effect of Regional Inequality by Personal Vote Rank, Latin America

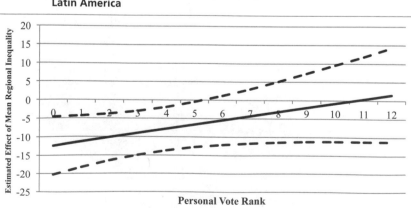

Figure 4.3 Marginal Effect of Interpersonal Inequality by Personal Vote Rank, Latin America

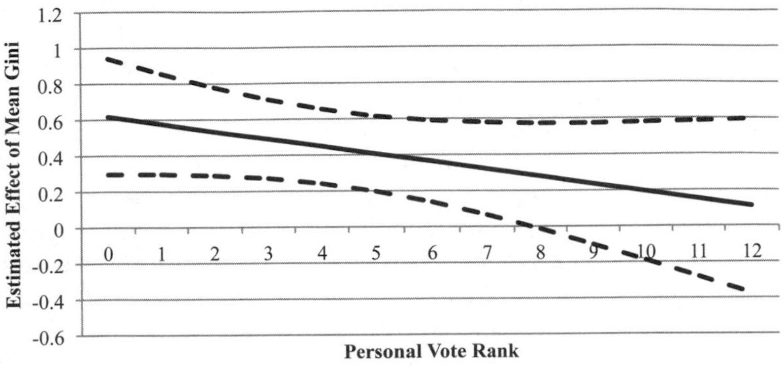

The conditional effects of inequality, based on the electoral system, are featured in Table 4.4. Recall that the personal vote was measured as a ranking of electoral systems by Joel W. Johnson and Jessica S. Wallack (2006). The higher the rank, the more personal vote oriented was that political system. The lower the rank, the stronger was the party vote. Accordingly, when interpreting the statistical effect of interregional and interpersonal inequality under different electoral systems, I looked for opposite signs to show similar effects and similar signs to show distinct effects. I expected interpersonal inequality to matter most in party vote systems (low personal vote rank) and interregional inequality to matter most in personal vote systems (high personal vote rank). Mattering within an electoral system, of course, may mean higher or lower spending or no effect at all. This is what I explored in the marginal effects. The results of interaction effects were not easily read through statistical output. Accordingly, I graphed the marginal effects of inequality, based on the electoral system, in Figures 4.2 and 4.3.

The results in Table 4.3 suggest several important things for the relationship between inequality and electoral systems in Latin America. First, the strong negative effect of regional inequality that I observed in all models is driven primarily by nationally oriented electoral systems. Figure 4.2 shows that in nationally oriented political systems (personal vote value is low), the effect of interregional inequality on government spending was significantly lower. Regionally oriented political systems (personal vote value is high) did not respond to regional inequality with lower spending—their spending was unchanged. Moreover, the overall effect of regional inequality to reduce spending was robust in all models. Second, the strong positive effect of interpersonal inequality on government spending in Latin America was also driven by those nations with nationally oriented electoral institutions, shown in Figure 4.3. In geographically oriented systems, increased interpersonal inequality had no statistical effect on government spending.

What do these results suggest about the relationship between electoral systems and inequality on government spending in Latin America? First, it is clear that interpersonal and interregional inequality have divergent effects on government spending in Latin America and these effects differ depending on a nation's electoral system. The results in the Latin American sample suggest that nationally oriented electoral rules (in all except Brazil, Colombia, and recently Bolivia) depressed spending as regional inequality grew. These same nationally oriented systems push spending up to deal with increasing interpersonal inequality.

Essentially, there was a null result for geographically oriented political systems to changes in interregional inequality. This finding is important in itself because it suggests a particular dynamic in political bargaining: namely, of resolving political conflict with pork barrel spending. Where politicians in nationally oriented political systems feel little motivation to redistribute to poor regions, in geographically oriented political systems it appears that rich regions are not able to cut off the poor regions. The most straightforward explanation for this outcome may be in party bargaining. While most national political parties are diverse in regional representation, they are often more coherently arranged on the issue of interpersonal inequality and redistribution. More simply, parties form precisely on the basis of individual income redistribution with broad regional representation. Accordingly, matters of interpersonal inequality are most often dealt with across parties while interregional inequality is a distinctly intraparty as well as interparty matter. These bargaining dynamics cannot be examined in this chapter, but are considered in detail in Rogers (2016).

Conclusion

What do these findings mean for the quality of democracy in Latin America today? Overall, I argue that regional economic differences impede national responses to inequality, and this may undermine the quality of democracy. Regions with distinct preferences have difficulty agreeing on policy reform and this may result in policy stagnation, even on pressing concerns over income inequality. At the same time, there is some reason for hope that governments will make serious efforts to lower income inequality. The quality of democracy in the region, and the parties representing lower income constituencies appear to be stronger than in the past. Nonetheless, significant structural barriers stand in the way of major redistributive reform in Latin America.

The results of my study suggest that regional inequality is an impediment to redistributive government spending. Indeed, in complementary results, regional inequality is shown to be a strong predictor of lower fiscal redistribution, measured as the percentage decrease in the Gini coefficient that results from government taxes and transfers (Beramendi, Rogers, and Diaz-Cayeros, forthcoming). The theoretical mechanism that links regional inequality to lower redistribution is differences in policy preferences. Economically dynamic regions want different policies out of national governments than do stagnating regions, and they have trouble coming together on a common policy. Not surprisingly, therefore, Latin American governments' responses have been limited in comparative perspective.

Yet Latin America's democracies have recently shown signs that addressing inequities is on their policy agenda. In the past decade, Latin American democracies have reduced income inequality and poverty to a significant degree through the efforts of their governments. Levy and Schady (2013) document how government programs to subsidize income to the poorest individuals in Latin America have resulted in substantial reductions in poverty (from 28 percent of the population below the poverty line in 1996 to 13 percent in 2011). Nora Lustig, Luis F. Lopez-Calva, and Eduardo Ortiz-Juarez (2013) show that higher and more progressive government transfers have contributed to reductions in income inequality in Argentina, Brazil, and Mexico. Some of the economic conditions that made these reforms palatable, such as a commodities boom that has put more money in government coffers, may be ephemeral. Nonetheless, the passage and implementation of these reforms reflects a potentially important political change in the region. Democratic leaders appear more attentive to the demands of the majority poor in the region than they have been in the recent past.

The sources of those changes, and the reasons for hope, come from improvement in the quality and functioning of many of Latin America's democracies. After decades of concern that parties in Latin America were populist machines devoid of programmatic content, we now see increasing evidence that parties offer distinguishable platforms and voters are able to discern those differences (Baker and Greene 2011; Zechmeister 2006). This is particularly important for advancements in redistributive policies. For the interests of the relatively poor to be articulated in the political system, they need parties able and willing to press for their demands. The rise of leftist parties and improved income distribution in recent decades suggest that democratic politics has encouraged the representation of a broader segment of the population (Huber and Stephens 2012).

This positive outlook needs to be tempered by severe lingering inequalities in the systems of representation that have clear implications for the likelihood of redistributive policy change. In particular, legislative malapportionment and enclaves of subnational autocracy limit the voice of the poorest in many nations of Latin America (Gervasoni 2010a; Gibson 2005). Moreover, both are inextricably linked to the structure of regional inequality.

Latin America, especially Argentina and Brazil, is a region with substantial malapportionment (Samuels and Snyder 2001). Not coincidentally, those countries with uneven development are also those in which political representation is often disconnected from the one person–one vote democratic ideal (Stepan 2004). Less populated and small regions have disproportionate political voice in these systems. This appears to be important for the distribution of interregional transfers and redistributive reform. For example, Martin Ardanaz and Carlos Scartascini (2013) show that nations with high malapportionment have low personal income tax collection. Low tax revenue and low progressivity in the tax structure limit redistributive options for governments. These authors argue that malapportionment allows antiredistributive elites to buy the support of politicians from less populated (and thus cheaper to buy) regions (see also Gibson 1996; Gibson and Calvo 2000).

Related to this, if regions are powerful actors in national politics, it is important who is representing the interests of those regions. Despite national-level democracy, some subnational regions continue to be governed by autocrats (Gervasoni 2010b). The quality of subnational democracy is much more variable than that of national democracy in Latin America (Gibson 2005). If politicians at the national level have incentive to treat all politics as local, and their local political environment is highly autocratic, then subnational autocracy may influence national democracy. One specific way this may occur is through decisions on interregional transfers.

While government support for the neediest individuals has often been lacking, many Latin American nations transfer considerable income across regions. In fact, intergovernmental transfers in Argentina, Brazil, and Mexico, as a percentage of GDP, are comparable to those found in highly redistributive nations such as Germany (Beramendi, Rogers, and Diaz-Cayeros, forthcoming). Economically productive regions subsidize the spending of less productive regions through centralized taxation. However, these transfers have not led to convergence in regional income (Russo and Delgado 2000). Malapportionment and subnational autocracy help to explain the limited redistributive effects of intergovernmental transfers. Transfers are not progressive, but reflect inequities in representation. Regional income is not a good predictor of regional transfers, but (low) population is a very strong predictor. Regional autocrats capture a high share of these transfers, which act like rentier resources (Gervasoni 2010a). Redistribution across regions thus reflects a specific political logic in many Latin American nations that is likely inimical to major initiatives to change existing levels of income inequality.

Notes

1. These behavioral assumptions have been questioned. See Ansell and Samuels (2010) and Dion and Birchfield (2010).

2. This is not to say that the preferences of individuals for redistribution are uncontroversial or straightforward. A lively debate in the US and comparative literature is working to sort out the psychological and political economy motivations for individual preferences for government spending.

3. A summary of variables and sources is shown in Appendix 1. The sample of the central government spending is smaller because of missing data in the dependent variable. No central spending data are available for Ecuador.

4. All fifty countries cannot appear in the empirical results because of missing data in the independent variables.

5. The results are also robust to alternative measures of regional inequality— the regional Gini coefficient and the unweighted coefficient of variance.

6. An arithmetical transfer from rich to poor regions reduces inequality.

7. With care taken to address the challenges of the data, discussed more below.

8. For a thorough description of the calculation of the Gini coefficient and the data collection process and methods, see Solt (2009).

9. Vote type = 1 if a vote for an individual is observationally equivalent to a vote for a party such as in single-member districts.

10. Carey and Shugart (1995) show that district magnitude interacts with ballot structure in proportional representation systems. As district magnitude rises in closed list systems, the personal vote declines. As district magnitude rises in open list systems, parties have more competitors from which to distinguish themselves, so the personal vote rises.

11. In additional models not shown here, I control for possible nonstationarity in the dependent and independent with moving averages in the inequality variables, and full estimations with five-year fixed and moving averages. A full empiric treatment of these data, including an instrumental variables approach, is available in Rogers (2016).

12. In the Latin American sample, in fact, the personal vote is negatively correlated with regional inequality. This may suggest that pork encourages regional convergence, or that regionally disparate societies purposefully choose nationalizing voting rules, or that they are unrelated.

5

Making the Military Accountable

David Pion-Berlin

How can the armed forces, which had been at the center of political power in Latin American authoritarian regimes, be irreversibly transformed into an administrative instrument at the service of a democratic state and society? What would that process be like, and how would we know progress when we saw it? It is now widely acknowledged that states attempting to consolidate their democratic gains, following periods of military-authoritarian rule, must have in place strategies for transforming their militaries from political predators into compliant partners willing to commit their resources and talents to whatever policy priorities are set by elected governments. The survival, development, and quality of democratic systems depend on governments making the armed forces their political servants and policy instruments rather than the other way around.

How will that be accomplished, and how will we know when it has been? Scholars agree that civilians must accrue political power so that they can design defense and security policies of their own choosing. One of the key arenas in which power displays itself is within defense institutions. Institutions are "collections of standard operating procedures and structures" that shape political behavior within their confines (March and Olsen 1984: 738; Steinmo, Thelen, and Longstreth 1992: 5–7). They are the instruments by which civilian control over the military can be achieved. Institutions have a tendency to persist, and if they can be arranged to maximize civilian leadership, authority, input, and oversight then control can be secured for the long haul.

In this chapter, I peer into one of those institutions—the Defense Ministry—which is arguably the most important executive branch organization for the setting of defense policy, the ordering of relations between government and the armed forces, and the harnessing of military knowledge and power for productive use. I first set out standards for assessing the quality of Defense Ministries, and then apply those standards to an analysis of four countries: Argentina, Brazil, Chile, and Uruguay.

Why did I choose these four Latin American countries? As members of the same subregion, they are geographically proximate. They share borders that once gave rise to geopolitical dispute—sometimes verging on war—that have since been settled diplomatically. This is now the most peaceful subregion in Latin America. That condition makes the choice of these four countries, in some sense, a difficult test for the reform of Defense Ministries. Because there is no realistic war scenario on the horizon for them, there is less incentive to invest time and resources in constructing or reconstructing Defense Ministries. To wit, few citizens care about territorial defense, let alone the work of the Defense Ministry. Without electoral incentives, it is difficult for politicians to summon any interest, let alone political will, to undertake institutional reform. Accordingly, if ministerial reforms could be enacted in this subregion, they ought to be doable elsewhere.

Military Intervention, Democracy, and the Need for Defense Institutions

Why should building defense institutions matter to the fate of democracy in Latin America? There is a long history of military political intervention in this region. Prior to the 1980s, the tenure of democratic leaders was repeatedly cut short by power-hungry generals who plotted coups and overturned governments at will. The coup d'état had become so common that it was thought of as an institutionalized means of resolving political crises (Fitch 1977). While there invariably were civilian coup supporters and even co-conspirators, there is no doubt that the armed forces themselves were the central protagonists in these unfortunate political dramas.

Most military regimes in South America came to an end by the mid-1980s, and in Central America by the early 1990s. But had the men in uniform completely forsaken political intervention? Politicians and scholars alike were not sure, but had cause to be skeptical. Having bitten into the fruit of politics for so long, it was unlikely that the military would suddenly vow political abstinence. Naturally, over time, we might expect the military to cultivate a set of beliefs more consistent with principles of political neutrality and subordination. However, in a region periodically plagued by military intervention, utter devotion to democratic authority is an acquired taste, one that comes after patterns of authority and conflict resolution have long been ritualized, not before.

Because compliance with democratic rules has rarely been principled or habitual in Latin America, scholars search for additional means by which the political reach of the armed forces can be shortened. Governments know that if their militaries are to faithfully execute policy, they must be subjected to institutionalized civilian control, and that control mechanisms must be initiated and constructed by policymakers rather than waiting (hoping) for soldiers to internalize principles of compliance. That civilian control is needed to restrain the military's political reach and strengthen democratic rule is a claim not specific to Latin America, but one that has been widely accepted and has in fact been built into the very definition of democracy. In an influential article, Philippe C. Schmitter and Terry L. Karl expanded on Robert A. Dahl's classic democratic procedural conditions to include the provision that elected officials must be able to govern without interference or overrides from military officers (1991: 75–88). Democracies that fail to fulfill this condition are placed in jeopardy.

It is also recognized that if civilian control is to endure, it must be institutionalized. It is not enough to exert short-term leverage over the military to gain some temporary advantage. Governments need a longer-term structured relation that induces stable supportive encounters between political officials and military personnel. For this, they need a set of strong, well-staffed, civilian-led organizations to devise, advise, and manage defense policies as well as to exert oversight on military operations. It is through defense institutions like Defense Ministries that leaders can enforce, routinize, and channel patterns of military behavior that support the policy preferences of democratic governments rather than undermine them. Defense Ministries then constitute one building block of civilian control and, as such, help to solidify democratic rule in a region with politically minded militaries.

Institutions and Defense Ministries

Civilian control is certainly about power, but institutions structure power relations (Bruneau and Tollefson 2006: 78). They do so by directing flows of influence, reducing points of entry, limiting veto options, and imposing bureaucratic distance between the military and centers of political authority, thus determining who is in or out of the loop and who gets to sit at the decisionmaking table. When it comes to civil-military interaction, the densest points of contact occur within the defense organizations of state. Nowhere else inside or outside of the state do so many actors from the two sides meet and work together (or collide) on a regular basis. Consequently, relations between civilians and soldiers are most frequent and most intense at this location. "Indeed," writes Martin Edmonds, "within the central organizations of defense of all states is found the very essence of civil-military relations within any society. . . . It is that locus where the armed forces meet and work with the political representatives" (1985: 2–3). It is those forums within which the creation, design, management, execution, and oversight of defense policies take place.

These executive agencies are critical because it is here that the president sits atop the civil-military chain of command. As such, the president presides over those defense organizations in and around this organizational ladder of influence, and it is there that defense plans are usually hatched. Within the executive branch, the Ministry of Defense is the key link in the chain. No democratic country can even pretend to have a stable civil-military relation—one that induces both civilian control and policy effectiveness—without a Defense Ministry. The Ministry of Defense is, according to Tom C. Bruneau and Richard B. Goetze, "perhaps the most indispensable mechanism for establishing [civilian control]" (2006: 78).

Many scholars would concur with this (Agüero 1995; Serra 2010). The Ministry of Defense is the organizational link between the democratic government and the military that allows politicians to translate policy preferences into military commands. To become and remain democratic, it is important that the ministry assumes key defense-related powers in defense and not relegate these to their armed service commanders. This has not always been true in Latin America, where many countries consign the Ministry of Defense to administrative tasks, leaving key strategic and operational decisions in the hands of the military brass (Pion-Berlin 2009). In sidestepping the ministry in this way, countries excessively defer to military judgments on politically decisive issues.

If a Defense Ministry is operating properly, then one of its primary purposes, according to Bruneau and Goetze, is to "structure the power relationships between democratically elected civilian leaders and the armed forces command" (2006: 78). One means of doing so is to serve as a buffer between presidents and their military commanders. Situated in the chain of command just below the president, the defense minister and his or her ministry prevent military commanders from occupying a position too close to the executive office where they could exert undue influence on the president and perhaps crowd out civilian points of view.

Effective governance is not, however, about keeping the military down and out. No worthwhile defense policy could ever be designed without informed input from the armed forces. Defense and military policy making is always a delicate balancing act between assuring that elected governments reign while also assuring that the military's voice is heard. That means designing institutions that induce high-quality interactions between political officeholders, civilian staffers, and uniformed officials to maximize informational exchanges and points of view—all within a hierarchical order that leaves no doubt as to who has ultimate authority. In short, civilian leaders want organizational designs that open up avenues of military communication, not political domination. Since military input is still valued, the ministry's additional task is to divide the labor, by rationally allocating duties between civilian and military officers along the ladder of influence, to ensure the president is kept well informed without being overwhelmed by formidable military advisers.

A general rule of thumb is that the ministry must be civilian led (Pion-Berlin 2009). The purpose of defense institutions is to prepare the armed forces to serve the policy goals of government, and not the other way around. Should military officers, either active duty or retired, occupy top positions within the defense sector, they inevitably exhibit divided loyalties. Civilianized institutions and leaders must be in place to ensure that policy preferences get translated into defense actions and to stand vigilant against military efforts to evade their duties. All of this implies having a critical mass of well-trained civilian personnel within defense institutions. In my appraisal below of progress on democratizing and strengthening the Defense Ministry, I looked for evidence that the agency was in the operational chain of command, had become civilian led, and was central to the formulation and management of defense planning and strategizing, not just administration; that it had reorganized its internal bureaucracy to take on expanded functions at the service of governmental priorities; and that departments within the ministry were, for the most part, headed by civilians.

Argentina

The Argentine Defense Ministry, founded in 1949 during the first Juan Perón presidency, has undergone substantial changes over the years. After the return to democracy in 1984, President Raúl Alfonsín (1984–1989) inserted the ministry into the chain of command, between the president and the armed forces, and the heads of each service were downgraded from commanders to chiefs of staff (FBIS-LAT 1983: B5). These organizational reforms immediately reduced the decisionmaking autonomy enjoyed by each branch while erecting a strong hierarchical vertebrae from the president to the defense minister to their military subordinates. The ministry would formulate and execute defense policies in conformance with the objectives set out by the chief executive, take over tasks (i.e., defense production) once relegated to the separate services, and formulate the military budget while overseeing the distribution of allocated funds (Argentina 1983: 1926–1927). As the ministry assumed more and more tasks hitherto reserved for the armed services, the bureaucracy expanded as well, reflecting a need to delegate more duties to subordinates.

If there was a legal basis, and an institutional architecture devised to grant the ministry capacity, that capacity tended to be grossly underutilized. Defense ministers under Alfonsín were consumed with managing military distress over the ongoing human rights trials and deep budgetary cuts (FBIS-LAT 1984: B7). Defense ministers under President Carlos Menem (1989–1999) had to contend with harsh austerity as well once the economic minister Domingo Cavallo's neoliberal economic plans kicked in. State shrinkage was the order of the day, as military firms were put on the chopping block, salaries reduced, training sessions cut back, and so forth. By the end of the Menem period, the designs for a new Argentine system of defense had yet to be written, nor would they be under Menem's successor, Fernando De la Rúa (1999–2001). This was true, despite the fact that the governments had the power to do so. After President Menem had successfully suppressed the last of the *carapintada* uprisings, the political balance of power had shifted again in favor of civilians (Norden 1996). The military were not in a position to throw their weight around, and they certainly did not stand in the way of government officials promoting ministerial and defense reform. The problem was that there was hardly any effort. For example, between 1990 and 2005 one strategic directive was produced, and that was written by the Joint Military Staff (Estado Mayor Conjunto) with no ministerial involvement (Montenegro 2013: 210).

This would change in late 2005, with the arrival of Nilda Garré as defense minister. Garré had long been associated with the left flank of the Peronist party, and became the first woman in Argentine history to hold the top defense post. Garré reflected the two faces of the Néstor Kirchner administration. The first was the one that pushed for human rights justice, castigating the military for its past record, and ensuring its continued political weakness. The second was a genuine effort to implement defense reform and transform the ministry in particular. Those dual priorities were pursued vigorously and sometimes clashed with each other. Changes were launched in June 2006 with the passage of regulations governing the 1988 Defense Law (Ley de Defensa Nacional [23.554], Law of National Defense). Eighteen years in the waiting, this new statute finally allowed for the implementation of defense changes in accord with the principles laid out in the 1988 law by specifying the duties of the Defense Ministry. This implementation law paved the way for major structural and procedural changes inside the ministry, permitting it to take charge of directing, planning, implementing, and supervising defense and military policy. The organizational design of the ministry changed, adding bureaucratic layers that reflected increased ministerial responsibilities. In 2000, before the arrival of the Kirchner administration, the ministry had two secretariats (one for military affairs and one for planning), a number of departments, but no undersecretariats. By 2005, the ministry had two secretariats, but had added three undersecretariat offices—military affairs, military institutional strengthening, and coordination (*Atlas Comparativo de la Defensa en América Latina* 2007: 110). By 2010, after the new impetus for reform had been in place for four years, the ministry had expanded to three secretariats and seven undersecretariats, which in turn had twelve departments under their supervision. In all, between 2006 and 2010, twenty-four new organizational units were created within the ministry at secretariat, undersecretariat, and departmental levels (Argentina 2010: 209).

These units gave the ministry authority over a broad array of functions, including strategic defense planning, defense industries, research and development, operational and logistical planning, human rights, education, and military intelligence, to name a few (Argentina 2010: 209). The benefit of this three-tiered bureaucratic expansion, and especially the addition of the second undersecretariat layer, is that it allowed for (1) expanded civilian control over internal ministerial agencies at the political, technical, and administrative levels; (2) more in-depth analyses and defense reform proposals; and (3) a more comprehensive and coordinated design and execution of defense plans that, in the past, had been relegated to the separate services or not performed at all (Argentina 2010: 206).

Accompanying these bureaucratic structural changes came procedural ones, including a planning cycle that outlined the sequential steps in the process of deriving defense plans, joining political, strategic, and operational components. The Defense Ministry is at the center of it all. The process moves from civilians to soldiers, from the defense minister to the secretariat of military affairs, and from there to the Joint Chiefs of Staff that formulate a military strategic plan before passing the baton to the heads of the army, navy, and air force (Argentina 2007, 2009).

The logic of bureaucratic expansion and the planning cycle make sense in terms of enhancing institutionalized civilian control over the process of designing defense plans, reducing military autonomy, and bringing together the myriad components of the defense system under one political-strategic umbrella (Battaglino 2013: 11). But had the ministry perhaps taken on too much change and too many responsibilities? The former secretary of strategy and military affairs, Germán Montenegro, believes it had. He argues that Minister Garré may have bitten off more than she could chew by not building up political and technical civilian staff that could keep pace with the new expansive ministry.[1] Argentina has struggled to equip itself with a civilian defense team large, stable, and knowledgeable enough to manage the myriad units and programs within the ministry.[2] Compounding this problem was one of budget shortfalls. Argentina had been slow to step up its funding to keep pace with ministerial ambitions. There was simply not enough budgeted to purchase the kind of military instrument needed to fulfill the defense objectives laid out by planners.

It is one thing to reorganize a ministry to create new bureaucratic units—a relatively inexpensive proposition. It is another to invest in the equipment, repairs, training, and supplies to translate ministerial progress into combat-ready forces on the ground. That raises the question as to why Argentine leaders would even bother pursuing ministerial strengthening if they were not prepared to commit the resources needed to convert institutional change into military action. One possibility is that bureaucratic strengthening achieved the objective of solidifying civilian control over the military and the defense reform process, and that was the main political priority of the time. But what was achieved in terms of greater civilian control has not as yet been balanced by consonant gains in defense readiness. Without ample defense funding, it will be difficult to sustain the gains already made. This will be made more difficult if the political leadership inside and outside of the ministry is absent. The defense ministers that have succeeded Garré have not shown any zeal for reform,[3] which raises the issue of whether the modernization of the Defense Ministry will be self-sustaining, or be held hostage to the shifting political whims of those in office.

That having been said, Argentina has made moderate progress in equipping, enlarging, and empowering its Defense Ministry. With new civilian-led secretariats, departments, and planning processes, the ministry is poised to lead the way on defense reforms. But it awaits greater funding and a more ambitious effort to staff the new ministry with able civilians.

Brazil

Brazil's Defense Ministry is the youngest of such institutions in the Southern Cone, having been formed in 1999 under President Fernando Henrique Cardoso (1994–2002). For years, resistance to its formation had been fierce, especially within the navy and air force, both of which feared the army would end up dominating the new ministry. It took presidential arm-twisting to seal the deal with the military. It was also a process that took place behind closed doors between the chief executive and top commanders only. There was no effort to involve civilians inside or outside of government, or to generate public interest in the matter (Saint-Pierre 2008).

Nonetheless, the ministry was born on solid political footing since its Complementary Law required passage in both chambers of Congress assuring widespread multiparty support. It was charged with managing all those aspects of the armed forces not reserved for the president. The president was to be served by a Military Defense Council on the actual use of military means. But in all other matters related to the military, he was to rely on the defense minister (Brazil 1999). In 2010, the Complementary Law was strengthened to assure a clear chain of command from the president to the defense minister to the separate services (Brazil 2010a).[4] The minister's powers over military selection were enhanced. Previously, the high command nominated officers for promotion and assignment, but that was now the minister's call who would present the nominees to the president. Amendments also gave the ministry more fiscal authority, requiring each branch to prepare its budget jointly with the Defense Ministry, with the latter responsible for consolidating these into a unified budget according to the priorities set by the National Defense Strategy. Both legally and structurally, the ministry appeared to be equipped to oversee a wide range of important tasks, including defense policy, strategy, doctrine, operations, strategic intelligence, defense education, budget, and mobilization (see Brazil 2012: 55).

Nelson Jobim (2007–2011), followed by Celso Amorim (2011–2014), raised the profile of the ministry considerably. As Octavio Amorim Neto points out, Jobim was an important figure in the governing coalition and thus received strong backing from President Luiz Inácio Lula da Silva to undertake defense reforms and to solidify the ministry's role (2012: 18–19). He, along with the secretary for strategic affairs, Roberto Managabeira Unger, spearheaded the writing of the 2009 National Defense Strategy for Brazil, and then launched the production of the nation's first White Book—completed under Amorim's tenure—heading up a governmental committee comprised of eight ministers and staff, along with members of the armed forces.[5] These documents demonstrated that the ministry was assuming responsibility for defining the nation's defense priorities, and for making transparent to the region and world what Brazil's intentions are in modernizing its defense systems.

Yet the military has retained considerable influence throughout this period and until the present day. There have been periodic confrontations between defense ministers and the military over human rights, military court jurisdictions, wage increases, and control over commercial aviation and airspace, and, in many cases, ministers have backed down or have resigned (Filho 2010). To wit, the first five defense ministers from 1999 to 2007 were politically weak figures who had difficulty asserting their authority over the military. Their weakness stemmed from the fact that they were not key figures in the governing party coalitions of either President Cardoso or President Lula (Neto 2014: 18–19). As a result, they did not receive sufficient support from the president in confrontations with the military, were circumvented in favor of other cabinet officials, or were abandoned entirely (Neto 2014: 16–20).

Also, the internal design of the ministry strongly suggests a dual work structure where civilian-led staffed agencies handle administrative issues while military-led staffed agencies handle strategy and operations. For example, two key secretariats, the Secretariat of Politics, Strategy, and International Affairs along with the Secretariat of Education, Logistics, Mobilization, Science, and

Technology, have been eliminated but their work is now subsumed within the Joint Chiefs of Staff (Brazil 2010b). Those secretariats had control over the formulation of defense policy, strategy, logistics, and mobilization—in essence, most of the essentials of defense planning. Those functions have passed from the civilian side of the ministry to its military side. What remains under civilian control are administration, defense industry and production, and personnel issues, education, and health. Defense production is certainly a vital component but, while the secretary of that division is a civilian, all of the department heads are military.

This dual work structure is likely to persist unless or until Brazil develops a civilian career track in defense to fill ministerial slots (Bruneau and Tollefson 2014).[6] Without that, it is difficult to populate the ministry with expert civilians, making it easier for military personnel to occupy the more important posts. In short, the ministry as a whole has acquired bureaucratic strength and complexity, and is charged with overseeing key defense functions. But it is still substantially dominated by military units and personnel, thus calling into question just how much civilian control the ministry can actually assert.

Chile

The Chilean Ministry of Defense is one of the oldest institutions in the government, having been founded in 1932. In fact, it is one of the few ministries actually mentioned in the constitution, referred to as the ministry in charge of national defense, with the armed forces being subordinate to it (Chile Constitution 1980, with amendments through 2012). But its age and legal stature disguise the fact that, until recently, it was at the margins of defense policy making. It had not been properly designed or utilized to create, promote, and execute the nation's defense plans. It had performed mostly administrative roles, leaving the military to do the strategic thinking, planning, and writing when it came to defense.

Indeed, the armed forces enjoyed considerable autonomy vis-à-vis the ministry. The Ministry of Defense had been eclipsed by the various national security and defense councils designed by the Augusto Pinochet dictatorship. With the passage of the 1980 Constitution, the National Security Council became the principal institutional vehicle with which the military made its preferences known. Its powers persisted into the democratic era, and the ministry was further diminished by the unwillingness of General Pinochet to acknowledge the defense minister, repeatedly circumventing him. Prior to the changes made in 2010, the ministry had fewer powers than the military commanders in chief. Before leaving office the military decreed the Constitutional Organic Law of the Armed Forces that gave to service commanders the authority to define the development of their service, leaving the ministry with comparatively less legal authority (Robledo 2013). All substantive decisions having to do with strategy, policy, equipment, training, and so forth resided in military circles, not within the ministry, and certainly not within any civilian-led agency. But even if the ministry had been relevant, it would have been structurally ill prepared to serve as the conveyer of government preferences. Its internal undersecretaries were all service based, thus giving primacy to the logic of and needs of the services.

The period 2005–2010 was one of institutional change, culminating in the February 2010 promulgation of the National Defense Organic Ministry Law (Chile 2010). The law gave the ministry the authority, structure, and tools needed so that the planning process reflected the political priorities of the democratic government, and not those of the separate service branches. Prior to this, the National Defense General Staff—a military unit—initiated the planning process. After the organic ministerial law went into effect, planning could be set in motion by the government's civilian appointees. The process is divided into three descending levels of priority: political, strategic, and operational. It is within the ministry's undersecretariat for defense that the political meets the strategic, where an analysis is to be conducted that assesses the nation's security environment—risks, threats, and opportunities—which then leads to the formulation of a national defense policy in response to that analysis. The plan is then sent to the Joint Chiefs of Staff and from there to the separate services that convert strategies into operational plans (Chile 2010: 179–180).

Several observations are worth making as to how this process manifests itself in practice. First, it is widely acknowledged that the ministry and its offices are headed up by skillful civilians who have the training, the career profile, and the commitment to assure that the ministry plays the central role in defense and military policy. Civilians can increasingly hold their own with their military counterparts. This is important because there is no clear division of labor between civilian and military personnel within the ministry. Even during the first phase of the planning cycle, where political orientations and analyses are conducted, the military is present. This is confirmed by the ministry's own website, where the undersecretariat's planning and policy division is described as "an *institutionalized space for civil-military integration*" that makes for more "effective advice on matters of defense and military policy" (Chile, "Subsecretaría de Defensa," emphasis added). If there is ongoing civil-military intermingling, all the more reason for civilians to be proficient in defense-related matters.

But this intermingling also makes it difficult to know how to assign weights to military versus civilian input—a problem exacerbated by the fact that there are no public data released on the proportion of officers to civilian personnel within the ministry. One scholar estimates that some 60 percent of the staffers within the two undersecretariats are retired military officers, many of whom have advanced university degrees.[7] Certainly, an intermingling of views from both sides can be enormously beneficial to the production of more informed policies. At the same time, it would be equally beneficial to have a much stronger civilian presence at the beginning of the sequence when drafting proposals and plans that allegedly reflect the politically strategic priorities of the government, and not those of the armed forces.

Second, and related to this point, it is difficult to know just how much of a lead civilians within the ministry take in actually drafting defense plans or priorities from square one. No such documents are posted on the ministerial webpage, and there are some scholars who believe that the ministry's departments have never drafted such documents. The reason is that the ministry may be more reactive than proactive; rather than design its own defense plans, it is evaluating those first proposed by the services, generally signing off on these though occasionally challenging them.[8] Thus, even though the aforementioned bureaucratic transformation has been extremely positive, it has not necessarily eliminated the problem of services. The commanders in chief of each branch still wield enormous powers. They determine how their forces will be organized and deployed, the doctrines that will guide their conduct, and the budgets to finance their operations, along with powers to approve the purchase, dismantling, and disposal of all weapons and weapons systems (Chile 1990).

Those powers are enshrined in the Constitutional Organic Law of the Armed Forces, which has yet to be annulled or reformed (Chile 1990). If the ministry sets the general political direction for the country when it comes to external defense, the manner in which this is translated into actual army, navy, and air force plans, both conceptual and operational, is largely in military hands. All in all, Chile has made substantial progress in fortifying its Defense Ministry. This is now a ministry that has the bureaucratic wherewithal to lead on defense, and a civilian staff with ample capabilities. And yet it needs to go further in placing its own civilian stamp on policies and reducing the policy impact of the services.

Uruguay

The Uruguayan Defense Ministry, which actually dates back to 1828 (when it was known as the Ministry of War and Navy), has a long history of institutional weakness. For decades during the twentieth century, the ministry did not weigh in on vital issues of defense strategy and planning. Its functions were restricted to matters of personnel administration, as evinced by its internal bureaucratic structure (Uruguay 1941a). Its one secretariat was divided into personnel, services, and accounting, and was headed by an army or naval officer. Within the hierarchy, the ministry was positioned along side of—not below—the president as part of a "Superior Command," meaning it was not in the chain of command.

Matters grew worse in 1974 when the revised Organic Military Law stripped out any actual ministerial functions, simply referring to the constitution (Uruguay 1941a). As Juan Rial suggests, the Ministry of Defense "practically disappeared as a relevant theme" by this time (1992: 77). It now had three bureaucratic units, two of which were entirely military in composition, and again the ministry was consigned to administrative duties. The president would work through the military commands to achieve national defense, bypassing the ministry and relying instead on the Junta de Comandantes en Jefe that advised him on all key defense matters (Uruguay 1941b).

Between 1974 and 2010, the ministry remained endemically weak and militarized. Most Ministerio de Defensa Nacional (MDN) employees had either military status or were civilians called *equiparados* who were given the equivalent of military ranks subject to military rules and discipline (Uruguay 1974). Promotion criteria had changed in 1958 to allow for more rapid and easier acceleration to higher ranks. The result was a surplus of officers who were not performing any useful or necessary defense role. And so many of these were absorbed into the Defense Ministry, a posting that became part of the normal rotation of assignments for active duty personnel,[9] thus crowding out space for pure civilian hires.

If the ministry was a link between the military and president, it was one that transmitted military preferences upward, not presidential preferences downward (Guyer et al. 2007: 134). Its ineffectiveness was captured by its structure, which was hierarchically flat. It had two political appointees—the minister and undersecretary—and directly below a huge number of departments (twenty-one in all) each headed and staffed by military personnel. This kind of structure left no bureaucratic space where the minister could, with the assistance of trained civilians, develop a public national defense policy (Guyer et al. 2007: 134).

During the first twenty years of redemocratization (1985–2005), ministerial structure and functions remained static, the product of political inertia. Then, with the coming to power of the first Frente Amplio government in 2005, Uruguay witnessed the stirrings of change. The Defense Ministry sponsored a series of public conferences and seminars that made defense a subject of attention. Following on the heels of these events, civilian equiparados were allowed to opt out of military ranks and into purely civil service ranks (Uruguay 2007).

The Tabaré Vázquez administration introduced a bill called the Legal Framework for National Defense, which finally passed into law in March

2010. This was the first significant piece of defense legislation since the 1974 Organic Law of the Armed Forces, and the first national defense law in the nation's history. It elevated the stature of the Defense Ministry, positioning it at the center of national defense policy making, and at the service of an elected president, not the armed forces. The ministry has all the power to exercise the direction and supervision of all defense-related activities not reserved for the president. The ministry has at its disposal a military general staff (see below) that elaborates a doctrine and coordinates all joint military action.

This defense law represents an important first step toward empowering Uruguay's Defense Ministry. But it is just that—a first step, and what was not enunciated in law is as important as what was. This defense law did not specify how the ministry was to be set up, nor was it intended to. Most defense laws do not; that task is typically left to ministerial laws that detail how the agency would be organized into undersecretariats and departments, and what their specific responsibilities would be. The difficulty is that Uruguay has yet to formulate such a law, meaning that the current ministerial composition is guided by an older regulatory decree (which has less force than a law) that has not been updated (Uruguay 2010).

Currently, the ministry has a minister, an undersecretariat, and under him or her five departments. While all of these departments were headed by civilians (as of 2014), the problem is that four of these are charged with performing administrative duties such as finance and accounting, budgets, personnel issues, benefits, and services. Only one department has to do with defense policy. This arrangement has traits similar to the organizational chart that dates to earlier periods. That is not to say that those currently inside the ministry are necessarily bound strictly to those parameters. According to a noted Uruguayan authority, there is a bit of improvising taking place, with operatives enjoying some margin for maneuver as the ministry tries to find its footing in moving from the old functions to new ones that are yet to be defined.[10] But it is also clear that the ministry has yet to fulfill the promise of the new defense law.

The civilian-led ministry retains a penchant for deferring to the military to make the more important decisions regarding defense policy, planning, and strategizing. So, for example, on the ministry's webpage its Department of Defense Policy references only one item having to do specifically with defense planning. That is a document ostensibly written by uniformed officers outside that department, within the ministry's Defense General Staff. There is no other evidence of work done by civilians within this department on the topic of defense planning (Uruguay 2015).[11] This is not a result of military resistance, but rather an absence of civilian initiative. And in that absence, the armed forces have filled a void.[12]

There is also a sense that the momentum generated by the defense symposiums of 2006 may have been lost, at least temporarily. For example, though the 2010 defense law called for the writing of a White Book, which has become an almost obligatory rite of passage for a nation striving to modernize its defense system and which would normally be coordinated by the Defense Ministry, no such book has been produced.[13] Minister Eleuterio Fernández Huidobro (2011–2014) undoubtedly had an understanding of or at least an appreciation for military issues, having been a former guerrilla leader of the Tupamaros. But he was unwilling to push the defense agenda very far, preferring to manage rather than lead and to keep his ministry off the front pages of the newspapers. In short, incremental progress has been made, but the ministry still attends largely to administrative functions and has a tendency to defer to military judgments on major defense issues.

Conclusion

Institution building is hard. Translating power into institutions capable of carrying out effective policies crafted by civilians is a difficult step. It requires a high level of commitment and follow-through on the part of political leaders and their appointees. They must care enough about the issues to set defense plans in motion, and to then properly staff and fund the agencies that will carry out the work. Where the armed forces put up resistance to institutional reform, those leaders must have the intestinal fortitude to push on nonetheless. Where the military does not contest, they must be properly motivated to fill the institutional voids once occupied by uniformed personnel.

All the ministries now assume key defense functions, rather than just attending to administrative and personnel matters. Bureaucratically, ministries have become more hierarchical, reflecting new layers of civilian authority that are more complex as they take on new responsibilities, and more functional as secretariats, departments, and planning processes carry out a singular defense agenda for the government, not the parochial agendas of each service. Hence, the ministries' roles have enlarged and their architecture has changed for the better. The ministries have established firmer civilian control as ministers have more power over policymaking, promotions, and budgets, and most joint military staffs are moved inside the ministries where they must answer to the defense minister. This is all good news for democratic governance as well.

And yet there has been an internal delegation of vital tasks to military agencies and personnel. This is most pronounced in Brazil and Uruguay, where the general and joint military staffs have taken on (or have been granted) the most important defense-related assignments, leaving it to civilians to handle administrative, personnel, accounting, and legal issues. Ironically, as democratic governments, through their ministries, have attained higher levels of political control over the armed forces, they have ceded authority to officers to do the actual work of defense planning within those very ministries. This is why, in my view, Brazil and Uruguay lag behind Chile and Argentina when it comes to ministerial development.

In Argentina and Chile, ministerial progress has been substantial, but some problems remain of a different variety. Both countries have seized control over defense planning from the military, housing those functions permanently within civilian secretariats and departments. Argentina's dilemma has been to recruit enough well-trained civilian staffers to effectively run those internal agencies, and to finance the reforms that have been scripted. Its bureaucratic expansion has been impressive, but has outpaced its growth of civilian personnel and funds. Chile does have an able well-trained team of civilians within the ministry, and has progressed further than any of the other countries under study. But it is still strongly influenced by the priorities of the services, and it is not clear how much of a stamp civilians within the ministry have actually placed on defense policies.

Why would Argentina and Chile have made greater strides in ministerial reform than Uruguay and Brazil? There is no single overarching answer to that question. Explanations are shaped by country conditions. Argentina could undertake reforms because, by the early days of the transition to democracy, the balance of power had shifted decisively toward the civilian side of the equation. That was not true in the three other states. Argentinian democratic leaders have always had the autonomy from military pressures needed to fortify civilian control elements within the ministry. It simply took an interest in ministerial reform to make it happen. That interest waxes and wanes because, as mentioned at the beginning of this chapter, defense is not a high priority for voters. But when governments bring the right defense team into the administration, as Nestor Kirchner and Cristina Fernández de Kirchner did by 2006, then change became possible.

Historically in Chile, there has been greater national preoccupation about defense than in most Latin American countries, owing to that state's geography; it lacks strategic depth and, thus, must be on its guard should there be an attack from the outside. But that also means the armed forces had readied themselves as the region's premier fighting force, and considered civilian input on defense matters to be redundant, if not irrelevant. Military autonomy has been historically formidable in this policy sphere, reinforced by the military's domination over the transition to democratic rule. Thus, the principal struggle in Chile had been to overcome the military's resistance to civilian participation in defense.

That resistance was overcome thanks to a strengthening of democratic collaboration at the beginning of the new century. It was triggered by the arrest and trial of Pinochet in London, in 1998–1999. The entire episode constituted a watershed moment for Chile, not only for its human rights policies but for the entire civil-military relation. The European judicial actions catalyzed change in Chile by deflating Pinochet's stature among Chileans of all persuasions. More pointedly, political parties on the right started distancing themselves from Pinochet and his authoritarian legacy to attract moderate Chilean voters. Once they did that, they were more willing to work with the center-left parties in Congress to pass vital defense reform legislation, including key constitutional reforms in 2005.

Uruguay has always been thought of as one of the strongest and most enduring democracies in the region. And yet, until 2006, Uruguay was notable for having made the least progress among its Southern Cone neighbors in the realm of military and defense reform. It would be difficult to lay the primary blame at the military barrack's door. Military resistance to reform has weakened over time. The problem lies more squarely on the civilian side of the ledger. Time and time again, political leaders failed to assume their burden of leadership.

That undoubtedly had something to do with political party ideologies. When parties of the center-right were in office, as they often were between 1985 and 2005, they had less interest in military-related issues. Once having settled the human rights dilemma with a 1986 amnesty law that was twice affirmed in national plebiscites, the more conservative parties and leaders followed a subdued strategy, one where they would keep military and defense issues off the front pages of the newspapers. Moreover, those parties received no pressure from their more conservative political bases to tackle defense-related issues. If party ideology had something to do with neglect of ministerial reforms, then it makes sense that it took the coming to power of the left-wing Frente Amplio party in 2005 to finally give national defense and military reform some attention.

Finally in Brazil, the armed forces have been able to throw their weight around ever since exiting office in 1985. When dealing with the military, Brazil's democratic leaders have not overcome their tendencies to accommodate the top brass. They press for reforms only so far, often backing down when they come up against too much military resistance. Where civilian leaders have made cautious advances, they have done so only when they receive military blessings. As in Uruguay or Argentina, there has not been sufficient public interest or electoral pressure to force politicians to take the bull by the horns and make more compelling ministerial changes that would bolster the civilian presence. But unlike Uruguay and Argentina, civilians would face a greater challenge from a more vocal and politicized military.

Notes

1. Germán Montenegro, e-mail communication with the author, July 27, 2014.
2. There also arises the problem of bureaucratic continuity and memory, when a new administration and minister bring in his or her team. Though these political appointees may have public administrative experience, most often they lack a specific background in defense. While career civil service employees are not filtering up, political appointees are filtering downward sometimes as far as the third tier (departments), which means that when they leave there is a void that again needs to be filled, disrupting policy continuity and the growth of learning curves inside the ministry. Montenegro e-mail communication.
3. Montenegro e-mail communication.
4. According to Lei Complementar 97, modified by Lei Complementar 136 on August 25, 2010.
5. In addition, the ministers reached out to various civilian experts (some 185 in all) who served as collaborators on the project. See Brazil (2012: 273–275).
6. At the time of this writing, there is talk of a defense career track being in the works.
7. Miguel Navarro, e-mail communication with the author, August 13, 2014.
8. Sebastián Briones, e-mail communication with the author, July 24, 2014.
9. The presence of military active duty soldiers in the ministry meant there was a double dependency. They were formally subordinate to the minister, but had to also answer to their respective commanders since military superiors selected them and would evaluate their performance at the ministry in determining their future career trajectories.
10. Félix Besio, e-mail communication with the author, July 26, 2014.
11. There is a manual on peacekeeping and human rights that seems to have been prepared mainly by civilians.
12. This perception is shared by two of the leading authorities on Uruguayan authorities on civil-military affairs. Julián González Guyer, e-mail communication with the author, December 16, 2013; Félix Besio, e-mail communication with the author, July 25, 2014.
13. This was confirmed by González Guyer and Besio e-mail communications.

6

Liberal vs. Popular
Models of Democracy

Gerardo L. Munck

Politics in Latin America continued to be about democracy after the democratic transitions in Latin America in the 1980s and 1990s. An old concern—securing the minimal standard of democracy that had served as the goal of democratic transitions –remained relevant. But a new concern –the attainment of more than a minimal democracy—transformed politics about democracy. Actors who supported and opposed neoliberalism, the key axis of ideological conflict, advocated and resisted political changes in the name of different models of democracy. And the conflict over which model of democracy would prevail shaped Latin America's post-transition trajectories, determining how democracy developed and, in turn, whether democracy endured.

The moral certainties and the bold, even heroic, actions that gave an epic quality to the democratic transitions in Latin America in the 1980s and 1990s are a matter of the past. The sweeping economic transformations initiated in the region in the late 1980s and early 1990s reduced the centrality of many of the protagonists of twentieth-century Latin American politics. Additionally, in the wake of successful democratic transitions, Latin American countries acquired the characteristic trademark of functioning democracies: the processing of political conflicts, as a matter of routine, according to widely accepted democratic rules. Thus, there is much truth to the statement that Latin American politics in the early twenty-first century revolved around the results of democratic elections, the institutional relationship between elected legislators and presidents, and the passing of laws regarding various policy domains (e.g., economy, health, education, justice, security). Yet politics in Latin America after democratic transitions was not limited to the processing of conflicts according to previously adopted and widely accepted democratic rules: politics within democracy did not bring an end to politics about democracy.

A key aspect of the democracy question concerned the endurance of gains made through democratic transitions. These gains could not be taken for granted and a novel question, one that subsumed this important but rather narrow concern, took shape. Increasingly, democracy was seen as hinging on much more than the minimal standard that served as the goal of democratic transitions. Actors who variously supported and opposed neoliberalism—the key axis of ideological conflict—advocated or resisted political changes in the name of different models of democracy. Frequently, the actors' preferred model was trumpeted as the more democratic one and invoked when advancing projects to democratize a country. But sometimes actors went further and criticized their rival's model as nondemocratic. Thus, the new struggle for democracy had some distinctive features. It was not just about the endurance of democracy but rather about whether democracy simultaneously developed and endured. Moreover, this struggle was driven by different visions of democracy. In a nutshell, the conflict over *which* model of democracy would prevail shaped Latin America's post-transition trajectories, determining *how* democracy developed and, in turn, *whether* democracy endured.

In this chapter, I address the travails of democracy in Latin America after its transitions from authoritarian rule—that is, in the post-transition period that began in roughly the late 1980s. To start off, I introduce the notion of post-transition Latin America and identify the novel problematic of democracy during this period. Then, I address theoretical-political discussions about democracy in post-transition Latin America, focusing on two alternative models of democracy: the standard liberal democratic model and what is labeled the popular democracy model. Thereafter, I turn to the record of four political-ideological actors—the right, center-right, center-left, and left—both in government and opposition, addressing their impact on the basic rules of electoral democracy as well as on the political institutions of government and the social environment of politics. Finally, I draw conclusions regarding democracy in Latin America and the broader study of democracy around the globe.

After Transitions from Authoritarian Rule

Latin America underwent a sweeping political change in the 1980s and 1990s (see Table 6.1, column 2). In 1977, only three countries in the region had democratically elected authorities. Yet starting in 1978 authoritarian, mainly military-based, rule came to an end as leaders elected in free and fair elections took office. By 1990, all of South America had democratically elected authorities. In the 1990s, the lingering issues from the Central American civil wars of the 1980s were resolved, and the left and right were fully incorporated into

Table 6.1 Democratization, Marketization, and Left Presidents in Latin America

Country[a]	Electoral Democracy (year of transition)[b]	Free Market (year of initiation)[c]	Left or Center-Left (years in office)
Costa Rica	1949	1986	2014 to present
Venezuela	1958	1989	1999 to present
Colombia	1958/1974	1987/1990	
Dominican Republic	1978	1991	2000–2004
Ecuador	1979	1990	2007 to present
Peru	1980	1990	2011 to present
Bolivia	1982	1985	2006 to present
Honduras	1982	1991/1992	2006–2009
Argentina	1983	*1977–1981*, 1988/1990	2003 to present
Nicaragua	1984/1990	1991	2007 to present
El Salvador	1984/1994	1990	2009 to present
Brazil	1985	1990/1991, 1995	2003 to present
Uruguay	1985	*1978–1982*, 1990	2005 to present
Guatemala	1985/2000	1986	2008–2012
Panama	1989	1994	2004–2009
Paraguay	1989	1990	2008–2012
Chile	1990/2006	*1975*	2000–2010, 2014 to present
Mexico	1997/2000	*1985*	

Sources: Author's elaboration, drawing on information on free-market reforms in Morley, Machado, and Pettinato (1999); Escaith and Paunovic (2004); and on presidential ideology in Murillo, Oliveros, and Vaishnav (2010).

Notes: a. Countries are ordered according to the year of their transition to electoral democracy through the holding of contested elections. The years correspond to the time when governments are formed; in some cases, the key elections were held in the previous calendar year (e.g., Ecuador) or even earlier (e.g., Bolivia).

b. For Colombia, though electoral politics began in 1958, free electoral competition started only in 1974. For El Salvador and Guatemala, though electoral politics began in 1984 and 1985, respectively, the left was able to compete starting in 1994 and 1999, respectively. In Nicaragua, though electoral politics began in 1984, the right competed only starting in 1990. In Chile, though competitive elections began in 1989, only in 2006 were all positions in the Congress filled through elections.

c. In three cases (Argentina, Brazil, and Uruguay), an initial process of market reform stalled and was resumed after a few years. The first date indicates when reforms were initially launched; the second date when they were resumed. Italicized dates (for Argentina, Chile, Uruguay, and Mexico) indicate that reforms were initiated by authoritarian rulers.

electoral politics in Central America by 2000. Thus, alternation in power in Mexico in 2000 capped an extraordinary wave of democratization in Latin America. For the first time in the history of government, democracy was the norm in a developing region of the world. Or, more precisely, through what was widely referred to as democratic transitions, nearly every Latin American country had become an electoral democracy; that is, had a political system in which elections were the only means of access to government offices, elections were based on the universal right to vote and the right to run for office without proscriptions, and elections were devoid of violence or fraud.

These democratic changes notwithstanding, the weight of the past was still evident. Though the pursuit of revolutionary alternatives through arms—a trend that spread from Cuba to many countries in the region in the 1960s—rapidly became a thing of the past, a democratic transition remained a pending challenge in authoritarian Cuba, the Latin American country where the legacy of the Cold War proved hardest to erase. (The guerrillas in Colombia were the other key enduring Cold War legacy in the region.) More generally, countries that made democratic transitions in the 1980s and 1990s could not take for granted that their democratic gains would not be reversed because the military—a dominant actor in Latin America from 1930 onward—remained a *poder fáctico* (de facto power) and actively challenged the authority of democratic leaders in many countries. Indeed, in the wake of democratic transitions, in countries where the agenda of transitional justice was salient but also in countries where the military was particularly entrenched, the military threatened or attempted— sometimes successfully, other times not—to carry out coups d'état.[1] In short, the past limited, and threatened the endurance of, democratic gains.

Nonetheless, in retrospect, it is clear that the wave of democratization in Latin America in the 1980s and 1990s was the final act of the conflicts that were generated in the course of the region's transition to popular politics initiated in the 1920s and 1930s (Touraine 1989; Collier and Collier 1991). Democratic transitions were the product of a compromise among the key actors of this old politics—soldiers, party leaders, industrial and agrarian economic elites, the middle class, organized labor, and occasionally guerrillas—who jointly accepted that key government offices would be filled through free and fair elections (O'Donnell and Schmitter 1986). But with the exception of a few stubbornly enduring legacies of the Cold War, the old politics was swept aside in the immediate aftermath of democratic transitions. Though some actors of the old system did not fully accept the democratic compromise and, in the short run, could impose some limits on the democratic transformations in Latin America, the state of democracy increasingly hinged on the conflicts at the heart of the new societies that were being shaped by the introduction of free-market reforms (Cavarozzi 1992; Garretón et al. 2003).

The break with the old came as somewhat of a surprise. A few countries had initiated free-market reforms, which brought about a rejection of the import-substitution industrialization model of economic development that had been the norm in Latin America since the 1930s and 1940s, in the context of authoritarian rule (see Table 6.1, column 3). Chile was the most prominent early example, and Mexico would follow several years later. Yet these countries appeared as exceptions. Their experience, along with those of Argentina and Uruguay, seemed to suggest that such reforms were associated with authoritarianism and hence were unlikely to be adopted in the new democratic age that was dawning in Latin America. But starting with Bolivia in 1985, the first country to show that it was possible for democratically elected leaders to implement radical economic reforms, a cohort of elected presidents of the right and center-right launched and then deepened free-market reforms in every Latin American country in the 1990s (Edwards 1995; Morley, Machado, and Pettinato 1999; Escaith and Paunovic 2004).[2] By the mid-1990s, the region had unexpectedly converged on the twin institutions of democracy and the market.

This was but a moment, however, not the final destination of history. And it did not end the relevance of the left-right distinction, understood here in rather narrow terms as revolving around the issue of economic inequality, seen as natural and acceptable by the right and largely socially constructed and unacceptable by the left.[3] First, protest movements resisted the implementation of free-market reforms and triggered major clashes with the authorities, including the Caracazo in Venezuela in 1989; the Zapatista uprising in Mexico in 1994; the water and gas wars in Bolivia in 2000, 2003, and 2005; and the riots in Argentina in 2001. Then, starting in Venezuela in 1999 and Chile in 2000, left and center-left presidents came to power through elections in nearly every Latin American country (see Table 6.1, column 4) and sought to offer more or less radical alternatives to unbridled free-market economics and the dominance of politics by economics (Edwards 2010; Flores-Macías 2012; Huber and Stephens 2012). Thus, the strong convergence on free-market policies in the 1990s gave salience to a neoliberal ideology that posited that all decisions in a society, and not only economic ones, are best left to markets or made subservient to market forces. But it also accentuated the divide between forces committed to neoliberalism and those who sought an alternative to neoliberalism. This divide rapidly became the key axis of ideological conflict in post-transition Latin America.

Divergence was not limited to the role of markets. A quick glance at the evolution of electoral democracy provides indisputable evidence that in post-transition Latin America politics was still about democracy and, moreover, that this politics was linked with the divide over neoliberalism.[4] Indeed, political actors committed to promoting and fighting neoliberalism repeatedly broke the rules of electoral democracy (see Table 6.2). The data show that these crises of electoral democracy were frequent and widespread: only six of eighteen post-transition countries did not experience crises that affected their status as an electoral democracy. In addition, although the decisive actions in these crises—a matter that goes to final responsibility—were carried out either by actors on the right or the left (Venezuela is an exception), the most grave problems were largely due to actions of incumbents seeking to imple-

Table 6.2 Electoral Democracy in Post-Transition Latin America[a]

Country	Nature of Problems			Source of Problems[b]			
				Right		Left	
	Electoral Process	Closing of Democratically Elected Legislature	Removal of Democratically Elected President	Disloyal Government	Disloyal Opposition	Disloyal Government	Disloyal Opposition
Problems of neoliberalism							
Peru	**2000**	**1992**		**1992, 2000**			
Guatemala		(1993)		(1993)			
Dominican Republic		**1994**		**1994**			
Venezuela		(2002)	(2002)		(2002)		
Honduras			**2009**		**2009**		
Paraguay			2012		2012		
El Salvador	2014				2014		
Problems of anti-neoliberalism							
Venezuela		1999	(1992)			1999	(1992)
Ecuador		2007	1997, **2000**, 2005			2007	1997, **2000**, 2005
Nicaragua	2011		(2005)			2011	(2005)[c]
Argentina			2001				2001
Bolivia			2003, 2005				2003, 2005
Mexico	2006, 2012						2006, 2012

Source: Author's elaboration.

Notes: a. The data include developments following democratic transitions and the initiation of free-market reforms; on this information, see Table 6.1. The more serious problems are highlighted in bold; failed challenges to the rules of electoral democracy are presented in parentheses.

b. The concept of "disloyal opposition," discussed by Linz (1978: 27–38), is adapted and extended to the government, which is considered disloyal inasmuch as it undermines the rules of electoral democracy.

c. In the crisis in Nicaragua in 2005, the conservative forces loyal to Arnoldo Alemán, as well as the leftist Sandinistas, were behind the push to remove President Enrique Bolaños Geyer.

ment neoliberalism (Peru in 1992 and 2000; Dominican Republic in 1994) or actions of opponents to governments committed to rolling back neoliberalism (Venezuela in 2002; Honduras in 2009).

These political developments showed that the gains made through democratic transitions could not be taken for granted and that ideological differences were very much alive in post-transition Latin America and affected support for democracy. But these developments were only the most overt manifestations of a conflict that revolved around two interrelated questions: What is democracy and should democracy be supported? The nature and value of democracy had been the subject of a theoretical-political debate in the 1960s, which revealed important disagreements within the left. Subsequently, disagreements were largely set aside in the context of the struggles for democracy in the 1980s and 1990s. Indeed, in part as a matter of strategic choice, political action in the context of processes of democratic transitions had relied on a decidedly minimalist concept of electoral democracy, centered on the holding of competitive elections with universal suffrage for key government offices. However, soon after democratic transitions led to the installation of elected governments, and especially as free-market economic reforms got under way, the nature and value of democracy again became a subject of discussion.

Latin Americans began to recognize that the work of building democracy had not been completed through democratic transitions. Moreover, they gave bite to rather generic statements about building democracy by asking the question, "Which democracy?" (Weffort 1992). And the response to this question was not a shared one. After a moment of consensus about the meaning of democracy in the context of struggles against authoritarian rulers, it became readily apparent that different ideological groups had different conceptions of democracy and that these differences affected support for democracy. Enthusiasm for building democracy was not unconditional; rather, it began to hinge more and more on which democracy was going to be built. Moreover, the endurance of democracy, even in its most basic electoral dimension, would increasingly depend on how projects for the continued democratization of Latin American politics unfolded (Caputo 2011).

The Theoretical-Political Debate

The first serious theoretical-political discussions about democracy in post-transition Latin America were framed by critical intellectuals, who focused on the decisionmaking process of governments, such as those led by Carlos Menem (president of Argentina, 1989–1999) and Alberto Fujimori (president of Peru, 1990–2000), that implemented radical neoliberal policies.

Particularly influential in this regard was the concept of delegative democracy (O'Donnell 1994). This concept recognized the democratic character of these countries—the basic minimal standard of electoral democracy was taken for granted—but portrayed the concentration of power in the hands of presidents, and the frequent recourse to rule by decree, as a deficiency from the perspective of a broader notion of democracy. In particular, emphasis was put on how strong presidents necessarily weakened parliaments, the prime site where parties can debate and decide on alternative policy options between elections.[5]

With the rise to power of the left in the 2000s, the discussion about democracy changed. Views about democracy were not voiced only by critical intellectuals. Now, partisan intellectuals weighed in. Moreover, though the discussion built on an element of consensus—democracy entailed, at the very least, the minimal standard of democracy that had served as a goal of earlier struggles for democracy—it revolved largely around sharp contrasts between countries seen as exemplifying a preferred and a less desirable model of democracy. Thus, a common critical diagnosis by opposition intellectuals was increasingly replaced by a debate about the merits and shortcomings of different, largely incompatible, models of democracy.[6]

In this debate, the liberal democratic model had a prominent status, serving as a somewhat obligatory point of reference. Furthermore, many defenders of liberal democracy in Latin America (Krauze 1984; Vargas Llosa 2009; Walker 2013: chapter 8)—in this region, they are correctly labeled as liberal-conservatives (Gargarella 2013: chapter 2, 197–199)—treated liberal democracy as more or less self-evidently the one legitimate version of democracy. But such a view was questioned by many on the left who proposed their own model of democracy as an alternative to the liberal democratic model.[7] In other words, the ideological divide between neoliberals and antineoliberals affected how democracy was understood in political discourse, and the old tension between liberalism and socialism crept back into the debate about democracy.

One axis of debate concerned the *political institutions of decision-making* required by democracy. The proponents of a liberal democratic model espoused a rather conventional view. They saw constitutionalism, an independent judiciary, checks and balances, and other means of both dispersing and limiting political power, as central features of democracy. In turn, deviations from these features were considered dangerous deficiencies. In contrast, the left suggested that this was not the only legitimate way to think about democratic political institutions. Indeed, the left rejected the blind embrace of rigid constitutionalism, for putting many issues of normal politics out of the reach of electoral majorities; it pointed out that the judges sworn to uphold the constitution are many times actually a *poder fáctico* (de facto power), much like the military; and it called for the sanctioning of new constitutions through plainly democratic processes such as a popular vote to set up a constituent assembly and to ratify the constitution proposed by such an assembly (Garretón 2007: chapter 10; 2012: chapter 12). That is, seeing the various mechanisms proposed by advocates of liberal democracy to limit the power of elected authorities as limits on democracy itself, the left proposed, as a way to make countries more fully democratic, a refounding of politics through constitutional change with popular participation.

The left also offered a perspective on the role of presidents that differed from the one provided in analyses of delegative democracy. Emphasizing how the blocking of programs for change by entrenched political elites and regional powers was a key problem of democracy in Latin America, some argued that a strong president, relying on plebiscitarian appeals for popular support, was needed to counter the bias toward the status quo (Unger 1987: 362–395, 449–480; 1990: 315–323, 356–360; 1998: 213–220, 264–266). Moreover, while some acknowledged that populism weakens the prospects of an organized civil society and sustained mobilization (Unger 1998: 66–70, 79–84), others maintained that populism was sometimes needed as a corrective to the tendency toward oligarchy and, additionally, that the dangers of neoliberalism were greater than those of populism (Laclau 2005, 2006). That is, the left favored institutions that, in seeking to accentuate the antioligarchic potential of institutional arrangements, courted some risks, but that were seen as ultimately more democratic than liberal democratic institutions in that they more fully empowered electoral majorities.

Beyond the difference between liberals and leftists regarding the institutions of democracy, a second axis of debate focused on what might be called the *social environment of politics*. In some ways, the differences concerning the social environment of politics were not as incompatible as those concerning political institutions. Advocates of liberal democracy in Latin America, as did their counterparts around the world, routinely included in their definition of democracy, in addition to a standard list of institutions, certain civil rights, including the freedom of expression, association, assembly, and access to information. And the left did not directly challenge this position. Thus, the distinctiveness of the left was not that it failed to acknowledge the importance of these rights to democracy. Rather, the particularity of the left was that it insisted on also addressing socioeconomic issues (Weffort 1992; Nun 2003; Caputo 2011), a point that had important implications.

First, it led the left to emphasize that political rights (e.g., to participate in an election as equals) could be effectively exercised only if economic power did not make a mockery of the democratic principle of political equality (Weffort 1992: 14–23; Nun 2003: chapters 14, 21, 22). Relatedly, it motivated the left to suggest that a liberal view of democracy was likely to downplay the extent to which the principle of political equality, central to democracy, was violated by the disproportionate power of economic elites. Thus, leftists argued that some aspects of the socioeconomic context had to be recognized as preconditions of a democratic process, much as liberals argued was the case of some civil rights. Second, the emphasis on socioeconomic issues was also behind the left's adoption of a different view of the standard civil rights included in liberal definitions of democracy. Seeing democracy and socioeconomic inequality as inextricably linked, the left questioned the liberal view that liberty always takes precedence over equality; contextualized what were seen, from a liberal perspective, as absolute rights; and asserted that democracy required regulation of the use of money in politics, public financing of parties and candidates, and free access to the mass media (Unger 1998: 122–123, 219, 265–266).

In short, in the wake of democratic transitions in the 1980s and 1990s, Latin American intellectuals engaged in a debate about what kind of democracy their countries had and what kind of democracy they wished their countries to have. The discussion focused on criteria of democracy beyond those included in the minimal standard of electoral democracy, and was both rich and divisive. While liberals adopted the standard liberal democratic model, the left argued for a different vision of the political institutions of decisionmaking—one that sees democracy as curtailed when elected authorities are weakened or when power resides in the hands of nonelected agents within the state—and the social environment of politics—one that holds that democracy needs some civil rights, but also requires measures to prevent the conversion of economic power into political power. In other words, this discussion essentially led to the proposal of two partly compatible, but also largely contradictory, models of democracy—the model of liberal democracy and what might be called the model of popular democracy—that introduced a fundamental evaluative conflict into discussions of politics. On the one hand, liberal thinkers argued that the liberal democratic model was the only legitimate model of democracy. On the other hand, thinkers on the left questioned that the liberal democratic model was the only model of democracy and countered by arguing that their model of democracy was actually a more democratic model of democracy.

The Record of Political-Ideological Actors

This theoretical-political debate about models of democracy did not translate directly into political practices. Political actors do not operate with pure models of democracy, sometimes act without an explicit model of democracy, and sometimes do not support any model of democracy. Furthermore, political actors are rarely in a position simply to implement their preferred model of democracy; the actual model of democracy is frequently the result of a mixture of conflict and cooperation among actors who support different models of democracy. Nonetheless, the Latin American debate about models of democracy was not just an intellectual exercise. Indeed, my selective survey of post-transition Latin America highlights cases where either distinctive or problematic trends were most evident, giving support to two points: Distinct political-ideological actors have had an effect on democracy not only through their support for the rules of electoral democracy, as indicated previously, but also through their impact on the political institutions of decisionmaking and the social environment of politics. Moreover, the impact of these actors on democracy can be attributed in part to their different views about the appropriateness of the liberal democracy and popular democracy models of democracy, and conflicts over the prevalence of one or another model of democracy.

The Right

The record of the right in post-transition Latin America can be summarized as follows (see Table 6.3a). Right-wing governments were characterized by hyperpresidentialism, a combination of concentration of power in the hands of the president and the personalization of power. More specifically, right-wing presidents implemented neoliberal reforms by frequently passing legislation through decree (even when this was patently illegal, as in the case of Menem before 1994) and sought, with various degrees of success, to concentrate power in their hands by, among other measures, reforming the constitution so as to allow for their own reelection and pressuring the courts to interpret the constitution so as to allow them to stand for reelection beyond what a strict reading of the constitution would allow.[8] Right-wing governments also routinely delegated decisionmaking power to technocrats, particularly within the economic ministries and the central bank. Moreover, these governments accentuated the top-down thrust of power by suppressing liberal freedoms.

The right's record of defense of the minimal standard of electoral democracy was also negative. President Fujimori's quest to impose his neoliberal agenda in Peru clashed with the free play of electoral competition and alternation in power, and led to two of the most unequivocal cases of full disregard for the standard of electoral democracy in post-transition Latin America: Fujimori's decision to close down the elected Congress in 1992 and essentially rule with the support of the military, and his later decision to commit outright fraud in the 2000 presidential election. But the

Table 6.3a Ideology and Models of Democracy in Post-Transition Latin America: The Right and Center-Right[a]

	Consequences of Models of Democracy			Cases[b]		
Ideology and Role	For the Institutions of Decisionmaking	For the Social Environment of Politics	For Electoral Democracy	Prototypical Cases	Other Central Cases	Other Cases
Right						
In government	Hyperpresidentialism, with delegation to technocrats	Limits on liberal freedoms	Removal of elected officials, electoral fraud	Peru (1990–2000)	Argentina (1989–1999)	Brazil (1990–1992)
In opposition			Removal of elected officials	Venezuela (2002, 2014)	Honduras (2009) Paraguay (2012)	Guatemala (2008–2012)
Center-right						
In government	Presidentialism, with checks and balances	Liberal freedoms, with occasional repression of dissent	Support of full electoral democracy, with some exceptions	Colombia (1990 to present), Mexico (2000 to present)	Venezuela (1989–1999) Bolivia (1985–2005) Argentina (1999–2001)	Chile (2010–2014)
In opposition			Support of unelected officials	Chile (1990–2005)		

Sources: Author's elaboration; drawing on information on presidential ideology in Murillo, Oliveros, and Vaishnav (2010).

Notes: a. The table covers developments following democratic transitions and the initiation of free-market reforms; see Table 6.1 for information on the dating of these events.

b. The lists of cases is not comprehensive; that is, it does not cover all Latin American countries or the entire period under consideration for the countries that are covered.

right also threatened electoral democracy, and did so more often, when it was in opposition rather than in government.

Once the left surged in post-transition Latin America and began to propose an alternative to the model of liberal democracy, the right went beyond placing the sort of legitimate limits on a government that correspond to an opposition. The right gradually articulated a dangerous argument against left presidents: even if a leftist president came to office by winning a contested and clean election, the minimal standard associated with electoral democracy, their removal from office was justified if such a president was seen as governing—according to their conception of democracy—undemocratically. And the right actually followed through on such an argument. In effect, as exemplified most clearly by the cases of Venezuela (2002 and 2014) and Honduras (2009), the right, at times working with the military, invoked the model of liberal democracy to question the legitimacy of presidents elected in contests that met minimal standards and to justify the removal of these presidents.[9]

In brief, right-wing governments deviated considerably in practice from the model of liberal democracy and only reluctantly espoused liberal democracy; the contrast between their trumpeting of economic liberalism and weak endorsement of liberal democracy was quite stark. Nonetheless, when in opposition, the right was persistent in criticizing the left's record in government for any deviation from the liberal democracy model and even went to the extreme of using those deviations as justification for removing duly elected presidents. The actions of the right, then, were shaped less by its support for the model of liberal democracy than by its opposition to the model of popular democracy.

The Center-Right

The center-right's record in the post-transition period was quite different from that of the right. While in government, the center-right supported a presidential system with checks and balances. Moreover, center-right governments defended some liberal freedoms such as freedom of the press. However, center-right governments deviated from the model of liberal democracy in various ways. Álvaro Uribe Vélez's presidency in Colombia (2002–2010) tilted toward hyperpresidentialism.[10] Several center-right governments responded to antineoliberalism protests with repression, leading to hundreds of dead in the Caracazo protests in Venezuela in 1989, some twenty-two dead in Argentina in 2001, and sixty deaths in Bolivia in 2003. Furthermore, in Colombia the killing of trade unionists was a recurring problem, and in Mexico violations of human rights were a major problem after 2006. With regard to electoral democracy, the center-right's record was more fully positive. The center-right never supported the outright breakdown of electoral democracy. Yet in the instance of Chile, it actively blocked full electoral democracy, specifically by resisting for fifteen years a reform to remove the unelected senators envisioned by Augusto Pinochet's constitution.

In sum, the center-right's record in the post-transition period was considerably more positive than that of the right. In particular, it demonstrated that a strong liberal-conservative alliance can provide the basis of support for a relatively consistent implementation of a liberal democratic model, even in a context such as Latin America. Nonetheless, it also showed that the center-right failed to protect some of the most basic liberal rights and, when convenient, supported blatantly undemocratic political institutions.

The Center-Left

The record of the center-left was largely positive (see Table 6.3b). Center-left governments were respectful of checks and balances. They stood out with regard to liberal freedoms; unlike other governments, they allowed dissent and did not resort to repression when faced with protests (e.g., Brazil 2013–2014). Moreover, the center-left had an impeccable record, both in government and in opposition, of support for electoral democracy. Indeed, since the record of the center-left was comparatively so positive, it is possible to convey it succinctly. Yet the record of the center-left was also full of irony and concealed costs.

One of the key features of the center-left in Latin America was that it did not challenge the model of liberal democracy traditionally espoused by liberal-conservatives in Latin America, and was actually rather successful at building real exemplars of liberal democracy. In effect, the center-left did more than any other political group to build liberal democracies. But this achievement hid an important trade-off. In making the model of liberal democracy its own, the center-left severely limited its ability to deliver on the left's traditional aspiration to address the economic conditions of participation and contain the transformation of economic power into political power. Thus, the center-left's compromise was good for liberal democracy but entailed a rather severe shortcoming, most evident in Chile: the failure to transform the preferences of electoral majorities into public policy (Garretón 2012).

The Left

The record of the left, in contrast to the center-left, did exemplify an attempt to build an alternative to liberal democracy in post-transition Latin

Table 6.3b Ideology and Models of Democracy in Post-Transition Latin America: The Left and Center-Left[a]

Ideology and Role	Consequences of Models of Democracy			Cases[b]		
	For the Institutions of Decisionmaking	For the Social Environment of Politics	For Electoral Democracy	Prototypical Cases	Other Central Cases	Other Cases
Center-left						
In government	Presidentialism, with checks and balances	Liberal freedoms, limited improvement in economic conditions of participation	Support of full electoral democracy	Chile (2000–2010, 2014 to present), Brazil (2003 to present)	Uruguay (2005–present), El Salvador (2009 to present)	Dominican Republic (2000–2004), Panama (2002–2009), Peru (2011 to present), Costa Rica (2014 to present)
In opposition			Support of full electoral democracy	Chile (2010–2014), Brazil (1990–2003)	Uruguay (1990–2005), El Salvador (1990–2009)	
Left						
In government	Hyperpresidentialism, with plebiscitarian dimension	Some leveling of economic conditions, tension with liberal freedoms; occasional repression of dissent	Removal of elected officials	Venezuela (1999 to present)	Bolivia (2006 to present), Ecuador (2007 to present)	Nicaragua (2007–present), Argentina (2003 to present)
In opposition			Removal of elected officials	Venezuela (1992)	Bolivia (2003, 2005), Nicaragua (2005)	Ecuador (1997, 2000), Argentina (2001)

Sources: Author's elaboration; drawing on information on presidential ideology in Murillo, Oliveros, and Vaishnav (2010).

Notes: a. The table covers developments following democratic transitions and the initiation of free-market reforms; see Table 6.1 for information on the dating of these events.

b. The lists of cases is not comprehensive, that is, it does not cover all Latin American countries or the entire period under consideration for the countries that are covered.

America, and thus deserves a more elaborate discussion. Left governments favored a distinctive set of decisionmaking institutions, overtly fostering the concentration of power in the hands of the president. That is, the left governed in similar ways to the right. Yet the record of left governments differed from that of the right. On the one hand, left governments went further in accentuating hyperpresidentialism than the right because incumbent presidents not only pushed actively for the right to run for immediate reelection, but also took steps to remove barriers to the indefinite reelection of the president.[11] On the other hand, left governments differed from right governments by rejecting technocratic rule and, more broadly, the placing of key questions out of the reach of voters. In this regard, the left actively confronted de facto powers both within the state and in society,[12] turned elections into referendums on the president's agenda, and even opened up other avenues for the population to weigh in on the president's agenda. In effect, one of the distinguishing traits of the left in government was its call to refound the country by initiating a process of constitutional change that called for popular participation to elect a constituent assembly and to vote on the proposed new constitution.[13] Thus, left governments such as those of Venezuela (1999 to present), Bolivia (2006 to present), Ecuador (2007 to present), and to a lesser extent Nicaragua (2007 to present) and Argentina (2003 to present), largely exemplified the model of popular democracy and are aptly characterized as cases of "plebiscitarian superpresidentialism" (Mazzuca 2013: 109–110).

Left governments also had a distinctive record concerning the social environment of politics. In various cases, these governments took measures that could be seen as correcting the excesses of neoliberalism and leveling the playing field: for example, by breaking up and deconcentrating the ownership of large media conglomerates and thus reducing the power of actors who are driven by economic interests and have a big impact on public opinion. In these ways, then, the left was somewhat successful in curtailing the political influence of powerful private economic actors. With regard to autonomous social associations and participation, however, the record of the left was decidedly mixed. Though the left facilitated the participation of the indigenous population in Bolivia, it placed restrictions on autonomous participation in Venezuela and Ecuador (de la Torre 2013; Gargarella 2013: 172–177, 192–194). Moreover, though the left did more than the right and the center-right to avoid criminalizing social protest and restricting political dissent, on occasion it engaged in overt intimidation of opponents and, in the context of the protests against the government in Venezuela during the first half of 2014, the Nicolás Maduro–led government was responsible for the killing of several dozen protestors, the imprisonment and even torture of protestors, and the arrest of opposition leaders. In sum, the left sought, with mixed success, to simultaneously address the economic conditions of participation and respect liberal freedoms.

Turning to the impact of the left on electoral democracy, some similarities with the right again deserve mention. When the left was in opposition, it frequently questioned the right to rule of presidents who had won contested and inclusive elections. For example, when Hugo Chávez, as an officer in the military, rose up against the government in Venezuela in 1992, he offered a distinct justification for his actions. In his view, the government's pursuit of neoliberal policies and repression of protests was evidence that it was a government that responded to elite and foreign interests, and this betrayal of democracy trumped any legitimacy due to the electoral origin of the government and justified his disloyal behavior as a coup plotter (Evo Morales echoed this view in Bolivia in 2003 and 2005). In turn, when the left came to power in Venezuela and Ecuador, it invoked the constituent power vested in the constituent assemblies that were elected soon after the elections that brought them to power to declare just-elected parliaments defunct. Thus, when the left was in opposition and taking its first steps in government, it invoked an alternative to the model of liberal democracy to justify overriding the basic standard of electoral democracy.

However, the potentially most serious threat to electoral democracy coming from the left emerged later on, once the left's grip on power became consolidated. There is evidence of the commitment of governments of the left to peaceful alternation in office. The left conceded defeat in Venezuela in a constitutional referendum in 2007, and in Ecuador in the municipal elections of 2014. Furthermore, the left conceded defeat in Argentina in the legislative elections of 2009 and, due to the result of the 2013 legislative elections, gave up on its ambition to reform the constitution so as to allow President Cristina Fernández de Kirchner to run for a third consecutive term.[14] Nonetheless, certain developments in countries with left presidents raise concerns about the future prospects of peaceful alternation in government. At times, the left has used state resources in ways that are reminiscent of practices of Mexico's Institutional Revolutionary Party during the twentieth century, and has relied on undemocratic practices in local races (e.g., committing electoral fraud in the 2008 municipal elections in Nicaragua, and banning opposition candidates in local races in Nicaragua and Venezuela). Moreover, as the events in Venezuela following the death of Chávez in 2013 showed, the problem of leadership succession in extremely personalistic systems exacerbates the most polarizing features of the model of popular democracy and opens up many dangers for electoral democracy. In short, the decided effort by the left to build an alternative to liberal democracy has generated distinct problems for democracy.

Conclusion

My analysis has important implications for our thinking about democracy in post-transition Latin America. I suggest that the problem is not that there are two different models of democracy. Rather, the problem is that political actors, regardless of the model of democracy to which they more or less explicitly subscribed, sometimes governed in ways that accentuated a top-down form of power that suppressed the role of parliament and extraparliamentary opposition. Indeed, this way of governing has occasionally been pushed to such an extreme that it has become imperative to confront the question, Have democratically elected governments in Latin America governed democratically? In turn, conflicts over the appropriate model of democracy have led to significant departures from the basic standard of electoral democracy. Legitimate differences over models of democracy have escalated to the point that political actors began to question the erstwhile non-negotiable status of electoral democracy.

More pointedly, the record in post-transition Latin America supports some generalizations. To a considerable extent, this record confirms Juan J. Linz's conclusion that "the breakdown of democratic regimes generally seems to be the victory of political forces identified as rightists" (1978: 15). After all, thus far the only indisputable breaches of a minimal standard of democracy (Peru 1992 and 2000, the short-lived coup in Venezuela 2002, and Honduras 2009) are due to actions of the right. But reinforcing a general point made by Norberto Bobbio (1996: 20–21), it is important to add that democracy has been put at risk and partially restricted by extreme versions of both the right and the left. Additionally, it is only fair to point out that, at least in Latin America, the center-right has also been a source of problems for democracy and that only the center-left has an unimpeachable record of support for democracy.

This analysis of post-transition Latin America also has implications for the future of democracy in the region. I suggest that there are grounds for paying particular attention to the cases where the left is currently in government and where efforts to build an alternative to liberal democracy have gone furthest. These are the cases where the conflicts between government and opposition are most bitter. And though these cases have not yet produced a breakdown of electoral democracy, as was the case in Peru in the context of President Fujimori's pursuit of a neoliberal agenda, concerns about the impact of the left on electoral democracy cannot be dismissed lightly.[15] The possibility that left governments will use their control of the state to prevent a peaceful alternation in government is very real. In sum, the future of democracy in Latin America largely hinges on the trajectory followed by countries where the left currently governs and is likely to govern in the immediate future: that is, Venezuela, Bolivia, Ecuador, and Nicaragua. (In Argentina, the Kirchners [Néstor Kirchner and Cristina Fernández de Kirchner] cycle will probably come to an end in late 2015).

The future of democracy does not depend only on the role of the left in government, however. The record of the right illustrates the tenuous nature of the alliance between conservatives and liberals that brought about the conservatives' acceptance of democracy, even when this acceptance of democracy was conditional on democracy being understood as a liberal democracy that withdrew key economic questions from consideration by electoral majorities. The right in post-transition Latin America has tended to adopt the old conservative approach to politics, introducing severe deviations from the model of liberal democracy, even stretching the liberal democratic model to the breaking point on many occasions, to enable the imposition of a neoliberal agenda. Thus, the possibility of a backlash from the right cannot be discounted. Moreover, the blatant weaknesses of democracy in two countries governed by the center-right, Colombia and Mexico, are as urgent as those where the left governs. In brief, it would be a mistake to focus solely on left governments and problems associated with the model of popular democracy, and overlook the internal contradictions of advocates of a liberal democracy.

The experience with democracy in post-transition Latin America could also be shaped by as yet untried options. No country in the region has been governed by a left-liberal alliance that does not relegate to a secondary status the left's concerns, among others about economic elites and other de facto powers. Furthermore, no country in the region has experience with a model of democracy that places legislative power firmly in the hands of parliament. Thus, the future of democracy in Latin America should not be envisioned only in terms of a repertoire of past experiences. The history of democracy in Latin America remains open.[16]

Finally, the analysis of post-transition Latin America that I provide in this chapter has some broader implications for our thinking about democracy. As stressed, once electoral democracy has been attained, it has to be defended. Nonetheless, it is important to avoid the common tendency to think about post-transitional politics in static terms centered on the defense of previously attained democratic gains. Democratization does not disappear as a political claim once electoral democracy has been attained. Rather, political actors continue to seek to build democracy, engaging in "democratic critiques of democracy" (O'Donnell 2007) that lead them to propose models of democracy that go well beyond the standard of electoral democracy. Moreover, the endurance of electoral democracy is strongly affected by the continued politics of democratization (Caputo 2011: 444–447). Indeed, conflicts over the appropriateness and legitimacy of different models of democracy play a key role in post-transition politics. In a few words, the outcome of the conflict over which model of democracy will prevail determines how democracy develops and, in turn, whether democracy endures.

Notes

I would like to acknowledge the useful comments that I received from Max Cameron, Mauricio Rivera Celestino, Juvenal Cortes, Joe Foweraker, Mariana Rangel, and Bárbara Zarate.

1. Coups were carried out in the course of transitions to democracy in Bolivia (twice in 1978, in 1979, and in 1980) and Paraguay (in 1989), and military revolts were carried out in a post-transitional context in Argentina (in 1987, twice in 1988, and in 1990) and Paraguay (in 1996 and in 1999). Moreover, the military maintained a strong influence over elected authorities in several other countries.

2. The case of Brazil under Fernando Henrique Cardoso (1995–2002) is a partial exception, in that free-market reforms were introduced along with an innovative social policy that involved some income redistribution.

3. Indeed, following Bobbio (1996: chapter 6), the difference between left and right is seen as hinging on the value of equality: the left is egalitarian, the right inegalitarian. However, since this chapter explores the link between ideology and democracy, and spells out this link in terms of different models of democracy, the concepts of left and right are understood here in terms of their position with regard to the more delimited matter of economic equality.

4. This idea that the post-transition period is a new period, in which the challenges and risks for democracy are not the ones of the past, is presented in Caputo (2011).

5. For a similar diagnosis, which highlights the concept of technocratic decisionism, see Bresser Pereira, Maravall, and Przeworski (1993: 4–10). A related debate focuses on the merits of presidential and parliamentary democracy (Consejo para la Consolidación de la Democracia 1988; Godoy Arcaya 1990).

6. For a review of conceptualizations of democracy in post-transition Latin America, see Barrueto and Navia (2013).

7. Many and varied democratic alternatives to liberal democracy have been proposed in Latin America (Unger 1987, 1990, 1998; Nun 2003; O'Donnell, Vargas Cullell, and Iazzetta 2004; Laclau 2005; Harnecker 2007; Caputo 2011). Thus, what follows is a selective depiction.

8. In Peru, Fujimori was able to persuade the Supreme Court to allow him to run for a third consecutive term, while Menem's attempt to do the same was blocked. In Brazil, Fernando Collor de Mello's tenure was cut short because he was impeached on corruption charges.

9. The problem in El Salvador in 2014 concerned the acceptance of an election's result, given that the right questioned the electoral process, with no evidence, and made calls for the military to prevent what the right claimed was a fraud to favor the left.

10. As incumbent president, Uribe successfully pushed for a reform of the constitution to allow for a second successive presidency. Though he sought to push through a reform allowing for a third successive presidency, the courts frustrated his ambition.

11. The indefinite reelection of the president has been allowed in Venezuela since 2009 and in Nicaragua since 2014 (earlier, the Supreme Court of Nicaragua had allowed Daniel Ortega to run for reelection in 2012, on highly dubious grounds). In Ecuador, the elimination of term limits for the president has been practically assured by the Constitutional Court ruling, in October 2014, that such a change is constitutional. In Bolivia President Morales ran successfully for a third consecutive and last term in 2014, a situation that has opened discussions concerning the elimination of term limits. Finally, in the case of Argentina, the Kirchner husband and wife team were able to get around the two consecutive terms limit by taking turns running for the presidency. But the death of Néstor Kirchner in 2010 ended this option and, though the possibility of indefinite reelection was discussed in Argentina, it was effectively blocked by the results of the 2013 election.

12. In Venezuela, however, a de facto power, the military, has been brought in to positions of influence in the government.

13. It is noteworthy that these constitutional changes broke with the pattern associated with governments that pursued a neoliberal agenda and are best seen as located within the tradition of constitutional radical democracy (Pisarello 2012: chapter 5, 193).

14. The lesson of the likely end of the Kirchners cycle in Argentina for the cases of Venezuela, Bolivia, Ecuador, and Nicaragua is limited, however. The waning power of Cristina Fernández de Kirchner is due to a counterbalance to executive power coming largely from the Peronist party that had initially supported the Kirchners, much as was the case with Menem in the 1990s. Thus, the problem for democracy in Argentina is not whether the left decides not to relinquish power but whether alternation between ideological groups occurs through candidates of one party, the Peronists, or alternation between different parties. An earlier instance when the left accepted electoral defeat in a race for president, the decision of Ortega to relinquish power in Nicaragua in 1990, also has limited applicability to the cases of Venezuela, Bolivia, Ecuador, and Nicaragua because the circumstances in Nicaragua in the 1980s were not the same as the current circumstances in Venezuela, Bolivia, Ecuador, and Nicaragua.

15. An assessment on the situation of Venezuela, the most discussed case of a left government, hinges on the complicated matter of what concept and criteria are used in such an assessment, a matter addressed elsewhere (Munck 2009: chapters 4 and 5). Though a careful discussion of Venezuela at the present time (December 2014) is beyond the scope of this chapter, Insulza's (2014) claim that Maduro was "democratically elected" is closer to the truth than the increasingly common statements that Venezuela is not a democracy. For a similar point of view, see Cameron (2014).

16. Along these lines, it is possible to posit a model that draws inspiration from the French Revolution and provides an alternative to the liberal democratic and popular democratic models by combining elements from liberal and socialist thought. This third model is arguably the most democratic model and actually has a tradition in Latin America (Gargarella 2010: chapter 1). However, in the current context, only a few scholars have defended this model (e.g., Gargarella 2010: chapter 4; 2013: 162–165, chapter 10).

7

Radical Claims to Accountability

Javier Corrales

What has happened to participatory democracy in Latin America? In the late 1990s, most countries in Latin America generated large political movements committed to revamping democracy to encourage participation. The idea behind participatory democracy was to make politics more directly connected to the people by relying less on delegation and traditional representation and by opening decisionmaking to previously excluded citizens and groups (Coppedge and Gerring 2011; De la Torre 2009). In this chapter, I focus on Bolivia under Evo Morales, Ecuador under Rafael Correa, Venezuela under Hugo Chávez and Nicolás Maduro, and to a lesser extent Nicaragua under Daniel Ortega's second administration. These administrations made some of the most radical claims about fostering participatory democracy, but their experiments eventually failed to deliver in varying degrees.

I examine these failures by comparing the projects and, in particular, by investigating their origins and tracing the subsequent evolution of government accountability, the model of political economy, and social policy. There were some—mainly early—successes. But in many respects the projects eventually led to reduced participation and representation and, hence, weaker accountability. Rather than intending to test new theories, I provide an assessment of more than a decade of experiments with radical attempts to advance participatory democracy.

Origins

Scholars of Latin American politics have devoted significant attention to studying the rise of the left since the late 1990s. Two themes have dominated this research enterprise: why the rise of the left occurred at this moment in history, and why the left split between a moderate and a more radical left. On the first question, research by political scientists has debunked several important myths. First, this is not the first time that the left has governed or taken the upper hand, as was initially assumed in the early 2000s. Research by Rosario Queirolo (2013) has demonstrated that this pink tide is not new. The region has had ideological cycles in the past, and the left was a previous favorite. Using survey and electoral data, Queirolo shows that the left was predominant in Latin America during a previous cycle (1969–1976) and at least as competitive as the right in another cycle (1956–1968). The second myth is the idea that the current cycle was a rejection of neoliberal policies (predominant in the 1990s) or conversely a sign of disadvantaged classes rising politically, or simply a reflection of economic indicators. Using data from 1980 to 2010, Queirolo found no confirmation for any of these variables.

Moreover, there is no correlation between the depth of neoliberal reforms and the pink tide. Consider the cases of Mexico and Peru versus Venezuela and Ecuador. In Mexico and Peru, neoliberalism went far in the 1990s, but the left did not achieve majority status in the 2000s, though in Mexico it became a major political force in the south. In Venezuela and Ecuador, the reverse was true (López Maya 2011: 214; De la Torre 2013). Regarding class, Queirolo (2013) found that successful leftist parties built cross-class coalitions, rather than relying exclusively on one particular class of have-nots.[1] And although radical movements in Ecuador and Bolivia successfully mobilized indigenous groups in what Madrid (2008) calls "ethnopopulism" (see also Yashar 2005), these movements also attracted the support of other strata of society, including the middle classes and leftist intellectuals. Finally, Queirolo found no clear correlation between macroeconomic or personal income variables and the vote for the left. The only economic measure that mattered was a high level of unemployment, but this variable was barely significant (2013: 51).

If it is not the rejection of the status quo or the rise of the have-nots, then the most likely explanations for the turn to the left might simply be mere democratic alternation (e.g., Murillo, Oliveros, and Vaishnav 2009; Panizza 2009)[2] and the search for parties that were less tainted by their links to the status quo (e.g., Queirolo 2013); the commodity boom of the 2000s that created the conditions for more fiscally expansive forces to come to power (e.g., Mazzuca 2013; Kaufman 2010); or a much-reduced fear of military intervention (Debs and Helmke 2010). In other words, the rise of the left had more to do with contingent and contextual conditions rather than a wholesale rejection of neoliberalism.

But what explains the divide between the moderate and radical left? Although definitions vary, the more moderate version encompasses leftist parties that have been willing to accept and even strengthen liberal principles in politics and economics. The more radical version consists of leaders who are willing to expand the power of the state and alter the status quo without necessarily seeking to preserve liberal principles (Madrid, Hunter, and Weyland 2010: 167; Huber, Pribble, and Stephens 2010: 82). By 2009 the moderate left was in office in Brazil, Chile, Peru, and Uruguay while the radical left governed in Bolivia, Ecuador, Nicaragua, and Venezuela, with in-between versions in Argentina, Honduras, and Paraguay.

Once again the incidence of neoliberalism is not the most compelling explanation for the rise of the radical left. Leftist parties of both the moderate and radical kinds have come to power in countries with previously high levels of neoliberalism (e.g., Chile, Argentina, Bolivia) (Huber, Pribble, and Stephens 2010: 82; Madrid, Hunter, and Weyland 2010: 168) as well as in countries with modest levels of neoliberalism (e.g., Uruguay, Venezuela, Ecuador) (Goldfrank 2011: 162; Etchemendy and Garay 2011: 301). Consequently, there is little correlation between the extent of neoliberalism and the rise of the left in general or the radical left in particular. Radicalism was not a response to a strong dose of neoliberalism. Nonetheless, the experience of neoliberalism does matter. The radical left was more likely to emerge if a country had a particularly traumatic experience with neoliberalism, whether a botched privatization program, a big increase in private monopolies and hence prices, a severe financial crisis after a period of austerity, or entrenched inequality and increasing poverty (Levitsky and Roberts 2011: 407; Debs and Helmke 2010). On the other hand, the prospects for the radical left were less favorable where there was less trauma of this kind. This may have been due to prior years of economic growth that created a new class of economic winners who were eager to change the current system by a turn to the left, but were cautious enough to prefer the moderate left. Or possibly it was simply that the absence of economic crisis left potential veto players in a position to moderate the policies of ruling left parties.

The latter point brings us to a vital observation about the institutional origins of the radical left: the radical left was more likely to set root where there was some sort of disruption in the party system, either across the board and affecting all parties or more selectively and affecting just key parties (Levitsky and Roberts 2011: 408; Kingstone 2011; Flores-Macías 2012). The connection between party system erosion and the rise of the radical left is complicated. On the one hand, the relationship might be seen as spurious. The very factor that leads to the demise of a party system, a severe economic crisis, is also the factor that leads to the rise of antisystem voting preferences. But on the other, the connection is also directly causal. It is one thing for a leader to want to break up the status quo; it is another to be able to carry it out. Only those parties facing fewer or weaker veto players will enjoy a clear path to radical reform. Countries with collapsed party systems offer such a clear path.

The Constituyente Moment

In Bolivia, Ecuador, and Venezuela, radical administrations started with a similar political decision. They focused on delivering new constitutions, rather than addressing economic ailments. This was remarkable insofar as it privileged the political and symbolic over the material, and so broke the pattern of the previous twenty years in Latin America of putting economic reforms first. This was because the economy in all three cases was in a shambles, and dealing with it would have meant breaking populist promises. But by pushing the constitutional process, these governments could be seen to fulfill these promises by empowering new actors and conferring new societal rights (see Nolte and Schilling-Vacaflor 2012; Negretto 2014). Table 7.1 provides a list of some of the new rights that these constitutions granted. There is no question that, in a number of important areas, these regimes began with formal institutional openings for nontraditional actors such as environmental groups, feminist groups, indigenous groups, nonpartisan/nongovernmental organizations, and even some lesbian, gay, bisexual, and transgender (LGBT) groups. Crucially, however, the constituent assemblies also created opportunities for the newly elected presidents to win more power for the executive (see Corrales 2013a) at the expense of their respective legislatures. The immediate motive for this was their lack of control of the legislature (Correa had no seats at all) and their need to win control in

Table 7.1 A Comparison of Constitutional Innovations

Constitutional Innovations	Bolivia	Ecuador	Venezuela
Impeachment of president	Yes	Yes	Yes
Recall of public officials	Yes	Yes	Yes
Direct elections of mayors and governors	Yes	Yes	Yes
Representation of indigenous peoples	Yes	Yes	Yes
Representation of ecological groups	Yes	Yes	Yes
Representation of women's groups in government	Yes	Yes	No
Explicit provision for women's rights	Yes	Yes	Yes
Recognition of indigenous languages	Yes	Yes	Yes
Same-sex civil unions	No	Yes	No
Institutionalized affirmative action	Yes	Yes	Yes
Antidiscrimination based on sexuality	Yes	Yes	No
Explicit rights to pregnant women	Yes	Yes	Yes
Social security benefits for homemakers	Yes	Yes	Yes
Citizen referendums for constitutional reform	Yes	Yes	Yes

the next round of elections by enhancing their own profile and prestige. So while the new constitutions certainly granted new rights to some previously excluded groups, the process itself was driven by the goal of rebalancing executive-legislative relations—as well as relations between the executive and subnational authorities—strongly in favor of the executive.

But there was variation that is best explained by different degrees of party fragmentation. The executive in Venezuela gained the most power, followed by Ecuador and then Bolivia. In Venezuela and to a lesser degree in Ecuador, the opposition was highly fragmented when it confronted the constitutional process and thus was unable to restrain the ambitions of the executive branch. In Bolivia, the opposition united during the negotiation process and mobilized against the ruling party and so was able—with the help of mediation by Brazil and Chile—to negotiate a more consensual outcome that was more respectful of opposition prerogatives. In Nicaragua, a previous pact with another party granted the Sandinistas considerable leverage (more on that below) and there was less incentive to call for a constituent assembly, so no constituyente was held.

The constitutional process reinforced the popularity of presidents among their followers, but generated significant discontent among the opposition. Rather than unifying the nation, the process was a polarizing event. The presidents' followers became more convinced that their new leaders were not going to betray them as previous leftist administrations had done by enacting economic austerity policies once in office. In contrast, the opposition began to recognize that the new ruling party was ready to concentrate power in the executive, curtail the freedom of action of opposition parties, and constrain communication with nonloyal actors. Thus, these presidents sought to ensure that only loyalists were appointed to key posts in the executive, to expand the clientelistic power of the state, and to denigrate the opposition as self-interested conservative groups that were only intent on blocking a long overdue redistribution of wealth and income. For its part, the opposition saw itself as attempting to defend institutional checks and balances while maintaining some semblance of pluralist politics.

Postfoundational Politics:
Vertical and Horizontal Accountability

After an initial honeymoon period, the politics of participatory democracy suffered a dramatic bifurcation. On the one hand these regimes made some progress toward better income distribution and more social welfare, but on the other they curtailed the participation of nonloyal groups and impaired checks and balances, so weakening vertical accountability. In the language of Robert A. Dahl (1971), the constitutional process soon led to general constraints on political contestation and a patchy and contradictory record of political inclusion.

Initially, all these regimes took advantage of the copious rents from commodity exports to boost the incomes of the poor. But at least some of this spending was either wasteful (realizing little benefit), or sectarian (channeled to loyal followers), or both. So while there was a real reduction in poverty in each case, the size of that reduction was not so significant considering their preexisting levels of poverty and the average reduction in poverty levels of other countries in the region (see Figure 7.1). The percentage of the population living in poverty decreased by 15 percent in Ecuador,

Figure 7.1 Incidence of Poverty, 2005 vs. 2012 (percentage of population)

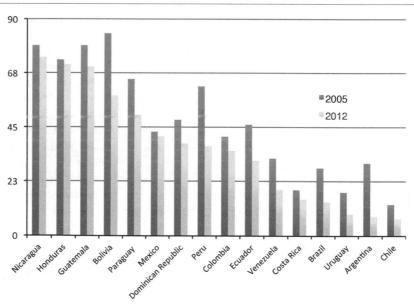

Source: ECLAC 2014. *Social Panorama of Latin America* 2014. United Nations, Santiago, Chile, available at http://repositorio.cepal.org/bitstream/handle/11362/37627 /S1420728_en.pdf?sequence=4.

Notes: Data for Nicaragua refer to 2005 and 2009; for Honduras refer to 2006 and 2010; for Guatemala refer to 2000 and 2006; for Bolivia refer to 2003 and 2011; for Paraguay refer to 2005 and 2011; for Mexico refer to 2004 and 2012; for the Dominican Republic refer to 2006 and 2012; for Peru refer to 2003 and 2012; for Colombia refer to 2008 and 2012; for Venezuela for 2005 and 2012 refer to urban areas; for Uruguay for 2005 refer to urban areas; for Argentina for 2005 and 2012 refer to urban areas; for Chile refer to 2003 and 2011.

5 percent in Nicaragua, and 13 percent in Venezuela between 2005 and 2012, compared to an average decrease of 11.5 percent across the region. Bolivia's reduction of 26 percent looks really impressive but less so in the light of the high starting point, which meant that a relatively modest real distribution could achieve a large percentage reduction. Furthermore, countries with nonradical or even nonleftist administrations achieved comparable or greater declines in poverty (compare Peru and Bolivia; Guatemala and Nicaragua; Uruguay and Venezuela; Brazil and Ecuador). Poverty alleviation was real among the radical cases, but not exclusive to them.

But any advance in economic redistribution was more than matched by the retreat from political participation as all these regimes moved to concentrate power and close down any political access available to the opposition. They did so, first, by undermining institutional checks and balances and, second, by imposing rules that prejudiced autonomous societal actors considered capable of challenging the regime.[3] The primary objective of the first was to curtail or eliminate the independence of the Supreme Court and of the councils or institutes responsible for regulating and monitoring elections. Strong attacks on the court occurred in Ecuador, Venezuela, and Nicaragua, but less so in Bolivia; the electoral bodies were largely neutered in Venezuela and Nicaragua, but less so in Ecuador and Bolivia. The rules intended to hinder and harass societal actors were characterized by what—in the case of Venezuela—I have called *autocratic legalism*: the use, abuse, and nonuse of the law to neutralize any resistance to the regime. In this way, these regimes systematically hampered horizontal accountability while slowly but surely impeding political pluralism.

The case of Nicaragua is distinctive insofar as the government successfully pursued similar ends, but without the springboard of a constituent assembly. The electoral weakness of the FSLN (Sandinista National Liberation Front) was evident from three successive election defeats, so its leader Ortega plotted his return to power by forming a pact with then president Arnoldo Alemán that sidelined the other opposition parties and left the FSLN and Alemán's PLC (Constitutional Liberal Party) in nearly complete control of both the executive and legislature. As a consequence, they were able to enact electoral reforms that lowered the percentage necessary for a presidential candidate to win an election to 40 percent of the popular vote, if the candidate beat the runner-up by at least 5 percent. To Ortega's great advantage, the opposition was divided and weak at the time of the elections while Alemán himself was serving a twenty-year prison sentence for fraud, corruption, and money laundering that had thrown his party into turmoil (Gooren 2010). In the election the liberal vote was split fairly evenly between the two main liberal parties, the PLC and the ALN (Nicaraguan Liberal Alliance), with 26 and 29 percent, respectively, so opening the way for Ortega to win the election and take up the reins of government in almost full control of the legislature, the Supreme Court, and the electoral authority.

Developmental Models

The developmental model adopted by these participatory regimes exhibits two common features that I call statism and neoextractivism. The former is more characteristic of this set of countries than others in Latin America while the latter appears to follow a regional trend. Both of these features have proved to be highly contentious, leading to polemical debates among scholars and the political publics of the countries in question.

Statism refers to the degree to which the state seeks to regulate, direct, control, curtail, or even eliminate market forces through state policies and state ownership of firms (Corrales 2003). One way to measure the degree of statism is the Index of Economic Freedom produced by the Heritage Foundation.[4] This index has been ranking countries according to how economically free government policies are since 1995. Figure 7.2 provides the scores from this index for the most important leftist administrations in Latin America in three separate moments: 2002, the year of Argentina's latest economic collapse that many scholars consider to be the peak of neoliberalism in the region; the starting year for each leftist administration in a given country; and the most recent data point, 2015 for all countries except Chile where it is 2010, the year that the leftist administration of the Concertación was unseated from office. The scores reveal a clear divide, with the governments of Bolivia, Ecuador, Venezuela, and indeed Argentina as the most statist for their low scores and for the extent of the transformation since the beginning of their terms in office. Evidently, these administrations have reversed many of the most important neoliberal reforms of the 1990s through a return to public ownership, reregulation, and price controls. The remaining countries took a different approach and sought to reverse neoliberalism only slightly or not at all. (It is noteworthy that Nicaragua falls into the category of the countries with more modest left turns in economic policy.) This forceful return of statism has repolarized this set of countries along conventional left-right lines, with the right arguing that this excessive degree of statism—especially when inspired by a government relatively unfettered by checks and balances—is a recipe for economic distortions, inefficiencies, and corruption while the left is less disturbed by the general direction of travel, but may be worried from time to time by policy excesses or poor implementation.

The second dominant aspect of these countries' political economy has been *neoextractivism* or *reprimarization*. The terms refer to heavy reliance

Figure 7.2 Index of Economic Freedom, Leftist Administrations, 1999–2015

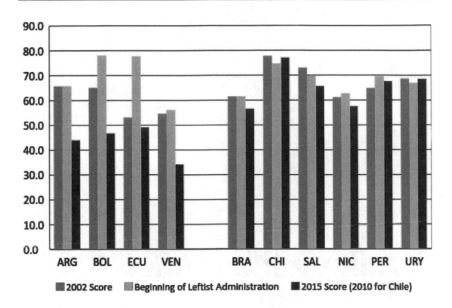

Source: Heritage Foundation, Index of Economic Freedom (various years), http://www.heritage.org/index/Index of Economic Freedom.

Note: Beginning of leftist administration is different for each country: 2002 for Argentina, 2006 for Bolivia, 2007 for Ecuador, 1999 for Venezuela, 2002 for Brazil, 2000 for Chile, 2009 for El Salvador, 2007 for Nicaragua, 2001 for Peru, and 2005 for Uruguay.

on the extraction of primary materials, especially land-based resources, for export. The term principally applies to governments that nationalize or overregulate the extraction of raw materials and use the surplus revenue from the exports to promote social development programs in the country (Hogenboom 2012; Burchardt and Dietz 2014). Figure 7.3 shows the top two extractive or agricultural exports as a percentage of total exports for various countries in the region. It is clear that most countries in the region have increased their dependence on primary products, but Ecuador, Bolivia, and especially Venezuela stand out for their high dependence on minerals, with the top two extractive or agricultural exports accounting for 53 percent of the total in Ecuador, 55 percent in Bolivia, and 97 percent in Venezuela. The only other country in the same league is Colombia with 59 percent, mainly as a result of its dramatic increase in oil production. The remaining

Figure 7.3 Percentage of Total Exports in 2006 and 2013

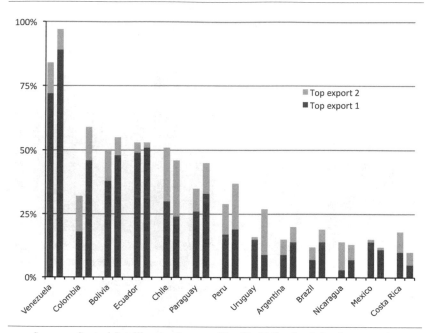

Sources: Central Intelligence Agency, *The World Factbook* (various years), www .theodora.com/wfb; *Atlas of Economic Complexity*, www.atlas.cid.harvard.edu.
Note: Left-hand bar 2006, right-hand bar 2013.

countries either have a much lower dependence or no dependence at all. Mexico and Chile have traditionally been dependent on mineral exports but saw a slight reduction in that dependence since 2006, with Mexico's oil exports dropping from 15 to 12 percent of the total and exports from the nonextractive transport industry increasing from 17 to 23 percent; similarly in Chile, the two main extractive exports, refined copper and gold ore, decreased from 51 to 46 percent of the total.

While Nicaragua has not exactly reprimarized, it has nonetheless developed its own version of neoextractivism in two main ways. First, Nicaragua has developed a high dependence on Venezuelan oil through PetroCaribe. Under Ortega, Nicaragua began receiving 11 million barrels of subsidized oil per year (Otis and Vyas 2015), in addition to $1.6 billion in aid from Venezuela over the years 2007 to 2011, with $511 million in 2010 alone (T. Rogers 2011). According to the Nicaraguan Foundation for Social and Economic Development (FUNIDES), 20 percent of Nicaraguan GDP in 2010 and 2011 was a result of Venezuelan aid (Central America Data 2012). Second, Nicaragua has also bet heavily on developing a canal, ceding full development rights to a Chinese investment vehicle, the Hong Kong Nicaragua Canal Development Company. This land-for-investment deal has increased the regime's dependence on foreign capital and has provoked widespread protests against what some see as a threat to national sovereignty. In effect, the government has given a foreign firm the right to alter and destroy vital natural resources, including freshwater supplies from Lake Nicaragua and Lake Cocibolca, as well as the power to displace over 100,000 Nicaraguans living near the construction site (Serrano 2015).

Neoextractivism in these countries provides a further stimulus to polarization. Whereas statism pits the left against everyone else, neoextractivism splits the left in two while doing little to captivate the right. Leftist support-

Table 7.2 A Five-Actor Model of Latin America's Political Economy, 1980s to 2010s

Key Actors	Neoliberal Era, late 1980s to late 1990s	Commodity Boom Era, 2012–2013	
		Radical Left	Nonradical Left
Ruling party	Very powerful (delegative democracy)	Very powerful (large electoral majorities; constituent assemblies that empower presidents)	Not as powerful (no foundational expansion of institutional powers)
Informal sectors	Demobilized (bearing the brunt of adjustment)	Mobilized, aligned with the ruling party, pitted against traditional parties	Less important for the ruling party
Traditional opposition parties	Varies: can be strong or weak vis-à-vis the ruling party	Very weak	Usually strong
International financial actors	Strong bargaining leverage; advocate austerity through loan conditionality	Weak veto player: role of international lending diminishes	Weak veto player: role of international lending diminishes
Transnational extractive industries	Winners through privatization	Winners through reprimarization and commodity price booms	Winners through reprimarization and commodity price booms
		Outcomes	
	High probability of changing the status quo in a market-oriented direction (with opposition from informal sectors)	High probability of changing the status quo in the direction of rentier populism and declining checks and balances	Low probability of changing the economic model or eroding checks and balances

Note: A gray cell indicates that the actor is helping to empower the executive.

ers of neoextractivism argue that there is nothing wrong with relying on state exploitation of resources if the main beneficiary is the local population rather than foreign capital—in other words, extractivism is ethically correct if it is handled by a distributionist state. Critics argue that not only is neoextractivism ecologically and demographically destructive but it also aligns the state with foreign interests, obliging it to comply with the demands of foreign investors and foreign buyers. Paradoxically, this dependency on foreign investors has compelled these regimes to enact policies that place foreign interests above the rights of local groups, particularly indigenous groups and the poor in general. As a result some of the regimes' most loyal supporters have turned into their most ardent opponents.

Critics also argue that gains from neoextractivism are being distributed in a sectarian rather than impartial fashion, and typically without any transparency. The press has alleged that Ortega and his Sandinista insiders have made business investments with funds supplied by foreign investors (T. Rogers 2009) while oil exploration in Ecuador's Yasuni National Park and mineral exploration of Bolivia's national parks demonstrate the irony of justifying extractivism under the banner of improving the welfare of the most marginalized groups. Bolivia's Supreme Decree 2366, in particular, which opened up previously protected national parks to the mining of hydrocarbons, will have adverse effects on the indigenous peoples who live in the area. Yet the law requires the company extracting the raw materials to contribute only 1 percent of its investment toward poverty reduction and economic development (Achtenberg 2015).

The antiextractivist left believes that this turn to neoextractivism represents a betrayal of leftist principles while the right sees extractivism—despite its reliance on international finance capital—as nothing more or less than a means of expanding the size of the state and its power over the market. And opposition to neoextractivism has led to some of the most serious conflicts faced by the leftist governments in Ecuador, Bolivia, Venezuela, and Nicaragua. The opening up of Yasuni National Park in Ecuador led to large street protests in 2013 when environmentalists, indigenous groups, and the political opposition took to social media and the streets to accuse the government of betraying its promises to protect the environment (Cevallos 2013). Correa responded by claiming that his opponents were exaggerating the adverse effects and misinforming the public while also cracking down on the media and NGOs, including the Fundación Pachama, one of the most prominent defenders of the rights of Amazon indigenous peoples (Pachamama Alliance 2013). In Bolivia, the plans to pursue economic growth at the expense of the environment and indigenous peoples' land rights have turned many of Morales's most loyal supporters against him. His support for a road project across the Amazon in the Isiboro Secure National Park and Indigenous Territory (TIPNIS) has led to numerous large protests since 2011, and four protestors died and many were injured during violent clashes between police and indigenous activists in August of that year (CNN 2011). Similarly, large protests against the Nicaraguan Canal project have provoked violent clashes with police. At least twenty-one protestors were injured and thirty-three arrested when police used rubber bullets to clear a roadblock in December 2014, and as of June 2015 there have been some forty-seven protests against the project (*Latin News* 2015) and against the expulsion of local inhabitants in particular (Al Jazeera 2014).

Modeling the Model

The contours of the political economy of these regimes are now clear. There initially was some progress toward vertical accountability of the kind generated by greater social inclusion and a more expansive social policy. But in other respects, vertical accountability suffered as opposition groups were excluded and pluralism declined while the erosion of institutional checks and balances saw a significant weakening of horizontal accountability. These contradictory developments can be described by a simple model comprising— following Mazzuca (2013) and others cited above—five main actors; namely, the ruling party, the informal sector, the traditional opposition parties, international finance capital, and transnational extractive industry (see Table 7.2). According to this model, radical leftist administrations can be characterized by the following:

1. A foundational electoral coalition in which the ruling party aligns with newly mobilized informal sectors.
2. A foundational institutional rupture (the constituent moment) in which the ruling party grants enormous formal powers (more legal prerogatives) and informal powers (more prestige) to the executive branch to the detriment of opposition parties.
3. Informal sectors and other rent-seeking groups that press the ruling party to engage in social spending, which creates pseudoaccountability in the form of rentier populism.
4. Traditional parties that decline or collapse early in the process and so find themselves incapable of defending horizontal accountability from the encroachments of the executive branch.
5. International financial actors with declining veto power. In the conditions obtaining in the era of neoliberalism—no commodity boom and a scarcity of rents—these actors could push their agenda of fiscal austerity

and respect for market forces, placing a veto on populism. But that power was lost once the governments after 2000 no longer needed outside financing.

6. Transnational extractivist interests that lost ground to the expanding power and intervention of the state (statism) but gained leverage as a result of reprimarization, which placed them at the heart of the development model that was increasingly shaped by foreign markets.

Table 7.2 depicts how this rentier-populist model compares with two alternative models: the neoliberal model that prevailed from the late 1980s to the late 1990s, and the social-democratic model that prevailed among the nonradical left in the 2000s. The key difference in the former model was that the executive branch was mainly empowered through delegation rather than through alliances with the informal sector or foundational constituent processes. In addition, the international financial actors insisted on austerity and the transnational extractivists supported the model insofar as they profited from privatization (rather than from reprimarization and high commodity prices, as was the case in the 2000s). Thus, the model was characterized by governments committed to neoliberalism and supported by international finance pitted against the informal sector and some opposition parties. The main difference in the moderate left model, in contrast, is that the informal sectors do not play such a decisive role in pressing the government toward populism and are not important allies of the executive while the opposition parties are far more capable of defending institutional checks and balances because they are not in a state of crisis. Hence, this model can be characterized as showing more continuity than change: inherited neoliberal economic policies continue, as do institutional checks and balances.

The Unexpected Rise of Social Conservatism

A discussion of the performance of participatory governance would be incomplete without mentioning social agendas. One of the most unexpected turns of these regimes has been toward social conservatism. These administrations came to power with the support of some of the most progressive movements in their countries. But once in office, all four regimes lost interest in pursuing a socially progressive agenda. This is most clear when looking at their stance on issues of gender and sexuality. In contrast to most moderate left administrations in Latin America since the mid-2000s, the radical left has become more conservative on these questions Thus, in Ecuador Correa won office by aligning himself with a wide spectrum of environmental, indigenous, and feminist movements, some of which called for expanding LGBT rights, and Correa's new constitution catered to some of these demands (Xie and Corrales 2010: 226). Similarly, Morales appealed to an array of leftist groups, including feminists who promoted a constitutional provision prohibiting discrimination based on gender or sexual orientation as well as laws against hate crimes and discrimination in employment. Chávez and Ortega did not explicitly mobilize feminist and LGBT groups, but did not initially reject them.

But each of these regimes became more conservative over the years. In Ecuador, Correa has repeatedly affirmed his strict opposition to abortion rights, even in cases of rape. And despite his initial show of sympathy toward LGBT issues, he has refused to allow any further progress on gender and sexual equality since 2008, going so far as to call gay marriage a "barbarity" (Miroff 2014). In Bolivia, Morales has refused to budge on the country's highly restrictive abortion laws (Kane 2013) and has made notorious homophobic comments, on one bizarre occasion linking being gay to eating chicken (Hernandez 2010), while gay marriage and adoption by gay couples remains illegal. In Nicaragua, despite the Catholic Church having been a strong opponent during Ortega's rule in the 1980s, Ortega entered into a sort of tacit pact with the church in the 2000s, backing a strict antiabortion law in 2006. Today, Cardinal Miguel Obando y Bravo accompanies Ortega and his wife to public events where he gives his blessing to government policy. In Venezuela, the regime is directly at odds with the Catholic clergy but has nonetheless embraced the kind of social conservatism supported by the church, refusing in particular to support laws protecting the rights of LGBT individuals. Although the president of the National Assembly recently declared that he would be in favor of same-sex marriage, the truth is that the Chavista governments have systematically refused to consider proposals for marriage equality or even civil unions, and congressional leaders have attacked opposition leaders with homophobic slurs and accusations. In sum, on questions of reproductive rights, the radical left has not been any different than the rest of the region; and on LGBT rights, the radical left could be said to have become far more conservative than the moderate left (Dilma Rousseff in Brazil, Cristina Fernández de Kirchner in Argentina, José Mujica in Uruguay) or even some moderate center-right administrations (Juan Manuel Santos in Colombia, Sebastián Piñera in Chile).

The regression to this kind of social conservatism by the hard left is open to various interpretations. One hypothesis is that it represents a sort of coming out experience. These regimes, some argue, were always intrinsically nationalist/militarist/machista movements, and this turn to religious conservatism is in character with that inherent conservatism. Others see it as one more example of these regimes' discomfort with pluralism: expanding gender and sexuality rights entails yielding to demands by NGOs that are no longer or never were loyal to the government. An alternative hypothesis is to see this as a political calculus. As more and more moderate progressive voters and leaders defect from these administrations, the leadership might feel the need to fill the political vacuum left by these desertions with new forms of support. Social conservatism allows these regimes to appeal to conservative groups, especially religious and nationalist leaders and voters, both in the countryside and in urban neighborhoods. Seen from this perspective, the sudden rise of social conservatism could very well be a survival strategy adopted by these regimes as their progressive coalitions fall apart.

Conclusion

The regimes most committed to radical forms of participatory democracy began with real political innovations, especially at the institutional level; and during the boom years of 2003–2013, the fiscal largesse they enjoyed allowed them to pursue policies of state intervention and income distribution that succeeded in bringing economic benefits to the poor and excluded. But over the years they curtailed political participation and rejected diversity, so that pluralism was replaced by sectarianism and institutional innovation reversed by efforts to entrench the status quo. In retrospect, this appears for what it is: a rather dramatic reversal of purpose, policy, and expectations that can accurately be described as the rise and fall of participatory democracy. I conclude with a few rather speculative reflections on why this occurred.

My guess is that the eventual reversal of the projects of participatory democracy was inscribed in their illiberal foundations from the outset. The deliberate rejection and removal of institutional checks and balances immediately restricted any effective form of accountability, so allowing these governments to act in a more or less arbitrary fashion. Initially, this permitted these regimes to deliver on their more populist promises, so pleasing their core constituencies and creating new supporters. But eventually, this arbitrary style of government and the lack of accountability led to increasing discontent and electoral defections, as it became apparent that there were no means of redress for perceived public wrongs and no way to be rid of tangible evils. By 2015 these discontents found public expression in graphic slogans like "#lasalida" (in Venezuela), "fuera, Correa, fuera" (in Ecuador), "no más Huevo"[5] (in Bolivia), and "#MiércolesdeProtesta" (in Nicaragua), demonstrating that many sectors of the opposition had turned into what Carlos Malamud (2015) described as avowed *destituyentes* for their commitment to dismiss the president and possibly even rewrite the constitution. It must be recognized that not all sectors of the opposition are destituyentes, and there is no doubt that in Bolivia and Nicaragua the opposition has been far less virulent than in Ecuador and Venezuela. But a radical and rejectionist opposition has begun to grow, and this has been true in Venezuela for over a decade now.

This groundswell of opposition was also owing to what might be called a typical populist trap. The initial economic boom generated by rentier populism spawned the growth of the middle classes, especially in Ecuador, which comprised the groups that became least tolerant of arbitrary rule. In this way, some of the regimes' most salient economic winners turned into its most embittered opponents. Furthermore, as the regimes eventually ran out of the resources to fund distributive policies (much earlier and more profoundly in Venezuela than elsewhere) popular discontent broadened, with former supporters defecting to the opposition and traditional opponents hardening their resolve. As we have seen, the regimes' response was to further restrict pluralism and subsequently align their political stance with a swathe of conservative forces, including nationalist and religious organizations, while simultaneously deploying the state apparatus to repress those groups that could mount a plausible challenge to the regime. And as the domestic economy retracted and domestic support dwindled, the economic model has had to rely increasingly on the bridge between international finance capital and neoextractivism. These survival tactics may serve to shore up the core institutions of these regimes over the short to medium term, but they are ineffective in stemming the tide of destituyente sentiments that now express widespread popular discontent.

Notes

1. See also Kaufman (2009, 2010).
2. See Panizza (2009).
3. Examples of these undemocratic tendencies are organized by country in appendixes that can be obtained by sending a request to Javier Corrales at jcorrales@amherst.edu.
4. The index measures economic freedom based on ten quantitative and qualitative factors, grouped into four broad categories: (1) rule of law (property rights, freedom from corruption); (2) limited government (fiscal freedom, government spending); (3) regulatory efficiency (business freedom, labor freedom, monetary freedom); and (4) open markets (trade freedom, investment freedom, financial freedom). Each of the ten economic freedoms within these categories is graded on a scale of 0 to 100. A country's overall score is derived by averaging these ten economic freedoms, with equal weight being given to each. See www.heritage.org/index/about.
5. A play on words merging Hugo (Chávez) and Evo (Morales) forming the word for egg, which stands colloquially for misstep or grand mistake.

8

Democracy and Human Rights

Todd Landman

The publication of the Brazilian National Truth Commission
Report on December 10, 2014, signaled another incremental step away from
the dark days of authoritarianism that characterized much of Latin America
between the 1960s and 1980s. The military regime in Brazil, which lasted
from 1964 to 1985, was arguably less brutal than its authoritarian counterparts in Uruguay (1973–1984), Argentina (1976–1982), and Peru
(1968–1978), or the personalistic dictatorships in Paraguay (1954–1989)
and Chile (1973–1989). While the National Truth Commission was long in
coming (see Olsen, Payne, and Reiter 2010), it once again revealed how
reasons of state, national security doctrine, and strong policies of counter-
subversion led to widespread abuse of human rights. President Dilma
Rousseff, no stranger to controversy for her role in leftist politics of the
time (and during her presidency), was tortured by the regime and presided
over a tearful release of the report, which not only shares accounts of atrocities committed by the Brazilian military but also the assistance and training
that were provided by the United States and the United Kingdom. The
report, like the many reports from other truth commissions in the region, is
a stark reminder of what political life was like before the advent of the third
and fourth waves of democracy that swept through the region from the late
1970s until the late 1980s (see Huntington 1991; Foweraker, Landman, and
Harvey 2003; Doorenspleet 2005; Landman 2013; Mainwaring and Pérez-
Liñán 2013). It is also a tribute to how the patience and meticulous docu-
mentation efforts of the human rights community can triumph over the
denials of those personnel that were part of the repressive state apparatus
responsible for committing these atrocities.

The story of the "precarious triumph" (Reiff 1999; Landman 2013) of
human rights and democracy in Latin America since the 1980s is one that
has been seen in other regions: (1) the somewhat easy installation of democratic institutions; (2) cycles of regular elections and the reasonable
chance for the opposition to unseat incumbent governments; (3) a public

133

reckoning with past wrongs; (4) more laggardly improvements in the protection of civil and political rights (Diamond 1999; Beetham et al. 2008); and (5) continued challenges around the progressive realization of economic and social rights. Developments in the region have indeed been achieved against the odds and stand in stark contrast to the pessimistic outlook articulated in much of the political science and economics literature in the 1980s and early 1990s. Economically, the 1980s in Latin America were characterized by many as the lost decade with the debt crisis, hyperinflation, and poor growth. Politically, the region adopted or resurrected institutional arrangements that combine presidentialism and proportional representation—a configuration that was seen to be inappropriate for the long-term consolidation, survival, and quality of democracy. Now, with the exception of Cuba, all countries in the region have elected presidents, elected legislative chambers, and judiciaries as well as various additional institutions for the protection of human rights. Latin America formed the core of the third wave of democratization (Huntington 1991) and has had few instances of democratic rollback (Landman 2013; Mainwaring and Pérez-Liñán 2013). The much-maligned institutional design has proved the critics wrong with sustained democratic governance and a range of governing coalitions that have remained wedded to the values and norms of democracy (see Linz 1990; Shugart and Carey 1992; Linz and Valenzuela 1994; Jones 1995; Foweraker 1998; Landman 2008). On September 11, 2001, in Lima, leaders from the region signed the Inter-American Democratic Charter, which affirms that democracy is the common form of government for all countries in the region (see www.oas.org/en/democratic-charter/).

Alongside the return to democracy, the region's own set of human rights instruments and institutions have developed significantly since the promulgation of the 1969 American Convention on Human Rights and with growing participation from all states in the region. The two main bodies for the inter-American system for human rights are the Inter-American Commission on Human Rights and the Inter-American Court of Human Rights, the issues, cases, and function of which make the system the second most developed regional human rights system in the world. The legal precedents set by the UK detention of General Augusto Pinochet in 1998 have unlocked human rights processes and buttressed the concept of universal jurisdiction in ways that have created the conditions for a domestic trial of the former leader of Guatemala, General Efraín Ríos Montt, and new developments in the case against the military in El Salvador for the 1989 murder of Jesuit priests and their housekeeper and her daughter. In this way, the long tail of accountability that stems from the proliferation of and participation in international and regional human rights instruments (Landman

2005a; Simmons 2009; Smith-Cannoy 2012) has meant that former heads of state are no longer immune from prosecution and that transnational advocacy networks can claim some success in bringing about positive change for human rights in the region (see Risse, Ropp, and Sikkink 1999; Hawkins 2002; Landman 2013).

At the individual political level, in addition to the case of Rousseff in Brazil, the political success of Michelle Bachelet in Chile is emblematic of the kind of positive changes that have taken place in the region. Bachelet was the first female president of Chile from 2006 to 2010 and was reelected in 2013. In 1974 she was taken by the Chilean internal security police (DINA) to the now infamous Villa Grimaldi detention facility in Santiago, where she was tortured as part of Pinochet's campaign against the political left (her father was a general who served under former president Salvador Allende). She spent many years in East Germany, but returned to Chile and served under President Ricardo Lagos before being elected president (see Politzer 2011). Both of these women suffered state repression for long periods of time and have since risen to occupy positions of political leadership and power. Bachelet and Rousseff, despite (or because of) their pasts, have become the first female presidents of their countries, a remarkable achievement given the continued prevalence of gender bias in politics across the world. No sensible assessment or commentary in the 1970s would have claimed that either or both of these women would have achieved top political positions in their two countries in the ways that they eventually did.

Against this backdrop of progress in the development of democracy and promotion of human rights, I present in this chapter a systematic assessment and set of explanations for the continued variation in the patterns of democratic governance and protection of human rights in the region. First, I provide a brief set of definitions of democracy and human rights as well as how the two concepts are related in theory and in practice. Next, I present comparative measures of democracy and human rights, where the advance of the institutional dimensions of democracy are mapped against the rights dimensions, including the protection of civil and political rights and economic and social rights. Then, I offer a series of explanations for the patterns that are observed across the countries of the region over time. In keeping with previous research (Landman 1999, 2006; Mainwaring and Pérez-Liñán 2013), my explanations focus less on the structural aspects of Latin American socioeconomic development and more on the political and contingent aspects of the changes that have taken place in the region. Finally, I provide a summary discussion and the implications of the analysis for the larger themes of this book.

Democracy and Human Rights

Any assessment of the state of democracy and human rights in Latin America must begin with an understanding of both concepts. Despite their different historical trajectories and "essentially contested" (Gallie 1956) nature, there is much theoretical and empirical overlap between democracy and human rights since both are grounded in shared principles of accountability, individual integrity, fair and equal representation, inclusion and participation, and nonviolent solutions to conflict. Modern conceptions of *democracy* are based on the fundamental ideas of *popular sovereignty* and *collective decisionmaking* in which rulers are in some way held to account by those over whom they rule (see Beetham et al. 2008). But beyond this basic consensus, there are many varieties of democracy, or "democracy with adjectives" (Collier and Levitsky 1997) that have been in use by scholars, practitioners, and policymakers. These definitions can be grouped broadly into (1) procedural democracy; (2) liberal democracy; and (3) social democracy—the delineation of which largely rests on the variable incorporation of different rights protections alongside the general commitment to popular sovereignty and collective decisionmaking. Aspirations for democracy and the ways in which Latin American elites and masses relate to these conceptions are important for any assessment of progress and any analysis of remaining challenges associated with democratic governance.

Procedural definitions of *democracy* draw on Robert A. Dahl's seminal work *Polyarchy* (1971) and include the two dimensions of *contestation* and *participation*. Contestation captures the uncertain peaceful competition necessary for democratic rule; a principle that presumes the legitimacy of a significant and organized opposition, the right to challenge incumbents, protection of the twin freedoms of expression and association, the existence of free and fair elections, and a consolidated political party system. Such a procedural definition of democracy can be considered a baseline set of conditions and a lower threshold that can be used to assess and count the number of democracies in the world, where Latin America is no exception in such an enumeration. Liberal definitions of democracy preserve the notions of contestation and participation found in procedural definitions, but add more explicit references to the protection of certain human rights. Definitions of *liberal democracy* thus contain an institutional dimension and a rights dimension (see Foweraker and Krznaric 2000). The institutional dimension captures the idea of popular sovereignty, and includes notions of accountability, constraint of leaders, representation of citizens, and universal participation in ways that are consistent with Dahl's polyarchy model outlined above. The rights dimension is upheld by the rule of law, and includes civil, political, property, and minority rights. Such a definition is arguably richer (or thicker) as it includes legal constraints on the exercise of power to complement the popular elements in the derivation of and accountability for power. Social definitions of democracy maintain the institutional and rights dimensions found in liberal models of democracy, but expand the types of rights that ought to be protected, including social, economic, and cultural rights (although some of these are included in minority rights protection seen in liberal definitions). This expanded form of democracy includes the provision of social and economic welfare and the progressive realization of economic and social rights. It also includes the protection of cultural rights, which are concerned with such issues as mother tongue language, ceremonial land rights, and intellectual property rights relating to cultural practices (e.g., indigenous healing practices and remedies that may be of interest to multinational companies). For Latin America, it is useful to consider social democracy defined in this way, particularly since the region has much variation within and between countries in terms of broad patterns of socioeconomic development reflected in levels and distributions of income as well as the associated problems of poverty and marginalization.

In their modern manifestation, human rights have become an accepted legal and normative standard through which to judge the quality of human dignity. This standard has arisen over many years through the concerted efforts of thousands of people inspired by a simple set of ideas that have become codified through the mechanism of public international law and realized through the domestic legal frameworks and governmental institutions of states around the world. Human rights are moral claims accorded legal recognition and states are legally obliged to ensure that they respect, protect, and fulfill these claims. Respecting human rights requires the state to refrain from violating them. Protecting human rights requires the state to prevent the violation of human rights by third parties such as private companies, nongovernmental organizations, paramilitary and insurgency groups, and uncivil or undemocratic movements (see Payne 2000). Fulfilling human rights requires the states to invest in and implement policies for the progressive realization of human rights.

Civil and political rights protect the personhood of individuals and their ability to participate in the public activities of their countries. Economic, social, and cultural rights provide individuals with access to economic resources, social opportunities for growth and the enjoyment of their distinct ways of life, as well as protection from the arbitrary loss of these rights. Solidarity rights seek to guarantee for individuals access to public goods like development and the environment and, as some have begun to argue, the benefits of global economic development (Freeman 2002; Landman 2006). Taken together, there is now a large number of human rights that have been formally codified and can be enumerated from the different treaties. As is evident from this brief discussion of democracy, conceptions of democracy vary precisely around the question of the degree of overlap and interaction between the institutional and rights dimensions. Thin definitions of democracy afford less space for human rights than thicker definitions. In the analysis of trends in democracy and human rights that follows, I consider different indicators for these different dimensions of democracy, where the period since 1980 has seen great variation across the different indicators within and between countries in the region.

Trends in Democracy and Human Rights

The Latin American tradition of democracy and human rights is much longer and deeper than many realize. The region has had a strong culture of constitutionalism, civic republicanism, and some argue a Latin American tradition of human rights (Whitehead 1992; Loveman 1993; Cleary 1997, 2007). The late nineteenth century saw periods of so-called oligarchic democracy, which gave way to personalistic dictatorships, populist democracy, or some form of corporatism that was representative but not necessarily free in terms of independent associations, and open and transparent mechanisms for vertical and horizontal accountability. After prolonged periods of authoritarianism in the 1960s and 1970s, the return to democracy during the third and fourth waves in many ways has embraced earlier traditions of liberal democracy while the electoral success of leftist candidates reopened debates and policy discussion around appropriate forms of social democracy for the region (Huber and Stephens 2012). New and resurrected constitutions have established in principle full democratic institutions, civil and political rights, and, in some cases, quite bold commitments to economic and social rights (e.g., the 1988 Brazilian Constitution). In practice, the region has had repeated cycles of elections and reasonably peaceful transfers of power between civilian leaders, and commentators agree that opposition parties have the opportunity to challenge incumbents and a reasonable chance of defeating them. Indeed, the victory of the National Action Party (PAN) in the 2000 Mexican elections signaled the end of the one-party dominance and electoral authoritarianism for which the country had become known (see Schedler 2013). In certain cases (e.g., Peru in 1992, Guatemala in 1993, Ecuador in 2000, and Venezuela since 1998), democracy has been overturned and undermined through the actions of elected presidents in autogolpes, or excessive centralization of executive authority founded on the mobilization (and eventual co-optation) of popular sectors.

Alongside the advance (or return) of democracy in the region, great strides have been made in the struggle for human rights. Again, in principle, countries in the region have committed themselves to a larger number of international human rights treaties (see Table 8.1) and a growing number of countries have committed to the various regional instruments (Table 8.2) while legal powers particular to the regional system have been increasingly exercised in ways that seek to confront abuses of rights. The region has also had a number of early exemplars of truth commissions (e.g., Argentina, Chile, Guatemala, and El Salvador), which were influential for truth commissions set up in other countries and which had innovative approaches to truth telling and data analysis (e.g., Peru and Guatemala) that have also been influential in the struggle for justice for past wrongs (see Hayner 1994, 2002; Landman 2006; Landman and Carvalho 2009). In practice, the region has been seen as a significant part of "the justice cascade" (Sikkink 2011), where the increase in the number of formal legal proceedings and institutions of accountability has led to an overall improvement in the protection of human rights (see also Olsen, Payne, and Reiter 2010; Landman 2013).

These positive developments in democracy and human rights have been captured quantitatively. Table 8.3 shows the historical trends in one measure of democracy and two measures of human rights. The democracy measure is the combined democracy score from the Polity IV dataset compiled at the University of Maryland (see Jaggers and Gurr 1995; Munck 2009;

Table 8.1 Main International Human Rights Treaties

Name of Human Rights Treaty	Parties (*N*)	Parties (%)
1966 International Covenant on Civil and Political Rights (ICCPR)	20	87.0
1966 International Covenant on Economic, Social, and Cultural Rights (ICESCR)	19	82.6
1966 Convention on the Elimination of All Forms of Racial Discrimination (CERD)	21	91.3
1979 Convention on the Elimination of All Forms of Discrimination Against Women (CEDAW)	21	91.3
1984 Convention Against Torture and Other Cruel, Inhuman or Degrading Treatment or Punishment (CAT)	19	82.6
1989 Convention on the Rights of the Child (CRC)	21	91.3
1990 Convention on Migrant Workers	14	60.9
2006 Convention on the Rights of People with Disabilities	18	78.3
2006 Convention for the Protection of All Persons from Enforced Disappearance	10	43.5

Source: Human Rights Atlas, www.humanrightsatlas.org.

Table 8.2 Participation in the Inter-American Human Rights System

Name of the Inter-American Human Rights Instrument	Parties (N)	Parties (%)
American Convention on Human Rights (1969)	25	74.5
Inter-American Convention to Prevent and Punish Torture (1985)	18	56.3
Additional Protocol to the American Convention on Human Rights in the Area of Economic, Social, and Cultural Rights "Protocol of San Salvador" (1988)	16	48.5
Protocol to the American Convention on Human Rights to Abolish the Death Penalty (1990)	13	40.6
Inter-American Convention on the Prevention, Punishment and Eradication of Violence Against Women "Convention of Belem Do Para" (1994)	32	94.1
Inter-American Convention on the Forced Disappearance of Persons (1994)	15	44.1
Inter-American Convention on the Elimination of All Forms of Discrimination Against Persons with Disabilities (1999)	19	55.9
Inter-American Convention Against All Forms of Discrimination and Intolerance (2013)[a]	0	0

Notes: There are a total of thirty-five countries in the inter-American system, but Cuba has not agreed to work within the rules and thus is not part of the total calculations.

a. There are only signatories and no ratifications for this instrument.

Coppedge 2012), where the movement in this more procedural measure of democracy sees the regional average score moving from a period of anocracy (i.e., scores between −5 and +5) between 1981 and 1993 to one of democracy (i.e., scores greater than 6) from 1994 onward, where this significant break point is marked in the table with a horizontal line. The human rights measures are the Political Terror Scale (PTS) coded from the US State Department and Amnesty International annual human rights country reports, where a score of 1 represents widespread and sustained protection of personal integrity rights and a 5 represents widespread and systematic abuse of human rights (see Landman and Carvalho 2009). Table 8.3 shows that the average score across both measures declined significantly between 1981 and 2012, indicating a mean regional improvement in the protection of this set of rights. Scores based on the Amnesty International reports are slightly less optimistic than those coded from the US State Department, but the long-term trends on average have improved.

Comparing country means of the data in Table 8.3 reveals that Costa Rica has had a high average democracy score with little variation (i.e., it has remained a democracy throughout the period) and Cuba has had a low average democracy score with little variation (i.e., it has remained authoritarian

Table 8.3 Democracy and Human Rights in Latin America Mean Scores, 1981–2012

Year	Political Terror Scale[a] (Amnesty Intl.)	Political Terror Scale[a] (US State Dept.)	Polity IV Democracy Score[b]
1981	3.63	2.71	−1.80
1982	3.80	2.62	−0.85
1983	3.59	2.62	0.10
1984	3.37	2.86	0.35
1985	3.33	2.62	1.90
1986	3.39	3.00	2.15
1987	3.42	2.90	2.05
1988	3.42	2.90	2.60
1989	3.20	2.95	4.45
1990	3.40	3.05	5.50
1991	3.20	3.05	4.90
1992	3.14	3.00	5.20
1993	3.00	2.95	5.40
1994	2.90	3.00	6.35
1995	2.76	2.81	6.35
1996	3.00	2.76	6.60
1997	2.60	2.62	6.65
1998	2.83	2.62	6.65
1999	2.95	2.67	6.50
2000	2.89	2.67	6.50
2001	2.65	2.57	6.65
2002	2.63	2.76	6.65
2003	3.00	2.76	6.65
2004	2.63	2.81	6.75
2005	2.68	2.67	6.90
2006	2.84	2.81	7.05
2007	2.78	2.52	7.00
2008	2.67	2.71	7.00
2009	2.78	2.81	6.60
2010	2.50	2.71	6.35
2011	2.40	2.71	6.67
2012	2.35	2.71	6.67

Notes: The horizontal line marks a break point indicating positive developments in democracy and human rights from 1994 onward.

a. The Political Terror Scale ranges from 1 (good rights protection) to 5 (systematic violations of human rights).

b. The Polity IV Democracy Score ranges from −10 (autocracy) to +10 (democracy).

throughout the period). All of the other countries in the region have shown great variation over time, with the most dramatic variation occurring in Chile, Guyana, Paraguay, Panama, and Uruguay in particular. Similar comparison of means for the two human rights scores reveal that some of the worst records for human rights abuse during this period have been seen in Colombia, Guatemala, Brazil, and Peru, where the greatest overall variation in human rights abuse has been in Chile, El Salvador (according the PTS Amnesty scores), and Peru. The level and variation in human rights abuse, despite advances in democracy, are discussed below, but it is clear that civil conflict of the kind that engulfed countries such as Colombia, Guatemala, and Peru during this period has taken a large toll on the protection of human rights. These various quantitative trends in democracy and human rights are consistent with single-country and comparative analyses of the region.

Beyond the procedural measures of democracy and narrow measures of civil and political rights, it is also possible to compare trends in the progressive realization of social and economic rights. Sakiko Fukuda-Parr, Terra Lawson-Remer, and Susan Randolph (2015) have developed a measure based on the relative achievement of countries to fulfill their social and economic human rights obligations. Using measures for food, education, health, and work, which are regressed on overall levels of national income (per capita GDP), the resulting Index of Social and Economic Rights Fulfillment (SERF Index) scores a country from 0 to 100 on the degree to which rights obligations have been fulfilled. The score reflects the notion of an achievement possibilities frontier (APF) that measures a country's performance based on its economic capacity. While there is a rising curve of expected performance across these different rights dimensions in line with levels of wealth, it is possible for countries to fall short of that expectation. The SERF Index thus captures the degree to which a country meets its expected performance. The index has been calculated for most countries in Latin America for the period 2000–2010.

Table 8.4 compares the mean scores of the SERF Index for each country for the period 2000–2010. The table shows that all countries in the region are falling short of their expected levels of performance (i.e., their scores are less than 100), where the underperformance rate varies from over 30 percent in Bolivia and Guatemala to under 10 percent in Uruguay. As this is a relative score, it represents both the underlying level of income and the realization of social and economic rights outcomes. This means that countries like Bolivia and Guatemala are struggling to achieve the realization of these rights commitments to a greater degree than Uruguay and other countries with relatively smaller degrees of underperformance. The overall change in performance between 2000 and 2010 is also of interest: Guatemala, Ecuador, and Honduras saw the most positive change; Chile and Peru the least positive change; and Guyana and Panama exhibited negative change, or a decrease in the realization in these rights. For the region overall across this period, the fulfillment index has increased from approximately 50 percent in 2000 to 83 percent in 2010.

These time series trends and theories about democracy and human rights suggest that these trends ought to be interrelated, where we might

Table 8.4 Index of Social and Economic Empowerment Rights Fulfillment (SERF Index) Mean Scores and Change, 2000–2010

Country	SERF Index	Change 2000–2010
Argentina	87.39	8.59
Bolivia	70.23	6.23
Brazil	85.24	5.69
Chile	89.58	3.87
Colombia	79.27	7.35
Costa Rica	89.68	4.84
Dominican Republic	83.46	3.01
Ecuador	50.09	10.67
El Salvador	76.68	10.09
Guatemala	65.51	9.93
Guyana	87.65	−1.80
Honduras	59.29	15.07
Mexico	81.68	10.86
Nicaragua	74.39	7.10
Panama	76.07	−0.85
Paraguay	81.67	5.75
Peru	75.26	3.70
Uruguay	92.69	10.48
Venezuela	78.37	7.88

Note: The SERF Index ranges from 0 (no realization of empowerment rights) to 100 (strong realization of empowerment rights).

expect that higher levels of democracy should be related to better human rights performance. Global analysis of human rights confirms this proposition in two important ways: (1) higher levels of democracy are associated with better human rights performance (Poe and Tate 1994; Poe, Tate, and Keith 1999; Landman 2005a, 2005b, 2013); and (2) democratic transitions have direct and quite immediate benefits for the protection of human rights (Zanger 2000). The relationship for Latin America is no different, where past analysis has shown a positive relationship (Landman 2006) that is again confirmed here using data for the period 1981–2012. Table 8.5 reports the correlation matrix for the measures of democracy and human rights, where it is clear there are significant correlations across the different measures. Latin America thus joins other regions in the world in which improvements in democracy are related to improvements in the protection of human rights, including civil, political, economic, and social rights.

Such significant relationships are encouraging for the protection of human rights in the region; however, closer scrutiny of the correlations reveals a human rights gap between the level of democracy and the protection of human rights. Throughout Table 8.5, it is clear that there are not perfect relationships between democracy and any of the measures of

Table 8.5 Correlation Matrix for Democracy and Human Rights in Latin America, 1981–2010

	Index of Social and Economic Empowerment Rights Fullfilment (SERF Index)	Political Terror Scale (Amnesty Intl.)	Political Terror Scale (US State Dept.)	Cingranelli and Richards Human Rights Data Project (CIRI)	Polity IV Democracy Score
SERF Index	—	−.102*	−.214***	.123**	.241***
Political Terror Scale (Amnesty Intl.)		—	.638***	−.588***	−.268***
Political Terror Scale (US State Dept.)			—	−.636***	−.379***
CIRI				—	.351***
Polity IV Democracy Score					—

Notes: The table reports Kendall's tau B correlation coefficients, the most appropriate measure of association for these kinds of data.
    * $p < 0.10$, ** $p < 0.05$, *** $p < 0.001$.

human rights, even though those relationships are significant. Reading down the final column in the table for the Polity IV measure of democracy, the absolute values of the correlations range from 0.24 to 0.37, suggesting that factors other than democracy alone explain the variation in human rights protection, where some countries perform well across both democracy and human rights and others do not perform as well. Comparative research has shown that such a gap between the rhetoric and reality of rights can act as catalyst for popular mobilization (see Foweraker and Landman 1997; Hawkins 2002; Risse, Ropp, and Sikkink 1999), where advocacy groups continue to make the case for better human rights protection alongside the advance of democracy and the more narrow focus on the cycle of elections. Next, I discuss how we might explain these developments, patterns, and relationships in the long-term trends in democracy and human rights, paying particular attention to the making of democracy and the struggle for human rights.

Explanations for Democracy and Human Rights

For decades, classic explanations for the variation in democracy and human rights have focused on structural variables relating to patterns in socioeconomic development. From the early writings on modernization theory by Seymour M. Lipset (1959, 1960, 1994) to the latest debates on endogenous and exogenous democratization (Przeworski and Limongi 1997; Boix 2003; Boix and Stokes 2003; Coppedge 2012; Landman 2013), there has been a strong tendency to see economic development as a strong driver for democratization and, by extension, an improvement in the protection of human rights (see also Fukuyama 1992; Poe and Tate 1994; Landman 2005b). But empirical analysis that uses data on only the region of Latin America has found no support for a relationship between levels of economic development on the one hand and democracy and human rights on the other, a set of findings that have been upheld for periods stretching back to the early twentieth century (Landman 1999, 2006; Mainwaring and Pérez-Liñán 2003, 2013).

Such a consistent set of findings leads me to reject modernization as a major paradigm to account for the growth of democracy and human rights in Latin America. The turn toward rational choice, with its focus on the strategic interaction of elites at moments of democratic transition, has been a welcome development to explain why and under what conditions different groups in society may wish to embrace democracy (see Przeworski 1991; Cohen 1987, 1994; Lichbach 2013). But such accounts ignore longer-term processes of democratic transformation (Rustow 1970; Foweraker and Landman 1997; Landman 2013), which afford greater weight to the making of democracy and the struggle for rights by popular groups from whom the human rights gap becomes a prime motivation for collective action. The emphasis on the struggle for rights from below and variations in state response from above suggests that democratic transformation involves what Dankwart Rustow calls a "long period of inclusive struggle" (1970).

Social mobilization around rights helps build the popular foundations for democracy, but there are no guarantees that such mobilization will necessarily lead to democracy, or that the establishment of democratic institutions will lead to a full protection of human rights. Rather, at a crucial decision phase, states can make concessions while maintaining the bulk of their authoritarian institutions (e.g., the passage of the 1980 Constitution in Chile). States may also crack down and seek to quash emerging movements (e.g., the state of siege in Chile in the mid-1980s), but such a move always brings with it the memory of the event and a long-term desire within the populace for regime change and justice (e.g., Brazil's latest truth commission). This interaction between society and the state suggests a much longer view on political change that involves both the macrovariables of economic modernization and the microvariables of choice and strategy (see also Mainwaring and Pérez-Liñán 2013). Democratic transformation takes place through several key phases, none of which is inevitable and none of which is irreversible, including mobilization and liberalization, moment of decision, consolidation, and habituation (see Landman 2013: 76–77 after Rustow 1970). Such a perspective suggests that history does not end with the installation of democracy. Rather, the return to democracy can both raise expectations for how the state ought to behave and provide additional political space in which popular actors can seek to address the human rights gap. For example, since the transition to democracy in Mexico in 2000, the state has been the subject of several large-scale mobilizations precisely around demands for greater rights protection and justice for the victims of state and nonstate violence (see below). And democratic Brazil has seen large-scale mobilizations around the amount of public expenditure in the run-up to the World Cup, where the discourse of protest centered on greater attention to social and economic rights.

Such an agential account of the struggle for rights and the making of democracy in my view provides a better explanation of the patterns in the data outlined in the previous section of this chapter. There have been extraordinary moments of mobilization against regimes in the region that have variously led to democratic breakthroughs, stasis, or regression. Agitation in Chile in the years of the debt crisis (early 1980s) led to a crackdown, but the 1988 plebiscite provided a new political opportunity for mobilization around the simple idea of "no!" Repeated mobilizations in Mexico from the 1968 Tlatelolco protests to the Zapatista rebellion in 1994 were managed by the PRI, but ultimately weakened its legitimacy to the point that democratic breakthrough was possible in 2000. Popular mobilizations have been the core support for candidates from the left such as Evo Morales in Bolivia. The Bolivarian revolution overseen by Hugo Chávez in Venezuela also shows the dangers of top-down mobilizations coupled with state power and resources that undermine the principles of democracy and human rights in the name of personal political power. These examples suggest that the region needs to be understood in more contingent and less deterministic ways, where choices interact with longer-term changes in society and the economy.

Lacunae and Challenges for the Future

While the positive developments that I outlined in this chapter are encouraging for the future of democracy and human rights in Latin America, it is necessary to remain attentive to many of the problems and outstanding challenges the region faces. The human rights gap is a real concern. After two or three decades of democratization, human rights protection remains precarious, where in many ways there has been a shift in organized violence from the state and public actors to society and nonstate actors (see Arias and Goldstein 2010). Violence can be legal or illegal and can be carried out by state or nonstate actors (see Landman 2010). Legal state violence involves everyday forms of violence required for maintaining law and order (i.e., the Hobbesian social contract). Illegal state violence involves the transgression of the rule of law and democratic norms expected of states, and includes such abuses as those committed in the name of fighting terrorism or subversion (either during the Condor years in the authoritarian states of the Southern Cone or during the post-9/11 war on terror). Legal private violence includes that which is carried out in a legitimate claim to self-defense while illegal private violence includes simple isolated criminal activity or the larger-scale organized criminal violence that characterizes the controlled areas of Brazil's favela communities and the turf wars between Mexico's drug cartels. The 2014 disappearance of forty-three students in Mexico appears to be a combination of state and nonstate illegal violence, where local government officials are alleged to have colluded with members of drug cartels to carry out atrocities against the students.

Beyond these more overt examples of the use of violence, there are longer-term patterns of inequality for which the region is well known that are related to systemic abuses of human rights. Land and income inequalities, and the social and cultural marginalization that come with them in both the urban and rural sectors, can create conditions under which human rights abuses continue unabated. Oligarchic patterns of privilege, differential access, and disproportionate political influence can lead to cultures of acceptability around the violation of the human rights of the less fortunate in society. Discourses of otherness and dehumanization make palatable state practices that include arbitrary arrest, detention, torture, and disproportionate sentencing of the urban and rural poor. Underinvestment in the justice system creates conditions of excessive caseloads, backlogs, the rush to conviction fueled by torture-induced confessions, and bulging prison populations without proper oversight and care. The connection between large-scale patterns of inequality and human rights abuse has been supported empirically (see Landman and Larizza 2009), but the ability for states to address such problems in the short run remains problematic. Redistribution, culture change, and judicial reform, which are required to address endemic patterns of human rights abuse, are long-term problems that will take time to address. Interestingly, democratic institutions, based on the power of the vote and representation of different interests, may well not be the best solution for these more intractable problems. Powerful lobby groups, political parties, and vested interests can hamper efforts at redistribution while, in federal systems (e.g., Mexico and Brazil), differential levels of power and responsibility complicate the kind of national-level policy reform initiatives required to address these structural issues.

Oligarchic power, inequality, and disproportionate abuse of human rights, however, are not isolated Latin American phenomena, as recent analysis and events in the United States have shown. Vested interests, disproportionate sentencing, and police violence in the United States affect African American and Hispanic populations more than any other sectors (Foweraker and Krznaric 2003; Sentencing Project 2014) while democratic discontent in the United States has been fueled by an increasing realization that the country is becoming more oligarchic than ever before (Gilens and Page 2014). It thus would be unfair to be overly negative about the remaining challenges with democracy and human rights in Latin America. Questions of democratic governance and the full protection of human rights remain challenges for a wide range of democratic countries and, as a region, Latin America has made extraordinary strides since the dark days of the 1970s. In this chapter, I thus sought to focus on the positive developments of the region that place it on a relatively positive footing in comparison to developments in regions such as Africa and Asia. Many lessons have been learned across periods of democratic transition, transitional justice, and the struggle for human rights. Fully accepting that much work remains to be done about key questions surrounding the quality of democratic life and the enjoyment of the full panoply of human rights, there is much to celebrate when taking the longer view as I presented here.

9

Quota Laws
and Gender Equality

Jennifer M. Piscopo

The most basic political rights have been understood as *el derecho de elegir y ser elegido* (the right to elect and be elected). Women throughout Latin America received the right to vote in the mid-twentieth century, beginning with Ecuador in 1929 and ending with Paraguay in 1961. Yet the right to be elected did not always appear simultaneously: in El Salvador, for instance, women received suffrage in 1939, but remained unable to stand for election until 1961.[1] Since women's formal incorporation into the polity depends on their ability to exercise both dimensions of their political rights, many Latin American women did not receive the formal entitlements and responsibilities of political citizenship until the 1960s. That women exercised these rights unequally in practice, however, did not come to the forefront until social movements and democratization processes swept the region in the 1980s (Craske 1999; Dagnino 2003; Molyneux 2003; Jaquette 2009). These efforts to reconstitute Latin American states as more just, inclusive, and multicultural implicated more than the political dimensions of citizenship, though the right to electoral participation and representation remained central to institution building in new democracies. The disappointingly low numbers of women elected to the legislature following democratization spurred the regionwide adoption of gender quota laws—statutes requiring that political parties nominate specified percentages of women to legislative office.

In 1991, Argentina famously became the first country in the world to adopt statutory gender quotas for its national legislature. All Latin American countries save Guatemala and Venezuela had followed by January 2015.[2] Seven Latin American countries—Bolivia, Ecuador, Costa Rica, Honduras, Mexico, Nicaragua, and Panama—have since moved beyond gender quotas, adopting parity laws that impose a strict fifty-fifty gender balance on the composition of the legislature and, in some cases, the executive and the judiciary. Scholars concur that quota laws remain the most effective mechanism for raising women's numerical presence in government (Dahlerup and Freidenvall 2005; Jones 2009; Jones, Alles, and Tchintian 2012; Schwindt-

Bayer 2009), but the statutes' qualitative effects remain controversial. Two critiques of gender quotas predominate: first, scholars highlight how the laws' numerous loopholes and lax oversight allow elites to violate either the letter or the spirit of the law, evasions that occur even in numerically successful cases (Baldez 2007; Htun and Jones 2002; Hinojosa 2012). Second, quotas have been unable to guarantee feminist or progressive policy change, let alone erode the patriarchal practices that continue to marginalize women from the centers of true political power (Franceschet and Piscopo 2008; Miguel 2012; Sagot 2010; Schwindt-Bayer 2010; Piscopo and Thomas 2016; Zetterberg 2008).

These critiques question the relationship between formal on-paper extensions of political rights and deeper in-practice transformations that unravel patriarchal (and classist and racist) power relations. The women's movements that participated in Latin America's democratization wanted more than to change the gender of political decisionmakers; they wanted state institutions to create and implement policies that would definitively upend complex systems of oppression (Randall and Waylen 1998; Molyneux 2003; Lebon 2010). Yet I argue that focusing on the failure of gender quotas to achieve this transformative goal leads scholars to mistake the proverbial forest for the trees. Since democratization, the Spanish- and Portuguese-speaking countries of Latin America have created an impressive legal architecture of gender equality, one that includes not just quota laws and parity mandates, but equal rights provisions set forth in constitutions and statutes. In fact, Latin American states' equality measures rival those of Scandinavia or continental Europe. Women's political rights are protected by legal regimes that establish states' liberal commitments to nondiscrimination and equal treatment, but also codify states' more radical obligations to compensate women for historical injustices and generate equality of outcomes. These efforts in particular distinguish women's political citizenship in Latin America.

In this article I center quotas and parity within this legal architecture of gender equality, arguing that Latin American states enforce women's political rights in proactive progressive ways. This enforcement both draws from and contributes to a normative vision of democracy as inclusive, representative, and gender balanced: even though this vision may not reach the daily lives of everyday citizens, its on-paper commitment provides female activists and female politicians with concrete avenues of redress when political rights are violated. To support this argument, I first sketch the normative relationship between gender quotas, political rights, and democracy. I then present evidence from nearly twenty-five years of gender quota strengthening across Latin America: the evidence shows that despite skeptics' consternation over quotas' exploitation and violation, quota reforms have consistently improved the measures' effectiveness by closing loopholes, demanding compliance, and raising thresholds. I situate this strengthening trend within Latin American states' broader constitutional and statutory commitments to gender equality, which have evolved over time to favor equality of outcomes rather than equality of opportunity. Irrespective of the gap between law and reality, gender balance in political decisionmaking has become a foundational permanent feature of Latin American democracies.

Political Rights, Democracy, and Gender Quotas

A vast body of scholarship has documented how women across different ethnic and class categories participated in Latin America's democratic transitions.[3] Yet as Georgina Waylen concludes in her hallmark analysis, "There is no necessary connection between playing an important part in any stage of the process of democratization and having any particular role during the period of consolidation" (1994: 329). The return to electoral politics in Latin America marked a return to business as usual: as protest politics, peace activism, and armed insurgencies were replaced by electoral competition and political parties throughout the 1980s, men reasserted their dominance in the public political sphere and women retreated (often involuntarily) to the private apolitical sphere (Baldez 2002; Franceschet 2005). In the founding democratic elections across the region, women attained, on average, a mere 6 percent of legislative seats; by 1990, the average percentage of female legislators hovered at 10 percent (Hinojosa 2012: 6). Women's presence in elected office was vastly disproportionate to their leadership roles in the social movements that had denounced authoritarianism and precipitated democratization.

These disappointing electoral results in democracy's early years coincided with powerful international discourses on women's rights. The international system, especially the UN World Conferences on Women in 1975, 1980, 1985, and 1995, played a significant role in shaping global narratives about gender equality, including women's right to participate in political decisionmaking. Affirmative action measures for women in public office, including gender quotas, were discussed as early as the 1975 Mexico City conference, though the final declaration fell short of recommending positive action. Rather, the Mexico City conference's World Plan of Action called for generic "special efforts" to increase women's presence in elected and appointed offices, meaning publicity campaigns, academic and government studies, and the recruitment of women to vacant offices.[4] Twenty years later, the 1995 Platform for Action adopted at the 1995 Beijing conference specifically listed "positive action" and "affirmative action" as desired mechanisms to achieve gender balance in public office.[5]

For democratizing Latin America, such a demonstrable commitment to gender equality would mark the new political regimes as nonauthoritarian nation-states—countries that belonged in the modern international community (Towns 2012). While the UN World Conferences on Women called for gender equality in all areas of life, from agriculture to child care, gender balance in political decisionmaking became an easily quantifiable target on which domestic activists and savvy politicians could set their sights. An important result of democratization in Latin America was the narrowing of channels through which social transformations could occur: economic neoliberalism accompanied electoral democracy, and together these processes weakened grassroots movements, privileged individual self-reliance over collective action, and shifted state builders' attention to institutional design and legal reforms (Lebon 2010; Jaquette 2009; Molyneux 2003; Piscopo and Thomas 2016). International discourses on gender equality, combined with a domestic emphasis on engineering effective government institutions, established the groundwork for quotas' adoption.

Thus, quota proponents across Latin America tied democratic development to gender equality. Argentine senator Margarita Malhorro argues, for instance, that parties "hold women back in the name of old, traditional prejudices more worthy of a feudal era than of modern times" (Towns 2012: 192). Mexican women called party leaders "dinosaurs" (Baldez 2004: 238). The inclusion of women, and the shedding of the sexist beliefs that previously discriminated against them, implied not simply a more fair democracy, but a better democracy. According to Mexican senator Gustavo Carvajal Moreno, "What is at stake is not just the inclusion of women in parliaments but democracy as such: our countries want to grow, our countries want more justice. Women are key actors for the renewal of democracy" (Towns 2012: 192). Across Latin America, quota debates were carried out in these normative terms, with opponents protesting that quotas violated liberal principles of individual merit and open competition, and proponents arguing that democracy depended on ending discrimination and rectifying women's historical disadvantage (Htun and Jones 2002; Marx, Borner, and Caminotti 2007; Schmidt 2011). In this way, the quota debates manifested the theoretical conflict inherent in any struggle over women's citizenship (Bacchi 2006; Krook, Lovenduski, and Squires 2009): Do women receive entitlements and responsibilities based on their universal sameness to men, or should entitlements and responsibilities reflect women's unique capacities, needs, and experiences?

This equality or difference debate has particular resonance in Latin America. In the mid-twentieth century, the extension of women's right to elect and be elected was framed in terms of republican motherhood: women could participate in civic life because their roles as nurturers of the family transmitted civic values to future generations and, thus, stabilized the nation (Lavrín 1995; Miller 1991; Molyneux 2000, 2003). These essentialist beliefs about women's caring capacities also permeated quota debates: quota proponents saw women's representation as fair, modern, and democratic, but also as consequential for ensuring that new democracies would further protect women, children, the poor, and the disadvantaged (Htun and Jones 2002; Franceschet and Piscopo 2008). Deep-seated convictions that women would express policy preferences that differed from those of men, and that these policy preferences would create a more just and equitable society, created clear expectations about what gender quotas would achieve. Argentina's quota proponents summed up this hope with the slogan, "With few women in politics, women change; with many women in politics, politics changes" (Marx, Borner, and Caminotti 2007: 67). If gender, race, and class oppression could no longer be addressed through revolution, widespread social ills could still be solved by placing women in office.

Irrespective of whether these hopes turn out to be true, the initial framing of quotas in normative and consequentialist terms created an important legacy for women's political citizenship in the region. Maxine Molyneux explains that the "compensatory feminism" and "strategic essentialism" represented by affirmative action signified how "citizenship could thus allow for principles of equality and difference to be respected even as it retained a broader commitment to universality of principle" (2003: 190). In other words, quotas make the universal nature of rights more effective while recognizing the parameters of women's difference: the same socially constructed gender identities that historically justified women's exclusion could now justify their inclusion. Women's difference both explains the need for and possible benefits of quotas while women's equality underscores their right to be elected under the same conditions as men. Gender quotas combine liberal notions of nondiscrimination with a more radical policy of positive action. As I document below, once Latin American states committed themselves to affirmatively guaranteeing women's political rights, two outcomes were inevitable: first, states would strengthen quotas until they became permanent features of the political landscape; and, second, the logic would shift from generating equality of opportunity (quotas) to manufacturing equality of outcomes (parity).

Quota Strengthening in Latin America

Gender quotas diffused rapidly across Latin America and the globe, though not at once. Scholars of quota adoption and diffusion recognize that quotas have appeared in generations or waves (Crocker 2011; Dahlerup and Norris 2014; Bauer 2014), with early-adopting countries constituting the first generation or wave, and late-adopting countries constituting the second. Adjusting this terminology to the Latin American experience reveals three distinct moments: two waves of gender quota laws followed by a third, still unfolding, wave of parity laws. First-generation quotas were adopted in the 1990s by pioneering countries such as Argentina. Initial quota laws were defined by their general weakness: significant loopholes and lax enforcement led observers to conclude that first-generation quotas constituted mere lip service to female activists and constituents (Htun and Jones 2002: 15). Second-generation quotas appeared in the 2000s, and consisted of two types: reformed laws from early-adopting countries that closed loopholes and improved enforcement, and initial quota laws in late-adopting countries that began with strong provisions. These quota waves provide considerable evidence that, contrary to proponents' claims about the transitory nature of affirmative action, the overall trend has been to affirm quotas' constitutionality, improve their ability to achieve gender balance in decisionmaking, and commit Latin American states to women's inclusion.

First-Generation Quota Laws

Table 9.1 identifies the twelve Latin American countries adopting quota laws in the 1990s: Argentina, Bolivia, Brazil, Colombia, Costa Rica, the Dominican Republic, Ecuador, Mexico, Panama, Paraguay, Peru, and

Table 9.1 First-Generation Quotas in Latin America

Country	Quota Rule at Adoption (%)	Year Adopted
Argentina	Both chambers, 30	1991
Bolivia	Both chambers, 30	1997
Brazil	Lower chamber, 25	1997
Colombia	Both chambers, 30	1998
Costa Rica	Unicameral, 40	1996
Dominican Republic	Lower chamber, 25	1997
Ecuador	Unicameral, 20	1997
Mexico	Both chambers, 30	1996
Panama	Unicameral, 30	1997
Paraguay	Both chambers, 20	1996
Peru	Unicameral, 25	1997
Venezuela	Both chambers, 30	1997

Sources: Crocker (2011); www.quotaproject.org; and author's research.

Venezuela. All first-generation quota laws, with the exception of Costa Rica's, set their initial thresholds for female candidates at 30 percent or below. The 30 percent target came from critical mass theories that first appeared in the late 1970s: adapted from studies of women in industrial organization, critical mass theories held that the representation of women's interests and perspectives would become possible only after women constituted a third of the legislature (Dahlerup 2006; Jaquette 1997). Though critical mass theories have since fallen into disfavor—with scholars acknowledging that policy change depends on myriad factors beyond just women's numerical presence (Beckwith and Cowell-Meyers 2007; Childs and Krook 2006; Dahlerup 2006)—the notion critically informed first-generation laws. Critical mass falls short of gender balance, but offers decisionmakers a more feasible target.

Proponents' strategy also included framing quotas as temporary or transitory. In Argentina, Brazil, Mexico, and elsewhere, legislators and ministers stressed that the mechanisms would eventually expire (Araújo 2003; Baldez 2004; García Quesada 2011; Towns 2012). Policymakers reasoned that the women boosted with quotas would quickly upend gender stereotypes, thus dissolving the barriers that held other women back (Htun 2004: 445). For example, the Costa Rican quota law contained a sunset clause: the quota would be cancelled for political parties that nominated women in proportion to their presence among registered voters (García Quesada 2011: 122). Political parties that independently demonstrated their modernity and inclusivity would not need quotas.

Low thresholds and implicit expirations combined with other weaknesses to reduce the numerical effectiveness of first-generation quota laws.[6] Most commonly, the laws—such as those in Costa Rica, Mexico, and Panama—lacked placement mandates for electoral lists, a loophole that allowed political parties to cluster the required proportion of women's names in the unelectable spots at the bottom. The measures also lacked sanctions (as in Honduras and Venezuela), or imposed impractical conditions for redress (as in Argentina and Brazil). The Argentine enforcement mechanism proved particularly unwieldy: excluded female candidates had to bring suit in provincial courts, which meant that, even if women were willing to commit professional suicide by litigating against their own parties, local judges needed to have awareness of, and be willing to enforce, federal law (Jones 1996).

Other loopholes reduced quotas' numerical impact by excluding Senate elections (Argentina, Brazil, and Ecuador); exempting political parties if they chose candidates via internal primaries (Mexico); applying the quota exclusively to primary contestants and not nominated candidates (Panama); allowing political parties to count alternate candidates toward the quota threshold (Venezuela); and requiring that candidate positions be reserved for women without stipulating that women actually fill them (Brazil).[7] In many countries, electoral institutes—the agencies charged with certifying candidate lists for quota compliance—simply ignored the statutes. Elsewhere, party leaders violated the spirit, if not the letter, of the law: female candidates often renounced their seats after the election, allowing their male alternates to enter (as in Mexico), or male candidates' names were inscribed as female candidates' names (as in Bolivia).

In no Latin American country did the initial postquota elections achieve the legally mandated threshold of women (Hinojosa and Piscopo 2013: 68). First-generation quota laws gave political party elites numerous escape clauses, a fact that largely explains why male-dominated Latin American legislatures would adopt quotas in the first place: leaders could gain all the public relations benefits associated with appearing fair, modern, and democratic—but without paying the actual cost of opening positions available to women. Elites' ability to evade quota laws fueled widespread frustration among proponents. As a male legislator in Peru observes, quotas "are mocked when women are consigned to the last list positions" (Gastañadui 2014). Female politicians in Mexico and Costa Rica likewise argue that quota laws placed more obstacles in the path of women's political rights because women suddenly needed to fight parties' skullduggery to secure their nominations (Piscopo 2016). Yet fight evasive practices they did: as female politicians and other domestic activists contested quotas' flaws, they won policy battles that made the measures not just more effective, but more permanent and enduring.

Second-Generation Quota Laws

Latin America's second-generation quotas contain reformed laws from early adopters, as shown in Table 9.2, and initial laws approved by late adopters, as shown in Table 9.3. Eleven of the twelve first-wave countries—all save Paraguay—reformed their quota laws at least once. Most commonly, reforms raised threshold percentages in an effort to raise the proportions of women elected, and imposed placement mandates to prevent political parties from clustering female candidates at the bottom of candidate lists.

Countries with thresholds previously set below critical mass—Brazil, the Dominican Republic, Ecuador, and Peru—raised their percentages to 30 percent or higher, and countries previously at critical mass increased their targets to 40 or 50 percent. In contrast to the convergence on critical mass in the 1990s, quota laws in the 2000s better reflected international discourses' emphasis on gender balance. In this new consensus, "percentages below parity now seem insufficient for achieving women's full inclusion"

Table 9.2 Reforms Creating Second-Generation Quota Laws in Latin America

Country	Final Quota Rule (%)	Reform Years	Reform Description (year)
Argentina	Both chambers, 30	1993, 2000, 2005	Placement mandate improved (1993, 2000) Extension to upper chamber (2000)
Bolivia[a]	Both chambers, 50	2009/2010	Threshold raised from 30% (2009/2010)
Brazil	Lower chamber, 30	2000, 2009	Threshold raised from 25% (2000) Quota positions must be filled, not just reserved (2009)
Colombia	Both chambers, 30	2000, 2011	*Declared unconstitutional* (2000) Applies beginning in 2014 (2011)
Costa Rica	Unicameral, 50	1999/2000, 2009	Placement mandate (1999) Threshold raised from 40% (2009)
Dominican Republic	Lower chamber, 33	2000, 2002	Threshold raised from 25% (2000) *Senate exempted* (2002)
Ecuador	Unicameral, 50	2000, 2008/2009	Placement mandate (2000) Threshold raised to 30% (2000), 50% (2008/2009) Extension to Senate (2008/2009)
Mexico	Both chambers, 50	2002, 2008, 2014	Threshold raised to 40% (2008), 50% (2014) Other loopholes closed (2014)
Panama	Unicameral, 50	2012	Threshold raised from 30% (2012)
Peru	Unicameral, 30	2000	Threshold raised from 25% (2000)
Venezuela	Both chambers, 30	2000	*Declared unconstitutional* (2000)

Sources: Crocker (2011); www.quotaproject.org; and author's research.
Notes: Italics indicate reforms that weakened the quota law.
Slash years indicate constitutional reform followed by implementing statutes.

(Franceschet and Piscopo 2013: 3). Indeed, two late-adopting countries—Honduras and Nicaragua—imposed gender balance. El Salvador, Chile, and Uruguay, by contrast, stirred considerable controversy as late adopters that chose quotas short of this mark (Piscopo 2016: 217). For instance, women's groups and other nongovernmental organizations released a statement explaining that 30 percent "does not resolve the problem of unequal conditions between men and women in politics" (El Salvador 2013).

In addition to seeking gender balance (discussed in more detail below) and establishing placement mandates, quota reforms eliminated other avenues of evasion. Reforms applied quotas to the senates in Argentina and Ecuador. In Mexico, reforms eliminated the exemption allowing political parties to avoid the quota by using internal primaries; these reforms also mandated that all primary–alternate candidate pairings be of the same sex, thus foreclosing on the practice wherein female legislators-elect renounced

Table 9.3 Late Adopters in the Second Generation

Country	Quota Rule at Adoption (%)	Year	Notes
Chile	Both chambers, 40	2015	Applies to elections from 2017 through 2029 only
El Salvador	Unicameral, 30	2013	
Honduras	Unicameral, 30 (with 5% increases each election)	2000	*Threshold fixed at 30% (2009)* Threshold increased to 40% (2012 law) Threshold increased to 50% beginning in 2016 (2012 decree)
Nicaragua	Unicameral, 50	2012	Applies beginning in 2016
Uruguay	Both chambers, 33	2009	Applies to 2014 elections only

Sources: Crocker (2011); www.quotaproject.org; and author's research.
Note: Italics indicate reforms that weakened the quota law.

their seats for their male alternates (Alcocer 2013). A 2009 quota reform in Brazil changed the statute's language from "reserve" to "fill": political parties could no longer reserve candidate positions for women that ultimately remained empty—they had to actually give women the candidacies.

Two features of second-generation quotas appeared when surveying the measures as a whole. First, a diverse array of state institutions strengthened Latin America's quota laws. In Argentina, for instance, activist groups contested parties' noncompliance in court, creating accumulated jurisprudence that led to the 2000 presidential decree that improved the placement mandate, stipulated that female candidates who withdraw must be replaced with female candidates, and extended the quota to the Senate (Marx, Borner, and Caminotti 2007).[8] Executive action also played a significant role in Honduras and Nicaragua: a presidential decree raised the Honduran Congress's statutory quota from 40 to 50 percent; and a presidential decree clarified that, when the Nicaraguan congress legislated "equal participation" in a 2008 law, this meant parity for candidate nominations.[9] Elsewhere placement mandates and threshold increases were established by electoral institutes (as in Costa Rica) or the legislature (as in Mexico, Brazil, the Dominican Republic, Panama, and Peru). Constitutional assemblies, themselves often elected under quotas, also played significant roles: in Ecuador and Bolivia, politicians wrote the principles of gender balance in decision-making into their nations' new constitutions. Together, these myriad avenues of reform indicate that, in each country, at least one state institution was predisposed to enforce and even expand quotas' reach—and savvy activists directed their efforts to these offices.

Second, despite proponents' claims about quotas' temporary nature, reforms that weakened or repealed quotas—indicated by italics in Tables 9.2 and 9.3—have not occurred. All cases of quota dilution except that of the Dominican Republic—where a 2002 legislative reform exempted the Senate from the 1997 quota law—have been followed by quota strengthening. In Honduras, the 2009 legislative reform did eliminate the gradual increase in the threshold percentage mandated by the 2000 law—though reforms in 2012 ultimately increased the quota to parity.[10] Quotas also returned in the two countries, Colombia and Venezuela, where high courts had declared the measures unconstitutional. The independent electoral tribunal in Venezuela has used its regulatory powers to demand parity—meaning the alternation of men's and women's names on the electoral lists—in national elections despite the Supreme Court's ruling (Madriz Sotillo 2012). In Colombia, 2009 constitutional reforms eliminated the Constitutional Court's objection that quotas interfered with political parties' autonomy: by stipulating that political parties are organized on the principle of gender equality, the new constitution legitimated positive action to guarantee this outcome.[11] Countries throughout the region have broadened, rather than narrowed, their commitments to women's political rights.

The Legal Architecture of Gender Equality

Latin American elites may have initially intended quotas to serve as symbolic rather than substantive measures, but the story of quota strengthening presented above indicates that the opposite trend occurred. Electoral institutes, legislatures, presidents, and constitutional assemblies have worked to improve the measures' numerical performance, with significant success, as shown by the current proportions of women in Latin America's legislatures. As shown in Table 9.4, Argentina, Bolivia, Ecuador, Mexico, Paraguay, and Peru all approach or exceed their quota thresholds. Women's representation averages 26.1 percent in the region's lower or unicameral houses, and 25.9 percent in the region's senates; in countries applying quota laws, these numbers increase to 27.2 percent for the lower or single houses and 32.0 percent for the senate. Overall, the proportion of female legislators in Latin America rose 15 percentage points between 1990 and 2015. Yet this change raises a further question: Why have political elites, who remain predominantly men, strengthened quota laws—especially when a stronger quota imposes a greater risk that these same male incumbents could lose their seats? The answer lies in the broad equality commitments Latin American states have made since democratization.

In many liberal democracies, quota laws are viewed as potentially

Table 9.4 Proportion of Women in Latin American Legislatures

Country	Election Year	Quota in Effect (%)	Lower House (%)	Senate (%)
Argentina	2013	Both chambers, 30	39.6	38.9
Bolivia	2014	Both chambers, 50	53.1	47.2
Brazil	2014	Lower chamber, 30	9.9	13.6
Chile[a]	2013	—	15.8	18.4
Colombia	2014	Both chambers, 30	19.9	22.5
Costa Rica	2014	Unicameral, 50	33.3	
Dominican Republic	2010	Lower chamber, 33	20.8	9.4
Ecuador	2013	Unicameral, 50	41.6	
El Salvador[a]	2012	—	27.4	
Guatemala	2011	—	13.3	
Honduras[b]	2013	Unicameral, 40	25.8	
Mexico[b]	2012	Both chambers, 40	37.4	34.4
Nicaragua[b]	2011	—	42.4	
Panama	2014	Unicameral, 50	19.3	
Paraguay	2013	Both chambers, 20	15.0	20.0
Peru	2011	Unicameral, 30	22.3	
Uruguay	2014	Both chambers, 33	16.2	29.0
Venezuela	2010	—	17.0	

Sources: Inter-Parliamentary Union Database, www.ipu.org/wmn-e/classif.htm.
Notes: a. Adopted quota law not yet in effect.
b. Parity threshold not yet in effect.

unconstitutional: quotas set aside opportunities for a specific social group and, in doing so, they violate norms of fair competition and fair access (Krook, Lovenduski, and Squires 2009). Latin America's democracies are better understood as hybrid citizenship regimes, in that they combine liberalism's normative commitments to individual equality and protection from unfair treatment with a more corporatist understanding that certain identity groups merit special treatment—which often includes special access to the representative institutions of the state.[12] This combination is expressed in Latin American states' broader efforts to address gender equality postdemocratization—that is, in the gender equality measures that undergird quota laws.

Every constitution in postdemocratic Latin America recognizes gender equality in some fashion.[13] Nearly all contain general equal rights clauses, meaning statements that women and men have equality before the law, or statements banning discrimination based on gender or sex.

For instance, the 1991 Colombia Constitution stipulates that "women and men have equal rights and opportunities. Women will be subject to no form of discrimination" (Article 43). These measures represent significant victories in the decades-long struggle to recognize women as citizens with the same entitlements and responsibilities as men. In some cases, this recognition appeared in the founding democratic constitutions, as in Colombia and throughout Central America. Elsewhere, women's full incorporation into the polity occurred after democratization. The 1980 Chilean Constitution did not include Article 19—"Men and women are equal before law"—until a 1999 act of Congress, and the 1917 Mexican Constitution, long heralded for its forward-thinking provisions, did not prohibit gender discrimination until 2011.

Equal rights clauses fulfill the liberal vision of women's citizenship by establishing states' negative role: states will protect women from unequal treatment, but this protection occurs retroactively, not proactively. Yet in ten Latin American constitutions, equal rights clauses exist alongside clauses that expressly guarantee women's political rights through the affirmative action of the state. The 1992 Paraguayan Constitution, for example, contains a general equality clause as well as a political rights clause: "The state will promote conditions and create mechanisms to make equality actual and effective, removing obstacles that impede or circumscribe the exercise of these rights and facilitating women's participation in all spheres of national life" (Article 48). Similarly, Argentina's 1994 Constitution—which postdates the 1991 quota law—stipulates that "the equality of opportunities between men and women for equal access to elective and party office will be guaranteed by positive action that regulates political parties and the electoral code" (Article 37). Similar positive action clauses with respect to women's political rights appear in Bolivia (2009 Constitution), Colombia (2009 Constitution), Costa Rica (1997 reform of 1949 Constitution), the Dominican Republic (2010 Constitution), Ecuador (2008 Constitution), Mexico (2014 reform of the 1917 Constitution), Nicaragua (1987 Constitution), and Peru (2005 reform of the 1993 Constitution).

Constitutional affirmations of women's rights, while perhaps unable to transform the daily sexism that affects women's lives, play crucial roles in establishing states' positive obligations toward gender equality. For example, in 2002, the Ecuadorian Constitutional Court—governed at the time only by an equal rights clause, as the political rights clause remained in the future—rejected any interpretation of the quota law's placement mandate that did not alternate men's and women's names on candidate lists. The court wrote that "the state has assumed the obligation to eliminate conditions of inequality in the electoral participation of men and women."[14] The Costa Rican Constitutional Court explained this obligation more plainly in a 2008 decision: responding to contestations that a party's formula for determining candidates' rankings violated the placement mandate, the court articulated a distinction between unequal treatment and systematic discrimination. *Unequal treatment,* reasoned the court, occurs in specific situations and can easily be remedied through straightforward channels; *systematic discrimination,* by contrast, is a "structural flaw" of "such a magnitude" that the state "must establish specific regulations" to correct it. Therefore, the "possibilities to be elected"—and not party procedures—must govern female candidates' list placement.[15] Costa Rica's Constitutional Court gave the state broad license to interfere in any party procedures that undercut quotas' numerical effectiveness, on the grounds that ending systematic discrimination requires proactive measures.

Thus, hybrid citizenship regimes made quota strengthening inevitable: gender quota laws were ruled consistent with states' constitutional commitments to advancing women's political rights. General equality laws—statutes passed by Congress or executive decree that affirm women's rights—further reinforced this mix of negative protections and positive guarantees. Found in twelve Latin American countries, general equality laws address women's rights across policy areas, including political participation and representation. For instance, Panama's 1991 equality law commits the state to the equal treatment of men and women (Article 1) while also specifying the state's obligations "to create the necessary conditions that lead to a more equal distribution of responsibilities in the public sector" (Article 4.5), including elected, appointed, and party offices (Article 7).[16] Echoing constitutional jurisprudence throughout the region, equality laws also establish that positive action does not violate liberal norms of fairness: the Peruvian statute, for example, specifies that positive actions "designed to accelerate the actual equality between men and women will not be considered discriminatory" (Article 4.3).[17]

Table 9.5 summarizes the legal architecture of gender equality in Latin America, showing where and when each country adopted its constitutional equal rights clause, constitutional political rights clause, first gender quota law, and general equality law. In most, equal rights clauses preceded quotas, and political rights clauses postdated quotas. Exceptions occurred in Colombia and Nicaragua, where constitutional commitments and general equality laws preceded the adoption of quotas, and Chile, where an equal rights clause predated quotas by nearly fifteen years. These chronologies suggest that Latin America's two countries without a quota law—Guatemala and Venezuela—may follow the path of other late adopters. In Guatemala, for example, the 1999 general equality law says the state will "promote effective, temporary, and gradual measures to achieve the full political participation of women" and "promote mechanisms that guarantee women's participation as parity representation in all institutions at the national, regional, or local level" (Article 23).[18] As Guatemala and Venezuela look to catch up, a third wave of quota reformers in Latin America have begun rejecting quotas in favor of parity.

Table 9.5 The Legal Architecture of Gender Equality in Latin America

Country	First	Second	Third	Fourth	Fifth
Argentina[a]	Q (1991)	CP (1994)			
Bolivia[b]	CE (1994)	Q (1997)	EL (1997)	CP (2009)	
Brazil	CE (1988)	Q (1997)			
Chile	CE (1999)	Q (2015)			
Colombia[c]	CE (1991)	Q1 (1998)	EL (2003)	CP (2009)	Q2 (2011)
Costa Rica[a]	EL (1990)	Q (1996)	CP (1997)		
Dominican Republic[b]	CE (1994)	Q (1997)	CP (2010)		
Ecuador[b]	CE (1996)	Q (1997)	CP (2008)		
El Salvador	CE (1983)	EL (2011)	Q (2013)		
Guatemala	CE (1985)	EL (1999)			
Honduras	CE (1982)	Q (2000)	EL (2000)		
Mexico	CE (2001)	Q (1996)	EL (2006)	CP (2014)	
Nicaragua	CE, CP (1987)	EL (2008)	Q (2012)		
Panama	CE (1972)	EL (1999)	Q (1997)		
Paraguay	CE, CP (1992)	Q (1996)			
Peru	CE (1993)	Q (1997)	CP (2005)	EL (2007)	
Uruguay	CE (1967)	EL (2007)	Q (2009)		
Venezuela[c]	EL (1993)	Q1 (1997)	CE (1999)		

Sources: Political Database of the Americas, http://pdba.georgetown.edu/Constitutions /constudies.html.

Notes: Q is the first-generation quota law. CE is constitutional equal rights clause. CP is constitutional political rights clause. EL is general equity law.

a. These constitutions contain a CP clause without a CE clause.

b. The CE clause was written in the nation's first postdemocratic constitution, and the CP clause appeared in the second postdemocratic constitution.

c. Colombia's quota law was repealed and repassed. Venezuela's quota law was repealed and not replaced.

The Third Generation: Parity Governments

As the data presented in Table 9.4 show, women's numerical representation continues to fall short of quota thresholds. Yet these outcomes—unlike in quotas first generation—result neither from political parties exploitation of loopholes nor from deliberate lax enforcement. Parties minimal compliance with quota laws, which often occurs alongside a complicated interaction between quota provisions and the electoral system, provides a better explanation at this juncture. For example, despite placement mandates governing the rank-ordering of women's names on electoral lists, parties continue to place women in the lowest-available—yet still legally compliant—spot (Jones, Alles, and Tchintian 2012: 354–355).

The Costa Rican case proves illustrative. Though the parity law requires that a female candidate appear in the first or second position, political parties typically do not allocate female candidates the top spot. In the

2014 elections, for example, 77 percent of all lists ranked men first; the trend was especially pronounced in districts with the fewest seats available. This minimal compliance meant that some Costa Rican provinces elected no women and, ultimately, lowered female legislators' representation well below parity (Murillo 2014). Yet this result, while disappointing, reflects less on the law's legal shortcomings (as was the focus on reforms in the first and second generation) and more on political parties ongoing recalcitrance to embrace the spirit of the laws.

This intransigence on the part of political parties has been described as the "masculine monopoly" of political power (Quispe Ponce 2014)—one that quota laws are unlikely to break. The third wave has thus emphasized electoral results, not candidate nominations. Six Latin American countries—Ecuador, Bolivia, Costa Rica, Honduras, Panama, and Mexico—have raised their quota thresholds to parity, and a seventh—Nicaragua—adopted parity outright. All justified this move by appealing to equality of outcomes, not equality of opportunities: in my analysis of these seven cases, I found that legislators and other parity supporters drew critical distinctions between parity and quotas (Piscopo 2014). Parity abandons the arguments about women's difference and temporary corrective measures that characterized quota debates; instead, parity offers a permanent vision of gender balance in government, one attained through the equality of electoral results. For instance, Mexican senator Adriana Díaz Lizama argues that parity "is not implementing a quota, it is sharing in decision-making so that together we [men and women] can be co-responsible for the true development and advance of democracy."[19] Parity advocates frame gender balance by appealing to the commonsense fact that, since women comprise half the population, they should comprise half the decisionmakers (Archenti 2011; Piscopo 2016; IDEA and CIM 2013).

An illustration comes from efforts to combat political parties' minimal compliance with parity in Costa Rica. The Women's Committee of the Costa Rican Legislative Assembly has introduced a horizontal parity bill, which would require political parties to place women in the first position on at least half of all their lists. Like their predecessors in the second wave, parity proponents in the third wave want legal reforms that improve performance; however, they are framing these revisions in different normative terms. The Women's Committee has argued that "parity norms remain insufficient unless they obtain the foreseen result."[20] The Legislative Assembly's technical service, asked to assess the bill's juridical merits, agreed with this emphasis on results. The technical assessors found that the bill "achieves the inclusion of women in *electable positions*," and that this inclusion meets the Constitutional Court's 2008 mandate to end systematic discrimination by guaranteeing women's election.[21] The 2008 decision was the first to articulate the goal as equality of results, a goal the Constitutional Court repeated in 2012: responding to a male candidate's claim that parity violated his individual right to be elected, the Costa Rican Constitutional Court ruled in 2012 that the right to be elected "is not just a right that affects a male citizen or a female citizen individually, but the democratic system as a whole."[22]

This framing echoes the normative link between democracy and women's political rights that undergirded quota debates in the 1990s, but without the emphasis on political modernity and individual equality. As Costa Rica's Constitutional Court made plain, electoral outcomes trump individual opportunity. Evolving jurisprudence now views gender balance in political decisionmaking not as an indicator of democracy, but as a constitutive feature of the system.

The fullest expression of this claim appears in Bolivia and Ecuador, which establish parity as a foundational principle of their governments. The 2008 Bolivian Constitution establishes that the country "adopts as its government representative, participatory, and communal democracy, with equivalence of conditions between men and women" (Article 11). The 2010 electoral code explains that *equivalence* means "parity" and the alternation in candidate lists for all government positions, and additional statutes passed that same year extended parity to all levels and branches of government, including all institutions of indigenous representation or self-governance.[23] The same parity regime was created in Ecuador by the 2008 Constitution. In particular, the charter specifies that all citizens have "the right to hold office . . . in a system of selection and designation that is transparent, inclusive, equitable, plural, and democratic, that guarantees participation according to equity and gender parity" (Article 61.7).

Other Latin American countries have likewise adopted the logic of parity government—that is, gender balance beyond the legislature—though more selectively than Bolivia and Ecuador. Parity also governs the election of Costa Rica's two vice presidents (of the two candidates presented by parties, one must be female), and the election of mayors in Costa Rica and Nicaragua (of the mayor–vice mayor candidate pairing presented by parties, at least one must be female). Costa Rica also adopted a gender balance rule for the boards of all voluntary organizations. Adopted in 2011, the statute requires that all civil society associations—from charities to sports governing bodies—must be comprised of 50 percent women; the Constitutional Court affirmed the statute's legality in 2014.[24]

Parity has also developed apace in Mexico. The 2014 constitutional reforms placed parity within the nation's charter. Subsequently, the federal Electoral Court stipulated that the country's thirty-two states must grant women the same political rights as the federal government: Mexico's subnational governments could not pass laws that negated their constitutional obligation to incorporate parity into their state constitutions and state electoral codes.[25] The court has also elevated parity above indigenous customary law, meaning that localities governed by *usos y custumbres* cannot invoke tradition to prevent women from entering public office.[26] Elsewhere at the subnational level, the mayor of Mexico City decreed parity for the entire public administration by 2019, including the popularly elected quasi-executive officials who administer the city's districts.[27] Finally, female legislators have proposed adopting parity within the federal Congress: that is, all leadership positions, committee secretariats, and committee memberships would be gender balanced (Notimex 2014). This measure would use parity not just to equalize women's numbers, but to equalize women's power: gender balance across Congress would eliminate the problem wherein women enter the legislature in greater numbers, but remain marginalized from prestigious committees and party leadership positions (Miguel 2012; Heath, Schwindt-Bayer, and Taylor-Robinson 2005; Schwindt-Bayer 2010).

Across cases, parity—like quota laws in the first generation—remains largely aspirational. Reforms are so recent that their kinks remain unknown or unresolved; their full effects remain in the future. Bolivia did become the second country in the world (after Rwanda) to elect a majority-female lower house in 2014 (see Table 9.4) but, in Ecuador, Costa Rica, and elsewhere, women's presence in elected and appointed office continues to fall short of gender balance. Yet even though change unfolds incrementally, the importance of these underlying constitutional and juridical principles cannot be understated. Parity dramatically updates the normative conditions through which women receive political rights. Earlier eras offered women electoral opportunities because their perspectives and talents were believed to enhance democratic outputs, but the parity wave guarantees women equal representation in the state because that is simply what democracy means.

Conclusion

The international conventions and domestic laws surveyed here knit together discourses on women's rights and political representation on the one hand, and democratic states' obligations to ensure these entitlements on the other hand. Notions of gender balance were explicit at the outset, from the 1995 Beijing Platform for Action to the general equality laws—like those in Guatemala and El Salvador—that mentioned parity rather than quotas. However, in this analysis I identified three distinct generations or waves of quota adoption in Latin America: an initial period of weak, largely symbolic laws in the 1990s; a second period of strengthening in the 2000s; and a recent shift toward comprehensive parity measures for all branches and levels of government. Only in the third wave have discourses fully embraced gender balance and parity: while the earlier waves emphasized that attaining certain proportions of female candidates would promote women's political rights and deepen democracy, the new wave seeks the fullest expression of democracy by demanding complete equality in the total number of women elected.

This new wave has important implications for women's political citizenship. First, unlike quotas, parity laws are not justified in consequentialist terms. Activists, observers, and scholars continue to hope that women will lead Latin American democracies toward adopting more fair, inclusive, and transformative public policies, but women's difference no longer establishes the terms on which they exercise their right to be elected. Second, this normative and legal evolution has occurred because political elites in Latin America unwittingly tied their own hands. Broad statements in constitutions and statutes about women's individual equality before the law, and about the state's positive obligation to guarantee women's political participation, provided concrete foundations for quotas' strengthening and permanency. On their own, each equality commitment may have been intended as a purely symbolic, conciliatory gesture toward female activists as democratization unfolded. Yet summed together, these equality commitments create a robust legal architecture of gender equality, one that places Latin America at the forefront of state-led solutions for women's underrepresentation in public office.

Notes

I wish to thank Malena Ernani for her invaluable research assistance and Magda Hinojosa for letting me draw on ideas and trends initially described in Hinojosa and Piscopo (2013).

1. See Women Suffrage and Beyond, "The Women Suffrage Timeline," http://womensuffrage.org/?page_id=69 (accessed January 5, 2015).
2. Though Venezuela applies quotas for subnational legislatures.
3. In this article, I could not survey the vast scholarship on women, social movements, and democracy in Latin America. Some key works are Baldez (2002), González and Kampwirth (2001), Jaquette (1994), and Waylen (2007).
4. See *Report of the World Conference of the International Women's Year,* (1975), paragraphs 57–66, http://www.un.org/womenwatch/daw/beijing /otherconferences/Mexico/Mexico%20conference%20report%20optimized.pdf (accessed January 6, 2015).
5. See "Platform for Action" (1995), http://www.un.org/womenwatch/daw /beijing/platform/decision.htm (accessed January 6, 2015).
6. Numerous scholars have documented these loopholes, including contributors to Crocker (2011), and Htun and Jones (2002), Hinojosa (2012), and Hinojosa and Piscopo (2013).
7. Brazilian parties can run more candidates than seats in each district (the

exact limit depends on district size and the configuration of party coalitions). If, for example, a party can run up to ten candidates for five seats, the party could reserve three spots for women, but just run five to eight men. Kristin Wylie, Mona Lena Krook, and Matthew Shugart provided the Brazilian data for this article.

8. This provision applies only to female candidates who withdraw during the election. After the election, a woman who renounces is replaced by the next candidate on the list who may be a man.

9. Honduras, Decree 54-2012; Nicaragua, Decree 29/2010.

10. República de Honduras (2012), Decreto No. 54-2012, *La Gaceta* No. 32,820, Tegucigalpa, May 15, 2012.

11. Constitutional Court Sentence C-371/00. Legislative Act 1/2009 modified Chapter IV, Article 107 of the Constitution. Corte Constitucional de Colombia (2000), Sentencia C-371/00, Bogotá, March 29, 2000; República de Colombia (2009), Acto Legislativo Número 1 de 2009, *Diario Oficial,* No. 47,410, July 14, 2009.

12. The literature characterizing Latin American democracy is exceedingly vast. I draw on Krook, Lovenduski, and Squires's (2009) presentation of citizenship regimes to characterize the Latin American case in broad terms.

13. All data on Latin America's constitutions are drawn from the archive at the Political Database of the Americas, http://pdba.georgetown.edu/Constitutions /constudies.html.

14. El Tribunal Constitucional (Ecuador) (2002), Decisión 028-2002, Quito. November 15, 2002.

15. Sala Constitucional de la Corte Suprema de Justicia (Costa Rica) (2008), Resolution 2008009582, San José, June 11, 2008.

16. República de Panama (1999). Ley No. 4 de 1999, Panama City, January 29, 1999.

17. Congreso de la República de Peru (2007), Ley No. 28983, Lima, March 12, 2007.

18. Congreso de la República de Guatemala (1999), Decreto Número 7-99, Guatemala City, March 9, 1999.

19. El Senado de Mexico (2013), "Proyecto de Decreto que Reforma y Adiciona Diversas Disposiciones de la Constitución Política de Los Estados Unidos Mexicanos, en Materia de Reforma Política," *Diario de los Debates*, No. 35, Mexico City, March 3, 2013.

20. Comisión Permanente Especial de la Mujer (Costa Rica), "Dictamen Afirmativo de Mayoría. Expediente 19.019," *La Gaceta* No. 58, San José, March 25, 2014.

21. Departamento de Servicios Técnicos, Asamblea Legislativa de la República de Costa Rica (2014), "Informe Jurídico," San José, May 28 2014, emphasis added.

22. Sala Constitucional de la Corte Suprema de Justicia (Costa Rica) (2012), Resolution 2012001966, San José; Sala Constitucional de la Corte Suprema de Justicia (Costa Rica) (2008), Resolution 2008009582, San José, June 11, 2008.

23. Asamblea Legislativa Plurinacional (Bolivia) (2010), "Ley 26," *Gaceta Oficial de Bolivia,* June 30, 2010.

24. Asamblea Legislativa de la República de Costa Rica (2010). "Ley 8901," San José, November 3, 2010; Sala Constitucional de la Corte Suprema de Justicia (Costa Rica) (2014), Sentencia 2014-004630, San José.

25. Tribunal Electoral del Poder Judicial de la Federación (Mexico) (2014), "Tésis IV," Mexico City, August 2, 2014.

26. Tribunal Electoral del Poder Judicial de la Federación (Mexico) (2014), "Tésis VIII," Mexico City, March 26, 2014.

27. Gobierno del Distrito Federal (Ciudad de México) (2014). "Decreto por el que se reforman diversas disposiciones de la Ley Orgánica de la Administración Pública del Distrito Federal," *Gaceta Oficial Distrito Federal* No. 1839, Mexico City, April 15, 2014.

10

Women's Rights, Indigenous Rights, and Social Cohesion

Jane S. Jaquette

A central debate in Latin American studies today is whether direct or participatory democracy—as practiced in Venezuela, Bolivia, and Ecuador—produces a higher quality of democracy for the poor and marginalized than traditional liberal democracy, which emphasizes checks and balances, party competition, freedom of the press, and other civil and political rights. In this chapter I address a somewhat different, but closely related, question that is raised by the increasing prominence and activism of indigenous movements in these and other countries: Can a plurinational democracy, allowing indigenous communities a high degree of local autonomy, address the crisis of representation while protecting human rights, fostering social cohesion, and strengthening the rule of law? I examine this question by focusing on the conflict between indigenous identity politics and women's claims to equal rights and an end to gender discrimination.

Indigenous Movements, Indigeneity, and Identity Politics

The political and economic exclusion of indigenous peoples became a critical issue in several countries of Latin America in the last decades of the twentieth century. Pressures from below have changed the contours of politics, most notably in Bolivia and Ecuador, but also in Guatemala, Peru, and Mexico (Van Cott 2008; Sieder 2002; Postero 2007; Yashar 2005). The indigenous demand for autonomy so that they may live according to their traditional *usos y costumbres* has received broad intellectual and political support.

Contemporary Latin American indigenous movements have organized through identity politics, emphasizing their differences from the dominant white/mestizo culture that surrounds them. Indigenous movements expand the language of rights to include collective rights, but they often fail to acknowledge discrimination and violence against women within indigenous communities. The indigenous answer to the demand for women's equality is to counter that gender complementarity protects and values women as women; Western notions of equality violate cultural norms.[1] This sets up a potentially serious conflict between indigenous rights and women's rights. How this conflict is addressed has implications not only for efforts to promote gender equity within indigenous communities, but also for the legitimacy of the core liberal values that undergird virtually all feminisms and inform broader concepts of liberal democracy, human rights, and citizenship.

Within Latin America and beyond, indigenous groups have become political actors, connecting through transnational organizations, through conferences at regional and international levels, and with environmental and antiglobalization groups. The United Nations sponsored the first International Conference on Discrimination Against Indigenous Peoples in the Americas in 1977, and subsequently declared two Decades for Indigenous Peoples (1995–2004 and 2005–2014). Following the International Labour Organization (ILO) Convention 169 on Indigenous Rights (1989), the UN General Assembly approved the Declaration on the Rights of Indigenous Peoples in 2007, which recognizes the right of indigenous groups to claim collective as well as individual human rights (Article 1) and reflects the demands of indigenous communities to maintain their autonomy against the ever increasing encroachments of the outside world. The declaration bars governments from employing coercively assimilationist policies while affirming that indigenous peoples have the same rights as all other citizens to the opportunities and resources of the wider society. Article 26 specifies that indigenous communities have rights to lands "traditionally owned or acquired," and Article 32 gives indigenous peoples the right to be consulted about any development of natural resources on these lands.[2]

Most Latin American countries have ratified the ILO Convention and many have incorporated consultation with indigenous groups into their constitutions. During the past decade, indigenous opposition has become a serious source of local disputes, as indigenous communities resist oil exploration and drilling and protest the opening of new mines, projects usually funded by foreign investment (increasingly Chinese) that produce primary products largely destined for export. The commodities boom (2003–2014), which brought about a period of rapid economic growth in South America, has increased the number and severity of these conflicts. This has created a painful dilemma for all governments but especially for the radical populist governments of Bolivia and Ecuador, which were elected with indigenous support yet rely on robust export earnings to fund generous social spending.

But indigeneity is more than a set of claims to be negotiated in competition with those of other marginalized groups. Kay B. Warren and Jean E. Jackson argue that it is a moral stance:

The pan-American discourses that emerged to celebrate indigenous other-ness often stress a nonmaterial and spiritual relation to the land, consensu-al decision-making, a holistic environmentalist perspective, and a reestab-lishment of the harmony of the social and physical worlds. Implicit in these values is a critique of occidental forms of authority, desires to con-trol and commodify nature, and the sovereign nation-state model with its accompanying power to define democracy, citizenship, penal codes, juris-diction, and legitimate violence. (2002: 13)

In its opposition to capitalism and the state, indigeneity suggests a post-Marxist avenue to pursue the Rousseauian ideal that remains deeply ingrained in the Western political imagination.

Gender and Indigeneity

Indigeneity as a political project challenges feminist moral capital by opposing gender complementarity to the liberal feminist demand for women's equality. Scholars have documented the ubiquity of gender com-plementarity in Andean societies, which is derived from, and reinforces, the emphasis on duality in the Andean worldview (e.g., Harris 1985, but see also Cervone 2002; Barrig 2006; Goodale 2009). The Andean couple unites opposites. Individuals are not accepted as adults in the community until they marry and complete each other. Complementarity reflects the need for cooperation between men and women to ensure survival, but also projects a cultural ideal of gender equality that is consistent with gender difference: although men and women perform different tasks and assume different roles in the community, these are equally valued.

Liberal feminists are generally skeptical of arguments that justify gender roles based on complementarity. Their concern that difference is rarely equal or even equitable is borne out in the evident gap between the ideal of comple-mentarity and the material reality of indigenous women's lives. Indigenous women are the most disadvantaged group in Andean and Mesoamerican soci-eties; they have the highest rates of extreme poverty and maternal mortality. Gender gaps in school attendance and literacy have virtually disappeared in much of Latin America, but not among the indigenous. In Ecuador, for exam-ple, 36 percent of indigenous women on average are illiterate, as compared to an average of 20 percent of indigenous men (Picq 2008: 278); in highland Peru, illiteracy rates for women are above 25 percent (Barrig 2006: 124).

Sarah A. Radcliffe, Nina Laurie, and Robert Andolina found that Ecuadorian labor markets remain segregated by race and gender, and that most indigenous women in Ecuador have unmet basic needs (2009: 198, 200). Women can hold title to land (Deere and León 2001), but the fact that women marry out of their communities and live in their husband's village denies them effective ownership of the land they have inherited as well as the right to participate in the rotating cargo system of community governance.[3] Men can travel outside the village, wear Western clothes, cut their hair, and are likely to speak some Spanish, but women's mobility is restricted by traditional norms such as the fact that they often need to have their husband's permission to leave the house (Barrig 2006; Picq 2008).

These distinctions are heightened by identity politics. Because they are the carriers of culture, Andean women are expected to wear the traditional *pollera* (layered skirt) and a hat appropriate to their village and to speak the indigenous language (Barrig 2006: 119). They should prepare and eat traditional foods, such as guinea pig and potatoes, while men may eat dishes like chicken and rice, which are associated with mestizo culture.[4] Men often migrate and engage in work outside the village, adjusting to "national norms and realities" while women remain "isolated from service facilities" and often fearful of interacting "with an outer world they [are] unfamiliar with." Since their behavior is constantly monitored, indigenous women are, in Manuela Lavinas Picq's phrase, the "guarded guardians of culture" (2008: 286).

Decisionmaking by consensus implies that all members of the community can participate in the forums in which community decisions are made. But women are often marginalized. Maruja Barrig (2006) reports that men exclude women by ignoring or ridiculing them, or by using Spanish to talk about the important things while reserving indigenous languages for discussing domestic or private affairs. According to Emma Cervone (2002), "Women's illiteracy is transformed into a condition of social and political inadequacy that silences them in public—even when meetings are held in their own vernacular in their own communities. This assumption of female inadequacy becomes part of a female identity ('women know nothing') that defines women as socially inferior to men" (2002: 182). Further, Cervone argues that, as modernization has led to greater contact between indigenous communities and the white/mestizo world, traditional power differentials between indigenous men and women have increased:

> The gendered symmetry between the androcentric and patriarchic national power structure, on the one hand, and the actual political control exerted by indigenous men within indigenous societies, on the other, has been further reinforced with the "modernization" of the Ecuadorian state and economy. . . . Although traditional forms of social and political prestige (such as the cargo system) still play a key role in the construction of leadership, formal education, experience in interethnic negotiations and, most recently, participation in development projects, have all become pivotal requirements for affirmation of local as well as national leaders. (182)

But women who are illiterate, lack a good command of Spanish, and are usually restricted to the house and the village rarely gain these skills. Public space "no longer refers to a specific place" shared by the community, "but to a space where Indians have to negotiate with white-mestizo society," and from which women are largely excluded (183).[5]

Reports from several NGO projects on women's empowerment show that, when asked, indigenous women put access to formal education, literacy, knowledge of Spanish, and public speaking high on their list of priorities, along with the prevention of domestic violence. This awareness offers one hopeful sign that indigenous women themselves may help bring about change from within their own communities.

Violence against women is often tolerated within indigenous communities, and reinforced by social control. Picq sees such violence as "intense and frequent, compromising women's physical integrity, sexual and reproductive health, and often putting their lives at risk" (2008: 280). Barrig reports that a woman's parents are likely to side with the husband should their daughter seek their support because her husband is alcoholic or abusive. In the communities Barrig studied, marriages are customarily arranged by parents, and strong pressure is placed on the girl to consent. In the southern highlands of Peru, mock abduction and trial marriages are practiced. Although these practices may at one time have offered some protections to women, Barrig suggests that this is no longer the case and that both are characterized by the Peruvian Penal Code as "violation[s] of sexual freedom" (2006: 123).

"Rape is often the first sexual experience of indigenous girls," according to Picq, who notes that indigenous women lack legal recourse outside the community while shame and fear of retaliation prevent them from seeking help within. Most women attribute violence to "male jealousy and alcoholism," but engaging in activities outside the home that "threaten men's power or image in the community" may also be a cause (2008: 281–282). Of course, violence against women is not limited to indigenous communities; Latin America and the Caribbean have some of the highest rates of family violence in the world (Dammert 2013: 83). Women's movements have made antiviolence legislation and enforcement a priority issue throughout the region, but indigenous autonomy makes it less likely that women will claim protection within their own communities or even against outsiders, such as the police and military, who have a long history of abusing indigenous women, particularly in times of civil conflict (e.g., Mantilla Falcón 2009).[6]

Responses of Stakeholders

The conflict between women's rights and indigenous rights has met with different responses from various actors with stakes in the debate: Latin

American feminist activists, environmentalist NGOs (both international and domestic), gender and development practitioners, and those who have studied—and often identify with—indigenous movements. Their approaches reveal some of the difficult choices facing those who are committed to addressing issues of inequality and social justice when cultural differences conflict with universal concepts of human rights, including women's rights.

Latin American feminist activists, whose successes are always vulnerable to misogyny and backlash, have found their equality claims can be challenged on "multicultural" grounds by those who resist the "homogenizing policies of the modern state" (Cervone 2002: 181). Where indigenous populations are a substantial voting bloc, feminists have found themselves on the defensive in debates over the content of new constitutions, in the setting of legislative priorities, and in implementing policies and laws that may be construed as insufficiently sensitive to multicultural views of gender.[7]

For their part, feminist development practitioners have concentrated on empowering women by increasing the resources available to them through training, microcredit programs, and leadership workshops.[8] "Gender and development" approaches have been deemed superior to "women and development" programs in part because they include men but staff in the field lack the ethical and social leverage to change male behavior, hesitating to impose gender criteria laid down by the development agencies when these might jeopardize other goals (Barrig 2006).

Environmental and antiglobalization movements tend to sidestep the conflict between women's rights and indigenous values as they encourage indigenous women to defy custom and take on leadership roles in transnational forums and in the media. Yet women indigenous leaders face strong constraints. The more conservative sectors of the indigenous movement "portray dissent as an act of disloyalty to the group," and women sometimes even perceive their own agency as a "threat to the collective foundations" of the movement (Picq 2008: 289), putting the issue of intersectionality into sharp focus.

Scholar-activists who are sympathetic to both indigenous and feminist demands find ways to reconcile positions that are in fact at odds. One way is to argue that indigenous communities are not by nature patriarchal, but have been contaminated by exposure to white and mestizo society. Barrig quotes Billie Jean Isbell's view that modernization is bad for indigenous women "to the degree that Spanish society, dominated by men, continues to displace the Andean order which is basically dual, complementary, and egalitarian" (2006: 114). This is consistent with the decolonial critique that sees contemporary evidence of gender discrimination as a result of the colonial past.[9] The imposition and reinforcement of social hierarchies have proved particularly devastating to women within their communities while stereotypes of indigenous mistreatment of women have been used to justify the colonial imposition of Western religious and cultural values (Chenault 2011: 22–33). For many who blame outside contamination or the perpetuation of colonial power hierarchies, there is no conflict between women's rights and indigenous customs because women who conform to traditional expectations are doing so by choice. Wearing the *pollera*, like wearing the veil, becomes "a heroic gesture of cultural resistance" (Barrig 2006: 120).

Radcliffe, Laurie, and Andolina (2009) found multilateral agencies and development NGOs to be a contemporary source of outside contamination. These have been "complicit in creating disparities in life chances" between indigenous men and women, they assert, because their "social capital" approach to development made women's "distinctive characteristics . . . the symbolic and material embodiment of ethnic communities" (204). These policies are "*transnational* constructs" and are "not reducible to traditional or local patriarchies" (213, emphasis in original).

Picq suggests that Latin American women's movements may deserve some blame: while they have been successful in eliminating discriminatory laws and passing new legislation to protect women's civil and political rights, they have left indigenous women behind. She notes, however, that indigenous movements themselves mobilized women to gain support but, once they gained political leverage, "women's voices were not heard." She concludes that the cultural realm is "particularly violent towards women" and that the "double standard of indigenous justice" leaves women with "virtually no rights" and "subjugated both to men and the community at large" (Picq 2008: 279–285).

Indigeneity as an Alternative to Liberal Democracy

The conflict between liberal and indigenous views of rights and justice can become a conflict of civilizations when indigenous values and practices are proposed as an alternative to liberal democracy and Western standards of justice.[10]

Shannon Speed (2008), rejecting June Nash's view that indigenous culture is "*necessarily* opposed to Western practices" (179, italics in original), applauds the ways in which indigenous communities in Chiapas "demand the right to maintain an alternative structure of power" based on "alternative logics of rule" (172) found in indigenous practices of collective and consensual decisionmaking, the concept of "rule-obeying,"[11] and the assertion of pluriculturality or diversity within the collective (162–173, 31–32).

When Zapatista communities assert autonomy by "refusing to grant the state the power to decide who are rights bearers and what rights they may enjoy," Speed asserts, they are articulating "a radically distinct discourse of rights" (2008: 167) and "reappropriating" the neoliberal language of subjectivity—the "right to self-control and autonomous self-production" (162–163)—in ways that are "subversive of Western liberal individualist discourse" (179). Drawing on Antonio Negri (Hardt and Negri 2000), Speed characterizes power in indigenous communities as potentia rather than potestas. *Potentia* is the "creative force of social struggle," whereas *potestas* is the coercive power of the sovereign (2008: 168–169). The Zapatistas are not challenging the state by proposing separatism; instead, they are offering "symbolic and material alternatives to neoliberal rule" (Speed 2008: 172).[12] Making clear that the real object of her critique is "neoliberal citizenship,"[13] Speed praises Zapatista discourse, which "does not lend itself well to market logics and to notions of rational-actor citizens out to maximize individual benefits, express their freedom of choice at the ballot box, and express their dissent in the courts of state" (2008: 172).

There are some problems with this vision. From a liberal standpoint, individualist discourse is not where the West went off the track; rather, it is the lack of universal application of liberal principles in systems where the strong have rights and impunity and the weak are denied both rights and dignity.[14] Further, although it is possible to imagine a pluricultural collective at the national level, at the community level (as we have seen in the case of women) diversity is discouraged and social control remains a powerful force. Nor is it clear that potentia (the power to create) can be so easily separated from the power to coerce,[15] or that the indigenous norm of consensus building (*mandar obedeciendo*) provides an adequate substitute for checks and balances, especially as indigenous communities become increasingly linked to the world of modern communications, commerce, and mobility. In Speed's (2008) account and others in this genre, liberal efforts to increase representation and voice or defend democratic procedures are thus dismissed as misguided and as barriers to new thinking while feminist concerns for women's rights as individuals are made to seem narrow and self-serving.

Finally, Speed (2008) finds that in unilaterally declaring their autonomy from the Mexican government, the indigenous groups of Chiapas are "challenging liberal conceptions of natural and positive law" by showing that rights "exist *in their exercise,* not as designations from God/nature or the state/law" (emphasis in original). But one might ask, why shouldn't dominant groups also contend that their rights exist in their exercise, unconstrained by God or natural law, thus eroding any distinction between might and right? Speed concedes that such rights might be exercised by groups "whose goals one finds abhorrent," for example, "right wing militia groups in the United States"; but she counters, "even in that case . . . such deployments might be challenging to neoliberal power" (173).[16] And that is all that counts.

Finding New Frames

The conflict between women's rights and indigenous rights is not easily resolved. There are moral arguments and social forces on both sides. Feminist movements have historically been committed to extending liberal values of equality and voice to women, who have long been denied these rights. Few feminists, even those who are critical of liberalism, are unlikely to be convinced by arguments that provide rationalizations for coerced complementarity, silencing women, or gender violence.

Recognition of the depth of the conflict between women's rights and indigenous views calls for more serious consideration of the options available to address it. Women in indigenous communities have themselves taken actions that empower them within their own communities and link them to the broader world. The gender lens employed by international financial institutions and development NGOs may not be the most effective approach. Venida Chenault suggests addressing violence against Native American women through empowerment based on participation that connects women to their communities as well as to the outside world, where women see themselves not as "victims" but as "members of a community." Such programs need to connect with "tribal healing practices" and "women's ceremonies," in addition to consciousness raising, education, and activism (2011: 41–42).

However effective, such measures may be focused too narrowly when what is needed is a critical perspective on the broader context of the conflict. Inspired by but adapting Albert O. Hirschman's schema in *Exit, Voice and Loyalty* (1970), I suggest three different ways to think about how this conflict might be addressed: exit, wait and see, and reframe.

Exit makes the assumption that indigenous communities will in fact achieve something like full autonomy and no longer engage in the national debate on women's rights or liberal democratic governance. This is not likely to happen, if only because rural-urban migration and ever closer economic, social, and political interaction between indigenous communities and the wider society will continue to draw indigenous peoples into contact with the white/mestizo world. But if it were to take place, the conflict between indigeneity and liberalism would be moot, and gender relations would be resolved on indigenous terms by indigenous communities themselves. From a feminist standpoint, there would likely be serious costs to indigenous women and, for the society as a whole, there would be a loss of diversity and opportunities for dialogue between white/mestizo and indigenous societies.

The fact that indigenous societies have begun to receive the benefits of both recognition and redistribution makes full exit unlikely. Yet partial autonomy for indigenous communities is widely accepted in practice and, when there are conflicts between autonomy and women's human rights, few states are willing to impose those rights in the face of cultural resistance. In addition, the more autonomy is seen by both indigenous and white/mestizo society as meeting indigenous demands, the easier it is for both sides to avoid dialogue. The trajectory of indigenous identity politics, with its emphasis on separating from the colonial center rather than changing it, creates incentives for powerful domestic and international groups to insist on an indigenous other who performs difference in ways that fit elite agendas, rather than making space for indigenous interests in all their complexity.[17]

A second approach is to *wait*. As contacts between indigenous communities and the wider society increase, both conflict and value change are inevitable. Today, indigenous identity politics is seen as an attempt to preserve traditional cultural practices. But in the longer run, indigenous identity politics may turn out to be more dialogic than confrontational, leading to a process of indigenous accommodation if not assimilation. Markets, migration, communications technologies—and even indigenous activism—will hasten these changes while the indigenous demand for control over indigenous lands will evolve under the pressure of competing forces. The issue to be decided will not be whether development will take place, but rather at what pace, under what conditions, and with what share of the profits going to the indigenous communities themselves. The wait and see approach does not directly challenge the discriminatory treatment of women; at best, it assumes that increasing female education and mobility will bring about pressures for change from within. In a climate of increasing attacks on liberal democratic values on a global scale, however, a weakness of wait and see is its failure to defend liberal values.

A third approach is to *reframe* the issue. The very real conflicts between indigenous and liberal feminist values cannot be resolved directly while wait and see too easily avoids confronting not only gender discrimination but the broader issue of racism and the negative effects of both on the quality of democracy. I suggest two proactive strategies that might shift the debate onto more productive terrain.

The first, in the spirit of Emile Durkheim, involves changing attitudes and behavior. It is now a commonplace that identity politics are about recognition in contrast to the class politics of redistribution. But not all ethnic politics are the same. Indigenous identity politics in Latin America are following a trajectory that is quite different from that followed by the black power movement in the United States. For US blacks, identity politics produced not only cultural recognition but also respect for African Americans as individuals and legitimized their claims to full participation in US politics and society. Black identity politics has not resolved problems of redistribution; African Americans still have lower incomes, lower life expectancies, poorer housing and medical care, and less access to good public education than the US average. Blacks have much higher incarceration rates and police brutality remains a serious problem. But the civil rights movement did address discrimination, not only as a structural issue (employment, Jim Crow laws, school segregation, affirmative action), but as a set of discriminatory practices carried out in face-to-face interactions on the street, in offices, in educational institutions, and in public and private venues of all types.

In Latin America, race and class are typically discussed in the abstract, and structural solutions are debated. But the power of identity politics is its potential to force changes in the micropractices of discrimination, the combined oppressions of racism and classism that indigenous people suffer daily in their contacts with the white/mestizo world. Carlos de la Torre captures a sense of this in his explanation for the repeated emergence of populist governments in Latin America:

> [The] socioeconomic distinctions between a few citizens, who not only enjoy all the privileges of living under a state of law but who can be above the law, and the majority, who are excluded from the benefits of their rights, explain the appeal of populist politicians. Like other politicians, populists have built political machines that exchange votes for goods and services. But, in addition to what other political parties have offered, *populist politicians have given back dignity and self-worth to those who are constantly discriminated against in their daily lives.* (2000: 142, emphasis added)

Until recently, indigenous rights have largely been demanded for, not by, the indigenous. There is no cultural equivalent of an Alex Haley, whose *Roots,* a best-selling book and popular TV miniseries about an African American's search for his African origins, helped reframe Negroes as African Americans. Many whites came to understand and empathize with the experience of being black from the inside out, as opposed to gaining an intellectual understanding from the outside in, as was true of the classic but emotionally distant treatment of US racism in Gunnar Myrdal's *An American Dilemma* (1944). Nor has an indigenous equivalent of a Martin Luther King emerged to articulate a compelling vision of citizenship that applies to all. It is true that these changes in the United States have not been enough to create full equality; the struggle continues. But they did give black culture, African American demands for access to education and jobs, and African Americans' insistence on being treated with respect a front and center role in US politics that contrasts dramatically with the trajectory of indigenous identity politics.[18] Race in Latin America has a different history and requires different tools of analysis.[19] But in the end, what has to change is the ways in which the individuals in dominant groups engage in micropolitics that enforce, on a day-to-day basis, the race and class hierarchies that mark so many aspects of Latin American life.

The second strategy takes the Weberian view that the quality of democracy depends on institutions as well as attitudes and behavior. It is not accidental that de la Torre begins his account of the effects of discrimination by referring to the rule of law. Of course, the term *rule of law* has become a cliché, and it may seem simplistic to invoke Western law as if it were self-evident when indigenous communities are demanding to be allowed to govern themselves according to their own traditions. Speed's (2008) position is part of a broader critique that sees Western law as part of the problem, a symptom of the ways in which liberalism takes illiberal forms in countries with different histories and cultures.[20] Of illiberal liberalisms, however, the distortion of law to serve the interests of the powerful and keep the poor (often identified by racial markers) in their place is surely one of the most perverse.

Indigenous Latin Americans are not alone in suffering the consequences of legal systems that fail to deliver justice. As Gary Haugen and Victor Boutros suggest in their article on the relevance of legal remedies to problems of poverty and marginalization, the international struggle for human rights has changed norms and legislation, but it has not changed the way legal systems affect the poor. For Haugen and Boutros, the struggle is not an "abstract fight over political freedoms or the prosecution of large-scale war crimes," but a matter of daily survival:

> It is the struggle to avoid extortion or abuse by local police, the struggle against being forced into slavery or having land stolen, the struggle to avoid being thrown arbitrarily into an overcrowded, disease-ridden jail with little or no prospect of a fair trial. For women and children it is the struggle not to be assaulted, raped, molested, or forced into the commercial sex trade. (2010: 51)

The issue is not the content of the laws—Latin American constitutions and legislation are often quite progressive—but the ways in which legal systems function to serve the interests of a few. Elites have little incentive to reform systems that work for them and, at the same time, provide legal cover for their privileges. It is not surprising, given how they have been treated, that indigenous groups are demanding more autonomy precisely from Western law. What is surprising is that the Latin American left and social movement activists have taken such little interest in the corrosive effects of letting constitutions represent scarcely more than good intentions and have tolerated the cynical abuse of their judicial systems.

Haugen and Boutros (2010) identify several ways in which the legal system could protect rather than repress the poor and marginalized, including "collaborative casework" linking human rights lawyers and law enforcement professionals with local officials to identify victims of abuse and prosecuting their cases in local courts. These kinds of measures would require changing the approach taken by human rights lawyers, redirecting resources in part to provide "caseworkers for the poor" and, in Latin America, to change the view, common in practice but rarely addressed, that the poor do not deserve effective legal rights. Their law-based approach goes beyond moralizing to provide concrete ways to build local capacity. Such an effort could mesh well with indigenous and other forms of activism and strengthen rather than delegitimize legal institutions, which have suffered not only from underfunding, corruption, and incompetence, but also from the failure of social movements to engage in institution building.

Real possibilities exist for constructive dialogue within a liberal frame. Donna Lee Van Cott, for example, suggests that Andean communities could serve as a model by offering

> an array of self governing practices that may prove useful in impoverished towns: collective work; incorporating local religious and cultural symbols to enhance the authority of new governance institutions; incorporating traditional methods of leader selection into formal election rituals; and providing mechanisms for community leaders to exercise 'social control' over elected authorities. (2008: 235)

Nor should it be assumed that indigenous groups reject Western law in its entirety. In a provocative study of highland Bolivia, Mark Goodale (2009) shows how indigenous Bolivians have used Bolivian law for centuries to negotiate their relations with white/mestizo society. Perhaps surprisingly, he found that women were the plaintiffs in more than 50 percent of the cases brought to the court he studied in northern Potosí (104).[21] At the international level, indigenous movements have called for dialogue. For example, in 2007 the Indigenous Caucus proposed that governments should consider "integrating traditional systems of justice into national legislations in conformity with international human rights law and international standards of justice."[22]

History has shown the immense capacity of liberalism to absorb new groups and ideas while preserving human rights and individual freedoms and strengthening the rule of law. In the end, as Goodale (2009) argues, liberalism is not going away. All counterliberal ideologies are in the shadow of liberalism; they are about the failure of liberalism to live up to its ideals. The conflict between women's rights and indigenous rights suggests the urgent need to think through how to strengthen effective democracy and build the institutions needed to further social justice.

Notes

This chapter draws on my contribution in *Sentido de pertenencia en sociedades fragmentadas: América Latina en una perspectiva global,* edited by Ana Soja and Martín Hopenhayn (Buenos Aires: Siglo XXI, 2011). I am grateful for constructive criticism from Sandra Harding, Jane Bayes, Ann Tickner, Breny Mendoza, Sarah Jaquette Ray, Abe Lowenthal, and the editors of this volume. I have thought deeply about their diverse concerns and have taken them into account. The biases and errors that remain are mine.

1. Western political theory has not always been egalitarian. As Saxonhouse notes, preliberal Western political theory did not see (male or female) individuals as equal, but put the emphasis "on complementarity, on differences, on the parts from which the whole is constructed" (1985: 9). The individual is not conceived of as autonomous; consequently, "the ancients had no conception of human rights as we understand them" (7).

2. This provision caused four developed countries with large indigenous populations (the United States, New Zealand, Australia, and Canada) to vote against the declaration on the grounds that it challenged existing property rights, but all have now endorsed it, including the United States, which in 2010 became the last country to do so.

3. Goodale points out that there is a pragmatic reason why women's land is taken over by the males in the family: if women retained their rights in absentia (having moved to the village of their husband), subsistence would be threatened. "In relation to landholding, women *must* be unequal to men . . . , not because this is compelled by local or moral discourse, but because a pragmatic inequality is necessary for sheer survival." He suggests that Westerners often think of indigenous or traditional values as rigid but, to Bolivia's rural population, the modern discourse of human rights, and particularly of gender rights, presents itself as "unyielding sources of normative knowledge that admit of no exception or nuance" (2009: 98–99).

4. For a more detailed understanding of food and gender in indigenous Andean communities, see Weismantel (1998).

5. For an earlier version of how women's roles may change, but their status does not, see also Bourque and Warren (1981).

6. In November 2014, women from San Juan Sacatepéquez in Guatemala marched in Guatemala City against the "occupation" of their city by police and military forces under a government-ordered "state of prevention," including "68 accusations of sexual harassment against women and young girls" (Abbott 2014). The state

of prevention was ordered to quell resistance to the construction of a cement factory by a Guatemalan company, Progreso Cement.

7. Corrales (2013a) has written about the political dynamics of constitutional change, particularly in the "radical populist democracies." His work also focuses on LGBT politics in Latin America, another set of rights in conflict with traditional *usos y costumbres*. See Corrales (2010a).

8. Also maternal and child health programs, which have in some cases made indigenous women the objects of "population control" measures; see Boesten (2010). Health practitioners may, consciously or not, reinforce class and ethnic patterns of dominance.

9. This argument is also made by Boserup (1970), who argues that women's status depended on their role in production and that many African groups had "female farming systems" that were undermined by modernization.

10. This intent is clearly reflected in Walsh's (2010: 78) choice of a quote from Franz Fanon to begin her essay on "decolonial thought": "Let's go, comrades, the European game is definitely finished, it is necessary to find something else."

11. This is a reference to the role an indigenous leader is expected to adopt, to *mandar obedendecio* (lead by following), a cultural expectation that is present in the Andes as well as Mesoamerica that community leaders can be made accountable through social control. This custom has been used to distinguish the leadership style of Evo Morales in Bolivia from that of Hugo Chávez in Venezuela or Rafael Correa in Ecuador.

12. See also de la Cadena (2015).

13. There has been an intense debate about whether efforts in Bolivia in the 1990s to integrate indigenous communities through a multicultural constitution and the Law of Popular Participation should be dismissed as co-optation, or neoliberal multiculturalism. The water and gas wars in Bolivia and the election of Morales suggest that indigenous groups instead took it as an invitation to activism. See Postero (2007).

14. For a decolonial critique of this position, see several of the essays in Mendoza (2014a, 2014b).

15. A similar debate about the difference between "power to" and "power over" has played an important role in feminist theory. See, for example, Hartsock (1983) and a critical discussion by Mansbridge (1996). Some feminists share Speed's (2008) ultimately utopian desire to find a form of power without violence or coercion. But social control (which in indigenous communities can involve the use of stocks and shunning) is certainly coercive. It may be that modern states can and should allow, and even learn from, indigenous concepts of justice; it is not necessary to portray them as utopian.

16. Critics too easily conflate liberalism with neoliberalism (a move that depends in part on the fact that liberalism in the United States is closer to social democracy than to classical liberalism). Over time, liberal practice and theory have increasingly recognized that economic and social preconditions are necessary to the exercise of political rights and to make life choices (see, for example, Nussbaum 1999). Liberal feminists are not Marxists; they do not reject capitalism out of hand. Nor are they marketeers because they know full well that women's lives and values are not limited to or measured by the market. Rather, they recognize the role of the state in limiting markets, and see the quality of democracy resting on strengthening liberal democratic institutions (checks and balances, freedom of the press, human rights, and the rule of law) rather than seeking their transcendence.

17. For a discussion of this phenomenon with regard to how Native Americans

become the "ecological other," precisely because they are expected to be "ecological Indians," as Krech (2000) argues, see Ray (2013: chapter 2).

18. The important contrast may be in terms of race (Afro-descendant vs. indigenous), not between the treatment of race in North America versus Latin America. The autonomy of reservations has also further marginalized Native Americans, whose use of territorial sovereignty to establish casinos has failed to provide a space where traditional practices can be reinforced or to make a dent in high levels of alcoholism and violence against women. An interesting window into some of the differences between black and indigenous strategies and their effects could be gained by comparing de Jesus's diary, *Child of the Dark* (1963) with Menchú's *I, Rigoberta Menchú* (1984), the debates over their authenticity, and the reasons why these books appealed to elites.

19. See Wade (2010).

20. The argument is that liberalism has become exhausted as a normative anchor for the region. As J. Franco writes, reviewing Ileana Rodríguez's book, *The Limits of Liberalism,* "Incongruous fantasies of liberalism (democracy, justice, and the common good), when transferred to cultures with different historical development, produce illiberal forms of liberalism" (2009). I would argue that lack of political will is the most important factor; it is not culture or history, but class and race interests that perpetuate illiberal uses of liberal institutions. My point here is that we need to distinguish problems that arise from the lack of fidelity to liberal principles from those that arise from cultural inappropriateness, which I see as a dynamic, not a static, arena of contestation and negotiation.

21. Goodale (2009) asks us to consider, however, what an indigenous woman must feel when she comes to the office of the mestizo judge and finds the walls covered with pornographic calendars, a racialized and sexualized exercise of male power.

22. From the Statement of the Indigenous Caucus, September 2007, and the Declaration of the Rights of Indigenous Peoples, available at www.iwgia.org/sw248 .asp. Arguments for moving away from universal conceptions of rights based on the individual to the concept of multicultural or group rights have been made by others. See Ivison, Patton, and Sanders (2000). The argument that the practices of indigenous and other groups claiming collective rights may be patriarchal and gender discriminatory can be found in Deveaux (2006) and Okin (1999).

11

Indigenous Peoples and Dilemmas of Electoral Participation

Neil Harvey

Since the late 1970s, Latin America has undergone significant political and economic change. The decline of authoritarian regimes and the shift to neoliberal policies have created contradictions for democratic participation. On the one hand, it can be argued that citizens have more opportunities to choose representatives and participate in competitive elections. On the other, the impact of economic restructuring has widened the income gap and raised questions over the supposed benefits of the political transitions. At the same time, accountability and human rights protections remain weak, particularly for poorer sectors of the population. As a result, the unevenness of democracy in the region continues to generate debate over the steps needed to improve its quality and reach.

In this regard, the position of indigenous peoples is particularly noteworthy. Until the 1980s, for the most part, indigenous peoples were not seen as politically significant actors in their own right. Theories of modernization tended to guide state policies that generally ignored the relevance of ethnic identities and sought to create a homogenous national identity through various strategies of assimilation. Similarly, most of the left saw revolution in terms of an urban educated leadership providing a unified vision and organization for socialist transformation in which ethnic identities would play a subordinate role to class consciousness.

Contrary to each of these assumptions, indigenous organizations became some of the most combative social movements in the 1980s and 1990s, leading to a series of institutional reforms that establish (at least on paper) the recognition of the multicultural nature of Latin American nations. At the same time, the end of the Cold War and the decline of leftist parties revealed a deep crisis within socialist thought and practice. In the face of globalization and the opening of markets for resource extraction, indigenous peoples have developed their own strategies of resistance, frequently occupying the space of anticapitalist alternatives that had been the sole preserve of the political left.

Scholars have tried to understand the significance of indigenous struggles by focusing on their emergence and impact, with comparatively less attention paid to internal practices. In this chapter, I examine different explanations for the rise and performance of indigenous organizations, ethnic political parties, and community-based autonomy movements. Due to the variety of strategies adopted by indigenous peoples, it is difficult to compare their degrees of success since each may have different objectives and priorities. For example, success can be measured in terms of local or national electoral performance, the achievement of constitutional reforms, or the creation of autonomous forms of government outside the formal political arena. Each of these strategies constitutes a different form of political participation and contributes in a different way to the quality of democracy that concerns indigenous and nonindigenous peoples alike. For this reason, it is important to understand the different contexts in which such struggles take place and how they are able to persist over time. While comparative analysis of movement emergence and impact is important, I argue that we need to give more attention to the internal practices that sustain or erode ethnic parties and indigenous organizations.

Attention to internal practices requires a closer analysis of the gradual construction of a political identity, the priority given to broad participation, and the willingness to address limitations and obstacles. In other words, I argue that participants have greater control over the internal life of their movement than they do over the wider political context with which they interact. For indigenous peoples, the practices they seek to uphold are often rooted in different conceptions of community governance that emphasize balance and consensus rather than individual competition and dissent. This is not always the case and anthropological literature has shown how rivalry and factionalism are also present in many indigenous communities. Particular practices do not spring automatically from assumed cultural differences, but require attention to the processes by which they are established, negotiated, and revised.

This chapter is structured in the following way. First, I briefly examine the emergence of indigenous movements in the 1980s and 1990s by highlighting their resistance to neoliberalism and their rejection of manipulative practices of traditional political parties. Next, I discuss different degrees of success of indigenous parties in the region, specifically in Bolivia and Ecuador. Following Raúl Madrid (2012), I highlight the importance of ethnopopulist appeals in explaining national-level impacts, in conjunction with institutional reforms, changes in the party systems, and social movement dynamics. Then, I turn to alternatives to electoral participation presented by indigenous autonomy, specifically the Zapatistas' efforts to build their own forms of local government in Chiapas, Mexico. To conclude, I summarize the main dilemmas of electoral participation and autonomy while noting the importance of learning from indigenous peoples and their conceptions of democracy.

Emergence of Indigenous Movements and Ethnic Parties

The limited appeal of traditional parties among indigenous people is not surprising if we consider the long history of discrimination in Latin America and the association of parties with urban-based nonindigenous elites. The recent struggles and demands of indigenous organizations and parties are not reducible to demands over land or linguistic diversity, but part of a deeper problem with the fact that, ever since the Conquest, indigenous peoples have been assigned to the lowest social position and denied the right to decide on their own forms of development. Indigeneity is therefore not simply a neutral fact of cultural difference, but a contested identity that modern forms of power have tried to represent as an obstacle or threat to modernity and progress (Wade 2010). Similarly, leftist parties were often accused of relying on an urban-based university-educated leadership that enforced strict adherence to party agendas, without allowing for debate or alternative proposals. In his study of relationships between the left and social movements in Chile and Peru, Kenneth M. Roberts (1998), for example, found that such relationships approximated the electoralist model or vanguard model. However, the rise of social movement activism in the 1980s and 1990s coincided with the decline of traditional left parties and opened up the potential for new organic party-movement relationships with stronger roots in community life (Van Cott 2005: 39).

This emergence of indigenous movements in the 1980s combined resistance to the loss of land to colonization, ranching, logging, mining, and oil exploration, with the affirmation of diverse cultural identities. To explain this emergence, Deborah Yashar (2005) emphasizes three broad factors: resistance to neoliberalism, the strength of transcommunity networks of affiliate groups, and the opening of new spaces for political mobilization. When these conditions were present, indigenous peoples organized to defend various degrees of autonomy with regard to landholding and community governance.

It is no coincidence therefore that the emergence of large and well-organized movements in Bolivia, Ecuador, and Mexico all cited neoliberalism as the main threat to indigenous peoples' livelihoods (Wade 2010: 114). For example, the Zapatistas' armed rebellion in Chiapas on January 1, 1994, was timed to coincide with the start of the North American Free Trade Agreement (NAFTA), which was seen as a framework to facilitate corporate exploitation of Mexico's resources and the concentration of land in private hands.

Dramatic events such as the March for Territory and Dignity by lowland indigenous communities in Bolivia in 1990, the simultaneous struggles of *cocalero* (coca grower) unions in Cochabamba against the government's eradication policies, and the Zapatista rebellion in Chiapas in 1994 all seemed to spell the end of politics as usual. In each case, traditional parties suffered from their declining ability to rule through clientelism and selective repression, and the opportunity seemed ripe for new parties and practices to emerge. This was particularly promising for indigenous movements that were not associated with electoralist or vanguardist parties and, therefore, could present themselves as cleaner and more genuinely in tune with popular aspirations. This was evident in the way that the Zapatistas were almost immediately welcomed by large sectors of Mexican civil society for whom the ruling PRI (Institutional Revolutionary Party) was no more than an authoritarian relic that had retained power in 1988 through widespread electoral fraud. Although most Mexicans disapproved of the use of arms, they openly sympathized with the Zapatistas and sought ways to provide solidarity in the face of the government's counterinsurgency efforts. Similarly, in Ecuador, the National Confederation of Indigenous Nationalities of Ecuador (CONAIE) mobilized thousands of supporters on several occasions between 1990 and 1994, blocking roads and causing economic disruptions that forced the government to back down on its plans to pass legislation to privatize communally held lands.

Indigenous movements could also count on a broadly favorable international context for advancing their demands. The massacre of thousands of Mayan indigenous people by the Guatemalan military in its counterinsurgency operations in the early 1980s spurred international attention to the lack of protection of minority rights (even if in this case, the Maya constitute a numerical majority). During the 1980s the International Labour Organization revised its formerly assimilationist Convention 169 on Indigenous Rights, culminating in the adoption in 1989 of a new version that favors stronger rights to indigenous autonomy within the context of existing nation-states. At a symbolic level, indigenous movements were able to gain global visibility through their region-wide campaigns to mark 500 years of resistance to conquest in 1992. In the same year the Nobel Peace Prize was awarded to Guatemalan Mayan activist Rigoberta Menchú, and in 1995 the first UN Decade for Indigenous Peoples was announced.

Despite this favorable attention and new international conjuncture, the impact of indigenous movements within different Latin American countries varied and depended on political environments that went beyond the control of any single organization. Donna Lee Van Cott (2001) compared the relative success of indigenous movements with regard to achieving constitutional reform. First, she noted how the opportunities provided in some countries by the election of Constituent Assemblies were unique and particularly conducive since indigenous organizations could lobby and participate in the drafting of new constitutions. Second, where movements were relatively unified and able to agree on a list of demands, the chances for success were great. Finally, reforms were more likely when organizations had firm allies within Constituent Assemblies. Van Cott added that these conditions existed in Colombia in 1991 and Ecuador in 1998, resulting in more responsive and inclusive national constitutions. In contrast, the Zapatista movement and its allies in civil society were less able to shape constitutional reform in Mexico. Despite negotiating a set of reforms with government representatives in 1996 (known as the San Andrés Accords on Indigenous Rights and Cultures, after the town where they were signed), the government failed to implement the accords and a watered-down version was passed in 2001, not only by the PRI and the conservative PAN (National Action Party) but also by the senators representing the center-left Party of the Democratic Revolution (PRD). The political and economic crisis in Mexico in 1994–1995 did not lead to the creation of a new Constituent Assembly. Instead, the main political parties negotiated new electoral rules that provided for a greater degree of alternation in power, leading to the loss of the presidency by the PRI in 2000, but tended to ignore the need for a new relationship between the state and indigenous peoples. Significantly, the Zapatistas pursued a more autonomous political strategy, distancing themselves from all parties, including the PRD and its presidential candidate Andrés Manuel López Obrador in 2006.

In sum, indigenous organizations made important political advances during the 1980s and 1990s in Latin America. They became political actors in their own right, articulating cultural as well as economic demands, including collective rights to land, bilingual education, and recognition of community governance structures. Their mobilization occurred at a time of deep economic crisis and the decline of traditional parties. Initially, indigenous movements preferred to keep their distance from electoral politics but, due to changing circumstances discussed below, in some cases they made the strategic decision to form ethnic parties. In doing so, they could draw on a prior history of organization that had developed deep roots in communities and regions and, in this regard, offered an opportunity to create more organic types of political parties than the electoralist or vanguard models that have often dominated in Latin America.

Dilemmas of Electoral Participation

Several scholars have noted that electoral competition can bring positive and negative effects for indigenous communities. On the positive side, it is argued that parties, particularly if they are rooted in community-led organizations, can be a vehicle to bring about policy changes and ensure that reforms are protected and implemented. On the other hand, as multicultural-ism becomes increasingly part of the mainstream agenda, parties seeking to garner indigenous votes may compete for allegiance of different leaders or groups, contributing to factionalism and internal divisions that may under-mine the strength of the grassroots organization. Van Cott (2005) also notes how, for example, the demands placed on party members to make decisions that may advance their negotiating position in local or national assemblies may often avoid the longer process of consensus building characteristic of many indigenous communities. Similarly, participation in political parties tends to favor younger community members who have some formal educa-tion and networks of support in urban areas or even internationally. In this way, decisionmaking authority is removed from village-level assemblies and traditional elders and placed in the hands of a new generation of leaders that may become detached from the day-to-day concerns of their home communities. While the outcome of such participation is not inevitable, the tensions it raises are very real and mean that community ambivalence about modern electoral democracy should not be taken as a sign of antidemocratic traditionalism, but instead as a call to consider the value of alternative forms of political participation.

Yashar (2005: 300–306) is also aware of some of the potential pitfalls of electoral participation. Drawing on her comparative case studies of six Latin American countries, she notes that indigenous movements can lose their most experienced leadership to parties and government posts. A related problem is that, once in government, indigenous leaders may be sidelined by more established political parties and coalitions, finding themselves with fewer allies and forced to participate in patronage politics to achieve some minimal gains. In Ecuador, indigenous representatives lost support from their core group of supporters in CONAIE precisely because of the per-ceived repetition of patronage politics (Yashar 2005: 304).

Despite these pitfalls, many indigenous organizations have continued to participate in the electoral arena. Their goal, according to Yashar (2005), is to press for three major changes that, taken together, comprise a postliberal challenge: (1) recognition of a diverse citizenry instead of assuming nation-al homogeneity; (2) advancing multiple modes of interest representation; and (3) devolution of power and resources to autonomous structures of indigenous government. In the struggle for such reforms, Yashar argues that it was not clear that refusing to participate in elections would have better results (307). While some indigenous movements preferred to continue organizing outside the electoral system, others opted to participate in and even create new political parties with the goal of ensuring that the new mul-ticultural reforms would effectively be put into practice.

In one of the pioneering studies of new ethnic parties, Van Cott (2005) draws attention to three sets of variables that, in various combinations, could explain the emergence of ethnic parties in Latin America. These are institutional reforms that made it easier for new parties, including those rooted in indigenous organizations, to gain registration and compete in local and national elections. Emergence was also enabled by changes in party systems, including the dealignment of voters from traditional parties, particularly those on the left. Finally, Van Cott notes how the strength and maturity of indigenous organizations contributed to the creation of viable ethnic parties. This latter factor is significant because it underscores the rootedness of the new parties in the communities and organizations that preceded them and that seek to monitor the actions of their candidates and elected representatives. As I have noted, such rootedness contrasts with the clientelistic forms of control exercised by traditional parties.

Van Cott highlights some key aspects of institutional reform that have been significant for the emergence of ethnic parties, including decentralization, improved access to the ballot, and (in Colombia and Venezuela) reserved seats for indigenous peoples. Decentralization measures do not always encourage ethnic party formation, but they were particularly important in Bolivia where the 1994 Law on Popular Participation established the first nationwide elections for new municipal districts, which were held in 1995. Participants from each of the three major indigenous organizations decided to form a political party to compete in the municipal elections. At the same time, electoral reforms established single-member districts for half of the 130 seats in the Chamber of Deputies, which opened up the possibility that an ethnic party could win in those districts where indigenous people were a substantial majority. The new party, known as the Assembly for the Sovereignty of the Peoples (ASP), had strong backing from the powerful *cocalero* unions, which argued for a more inclusive strategy that won support from Aymara organizations in the western highlands and indigenous groups in the more sparsely populated eastern lowlands and after 2000 also appealed to the nonindigenous poor and middle-class groups in urban areas (Madrid 2012: 53–62).

The ASP therefore gained strength in local elections, but was able to grow and gain support outside of its core area. This was vital to its ability to compete at the national level and, using the registration of the Movimiento al Socialismo (MAS), led to a strong performance in the 2002 general elections. In that year, Evo Morales, a former *cocalero* union leader, came a close second in the presidential race while MAS gained 20.9 percent of the vote and became the largest opposition party in Congress. MAS continued to gain strength, with Morales winning the presidency in 2005 with 53.7 percent of the vote (the largest since Bolivia's return to democracy), and

MAS winning a majority of seats in the lower house. This allowed Morales to call for a Constituent Assembly and the writing of a new constitution, which was approved by 62 percent of the population in a national referendum in early 2009. Morales was reelected at the end of that year with 64.2 percent of the vote and MAS won 88 of 130 seats in the Chamber of Deputies and 26 of 36 Senate seats. A similar result was achieved in 2014, with Morales winning just over 61 percent of the vote, and MAS retaining eighty-eight seats in the lower house and twenty-five seats in the Senate.

Access to the ballot is also conducive for new party formation. This was evident in Ecuador in 1994 when, just as the national indigenous movement was reaching its peak, institutional reforms were passed that included removing a provision that parties had to register members in ten provinces and run candidates in twelve provinces to participate in national elections. In addition, the 1994 reforms allowed for the registration of independent candidates and organizations, removing the need to rely on the traditional political parties to gain office. With these changes, the CONAIE found that it was possible and attractive to form its own party, the Pachakutik Movement of Plurinational Unity (MUPP, or Pachakutik), to compete in the 1996 elections. Ecuador's electoral system already included single-member districts, so it was possible for indigenous candidates to win in heavily indigenous provinces and municipalities once the 1994 reforms removed the earlier requirements for broader national presence.

Similarly to the ASP and MAS in Bolivia, the MUPP emerged in alliance with nonindigenous sectors, including labor unions, urban social movements, and members of leftist parties that began to see the new ethnic parties as the strongest political expression of antineoliberalism. In short, the electorally successful ethnic parties were not exclusionary. On the contrary, they were born in broader opposition struggles against highly unpopular governments and led to impressive gains. In 1996 MUPP participated in national elections for the first time, in alliance with Nuevo País (NP), a coalition of labor and social movements that had mobilized alongside CONAIE in the antineoliberal protests of 1994–1995. The MUPP-NP presidential candidate finished third with 20.6 percent of the vote while the alliance won eight seats in the eighty-two-seat National Congress, becoming the fourth-largest bloc in the legislature. The MUPP-NP also won seven of every ten local election races that it entered, and ran candidates in thirteen of the country's twenty-one provinces. Most analysts saw this as a successful first election and demonstrated the value of the organic links that had been built between movement and party. CONAIE and Pachakutik continued to play a central role in national politics, organizing demonstrations that led to the ouster of President Abdalá Bucaram in 1997 and the election of a Constituent Assembly. Pachakutik was the third-largest force in this assembly and used its position to make alliances and gain support for indigenous rights, including ratification of ILO Convention 169 (Van Cott 2005: 125).

In both Ecuador and Bolivia, the emergence of ethnic parties was facilitated by institutional reforms and the crisis of traditional parties that were blamed for economic austerity and the negative impacts of neoliberal reforms. However, as Madrid (2012) argues, the electoral performance of ethnic parties is best explained by the type of appeals they make rather than institutional factors. He notes, for example, how some ethnic parties failed to increase their share of the vote, despite having the same opportunities to do so. This was due to their more exclusionary ethnonationalist discourse, which has alienated most nonindigenous voters as well as many indigenous voters. In Latin America, although discrimination still exists, ethnic boundaries have generally been blurred by centuries of *mestizaje* (racial mixing). This allows us to understand how urban-based mestizos may vote for candidates of ethnic parties, if the latter adopt a more inclusive strategy and discourse. While ethnonationalist parties may appeal to a locally strong sentiment, they have not performed well outside their core areas. For example, the Movimiento Indígena Pachakuti (MIP) in Bolivia has a strong Aymara nationalist platform. Its share of the national vote peaked at 6.1 percent in 2002, but declined afterward to 2 percent in 2005, and the party has since disappeared (Madrid 2012: 42).

Ethnic parties in Latin America have also tended to do better when they could rely on networks of indigenous organizations. This was vital to the MAS's success and provides a contrast with parties that have either lost their earlier grassroots support (e.g., the traditional parties that backed neoliberal austerity policies), or new populist parties that depend on the charismatic appeal of leaders who fail to build strong organizational ties to existing organizations. In the case of the MAS, the mostly Quechua-speaking members of the *cocalero* unions of Cochabamba became the strongest and most active organization in Bolivia in the early 1990s, managing to gain control of the older Confederación Sindical Única de Trabajadores Campesinos de Bolivia (CSUTCB) that had traditionally been dominated by Aymara leaders. However, the *cocalero* leaders were successful in reaching out to many Aymara and other indigenous organizations, including the national Women's Peasant Confederation, and helped create a new network of support for the MAS as it began competing in elections. The rootedness of the MAS has distinguished it from the traditional parties in Bolivia (and, I may add, from most parties in Latin America).

By rooting itself in long-established popular movements, the MAS ensured it would gain majority support in indigenous areas. However, it has also succeeded among mestizo and middle-class voters in urban centers by making populist appeals to people disaffected by government corruption and foreign dependency. In this regard, Madrid highlights three aspects of populism: the personalistic appeal of party leaders, a strong antiestablishment discourse, and a nationalist rejection of foreign control or interventionism. In the case of the MAS, Morales was able to extend the party's appeal by presenting himself and the MAS as the opposite of the existing government: a candidate of the people, opposed to the US-backed elite and its policies favoring foreign commercial interests. The rise of the MAS is therefore the rise of a form of ethnopopulism, which, given its rootedness in society, may allow the party to persist much longer than other populist parties.

While the more inclusive nature of ethnopopulist appeals seems to explain the electoral successes of MAS and Pachakutik, it is also important to consider the practices that characterize party-movement interactions. It is this relationship that I earlier identified as significant for understanding differences between vanguard, electoralist, and organic parties. If new ethnic parties are to develop as organic parties, attention must be given not only to how well these parties do in national elections, but also to the conflicts and debates that emerge over policymaking and implementation. It is one thing for an indigenous movement to protest the failure of traditional parties to follow through on their electoral promises, but expectations are inevitably raised when one's own candidates become public officials.

The failure to meet such expectations in Ecuador led to a severe crisis for the national indigenous movement, CONAIE. Despite sharing many similarities with the early years of the MAS, such as the inclusive nature of its discourse and the alliances with many antiestablishment social movements, the Pachakutik party has had more tense relations with its indigenous support base. For example, CONAIE leaders were upset by the way that Pachakutik deputy Nica Pacari allied with parties of the governing coalition and even right-wing legislators to secure the second vice presidency of Congress in 1998. Many grassroots activists felt that their newly elected representatives did not behave much differently from the traditional parties with whom they now negotiated in Congress. On the other hand, the continuing strength of CONAIE may have constrained Pachakutik legislators who felt marginalized when CONAIE sought to negotiate directly with the government. Tensions between movement and party were exacerbated in January 2000 when CONAIE participated in a popular revolt, with support from some military officers, that led to the ouster of President Jamil Mahuad. Although the revolt revealed the political influence of CONAIE, it also divided the movement since the leadership had acted without grassroots support. The movement remained divided for the next two years and, to try and maintain as much unity as possible, decided not to field a presidential candidate in the 2002 elections. Instead, CONAIE backed Lucio

Gutiérrez, candidate of Partido Sociedad Patriótica (PSP) and the PSP-Pachakutik alliance in provincial elections. The alliance strategy was successful in that Gutiérrez won the presidency and appointed several CONAIE and Pachakutik leaders to his cabinet. It seemed that the indigenous movement would now have a strong influence in policymaking; however, within a few months of the new government taking office, Gutiérrez announced austerity policies and other measures that were strongly opposed by CONAIE, leading to the resignation of some Pachakutik appointees and eventually the decision by Gutiérrez to fire the others in August 2003.

In contrast to Bolivia, participation in the electoral arena did not produce a strong, unified, and dominant ethnic party, but rather a weaker and more divided party and movement. CONAIE continued to protest against the policies of Gutiérrez, but the electoral performance of Pachakutik declined and its presidential candidate Luis Macas won just 2.2 percent of the vote in 2006. Part of the reason for this decreased share of the vote is that Pachakutik decided to field its own candidate, rejecting proposals to form an alliance with Rafael Correa, of the Alianza País, precisely because of the negative results of its previous alliance with Gutiérrez. Madrid adds that Pachakutik also shifted away from its earlier ethnopopulist appeals and adopted a more exclusive ethnocentric position that alienated its former supporters in peasant organizations and labor unions (2012: 102–103). In the 2006 election, it was Correa and Gutiérrez who positioned themselves as populist candidates that could represent the aspirations of the indigenous peoples of Ecuador. Correa made it to the runoff stage and, at that point, Pachakutik gave its endorsement to his candidacy. Correa won with 57 percent of the vote and has since consolidated his position, convening a Constituent Assembly in 2007 and gaining passage of a new constitution the following year. Correa was reelected in 2009 and again in 2013 while Pachakutik failed to stem its electoral decline, receiving less than 2 percent of the vote in the 2009 presidential elections.

Similar to the experiences noted here for Ecuador and Bolivia, most indigenous parties in Latin America do not contribute to ethnic polarization. Unlike other areas of the world, they do not threaten national unity with secessionist claims; on the contrary, they contribute to national unity by achieving, in gradual and locally contingent ways, collective rights of indigenous peoples within multicultural societies. Indigenous movements and ethnic parties have had a positive impact in increasing voter registration, increasing electoral turnout, translating materials into indigenous languages, and the running of indigenous candidates for office. More generally, they have placed indigenous demands on the political agenda, obliging almost all parties to include some of these demands in their own campaign platforms, electoral alliances, and legislative coalitions.

Indigenous movements and parties have therefore contributed to greater vertical accountability between voters and elected officials, but ethnopopulism has had more negative impacts on horizontal accountability between government institutions. Madrid (2012) notes how, in Bolivia, the Morales government has reduced the independence of the judiciary and electoral courts, concentrating power in the executive and the MAS-dominated legislature. While supporters of the MAS may defend such steps as necessary to ward off threats from traditional elites who now find themselves in the opposition, the weakening of accountability can also erode confidence in the system among all sectors, including those who had initially supported Morales.

It is important to note that concerns over the quality of democracy in Latin America have less to do with ethnic parties or indigenous movements, which in most cases enhance participation and representation of previously disenfranchised populations, but more to do with populism as a style of governance (Madrid 2012: 162–163). At a certain point, populism also weakens vertical accountability as decisionmaking becomes the preserve of a small elite group of party leaders or technocrats with close ties to the president. For indigenous peoples, this is nothing new, as the use and abuse of their lands by public and private corporations has traditionally been carried out by whichever party has been in power. However, conflicts have arisen in recent years in Bolivia, Ecuador, and Peru between governments that profess to uphold indigenous rights and ecological practices while also promoting extractivist industries in oil, natural gas, and mining. In some cases this has led to repression of indigenous protestors, while more generally revealing a deep gap between different visions of development (Achtenberg 2013; Chimienti and Matthes 2013; Renique 2013).

Dilemmas of Indigenous Autonomy

Indigenous peoples have also organized outside of the electoral arena and sought to build alternative forms of government independently of political parties. Such a strategy has arisen from indigenous efforts to go beyond petitioning the state for land rights and to view land itself as a part of the broader concept of territory. As Peter Wade argues, indigenous movements in Latin America often emphasize the importance of territory for the reproduction of a cultural way of life and the ecological conditions that permit the continuity of ethnic identities (2010: 124–126). Such struggles over the political authority to claim, recuperate, and govern indigenous territories involves the remaking of internal practices. Examples can be found among the Mapuche in southern Chile (Marimán and Aylwin 2008), the Uros people in southern Peru (Wade 2010: 124), and the indigenous peoples of the Cauca region of Colombia (Zibechi 2012: 166–169).

Here, I examine one such struggle for indigenous autonomy: the Zapatista movement in Chiapas. As noted earlier, indigenous movements in Mexico failed to win significant constitutional reforms in the 1990s, partly due to the convergence of all major parties in passing a watered-down version of the San Andrés Accords in 2001. This led the Zapatistas to focus all their efforts on defending and promoting their own de facto autonomy.

In August 2003 the Zapatistas announced the creation of five cultural and political centers, called *caracoles,* which would house the Zapatistas' new *juntas de buen gobierno* (Councils of Good Government, or JBGs) (Muñoz Ramírez 2003; Subcomandante Marcos 2003). Subcomandante Marcos explains that this new structure would allow the civilian bases of the movement to exercise authority without the interference of the military commanders of the EZLN (Zapatista Army of National Liberation), and would also promote a more equal relationship with outside solidarity groups and greater inclusion of more distant Zapatista communities within Chiapas. One of the challenges that the new JBGs have had to confront is how to ensure that the social and economic projects of solidarity groups reach the more remote communities and do not continue to disproportionately benefit those communities with easier access and longer relationships to external groups.

With regard to the practice of autonomy, several achievements and obstacles were discussed at a meeting of Zapatistas, allies, and supporters in July 2007. Almost 200 indigenous Zapatista authorities spoke at this week-long gathering. Although they referred to different issues and local contexts, they all noted that their autonomy is based on the existence of twenty-seven rebel municipalities, Municipios Autónomos Rebeldes Zapatistas (MAREZ). The uprising in 1994 allowed the Zapatistas to recuperate lands when the private landowners fled the conflict zone. With this territorial base, the Zapatistas were able to create new projects in the areas of health care, education, and agriculture, in which women have the right of participation and work as promoters alongside Zapatista men. It should be noted that none of the people who occupy positions of authority within the MAREZ receive a salary, and they can be removed through decisions made by community assemblies.

Collective production projects make up a central pillar of Zapatista autonomy. These projects are carried out on the lands recuperated after the uprising and include a wide variety of products and services. Gains from these projects are used to cover the expenses of the health and education promoters. For example, in the Caracol of La Realidad in the border region, the Zapatistas created projects to produce coffee, honey, citrus fruits, vegetables, chilies, corn, beans, bread, and services such as transportation, pharmacies, and small taco stands. These projects are important for sustaining the unsalaried work of the health and education promoters. The Zapatistas have to compete with the government by providing good quality services to the local population, whether Zapatista or not. The Zapatistas reject government programs because they see them as attempts to dilute their struggle. As a result, they have sought support from solidarity groups while also training their own members in different areas.

Deficiencies in health and education had long been a problem that indigenous organizations denounced before 1994. Following the uprising, the Zapatista communities selected and trained their own promoters in these areas with the goal of providing better services that take into account the particular histories, cultures, and languages of the communities themselves. For example, some communities are recuperating practices of traditional healing to make use of local medicinal plants and, in this way, support the work of midwives, bonesetters, and herbalists (Forbis 2011). In the autonomous municipalities, teachers come from the same communities rather than from the cities and share the same economic conditions and cultural practices as the families of their students. For example, Bruno Baronnet (2011) shows how communities, through their assemblies, support and assess the work of those who carry out the tasks of an education promoter. This relationship is different from the practice of teachers employed by the federal government who assume the power to decide the content of the curriculum in a way that excludes the community and the recognition of its own needs.

Although the Zapatistas have achieved some advances in building autonomy, the question of sustainability remains an important one. On the one hand, the creation of new spaces for autonomous government is seen as a positive change by Zapatista supporters because the relationship between the community members and their authorities is a more horizontal one. They tend to share the same economic conditions, speak the same language, and have participated together in the same political struggles. Although the Zapatista authorities do not have all the resources they need to resolve the problems presented to them, in comparison to the authorities of official municipalities and government teachers they at least are seen as accessible and respectful of those who seek their support (Van der Haar 2001: 233; Baronnet 2011: 209–211). The new autonomous institutions have also, in several cases, gained greater legitimacy than the official system of government. In many instances, even those community members who are not affiliated with the Zapatistas turn to the autonomous authorities to resolve conflicts. This is due to various factors such as the fact that the Zapatistas do not charge for their services and they are not corrupt, they speak the same language, and they use restorative rather than punitive forms of justice (Stahler-Sholk 2011: 443).

The Zapatistas are constantly dealing with new challenges and, in the process, seeking solutions that help sustain autonomy. For example, the collective production projects allow them to generate some savings for investment in education and health programs. They also charge outside contractors a fee of 10 percent on the value of their projects if they are to be implemented in areas with a Zapatista presence. Since 2010 the Zapatistas have also operated their own banking system, which allows members to request loans with a 2 percent interest rate to cover emergency expenses that are often related to serious health problems. The *bancos zapatistas* also allow for some funds to be invested in new collective projects to create options for youth and women. Another approach has been to reallocate funds with the autonomous municipalities. For example, in the Caracol of La Realidad, some of the resources that were not being used by a Zapatista hospital in the area were reallocated for the repair of a warehouse that the government had left abandoned (EZLN 2013a: 13).

Even when the community finds a way to support the young unmarried men who are carrying out some task on its behalf, it is more difficult for women with children to fulfill the same roles due to the household division of labor. Gender equality continues to be an ideal that is expressed in political declarations such as the Revolutionary Women's Law of 1993. For example, the fourth point in the law states that "women have the right to participate in the affairs of the community and occupy positions if they are elected freely and democratically" (EZLN 2013b: 26).

In each of the *caracoles*, the number of women participating in the Councils of Good Government has been increasing since 2003. However, it is often more difficult for women to carry out their duties as members of the JBGs (Zylberberg Panebianco 2006). This is due to several factors, including *machista* attitudes of some spouses and fathers, lack of support in the home and in looking after children, fear of making mistakes, low levels of literacy in Spanish, and lack of other skills. As a result, there are situations in which women formally occupy the same number of positions as men but, in practice, they are unable to have the same influence in how different tasks are carried out and they begin to reduce their level of participation. According to a former member of the JBG in La Realidad, it is difficult for a woman to take on responsibilities at the municipal or regional level if they have never had a position within their community (EZLN 2013b: 7).

The Zapatistas have adopted different strategies to try to deal with this problem, including efforts to show the importance of family planning and the need for men to give support at home and in caring for children as well as encouraging women to participate so that, once they are integrated into community work, they will begin to see that they can indeed resolve problems and continue to learn.

It should be noted that many men stop participating when the workload gets too heavy. Besides promoting women's participation, some Zapatista municipalities have seen the need to reduce the duration of the time that they spend as authorities, which also allows for more individuals to participate and gain experience. However, some women complain that the time may be too short and this prevents them from really learning how to govern and, therefore, from advancing as much as they would like (EZLN 2013a: 70–71).

The Zapatistas also argue that the obstacles to women's participation are rooted not so much in indigenous cultures but in the consequences of colonialism and capitalism, particularly the ways of their former employers on private coffee plantations. By situating gender inequality in a broader critique of patriarchy and class exploitation, the Zapatistas seek to counter the argument that women's rights and indigenous cultures are inevitably incompatible. Approaching the issue in this way allows for men and women to work together in changing different practices of oppression and discrimination in all areas of society, including their own homes and communities.

The Zapatistas have had to learn as they go, without a manual or guide. Although this lack of a clear model makes the construction of autonomy a difficult task, it has the advantage of being something that they assume as their own project, rather than an outside imposition. As autonomous governance gradually provides concrete results for community members, the Zapatistas are able to reject the offer of projects from government agencies and political party candidates. In their eyes, the government produces only division and dependency, obliging people to affiliate with a party to compete for access to the limited resources that are provided for agricultural or livestock production.

In the context of weak constitutional reforms, the impact of Zapatismo is felt more through changes within indigenous communities as well as the lessons that other indigenous peoples and social movements have taken away from Chiapas. It is the practice of autonomy that will determine the longer-term viability of the Zapatista movement. The ability of autonomous governments to offer health and education services, resolve disputes, and provide access to land of course will vary according to different local contexts. Nevertheless, for two decades now, the Zapatistas have shown that it is possible to build more accountable forms of governance independently of political parties and state institutions. This is their main contribution toward improving the quality of democracy in Latin America.

Conclusion

During the past three decades, indigenous peoples have mobilized for political change throughout Latin America. Resisting exploitation, repression, and manipulation, they have built organizations and parties that continue to demand more responsive, inclusive, and accountable democracies in the region. In doing so, they have opened new opportunities for participation, leading to higher levels of voter registration and electoral turnout. In short, the third wave of democratization in Latin America was simultaneously an indigenous wave.

Despite this heightened level of participation, whether in terms of ethnic parties or autonomy movements, their sustainability depends on the effectiveness of internal practices for addressing several dilemmas and challenges. First, indigenous organizations need to affirm greater control over how their leaders act as candidates, elected representatives, and cabinet ministers. The lack of consultation between leaders and their base in the case of Pachakutik and CONAIE led to serious divisions that weakened the grassroots movements as well as subsequent electoral performance. If one of the distinguishing features of ethnic parties is their comparatively greater degree of rootedness in society, there remains the possibility of learning from the past and building more organic ties, even if this takes longer than an electoral cycle. Second, I noted how differences over development policies can also strain relations and lead to conflict between some indigenous organizations and ethnic parties in government. The continued threat of environmental damage and dispossession due to mining, oil operations, and commercial forestry clashes with indigenous demands not only for consultation, but also for greater recognition of indigenous cosmovisions and decisionmaking authority in how their lands and resources are to be used and conserved. Third, the meaning of indigeneity has also been contested and appropriated by an increasingly wider array of social and political actors. The MAS, CONAIE, Pachakutik, and Zapatistas are not the only organizations that express indigenous demands and have to compete in complex and changing political landscapes in which different expressions of indigeneity coexist and clash. The use of indigenous themes by presidents as diverse as Alberto Fujimori, Alejandro Toledo, Alan García, and Ollanta Humala in Peru, or Gutiérrez and Correa in Ecuador, should alert us to the ability of mestizo politicians to draw sufficient support from the newly enfranchised indigenous voters to defeat the more organic ethnic parties.

Given these dilemmas of electoral participation, the construction of indigenous autonomy is a more effective way to produce deeper-rooted political organization and achieve greater accountability of elected authorities. The emphasis given by the Zapatistas to broad participation of community members, close oversight of the work of education and health promoters, and the opportunity to recall authorities who fail to carry out assembly agreements are all practices that contribute to the quality of democracy and stand in stark contrast to the high levels of corruption that Mexican citizens associate with political parties and all branches of government. It is clear that, for the Zapatistas, there is nothing to be gained by allying with any political party in Mexico. While this may appear to limit their political significance, it has enhanced their position with other communities and organizations that are similarly disenchanted with political parties and the electoral system. In fact, many indigenous groups do participate in the National Indigenous Congress (CNI), which was established in 1996 as an independent network that supported the Zapatistas in drawing up their demands for national reforms to recognize indigenous rights and cultures. The CNI continues to unite communities in their resistance to official development plans and threats of dispossession. Similarly, for nonindigenous activists, the attractiveness of movements such as that of the Zapatistas derives from their commitment to more accountable practices that can build an alternative democratic politics from below.

In conclusion, when viewed through the experiences of indigenous peoples, the quality of democracy involves at least two considerations. On the one hand, there remains a significant gap between constitutional recognition of indigenous rights and the actual implementation of such rights. While this may be a more general problem with democratic performance in Latin America, for indigenous peoples it has the added significance of representing continuity with a long history of discrimination and undermines confidence in the responsiveness of government institutions, particularly where ethnic parties have little independent weight. A second consideration is the need to include indigenous perspectives and experiences in how we conceptualize democracy and, by extension, the debate over how to improve its quality. I noted how indigenous organizations and ethnic parties have deep social roots and promote more deliberative and participatory forms of representation than traditional political parties. As revealed by the Zapatistas, this does not mean that tensions and limitations are absent, or that communities have not evolved and created new internal practices. On the contrary, they have been adept at meeting new challenges while also insisting on the centrality of equal participation in the complex and unending process of democratic learning. In this regard, intercultural dialogues and exchanges can help nonindigenous activists and scholars gain new insights on the dilemmas of democratic participation in highly unequal multicultural societies.

12

The Changing Profile
of Party Systems

Will Barndt

All agree that Latin American party systems have undergone profound transformations over the past few decades. Yet few agree on what has become of those systems. The best recent work (e.g., Kitschelt et al. 2010) has struggled to find new dimensions of programmatic competition within them. Many others lament the dissolution of party systems into fleeting personalist campaign devices, unable and unintended to anchor the partisan arena across multiple electoral cycles (Levitsky and Cameron 2003). Understandably, some have even begun to describe frameworks of electoral competition in Latin America as "party *non*-systems" (Sanchez 2009, emphasis added).

In this chapter, I suggest that our collective difficulties in perceiving meaningful patterns within Latin American party systems come, in part, from looking in the wrong places. Shifting our attention to *party building*—to how parties are built, by whom, with what resources, and to what ends—promises to open new windows into ongoing transformations in the region.[1] Such refocusing helps reveal how Latin American party building has been increasingly privatized in recent decades—a process with enormous potential effects on the stability and performance of party systems and democracy.

In the first half of this chapter, I make the case that the dominant trend in Latin American party systems is toward electoral conservatism. In recent decades, Latin American parties have converged on an electoralist model of organization in which campaigns have an increasingly prominent role. These electoralist parties are constructed around five key capacities: core, recruitment, financial, publicity, and networking. All five of these capacities require considerable resources to build and maintain. Yet the range of resources available to Latin American electoralist parties has shrunk in the region, leading to a deep and growing dependence on private sector financing.

In the second half of the chapter, I untangle the implications of electoral conservatism in the region. As many electoralist parties have adopted a strategy of maximizing private donations, they have come to resemble classic conservative parties with broad-based core constituencies in the business class (Gibson 1996). Yet it turns out that not all businesspeople are content with such broad-based classic conservative parties. Faced with the difficulty of making their particular interests heard in such parties, individual businesspersons have begun to build their own new parties directly on the assets of their own particular businesses. This has become possible because the resources and capacities controlled by particular business conglomerates are often the same resources and capacities needed to construct viable electoralist parties. Consequently, individual businesses have become capable of sponsoring their own corporation-based political parties.

In these ways, significant segments of contemporary party systems in Latin America have effectively become the realm of businesspersons. The persistence of electoral conservatism within Latin American party systems poses a serious challenge to the possibility of democratic elections—and to quality and stability of democracy—in the region.

The Electoralist Imperative

Over the past two decades, a growing consensus has emerged over the basic trajectories of party organizational change in Latin America. Until the late twentieth century, many scholars would now agree, Latin American party systems could be divided into two basic types: what Kenneth M. Roberts has termed "labor-mobilizing" and "elitist" (2002, 2007, 2015). In the late twentieth century, parties in both of these systems faced an onslaught of challenges. The shift toward economic liberalization undermined the societal organizations—like unions—that had helped to ground labor-based parties (Roberts 2007; Levitsky 2003). The growing emphasis on competitive elections as a means of accessing power (Mazzuca 2010)—inherent in the regionwide wave of democratization— pushed parties to privilege those components of their organizations attuned to electioneering (Boas 2010). An increasingly fluid electorate transformed the more rigid aspects of older party organizations from assets into potential liabilities (Levitsky and Burgess 2003). The spread of new communications technologies rewarded parties that incorporated those technologies and privileged them in their organizational schema (Mancini and Swanson 1996; Plasser 2002). All these changes were attended by the growth of a Latin American class of campaign experts, often trained in US techniques, who pushed older party organizations to focus more on campaigns (Boas 2010; Plasser 2002).

Parties throughout the Americas have thus faced a growing imperative to compete in this new political environment. One important response to this imperative has been organizational adaptation (Levitsky 2003). Evidently, organizational change is not always an easy or fluid response to changing environmental circumstances. But many parties that have excelled in this new electoral environment are those that have been able to adapt to its new demands (Hunter 2010; Greene 2007).

Of all the adaptations that parties have made, the most fruitful has been their shift toward an electoralist model of party organization, a model in which campaigns and elections take center stage in party life and the (formal or informal) organizational encapsulation of voters is increasingly replaced by direct links to individual voters (Roberts 2007; Levitsky 2001: 105–106). Electoralist parties are thus campaign-oriented parties (Farrell and Webb 2000), constructed to compete in the era of the electoralist imperative.

To this end, electoralist parties become robust organizations only during electoral campaigns (Farrell and Webb 2000). They rely not on the contributions of mass memberships or linkages with mass organizations, but rather on direct and technologically mediated ties to voters. They forge these direct connections using both older and more recently developed techniques (De la Torre and Conaghan 2009; Waisbord 1996). From one direction, electoralist parties distribute goods and services to prospective voters through mass (often clientelist) networks (Mainwaring 1999; Stokes 2007). From another, they use polling, political marketing, and mass media advertising to connect with individual voters (Zovatto 2001). To carry out all these tasks, electoralist parties depend not on a permanent party staff or volunteers, but instead on professional experts in media and marketing (Plasser 2002). These tasks—particularly media access—are quite expensive, leading electoralist parties to seek out reliable and substantial sources of financing (Zovatto 2001; Mancini and Swanson 1996: 14; Barndt 2014).

Disparate kinds of Latin American parties have converged on this electoralist model of party organization in remarkably short order. Older labor-mobilizing and mass parties have loosened their organizational and programmatic ties to organized societal actors (Roberts 2007; Levitsky 2001, 2003; Levitsky and Burgess 2003; Levitsky and Roberts 2011). Though they faced less daunting adaptive challenges (Roberts 2007), older elitist parties adopted, for example, new campaign technologies to compete among politically and socially dislocated voting populations. At the same time, new parties have emerged, constructed from scratch around the prerogatives of elections and campaigns. Electoralist organization has thus become the model form of party organization in Latin America today

(Alcántara Sáez and Freidenberg 2001; Angell, D'Alva Kinzo, and Urbaneja 1992; Waisbord 1996; Plasser 2002; De la Torre and Conaghan 2009; Boas 2010; Levitsky 2001: 106).

Building Electoralist Parties

At first, the rise of the electoralist model of party organization seems incontrovertible. Yet as Steven Levitsky rightly argues, the very fact that so many parties seem to fit this model may undermine its usefulness. At the turn of the century, he notes, the model already had become so conceptually stretched that seemingly all parties could be categorized as electoralist (Levitsky 2001). This is not an unreasonable critique. In part, scholars responded to the rise of the electoralist imperative by labeling all (surviving) parties "electoralist." The challenge, as Levitsky recognizes, is to reconcile the ongoing diversity of Latin American parties with the fact that the electoralist imperative has forced significant convergence among them.

This chapter provides a partial response to this challenge, arguing that the most relevant variation among Latin American parties today is not which organizational model they adopt—again, most are electoralist—but rather how they obtain the resources that sustain viable electoralist organizations. The argument rests on the following premises. First, all viable electoralist parties must develop a well-defined set of organizational capacities. Second, developing these capacities entails the accumulation of particular types of resources. Third, while all electoralist parties must develop the same capacities, they differ in where they obtain the resources necessary to build those capacities. Consequently, electoralist parties can be differentiated according to the locations from which they draw these necessary resources. Beginning with resources and capacities lays the foundation for a theory of parties centered on the different ways in which parties assemble those resources.[2]

Electoralist parties across Latin America today seem to be built around five key capacities.

1. Their *core capacity*. Electoralist parties are first and foremost organizations. They must register with the state, collect signatures of party members, maintain some geographical coverage, navigate legal issues, and conduct basic administrative tasks. As such, they require the basic resources associated with any modern organization: office space, information technology networks, transportation, and an administrative staff.

2. Their *recruitment capacity*. An electoralist party must field viable

candidates for multiple levels of office and, should it win, appoint individuals to key government positions. It must also recruit high-level professionals capable of navigating a diverse set of legal, political, advertising, and other issues.

3. Their *publicity capacity,* which enables them to conduct polls, develop advertising strategies, and secure media access. As noted above, contemporary electoralist parties rely heavily on polling, political marketing, and mass media advertising to connect with individual voters. They therefore require specialized marketing organizations as well as the ability to place their advertising in appropriate forums.

4. Their *networking capacity,* which includes the targeting, transportation, and delivery of goods, services, and promises to prospective voters at the individual level. Consequently, electoralist parties must develop the capacity to identify potential voters—as well as the ability to generate the goods and services those voters demand.

5. Their *fund-raising capacity,* which allows parties to accumulate the financial resources they need to compete effectively.

All successful electoralist parties in Latin America must develop organizations capable of performing these five tasks. These different capacities may be developed formally or informally (Levitsky and Helmke 2006), and they may be institutionally differentiated or not. But all five are critical to the success of an electoralist party. Of course, many electoralist parties develop additional capabilities: organizational spheres dedicated, for example, to policy formation or coordination once in government. Others retain vestiges of other models of party organization, including formal linkages with mass actors like unions. Nonetheless, these five capacities are sufficient to constitute a viable electoralist party in the Americas today.

The prospect of building or sustaining an electoralist party is thus a question of acquiring the resources necessary to develop these capacities. Historically, electoralist parties in Latin America have turned to five tactics to raise their resources: ownership, membership, state funding, commercial transactions, and private donations. Yet as the following analysis demonstrates, resources in many of these places have become increasingly scarce.

The Insufficiency of Ownership, Membership, State Funding, and Commercial Transactions

Some parties have the good fortune of having developed the resources they need to compete within their own organizations. A handful of parties, for example, continue simply to own relevant resources, including offices, media outlets, and survey firms (Salas Alfaro 2001; Santiuste Cué 2001; Artiga

González 2001; Garretón 2005; Gibson 1996: 150; Agosto and Cueto Villamán 2001; Hunter 2010: 38–39, 129). Others continue to depend heavily on members—both elite and mass. At the elite level, politicians and officials in many parties are required to donate some of their salary to the party (Hunter 2010: 40), to maintain and finance local offices (Hernández Sánchez 2001; Freidenberg 2001: 379), or to build their own campaigns (Mezrahi 2003: 83–84; Mainwaring 1999: 147). And throughout much of the region, mass members are still, at least formally, required to pay dues to the party or to volunteer during election campaigns (Griner and Zovatto 2005; Alcántara Sáez and Freidenberg 2001).

Beyond ownership and membership, states (especially rentier states) remain a major provider of resources to Latin American electoralist parties—formally and informally. Formally, many Latin American states provide some form of public financing to campaigns and parties, endowing them with greater finance and publicity (Casas-Zamora 2005a; Zovatto 2001; Griner and Zovatto 2005). Yet informal access to state resources is much more important throughout the region—especially when it comes to developing fund-raising and networking capacities (Jones 2008: 48–49; Mainwaring 1999; Samuels 2001; Greene 2007; Ajenjo Fresno 2001; Hunter 2010: 41–42, 148; Roberts 2006; Conaghan 2006: 166). For example, the state can provide parties with the resources they need to develop key core capacities—including offices, technology networks, and transportation—and publicity capacities through party control of state-run and state-manipulated media (Garretón 2005: 174; Roberts 2006: 94–95; Hernández Sánchez 2001: 416; Conaghan 2006: 165–166; 2011; Bautista Urbaneja and Alvarez 2005: 143).

When these resources fall short, electoralist parties may have yet another potential tactic at their disposal: renting the capacities they need to compete. Most directly, parties can simply borrow money from commercial banks, a practice that has led to high levels of party indebtedness in Chile and Paraguay (Garretón 2005: 164–165, 173; Hernández Sánchez 2001: 386). Indeed, renting has long been central to electoralist parties' development of publicity capacities. Throughout the Americas, electoralist parties regularly hire outside firms and consultants during campaigns (Alcántara Sáez and Freidenberg 2001; Boas 2010; Plasser 2002)—and pay commercial media to broadcast their political messages (Mancini and Swanson 1996: 16). The Brazilian PT (Partido dos Trabalhadores, or Workers' Party) and Ecuadorean Alianza PAIS, for example, have hired well-known publicists and public relations firms to run their campaigns (Hunter 2010: 38–39; Conaghan 2011: 268–269). Throughout the region, in fact, the importance of externally contracted political consultants has skyrocketed over the past two decades (Angell, D'Alva Kinzo, and Urbaneja

1992: 43; Waisbord 1996; Plasser 2002: 271–273; Boas 2010). Beyond publicity, parties regularly rent the resources they need to maintain core capacities, as has occurred in Costa Rica and Venezuela (Molina et al. 2001: 551).

In theory, electoralist parties could be using all four of these tactics to gain access to the resources they need. In practice, however, the availability of these kinds of resources has seemed to diminish as electoralist organization has grown in prominence. Long-standing parties no longer own as many assets—perhaps due to the combination of economic crisis and authoritarian repression during the 1970s and 1980s. Mass membership is not a viable source of substantial resources for most parties—not least because of the enormous administrative costs entailed in collecting those resources (Garretón 2005: 164–165). Even where mass memberships persist (Levitsky 2003: 30, 67, 69; López Maya 2011: 218; Roberts 2006; Freidenberg and Levitsky 2007), few parties are able to rely primarily on those memberships for substantial resources in the electoralist era. And while elite members can provide significant resources to their parties, in doing so they often gain a problematic degree of autonomy from the party, undermining its cohesion.

Similarly, while the state remains a major source of resources (especially informal resources) for some parties, the quantity of state resources available to parties in many countries decreased as states withdrew from participating in firm-like ways in their economies (compare with Greene 2007). Moreover, many informal state resources are usually available only to parties already in power: they are thus not a viable option for new parties. At the same time, formal state resources, such as public funding for parties and campaigns, are generally insufficient for parties to remain competitive. (I discuss the special case of rentier states in the Conclusion.)

Relying on commercial transactions also has clear and often unsustainable costs. Most importantly, the ability of electoralist parties to borrow or rent resources depends on their ability to pay for those resources. Renting in perpetuity is therefore not a viable option for parties unless they maintain other strategies for raising resources—particularly financial resources. Commercial transactions are thus at best a temporary fix for the deeper problem of declining access to historically important resources used to build parties in the region.

The Rise of Private Donors

Given the insufficiency of other tactics, many Latin American electoralist parties—especially new parties—have come to depend increasingly on private donors. Indeed, fund-raising from private donors is critical for parties in every single country in Latin America (Alcántara Sáez and Freidenberg 2001; Zovatto 2001; Griner and Zovatto 2005; Malamud and Posado-Carbó 2005; Casas-Zamora 2005b; Del Castillo and Zovatto 1998; Alcántara and Barahona 2003; Burnell and Ware 2007; Austin and Tjernstrom 2003). Such fund-raising occurs in at least three different ways. In some countries, private donors are recruited to fund-raise for the party. In Uruguay, for example, parties assemble businessperson-dominated finance commissions at the outset of each campaign season (Casas-Zamora 2005a: 222; Gibson 1996: 160, 163). In other countries, parties have built fund-raising capacities that are constantly tapped into the private sector, as in the case of Chile (Luna 2010). In still other countries, parties rely on private donors to finance the party indirectly—as, for example, occurred in Mexico (Camp 2012: 321). Through all these channels, private financing has poured into electoralist parties in recent decades.

While financial resources are the most regular form of support, private donors can help parties develop other types of capacities as well. Publicity capacities, for example, are also often buttressed informally by private donors (Middlebrook 2000: 26), as amply documented by Edward L. Gibson (1996: 155). Similar dynamics have played themselves out in Colombia, Uruguay, and Peru (Cepeda Ulloa 2005: 137; Casas-Zamora 2005b: 214; Conaghan 2006: 18–19). When parties cannot access sufficient commercial airtime, private allies in local radio can also help supplement their publicity capacities—as has occurred in Peru and Ecuador (Bowen 2002; De la Torre and Conaghan 2009: 9–10). Private donors can also provide resources for core capacities. For example, the Costa Rican PUSC's central offices were in an old house owned by a rich family that supports the party, and COPEI in Venezuela depended on real estate companies to provide local offices for the party (Salas Alfaro 2001; Molina et al. 2001: 536). Moreover, where private donors have access to mass support, they can help parties develop network capacities. In 1989 and 1994, for example, Salvadoran landholders mobilized resident employees of their agribusinesses in support of ARENA (National Republic Alliance) (Middlebrook 2000: 40).

Many—probably the majority of—Latin American parties are heavily dependent on private sector donations for the resources they need to develop and maintain the capacities associated with viable electoralist organization. While such donations can come from various types of private donors and help to build various capacities, the most common and important form of private donation seems to be financial contributions from businesspeople, businesses, and other wealthy individuals. These financial resources are then used to rent or buy the other capacities parties need to compete effectively.

The Rise of Electoral Conservatism
and the Problem of Influence

Over the past two decades, the trend toward electoralist organization and the trend toward private donation have combined to transform the landscape of Latin American party systems. The model strategy for electoralist parties that have not benefited from access to state resources is now to maximize donations from the private sector. Given this dependence on private finance, many electoralist parties tend to fund-raise widely, seeking financial resources from broad swaths of the private sector. Such behavior has been documented throughout much of Latin America including in Chile, Brazil, Mexico, Venezuela, Uruguay, Bolivia, El Salvador, and Panama (Luna 2010; Samuels 2001; Mezrahi 2003; Coppedge 2000; Casas-Zamora 2005a; Wood 2012; Brown Araúz 2009).

Such behavior seems to lead toward electoral conservatism. When an electoralist party depends heavily on widespread funding from businesspeople for its viability, business becomes what Gibson has called a core constituency of that party, transforming the party into a vehicle of conservative representation. Indeed, as Gibson argues, "The sources of a party's financial support are one of the most telling indicators of a core-constituency relationship" (Gibson 1996: 14).[3] The many contemporary electoralist parties in the region today that depend on businesspeople for their resources are thus well described as Gibsonian conservative parties with their core constituency in the private sector. Let us call these parties that receive the lion's share of their resources from many businesspeople "classic conservative parties."

Unsurprisingly, classic conservative parties often tend to pursue policy agendas in line with the demands of their core constituents (Gibson 1996: 8–14). For example, a party that appeals to the business class as a whole for financial resources should be expected to support general pro-business policies such as the preservation of private property, low taxation, stable currency, predictable regulation, and the weakening of organized labor. In line with these expectations, some contemporary classic conservative parties have been highly effective and stable vehicles of representation for the business class—as is most clearly evidenced by the UDI (Independent Democratic Union) in Chile and ARENA in El Salvador (Luna 2010; Wood 2012: 223–254). The spread of such parties—most not nearly as stable as the UDI or ARENA—throughout many countries the region represents a rise in electoral conservatism.

Notice, however, that the advantages derived by particular business conglomerates from financing a classic conservative party are not always as clear as might be imagined. Indeed, classic conservative parties can present particular businesses with a real dilemma of influence. This is because particular businesses, as the growing scholarship on political finance has documented, often donate resources to parties not only to support a stable business environment but also to secure individual advantages for themselves (Faccio 2006; McMenamin 2012; Stratmann 2005; Scarrow 2007; Claessens, Feijen, and Laeven 2008; Cooper, Gulen, and Ovtchinnikov 2010). Ironically, classic conservative parties often turn out to be devastatingly ineffective representatives of the interests of any particular business conglomerate.

While the leaders of classic conservative parties must keep many of their business constituents content, they need not keep them all content. Broad-based fund-raising within the business class thus provides party leaders with a measure of autonomy from the demands of any particular business donor.[4] Even worse from the standpoint of any particular business donor, party leaders must divide up whatever concrete benefits they are able to offer among the many different businesses that have donated to the party.

Business supporters of electoralist parties are thus faced with a curious dilemma. As electoralist parties come to depend more on private donations, business influence within them increases. Yet the rise of such electoral conservatism forces individual businesses to struggle with one another for influence within parties. The broader the support for the party among the business class, the lower the probability that any given business will receive significant favors—and the smaller those favors are likely to be. The rise of privately funded electoralist party organizations—of electoral conservatism—is thus not exactly the unmitigated blessing for businesses that it is sometimes made out to be.

Consider, by way of example, the case of Panama—and particularly the case of Panamanian businessman Ricardo Martinelli. By 1994, Panamanian parties had converged increasingly on electoral conservatism. Even the old military party, the Party of the Democratic Revolution, had been taken over by its business wing, the Frente Empresarial (Brown Araúz 2009: 51). Indeed, in 1994 the PRD successfully ran Ernesto Pérez Balladares, leader of its business wing, for president of the republic. On coming to power, the PRD entered into coalition with the tiny new Solidaridad (Solidarity Party), which had been formed by Samuel Lewis Galindo, a beer and bank magnate. Solidaridad also drew on the support of a wide range of Panamanian businesspeople and political elites, including Martinelli, the owner of a diversified business conglomerate centered on the Super 99 supermarket chain. Martinelli served as a spokesperson for Solidaridad in 1994 and was subsequently appointed general director of the Panamanian Social Security Office (Caja de Seguridad Social).[5]

Martinelli's tenure at the Social Security Office was filled with controversy over a variety of items, including his attempts to privatize some of its functions—controversial within the Panamanian business community. As a result, President Pérez Balladares pressured him into leaving the post after less than two years in office. On leaving, Martinelli declared that he had "not received the support of his party [Solidaridad]" and suggested that Lewis Galindo wanted his job, provoking a public spat between the two men (Aguilar 1996). Faced with intransigent resistance to his policy initiatives within Solidaridad, Martinelli decided instead to resign his position and abandon the party. He became, like so many other Latin American businesspersons, a casualty of a fight between highly politicized business interests within classic conservative parties. Interbusiness conflict within classic conservative parties in Panama, as elsewhere in the hemisphere,[6] led to the exclusion of particular businesspersons from the partisan arena—at least for a moment.

The Possibility of Corporate Sponsorship: Resolving the Problem of Influence?

Confronted with the difficulty of making their particular interests heard in classic conservative parties, particular economic conglomerates in the Americas have turned to a new strategy. In short, they have begun to build their own new parties and party factions directly on the assets of their own particular business conglomerates—assets that include fund-raising, core, recruitment, publicity, and networking capacities. They have, in other words, turned from more broadly based classic conservative parties to more narrow "corporation-based parties" (Barndt 2014). When a particular businessperson constructs a new electoralist party on business assets that he literally already owns, the problems of political influence discussed above are attenuated, to say the least.

Corporation-based parties have become a real possibility in the region because the resources and capacities controlled by particular business conglomerates are often the same resources and capacities needed to construct viable electoralist parties. By repurposing the capacities they have already developed for the use of particular parties (or party factions), particular businesses can come to sponsor those parties. Businesses have significant financial resources that can be used for fund-raising. They can provide infrastructural core capacities out of their existing offices. They can draw on their personnel to recruit loyal party officials. They can use their existing media holdings and market research units for party publicity. And their existing customer, supplier, logistical, and philanthropic networks can be repurposed for partisan support. The building of such corporation-based parties, it turns out, has become quite common across Latin America (Barndt 2014).

Given party finance regulation that is weakly enforced, major Latin American business conglomerates regularly find themselves in a position to provide some or all of these capacities directly to a particular political party. Because these capacities already exist in-house, all are readily repurposed from the economic ends of the business to the political ends of the party. Such repurposing can pay significant dividends for a business: the more a party depends on a particular business for its key capacities, the less autonomy the party has from the particular interests of that business, and the easier it is for that business to monopolize whatever benefits accrue to the party.

In corporation-sponsored parties, that is, the particularistic benefits that run through the party flow first and foremost to its sponsoring corporation. Unlike in classic conservative parties, corporations that sponsor their own parties do not need to contend as robustly for influence within the party—especially (as is often the case) when the party is led by the owner or manager of the business that sponsors it. As such, corporation-sponsored parties can be highly effective representatives of the interests of particular businesses.

Consider again the case of Martinelli. Faced with his exclusion in the mid-1990s from newly (re)founded classic conservative parties, Martinelli struck out on his own. In 1998 he formally announced the formation of a new party, which he called Democratic Change and over which he presided. Martinelli was uniquely positioned to build this viable new electoralist party, given that he owned a major business conglomerate centered on the Super 99 supermarket chain. Martinelli was, in short, able to construct his Democratic Change party squarely on the preexisting assets of his conglomerate, drawing on it for all five capacities necessary to the success of electoralist parties (Barndt 2014).

Since its founding, Democratic Change has participated in four elections (1999, 2004, 2009, 2014), and in 2009 Martinelli himself was elected president of Panama. On taking office that year, the Democratic Change government was able to enact a variety of policies seemingly tailored to the interests of a supermarket chain, including the creation of a sub-secretary of refrigeration (charged with building a state-subsidized chain of refrigeration stations that could efficiently move produce from the countryside to urban centers), the building of a new metro in Panama City (with stops conveniently located adjacent to multiple Super 99 stores), and the ratification of a free-trade agreement with the United States (an addendum to which declares that retail operations like supermarkets can be owned and managed only by Panamanians). The Democratic Change government of 2009–2014 clearly demonstrates, if nothing else, the particular policy benefits that can accrue to a business conglomerate that sponsors its own party. Once Martinelli founded Democratic Change, he no longer had to squabble within a classic conservative party for influence: the party to which he belonged was, in point of fact, his own.

This story has been repeated over and over again in many Latin American party systems. Parallel events can be found in Argentina (Mauricio Macri and the PRO [Republican Proposal]), Bolivia (Max Fernández and the UCS [Soldarity Civic Unity]), Brazil (Paulo Maluf and the Partido Popular), Chile (Javier Errázuriz and the UCCP [Union of the Centrist Center]), Ecuador (Álvaro Noboa and PRIAN [Institutional Renewal Party of National Action]), Paraguay (Guillermo Caballero Vargas and Encuentro Nacional), Peru (César Acuña and Alianza para el Progreso), and Guatemala (Ricardo Castillo and the Partido Patriota).[7] And similar conflicts have wracked classic conservative parties in El Salvador (ARENA), Colombia (Liberal Party), Mexico (PAN), and Nicaragua (Liberal Party).

In short, the fact that most Latin American party systems are dominated by privately financed electoralist parties gives rise to manifold partisan fights and divisions between highly politicized business interests. These conflicts are, perhaps, what almost all current Latin American party systems most clearly share in common: incessant squabbling over the extent of influence of major conglomerates within classic conservative parties and regular attempts by particular conglomerates to rise above the fray by forming their own particular corporation-based parties.

The Condition of Latin American Party Systems and Latin American Democracy

Over the past few decades, a majority of Latin American parties seem to have converged on an electoralist model of organization and on private donations as a primary means of constructing those parties. This trend has given rise to an electoral conservatism, in which classic conservative parties—parties that depend heavily on the collective financing of many business interests—dominate many party systems. Yet the widespread emergence of classic conservative parties has also produced new dynamics within party systems, which have increasingly become arenas for highly politicized businesspeople to fight with one another over the extent of their own particularistic benefits. These dynamics give good reason to worry about the quality of democracy in the region—today and into the future.

Conservative Instability, Business Populism, and Oligarchy

First and foremost, the rise of electoral conservatism puts hard limits on the scope of policy innovation within contemporary Latin American democracies. When party systems are built and rebuilt with private donations, policies that might fundamentally challenge the sources of those donations become extraordinarily difficult for parties to pursue. Much attention has been paid to the ways in which external forces—for example, foreign capital markets and international financial institutions—may constrain policy choice. Yet just as central may be the increasing need for parties to appease those private domestic interests that dominate party building in many places today.

This need has real consequences on the structure and stability of party systems. Absent windfall state revenues from international commodity prices, most parties have had great difficulty advancing redistributive policy agendas—other than the popular, acceptable, and often effective Conditional Cash Transfer programs. These difficulties have led old and new left parties to reach into more shadowy places for their funding. More specifically, left parties have turned to funds from state-based kickback schemes—as became public in recent years in Chile and Brazil.[8] These examples demonstrate the extent to which a regular choice for parties may now be either to sacrifice important parts of their agenda to the rise of electoral conservatism or to engage in particularistic state-based corruption rackets to supplement their resources.

This tension has potentially serious implications for democratic stability. When these kinds of schemes become public, it is precisely those parties that have resisted electoral conservatism that are faced with voter outrage. Such schemes not only undermine left parties' claims to be purveyors of public goods, but also increase voter dissatisfaction and distrust of the parties that are (partially) challenging the privatization of party building in the region. The fund-raising imperatives introduced by the rise of electoral conservatism are further contributing to the destabilization of party systems—as illustrated by ongoing events in Brazil today. Ironically, this kind of destabilization opens even more space for private donations to dominate party building. In the vacuum of party system instability, particular businesses are especially well placed to enter partisan politics for a moment, temporarily repurposing their assets into campaigns to reap the short-term benefits of electoral disarray that attend delegitimizing corruption scandals. Arguably this was an important dynamic, for example, following the collapse of the Bolivian left in the 1980s, the defeat of the FSLN in Nicaragua in 1990, and the fragmentation of the Peronists in Argentina in the 2000s.

These destructive competitive dynamics inherent to electoral conservatism may, ironically, be producing yet another wave of populism in the region. Much as a populist resurgence accompanied the destabilization of labor-based parties in the 1990s, a new kind of corporation-based populism may also accompany the destabilization of party systems today.

Corporation-based parties in Panama, Bolivia, and Ecuador, for example, have explicitly combined direct appeals to the people with the antielite discourses associated with right- and left-wing populism more globally. More importantly, corporation-based parties are ideally suited to engage in populist electoral strategies given their ability to engage in massive spending on direct connections with individual voters.

Indeed, builders of corporation-based parties are finding that they are just as—if not more—adept at combining their own particularistic conservative agendas with populism as Alberto Fujimori, Carlos Menem, and Fernando Collor de Mello were at combining neoliberal agendas and populist appeals a generation ago (Weyland 1999). Unlike the electoral populism of these earlier leaders, however, corporation-based populism is characterized by a high degree of organization in civil society: business organization. Structurally, that is, corporation-based populism is oddly not entirely unlike earlier forms of labor-based populism (Roberts 2006). Today, however, it is business conglomerates, not unions, that are organizing and mobilizing the masses on behalf of populist leaders. This era of electoral conservatism may well be an era of apparent conservative instability—characterized by bickering within classic conservative parties and the rise and fall of corporation-based parties, some of which adopt populist strategies and appeals.

Yet this instability threatens to disguise what Robert A. Dahl once called "competitive oligarchy" (1971). Indeed, it is in countries or regions where a small number of business conglomerates dominate the economy that electoral conservatism seems to have become most pronounced: nationally in Panama, Guatemala, Honduras, and El Salvador; regionally in Bolivia, Ecuador, and Peru. In places like these, oligopoly in the marketplace may come to be closely paralleled in the electoral sphere. The real concern here ought to be that a concentration of economic power in a particular place could produce similarly concentrated political power in the same place, as John Gaventa (1980) described in another context years ago. Such concentration of power does not bode well for the representativeness, accountability, or legitimacy of democratic systems. In countries with more competitive markets, conversely, such oligarchy may be more difficult to sustain. That is, where businesses find themselves regularly challenged (and, indeed, destabilized) by market competition, it should be more difficult to transform conservative party systems into instruments of oligarchic rule.

A New Model of Citizenship?

Yet oligarchy is not the only possible outcome of the privatization of party building in Latin America. As the primary organizations that mediate between state and society, political parties also generate new models of citizenship. Most intriguing is perhaps the role of corporation-based parties in suggesting a new model of "consumer citizenship" in Latin America (García Canclini 2001). Over the past two decades, the old capitalist-worker divide in Latin America has been replaced by a new consumer-producer cleavage (Baker 2010). In countries like Brazil, this change is sorting consumers and retail businesses into low-price alliances—alliances that may well be repurposed effectively into corporation-based parties. Indeed, a number of corporation-based parties—particularly in Panama and Bolivia— have already appealed directly to their consumers as potential partisans, suggesting openly that voters should understand their consumption and political preferences as intersecting. Mobilizing voters as consumers would be a novel addition to the Latin American electoral repertoire. And such a model might well be more durable than the alternative visions of citizenship articulated by other parties in recent years.

Consider, by way of contrast, the two most serious partisan challenges to electoral conservatism in the past quarter century: parties built by and on indigenous movements (most notably, Pachakutik in Ecuador and the MAS in Bolivia [Van Cott 2003; Madrid 2014; Harvey, Chapter 11, this volume]) and parties built with the windfall profits from state hydrocarbons companies (most notably, Alianza PAIS in Ecuador and the MVR/PSUV [Fifth Republic Movement/Union Socialist Party of Venezuela] in Venezuela). These kinds of parties have tried to supplement the electoralist model of party organization—to recover, for example, standing membership as a key component of partisan life—and to diversify the resources with which parties are built—while Alianza PAIS and the PSUV draw extraordinarily heavily on state support, Pachakutik and (initially) the MAS drew heavily on the collective memberships of the indigenous organizations that launched them. In so doing, these indigenous and rentier parties challenged electoral conservatism within Latin American party systems.

Yet neither indigenous-based nor hydrocarbons-based rentier projects seem imminently poised to recapture party systems from privately financed electoralist parties. Almost nowhere have indigenous parties met with lasting success in capturing and holding state power—due to internal conflicts about what it might mean to be an indigenous party and the difficulty of such parties in attaining sufficient resources to persist across time. And parties built on oil and natural gas revenues are everywhere teetering as historic price spikes crash to the ground. As noted above, moreover, such parties depend for their resources on actually being (and staying) in power. With the sole clear exception of Bolivia, where Evo Morales's MAS has carefully and successfully (to the moment) balanced indigenous and state support, parties (and thus party systems) across the region remain organized, at least in part, by businesses.

If the dynamics that I described in this chapter are to be countered or reversed, new kinds of partisan vision and partisan strategies are desperately needed. It is this task, as much as any other, on which the future quality and stability of Latin American democracies may rest.

Notes

1. These dynamics are beginning to be discussed in more detail. See, for example, Levitsky et al. (2016).
2. Several important scholars have responded to this challenge (e.g., Greene 2007; Levitsky 2003; Hunter 2010; Van Cott 2003; Roberts 2006).
3. For an alternative approach to identifying and analyzing right politics in Latin America, see Luna and Kaltwasser (2014).
4. Perhaps helping to explain the difficulty that scholars have had conclusively demonstrating a link between campaign finance contributions and favoritism. See, for example, Stratmann (2005).
5. Interestingly, Martinelli also gave money to the 1994 Pérez Balladares campaign, even though he was a member of Solidaridad.
6. Similar dynamics occurred with the Salvadoran ARENA in the mid-1990s, the Nicaraguan UNO (National Opposition Union) coalition in the early 1990s, the Colombian Liberal Party in the mid-2000s, the Guatemalan PAN between the mid-1990s and the mid-2000s, the Brazilian ARENA in the mid- to late 1980s, the Bolivian ADN-MNRH (Nationalist Democratic Action–Historic Revolutionary Nationalist Movement) coalition in the late 1980s, the Chilean MUN (National Unity Movement) in the mid-1980s, and the Peruvian FREDEMO (Democratic Front) after 1992. See Barndt (2016).
7. For more detail, see Barndt (2014, 2016).
8. The Chilean Concertación and Brazilian PT both engaged in elaborate municipal kickback schemes in the late 1990s and 2000s. For more detail, see Luna (2010: 342–343) and Hunter (2010: 102–104). The Brazilian *caixa dois* scandal is particularly relevant here, though (as mentioned later in text) the Petrobras scandal is effectively the same practice on a grander scale.

13

A Democratic Paradox:
More Governability, Less Trust

Roderic Ai Camp

When the Institutional Revolutionary Party won the presidential
elections of July 2012, reestablishing its control over the executive branch,
pundits and politicians alike wondered what this would mean for democratic politics. The most extreme positions appearing in the media in response
to this event suggested implicitly or explicitly that the PRI would return to
some of its predemocratic behaviors, or that the country would witness a
dramatic rise in political corruption. Instead, the day after taking office on
December 2, President Enrique Peña Nieto announced an extraordinary
agreement among the three major parties. Labeled the Pact for Mexico
(hereafter the Pact) this agreement dominated congressional policymaking
for the first fourteen months of his administration. Indeed, I would argue
that the PRI's most significant achievement to date is the passage of policy
reforms that may contribute to major alterations in social, economic, and
political conditions. Depending on the extent to which these reforms are
actually implemented, it may well become the most important political
achievement since an opposition party won the presidency in 2000. But paradoxically the potential legitimacy earned by all three major parties that
agreed to the Pact has been undermined by widespread violence and official
corruption. The level of disenchantment with political institutions has
reached the point where the very legitimacy and prestige of the democratic
political model has been called into question.

The Policy Content of the Pact

The Pact for Mexico is a nineteen-page agreement signed by the presidents
of the PRI, the National Action Party, and the Party of the Democratic
Revolution as well as the president of Mexico himself. Among the key
reforms are those aimed at breaking up monopolies, increasing economic
competition, expanding the pace of antipoverty programs, and opening up

223

petroleum exploration and extraction to domestic and foreign private investment. Additionally, the Pact highlights the need for major alterations to public education, increasing access to education at the elementary level, improving the quality of teaching, and increasing the percentage of Mexicans who complete secondary and higher education. It also includes such difficult political issues as expanding and clarifying the state's role in human rights, removing special legal privileges for the armed forces that go back to the colonial era, and reforming the national legal system with a unified code. Finally, the Pact incorporates proposals focused directly on democratic procedural issues such as eliminating the prohibition against reelection in the legislative branch at the federal and state levels and eliminating the five-month lag in time between the presidential election in July and the victor's inauguration in December.[1]

Peña Nieto has already put some of these measures into law. The most prominent to date include, first, radical educational reforms, which if fully implemented would exercise a decisive influence on the quality of education, the level of poverty, and economic growth.[2] The second involves relaxing the state's control over subsoil mineral rights, specifically the petroleum industry, traditionally the most widely supported principle in the 1917 Constitution, thus allowing domestic private and international investment in the exploration and extraction of oil, a major source of revenue to the federal government.[3] And the third reverses another constitutional heritage: the concept of no consecutive reelection in the legislative branch at the national and state levels, in addition to a more radical provision that allows mayors, who are elected and executive officeholders, to be reelected for another term.[4]

The latter legislation is particularly noteworthy in terms of Mexico's ability to consolidate democracy.[5] Specifically, the law would allow members of the Chamber of Deputies, Mexico's lower house, to be reelected three consecutive times, thus allowing members of Congress to serve through two complete presidential terms (twelve years). For members of the Senate, who currently serve a six-year term, the law would allow them to repeat that tenure for another six years. These regulations go into effect in 2018.[6] These tenure changes are essential to strengthen the legislative branch, which historically has been weak in initiating legislative proposals and dominated by a powerful executive branch (Casar 2010: 117–120). In the eyes of most Mexicans, and elsewhere in Latin America, there exists little confidence in the legislative branch of government. Indeed, Mexicans rank third among Latin American political systems in their support for presidential decisionmaking without a legislature.

But contrary to what most observers believe, constitutionally the Mexican presidency ranks among the weakest in Latin America. As a leading expert on the legislative branch argues, Mexico's president has only a partial veto power, thus the presidency is on par with such countries as Honduras and Costa Rica (Nacif 2012: 235–237). During the reign of the PRI, past presidents exercised what legal experts have described as meta-constitutional powers, powers that relied on the PRI's control over both legislative and judicial branches. But since 2000 the strengthening of legislative opposition means that legislative decisionmaking has begun to reflect these constitutional limitations, so Mexican presidents now have to rely on weak or nonexistent constitutional provisions while their counterparts in Argentina, Brazil, and Colombia can actually decree new legislation (Shugart and Haggard 2001: 73). In Chile, the development of what has been labeled "coalitional presidentialism" has led to the party pacts being described in terms that are familiar to any observer of predemocratic Mexican politics: "The authority of coalition leaders over nominations is effectively the authority to control the political careers of rank and file legislators" (Baldez and Carey 2001: 118). What we see here is a democratic version of the control the PRI exercised during its lengthy period of semiauthoritarian rule.

What is different about the Mexican experience in the first two years of Peña Nieto's term from that of coalition presidentialism in such countries as Chile and Brazil? In Brazil, David Samuels notes that Luiz Inácio Lula da Silva used cabinet appointments from numerous parties to achieve a consensus; indeed, his government had the most extensive multiparty composition in Brazilian history, far exceeding the degree of fragmentation currently observed in Mexico (2008: 152–176). In Argentina, control over legislators is in the hands of local political bosses and party leaders, not the national party leadership, thus significantly complicating coalitional behavior at the federal level (Jones 2008: 73–75). Furthermore, it is observed that choosing cabinet members from other parties is a two-edged sword because a president risks losing control over those ministerial departments led by other party members. Indeed, presidents in Latin America, including recent Mexican chief executives, have frequently relied on nonpartisan appointments to their cabinets to minimize these risks[7] (Martínez-Gallardo and Schleiter 2014).

The reelection of mayors—the only elected executive position at the local level—is equally important[8] because it allows the electorate to pass judgment on incumbents' performance in office, so reinforcing accountability. In the past, the lack of accountability could invite corruption and abuse of office as mayors sought to take advantage of their only opportunity for self-enrichment. As Andrew Selee suggests in his thorough examination of local governance, although many cities "have competitive elections, representative institutions do not appear to be the primary means for making demands, nor do they ensure accountability at the local level in any of them" (2011: 165).

The political path that Peña Nieto has taken differs greatly from that of his PRI predecessors, or President Vicente Fox for that matter, primarily because his party only has a plurality of congressional seats. Consequently, he chose an imaginative and novel strategy to pursue his controversial set of reforms. Similar to the religious reform bill of President Carlos Salinas de Gortari, numerous individual members of his party oppose the petroleum reform despite the party's official decision to back the reform at a national assembly in March 2014.[9] Moreover, in contrast to the overwhelming popular support for Salinas's religious reforms, at least a third to as many as two-thirds of Mexicans opposed the petroleum reforms (Carta Paramétrica 2013d). The nation's oil is linked in the minds of many citizens to the mythology of the 1910 Mexican Revolution, the legitimacy of the 1917 Constitution, and perhaps most important of all, to national sovereignty inherent in President Lázaro Cárdenas's dramatic 1938 nationalization of the oil industry, the most unifying political decision in Mexico since 1920.[10] If Peña Nieto succeeds in implementing each of these reforms, in addition to other legislation already passed, not only will there be a dramatic impact on Mexico's political and economic development, but successful implementation will bolster and legitimize the president's novel strategy for garnering cross-party support for the reforms.

This collaborative approach is very different from the PRI's record as the opposition party with the largest plurality of seats in the legislatures of 2003–2006 and 2009–2012. Flushed with its electoral comeback victory in 2003, far from seeking collaboration with the executive branch and the PAN's deputies in Congress, it watered down important legislative proposals rather than cooperating to achieve the significant structural changes that Mexico required on most policy fronts.[11] Six years later, after again winning the largest plurality with 223 seats, the PRI repeated the same behavior. Only after winning the presidential election of 2012 with a small plurality of the vote but with the largest plurality of seats in Congress did Peña Nieto and his advisers change tack by beginning to negotiate the Pact before the president assumed office, thus focusing simultaneously on policy goals and the strategic path to achieve those goals. It was this combination of political means and ends that made the major reforms possible, something that the relevant survey results show was clearly understood by the voting public. Thus, half of the survey respondents saw the PRI as opposing President Fox's legislation while over 60 percent saw the PRD as opposing President Felipe Calderón's legislation, but in 2013 only 25 and 10 percent of respondents, respectively, viewed the PRD or PAN as opposing Peña Nieto's legislation (Bimsa 2006). In effect the strategic switch allowed all parties in power—and indeed the government rather than the president alone—to share in responding to voters' aspirations and preferences.

The Social, Political, and Cultural Challenges to the Pact

Why place so much emphasis on the strategy and tactics of the PRI government? Every political analyst I know believes Mexico achieved an electoral democracy in 2000, which was reinforced in the 2012 election by the most widely used measure of democratization, an opposition party victory in a national election. But equally Mexico is not generally considered to be a consolidated democracy since it lacks a culture of law,[12] adequate transparency,[13] and sufficient accountability.[14]

Despite the media speculation that the 2012 electoral victory would mark a return to the pre-2000 semiauthoritarian model of PRI dominance, the process of making the Pact and implementing the agreed reforms does not confirm this prediction. What it does confirm, in contrast, is the PRI's characteristic preference for pragmatism over ideological stances of any kind, and a recognition that the PRI is now part of a highly fluid three-party system where all the parties have a clear capacity either to win the presidency or to come within a percentage point or less of the popular vote of doing so. Fox won with 43 percent of the vote, Calderón with 36 percent, and Peña Nieto with 39 percent. The PRI was the second-strongest party in 2000, as was the PRD in 2006 and 2012. In this circumstance, the leaders of all three parties recognized that the only way to enact reform legislation was to forge cross-party alliances.

The composition of Peña Nieto's first cabinet in 2013 confirms this preference for collaboration because this was the most multiparty cabinet of the past eighty years. It included a former president of the PRD, Rosario Robles;[15] a leader of the Green Party—a frequent PRI ally—who was a former mentor of the president when he was governor of the state of Mexico; a former treasury and energy secretary under President Calderón, José Antonio Meade Kuribreña, as secretary of foreign relations;[16] and the former PAN secretary of public security and attorney general under Fox and Calderón, respectively, Eduardo Medina Mora, as ambassador to the United States. Furthermore, this cabinet also demonstrated diversity in the choice of PRI members, including the former PRI president and candidate for the PRI presidential nomination in 2012, Beatriz Paredes, and combining technocrats and party militants in the hybrid tradition that stretches back to the administrations of Miguel de la Madrid and Salinas. Financial leadership remains in the hands of technocrats such as Pedro Aspe, who was Salinas's treasury secretary, while some of the more politically oriented cabinet posts went to former presidential contenders such as Alfredo del Mazo, Francisco Labastida, and Cuauhtémoc Cárdenas.[17]

Despite these positive signs of political progress Peña Nieto faces important contextual challenges that may undermine the ability of the federal administration, state governors, and municipal mayors to strengthen democratic governance and assure continuing democratic consolidation. As of May 2014, surveys suggested that almost 60 percent of Mexicans believed the country's economic situation was the most important challenge while 37 percent saw security as the most critical issue (Consulta Mitofsky 2014); and it is these two issues that have worried Mexicans most over the past fourteen years, with the security situation overtaking the economy in both 2011 and 2012. Equally telling was that seven out of ten Mexicans saw both issues as getting worse, not better (Consulta Mitofsky 2014). At the same time fully 60 percent of respondents put Peña Nieto's electoral victory in the same category as that of President Fox in 2000—as constituting a change not just of government but of the political system overall. Clearly, there was reason to do so in 2000, after seven decades of PRI rule, and the similar view of the 2012 result suggests a strong popular expectation that Peña Nieto's government will address the problems besetting both the economy and security with policies to reinforce the antidrug strategy, generate employment, combat poverty, and build schools.

So how can the reforms identified in the Pact for Mexico respond to these overriding economic and security concerns and, thus, satisfy citizens' expectations? The most novel aspect of the Pact is that it is imagined as a grand strategy that links these issues together in the recognition that no progress can be made without structural changes that will impact different policy arenas. For example, the Pact focuses on economic growth and the historical obstacles to it because of the perceived link between unemployment and organized crime. In a conversation organized by David Shirk, director of the Trans-Border Institute at the University of San Diego, between the chief of police in Tijuana and a small group of scholars during the latter years of the Calderón administration, we asked the police chief to characterize the typical cartel member that he and his officers encountered. He described the cartel member as a young man with a low level of formal education who usually was unemployed. The chief's description replicates other sources such as the US intelligence community, which has suggested that some 450,000 Mexicans are employed directly or indirectly in organized crime, prompted in part by the high rates of unemployment during the past two administrations.[18] Moreover, the problems of comparatively poor economic growth and low productivity are often attributed to the failures of the educational system, which itself is seen as partly responsible for the persistent poverty of a large minority of families, particularly as measured by low income levels. Using more sophisticated measures of poverty, based on inadequate income to achieve certain capacities, the 2010 census also reported that 19 percent of Mexicans were suffering from nutritional poverty, 27 percent from health and educational poverty, and 50 percent from housing and transportation poverty—with none of these measures having shifted much since 2002 (Coneval 2014). Bizarrely, organized crime in Mexico recognizes this poverty and the lack of employment opportunities by openly advertising for new recruits, often emphasizing economic benefits including life insurance policies (Roig-Franzia 2008)!

The Mexican government has attempted to address poverty in several ways. Social expenditure began to increase significantly under Ernesto Zedillo's administration (1994–2000) and this continued under the succeeding PAN administrations of Fox and Calderón. Although the proportion of Mexicans living in poverty had declined slightly by the end of the Fox administration, the figure began to rise again with the global recession.[19] By the last year of the Calderón administration, 57 percent of government expenditure fell into the social category while social and economic spending combined reached 91 percent; these figures increased to 60 percent and 93 percent, respectively, in Peña Nieto's first year in office (Mexico 2013: 366). But even if it alleviated poverty in some degree, this spending did not have a perceptible impact on unemployment, low rates of productivity, lack of competitiveness, and slowing economic growth, all of which many attribute—inter alia—to deficiencies in public education. For this reason the education system was the object of the Pact's first reform in 2013, creating the Professional Teaching Service, an agency that would henceforth control the hiring, promotion, and continued employment of teachers, thereby removing these decisions from the powerful National Teachers Union (SNTE). At the same time the Oportunidades program had earlier recognized the close relationship between poverty and time spent in education, and so required low-income families to keep their children in school between the third grade and the third year of high school as a condition of continuing to receive cash transfers.[20]

These efforts by the federal government have to compete with the drug cartels' high-profile strategy of investing in local communities by constructing local municipal buildings and sports facilities while also donating directly to Catholic parishes whenever this suited their agenda. As a consequence, a large minority of Mexicans living in smaller rural communities where cartels have been active believed that organized crime has done more for them than local government, and that it is drug trafficking that drives progress at the community level (see Table 13.1).

Similarly, there exists no stronger illustration of Mexicans' lack of faith in public institutions or in their capacity to maintain stability and security than the growing trend among rural Mexicans to establish their own police forces recruited from ordinary citizens. Fully two-fifths of Mexicans believed that such forces can best protect their communities against one-fifth who kept faith in local or state police, while 70 percent

Table 13.1 Mexican Attitudes Toward Drug-Trafficking Organizations

Questions	Percentage Answering Yes
Listened to a *narcocorrido* (song about traffickers)	90
Narcocorridos reflect reality	69
Drug trafficking generates employment	41
Listened frequently to a *narcocorrido*	37
Drug traffickers do more public works in communities than their own governments	34
Drug trafficking generates progress in the communities where drug traffickers live	33
If drug trafficking weren't violent, it would be a beneficial activity to your state	27
Narcocorridos distort reality	24
Drug trafficking is a necessary evil	23
Don't know if they are heroes or criminals	17
Drug cartel leaders are heroes	15
It is not bad to produce or sell drugs	11
It is not a bad thing to consume drugs	10

Source: Carta Paramétrica (2011); 400 respondents, +/− 4.9 percent margin of error.

favored locally recruited or a combination of such local and regular police (the same percentage who judged both local and state police to be ineffective in fighting crime). Unsurprisingly, such community forces in the shape of self-defense groups had begun to multiply quickly by early in 2013 (Carta Paramétrica 2014a).

Since both the US and Mexican governments were also skeptical of the capacity of police to fight the drug cartels, the Mexican government has turned increasingly to its armed forces to take primary responsibility for this task. Over time, these cartels have evolved into sophisticated criminal organizations involved in kidnapping, human trafficking, extortion, bribery, and torture, with public officials, journalists, small and large businesses, police, soldiers, and ordinary citizens among its victims—as well as the members of rival cartels. Worse yet, they can commit even the most cruel of crimes with impunity since less than 2 percent of all crimes reported to the police are ultimately prosecuted (Seelke 2013: 14). But ordering the military to take the lead in combating criminality can create its own problems, most notably a vertiginous increase in human rights abuses. Most of the alleged violations by the military—who have no police training—have gone unpunished, so reinforcing popular perceptions of the judiciary as ineffective and the military as increasingly unaccountable. According to the attorney general, some 26,000 Mexicans had disappeared in drug-related violence during the six years of the Calderón administration; and, despite the 5,600 alleged cases of military abuse investigated by the armed forces from 2007 to 2013, only 38 individuals have been punished (Human Rights Watch 2014).[21]

The level of criminal violence also has produced a chilling effect on journalists, one of the most influential actors in securing accountability and a key component of a consolidated democracy. Comparative studies have revealed that a free press is bad for corruption but good for political accountability and the rule of law (Stanig 2014: 1; Tella and Franceschelli 2009; Manzetti 2014: 193), and equally that for many years Mexico has been one of the most dangerous countries in the world for journalists. As Emily Edmonds-Poli observes, the most reliable reports focus on the actual motive for a journalist's murder, and they suggest that seventy-four journalists and media support workers "lost their lives between 2000 and 2012" (2013: 5).[22] Yet only one culprit has been brought to book since 2006, again reflecting an almost complete impunity for these crimes (2013: 11).[23]

Violent Crime, Corruption, and the Legitimacy of Mexican Democracy

There is no doubt that Mexico is finding it difficult to change its political culture to achieve a greater degree of accountability and transparency within an effective legal framework, a challenge that is commonplace across Latin America and especially in its near neighbors, Guatemala and Honduras. At the same time, the criminal violence of the drug cartels has rapidly reduced popular trust in government institutions and popular faith in democratic government. In the recent past, just before Calderón won the presidential election of 2006, half of all Mexicans judged government institutions to be strong while nearly 30 percent thought them weak. Only six years later, following Calderón's violent war on the drug cartels, perceptions were reversed, with 47 percent thinking them weak and only 32 percent believing them strong (Carta Paramétrica 2012). Moreover, while 40 percent of Mexicans continued to see the federal executive as the country's most influential institution, fully 30 percent believed it was the drug cartels (see Table 13.2), with Congress a distant third with 9 percent. And as of 2013, according to Carta Paramétrica (2014b), only one in three Mexicans believed the government to be capable of defeating the cartels.

**Table 13.2 Institutions or Groups That Have the Most Influence in Mexico
(percentage of responses)**

Institution	2008	2009	2010
President	37	43	41
Drug cartels	34	28	29
Congress	9	9	9
Armed forces	5	4	4
Catholic Church	6	4	5
Large companies	4	4	4
Media	2	5	4
Unions	2	0	1
Don't know	1	3	3

Source: Carta Paramétrica (2014b).

Similar results are found in surveys focusing on the state and local levels. Within individual states 37 percent of respondents said it was the governor who wielded most power, but 28 percent pointed to the drug cartels, with the army a distant third with 9 percent. Equally, 84 percent acknowledged that organized crime was present in their state, but only 30 percent thought the state government had the capacity to confront it. Popular perceptions at the local level were even more pessimistic with only 21 percent convinced of the municipality's ability to challenge organized crime (Carta Paramétrica 2013e). The lack of faith in the strength of local, state, and national institutions to fulfill their responsibilities for public safety is further reflected in the belief that criminal organizations already control 10 percent of Mexico's cities (Sullivan 2014). It therefore is no surprise that in 2012 more than 40 percent of Mexicans considered crime to be their biggest problem, the fifth-highest response in Latin America (Seligson, Smith, and Zechmeister 2012: 130). In the same year, one in three Mexicans reported that a member of their household had been a victim of crime, rising to one in two in Mexico City (Seligson, Smith, and Zechmeister 2012: 144–145).

The level of crime in Mexico adversely affects economic growth, investment, employment, and social development (Sohnen 2012: 8). According to the Global Peace Index, Mexico spent $173 billion to fight organized crime in 2013, which is over 9 percent of the country's gross national product (GNP), or $1,430 per person (Institute for Economics and Peace 2014: 69). Indeed, it has been calculated that a 10 percent decrease in the homicide rate would translate into a 1.1 percent increase in per capita GDP. Furthermore, by 2014 Mexico ranked fifth after Venezuela, Honduras,

Guatemala, and Haiti as the most dangerous country in Latin America for doing business. These are strange bedfellows for a middle-income OECD country (FTI Consulting 2014). But the most important adverse effect has been on levels of trust among ordinary Mexicans for each other and for the institutions of democratic government, with many Mexicans willing to replace democracy with authoritarian rule if it would reduce the levels of violence, both real and perceived. In a comprehensive analysis of the relationship between violence and trust, Miguel Carreras identifies three explanations for declining support of political institutions:

> First, Latin American citizens become disenchanted with a political system that is unable to respond efficiently to one of their main concerns (public security). Second, individuals who are victims of violence or who perceive violence as high are dissatisfied with judicial systems that fail to punish those responsible for the increased violence. Third, exposure to criminal violence has a negative impact on interpersonal trust, which in turn negatively affects system support. (2013: 100–102)

In the case of the Dominican Republic in particular, it was found that there was "less system support among those who had been the victims of crime, those who perceived greater insecurity, those who had been the victims of corruption, and those who perceived higher levels of corruption" (Morgan and Espinal 2010: xxxii).

Similarly, it has become clear in Mexico, as in Central America, that "both personal victimization and fear of crime in the neighborhood emerge as important predictors of citizens' willingness to allow authorities to act on the margin of the law" (Malone 2010: 14).[24] Regardless of whether a person is an actual crime victim or fears becoming a victim, it increases their tolerance for human rights abuses, so undermining the rule of law. In 2014 nearly a fourth of Mexicans indicated that, if acting as members of the police or armed forces, they would prefer to execute drug traffickers rather than hand them over to the proper authorities (Carta Paramétrica 2014g). Fear of crime and violence has also pushed 2 percent of the population aged eighteen years and older to move somewhere else, whether within Mexico or abroad, from 2006 through 2010, with over 265,000 Mexicans fleeing to the United States for the same motive (Rios Contreras 2014: 208). In neighboring El Salvador, Nicaragua, and Guatemala perceptions of increased crime, being a victim of crime, and the level of corruption have been shown to be statistically significant in predicting patterns of migration (Hiskey, Malone, and Orcés 2014: 6).

Such is the level of disenchantment with institutions in Mexico that support for democracy itself is being steadily eroded, as is evident from participants' responses to three key statements from the Latin American

Barometer, namely, "Democracy is preferable to any other form of government"; "In some circumstances, an authoritarian government is preferable to a democracy"; "To someone like me, a democratic regime is the same as an authoritarian regime." During Zedillo's administration (1994–2000), preferences for a democratic system remained quite stable at about half of all Mexicans (see Table 13.3), they unsurprisingly rose to their highest recorded level of 63 percent one year after Fox's inauguration, and they remained stable at over half until the end of Fox's term. But in the subsequent years of the Calderón administration, support for democracy declined through 2011, with a strong rise in the proportion of Mexicans who viewed democracy and authoritarianism as equally preferable. Some 44 percent came to see their democracy as problematic, a view that was more pronounced among those on lower incomes, but it must be recognized that this tendency is reflected in greater or lesser degrees across many Latin American countries, including Guatemala, El Salvador, Honduras, Nicaragua, Costa Rica, Panama, Colombia, Ecuador, Bolivia, and Peru (Carlin et al. 2012: 211). One interesting consequence of this declining faith in democracy is the increasing support for a different form of democracy—namely, direct democracy—as measured by the responses to a question in the Latin American Public Opinion Project (LAPOP) survey of 2012 asking whether the "people should govern directly rather than through elected representatives?" Mexico ranked fifth across Latin America in its support for such a system at a level similar to those of Bolivia, Ecuador, Paraguay, Guatemala, and Peru. In good part, this simply confirms Mexico's low levels of trust in political parties (equal numbers of Mexicans believe that parties are and are not necessary to democratic government; Carta Paramétrica 2014f) and the institutions of electoral democracy more broadly writ.

Although the policy package endorsed by the Pact for Mexico attempted to address some of the most pressing problems giving rise to these negative

Table 13.3 Support for Democracy in Mexico, 1995–2013

Presidency	Range of Support for Type of Regime (percentage)		
	Democracy	Authoritarian	No Difference
Ernesto Zedillo	44–53	15–34	15–22
Vicente Fox	46–63	13–35	14–30
Felipe Calderón	42–48	10–15	30–36
Enrique Peña Nieto	37	16	37

Source: Carta Paramétrica (2013f).

perceptions, it did not tackle what many view as the crucial problem—the depth and extent of corruption, a condition that affects public life, the implementation of public policy, and the health and growth of Mexico's economy (see Table 13.4). In other words the Pact's program of institutional reform was designed to improve the formal political and legal framework governing economy and society, but could not reach or reform the informal rules that undermine institutional performance and the effective implementation of public policy. And this is reflected in the popular belief, according to Carta Paramétrica data, that the key to victory over organized crime is not reducing the US demand for illicit drugs, but rather reducing political corruption.

Nobody questions that corruption is pervasive throughout Mexico at the level of paying bribes to mollify the police, making side payments to ensure the supply of services, and so forth. But the nub of the problem is the characteristic presence of individual and institutional clientelism (Bardallo Bandera 2014: 121), and the consequent perception among Mexicans that others illegally use their personal connections to receive special attention or treatment. Indeed, 90 percent of respondents in a survey of 2013 were convinced that this was routinely occurring at one or all levels of government (Carta Paramétrica 2013c) while 30 percent suggested that the situation was no different in the private sector. Moreover, nearly half of the respondents said that corruption of this kind is not reported for fear of reprisals, suggesting that such corruption consistently erodes trust in the judicial system and, by extension, in political institutions more generally (Carlin et al. 2012: 199). And attitudes toward corruption become more permissive—or simply resigned—where citizens lack confidence in these institutions, so creating a vicious circle of mistrust (Lavena 2013: 361). This is what drives the low level of support for the rule of law in Mexico—low even by Latin American standards.

Table 13.4 Mexican Views on Public Policy Issues

How Big of a Problem Is . . . ?	Percentage Responding Very Big
Crime	81
Economic problems	75
Illegal drugs	73
Corrupt political leaders	68

Source: Pew Global Attitudes Project (2009). One thousand interviews conducted nationally, May 26 to June 2, 2009, +/− 3.0 percent margin of error.

Conclusion

The policy initiatives endorsed by the Pact for Mexico, supported by the United States through the Mérida Initiative, and subsequently pursued by the current PRI administration have promoted an important process of institutional reform,[25] but the reforms have not reached the intractable informal rules that determine the practical effectiveness of government institutions in Mexico. For this reason the World Bank's time series indicators of accountability, rule of law, regulatory quality, and so forth show that since 2000 there was virtually no improvement in transparency; control of corruption remained stagnant; government effectiveness, regulatory quality, and the rule of law declined—the latter significantly; and political stability fell by almost half (see Table 13.5).

The Pact expressed a tentative move toward the kind of coalitional presidentialism that has characterized executive-legislative relationships in Brazil and Chile, and also in Uruguay and Bolivia in some degree, and it succeeded in similar fashion in bolstering governability in the narrow sense of pushing through a reforming legislative agenda. But on the evidence mustered here, this increased governability has been recurrently compromised by a popular distrust of government institutions, not least political parties. This lack of trust derives in large part from a radically imperfect rule of law and rampant corruption, which together have reinforced the sense that government in Mexico remains largely unaccountable. These failings eventually leach legitimacy from the political system overall as popular support for democracy inevitably declines. Thus, although electoral

Table 13.5 Governance Indicators for Mexico (percentage)

Indicator	1996	2000	2006	2009
Voice and accountability	44.0	54.8	51.0	53.6
Political stability	17.8	43.8	29.3	22.2
Government effectiveness	55.3	63.1	58.7	60.5
Regulatory quality	70.7	64.4	63.9	61.0
Rule of law	35.2	43.3	42.9	34.0
Control of corruption	41.7	47.1	49.5	49.0

Source: World Bank Governance Indicators, 2011, www/info.worldbank.org/governance.
Note: Percentages refer to the percentage of countries globally that Mexico scored above. The higher the percentage, the better the ranking. The governance indicators presented here aggregate the views on the quality of governance provided by a large number of enterprise, citizen, and expert survey respondents in industrial and developing countries. These data are gathered from a number of survey institutes, think tanks, nongovernmental organizations, and international organizations.

irregularities have been few and far between in every election since 2000 (Cantú 2014: 12), nonetheless the same percentage of supporters of the strongest losing candidate in each election have believed the election to be fraudulent and democracy in Mexico a sham (Camp 2013b: 471). For these voters, electoral outcomes are to be trusted no more than any other government activity; and, without trust in government institutions, there is no way to defend the legitimacy of the democratic system overall.

Can trust in government institutions be restored in some degree? This will necessarily depend on whether government policy can resolve the issues that most affect the citizenry's life chances, and especially its sense of personal security. Trust clearly cannot be repaired while numerous sections of the population have to change their daily routines and social interaction in response to criminal violence or their perception of the likelihood of criminal violence. The conditions for trust cannot flourish if citizens have to calculate whether they can go shopping, take public transportation or drive their car, go out for an evening walk or to the movies, or join friends and family for an evening meal. This represents a huge challenge for the government because, as I argued throughout this chapter, it requires an effective response to the problems of several interrelated policy areas, including the criminal justice and education systems, as well as measures to improve the productivity of the economy and rates of employment while simultaneously bearing down on corruption, especially in federal and state police forces and in the administration of government.

Notes

1. For the complete agreement as well as for discussion of the initial five reforms in 2013, see Pacto por México (2013).

2. These reforms received widespread support from the public, according to the survey data in Carta Paramétrica (2013a and 2013b).

3. See Instituto Tecnológico Autónomo de México and the Mexico Institute, Woodrow Wilson International Center for Scholars (2012).

4. Legislative reelection, contrary to public opinion, was not a principle that emerged from the 1910 Mexican Revolution, expressed in the mantra "Effective Suffrage, No Re-election." Instead, it was a constitutional amendment introduced by President Cárdenas, and went into effect with the 1934–1937 congressional session. However, the change in allowing a mayor to be reelected one additional term does fit in with the broader principle of no reelection of the president or a state governor. A specific justification for making that change is that a mayor serves only half as long as a governor or a president, just three years.

5. Critics have rightly noted that two other political reforms—replacing the Federal Electoral Institute with a new untested federal agency, some of whose responsibilities are unclear, as well as allowing election results to be overturned for violations of spending rules—are likely to open the doors to greater rather than decreasing postelectoral conflict (Starr 2014: 54).

6. These involve changes to Article 59 of the 1917 Constitution.

7. The countries studied were Argentina, Bolivia, Brazil, Chile, Colombia, Costa Rica, Ecuador, Mexico, Uruguay, and Venezuela.

8. The reelection of mayors and local deputies (state legislators) will apply to the next individual who holds those positions since local elections occur in different years. This affects Article 115 (mayors) and Article 116 (state deputies). For the best current explanation of how the laws will be implemented, and the restrictions against their abuse, see Dominguez (2004).

9. The PRI's own bylaws prohibited its members from voting on any changes in the management of the state oil company, Pemex. After Peña Nieto requested the party to alter its internal regulations, the assembled party membership (several thousand) at its annual meeting voted unanimously to make those changes (Wilkinson 2013a).

10. Forty-four percent of Mexicans were still opposed to the petroleum reform in June 2014 (Carta Paramétrica 2014c). In a survey completed in July 2014, two-thirds or more of Mexicans indicated that the PRI supported the six major reforms to date and fewer than half, with the exception of the energy bill, believed PAN supported these reforms (it supported all six). And except for the education reform, only 21–25 percent of Mexicans believed the PRD supported any of the bills (Carta Paramétrica 2014d).

11. The representatives of the PRI in Congress, under the leadership of then PRI secretary general, Elba Gordillo, the powerful teachers' union leader, invited me to speak to the 224 PRI members of that body on democracy and legislative responsibilities. In my presentation titled "Walking the Democratic Line in Mexico, Whose Democratic Anyway?" I urged the audience to pursue a statesman-like strategy, placing the interests of the country above their partisan interests. To their credit, the PRI congressional leadership at that time wanted to collaborate with President Fox, but Gordillo and her group were forced out of their leadership positions shortly thereafter, ending any real possibility of such cooperation. My presentation was published in Camp (2003: 4–10).

12. In a survey by Carta Parametríca in December 2013, 73 percent of Mexicans believed that laws in their country were not applied equally, two-thirds disagreed that the rights of those accused were respected during the entire legal process, and that honesty and justice prevailed in the courts (Carta Paramétrica 2014c). Moreover, the World Justice Project's Rule of Law Index 2014, which ranked the pervasiveness of each country's rule of law, quality of governance, and criminal justice system, ranked Mexico seventy-nine out of ninety-nine countries (World Justice Project 2014).

13. For example, in the early discussion of the transparency reforms in the fall of 2012, three-quarters of Mexicans did not know what IFAI (Instituto Federal de Accceso a la Información y Protección), the agency responsible for access to government agency information, was. Moreover, six out of ten citizens considered such information as government expenditures and the salaries of officials to be opaque and difficult to find out (Carta Paramétrica 2012). For an insightful analysis on how an organization, the Citizen's Movement, has been able to achieve far greater transparency in some ninety municipalities in Mexico, see Tucker (2013).

14. The most comprehensive account of accountability in government agencies is Merino (2013).

15. To his credit, Fox attempted to incorporate representatives of the PRD in his cabinet, but the party refused to allow its members to join Fox's government. It is also important to note that both PAN administrations included individuals who had

served in Zedillo's cabinet such as Luis Téllez Kuenzler, a former secretary of energy and chief of staff, as Calderón's communication and transportation secretary, and Francisco Gil Díaz, former assistant secretary of the treasury under Salinas and Fox's secretary of the treasury. Most of these individuals could be identified as technocrats rather than politicians.

16. Although considered a political independent, his father (Dionisio Alfredo Meade García de León) pursued a distinguished career in public service, concluding it as assistant secretary of legislative liaison in government at the end of the Fox administration. His wife (Lucia Kuri Breña Orvaños) is the niece of Daniel Kuri Breña Gordoa, a cofounder of PAN and a member of the National Executive Committee from 1939 to 1949. Moreover, he served as the first rector of the Instituto Tecnológico Autónomo de México in 1946 and was a student leader in the historic movement supporting José Vasconcelos's 1929 opposition candidacy for the presidency (R. P. Franco 1979: 197–198). He also is the grandson of the distinguished sculptor and artist, José Kuri Breña.

17. For a detailed analysis of the composition politically and demographically, and its significance, see Camp (2013a).

18. In addition, "official estimates suggest that drug trafficking activities now account for 3 percent to 4 percent of Mexico's more than $1 trillion GDP" (Shirk 2011: 7).

19. The first dramatic increases in social expenditures actually happened under Gustavo Díaz Ordaz (1964–1970), whose administration's social expenditures averaged 32 percent, compared to only 19 percent for his predecessor. This percentage did not change significantly until de la Madrid's tenure (1982–1988), when it reached a new peak of 41 percent, followed by Salinas, who again increased it significantly to half of the total expenditures. The next three administrations all have assigned 56 percent or more to the social category. Since 2000, 90 percent of federal expenditures have fallen into the combined economic and social categories (Mexico 2011: 127–128).

20. For the limitations of the program, see Molyneux (2006: 425–449).

21. One of the important changes that should help reduce the level of impunity by the military is to remove cases involving civilians from military jurisdiction. Amnesty International is even more critical, concluding that of the more than 7,000 complaints of mistreatment and torture directed to the National Commission on Human Rights between 2010 to 2013, not one resulted in a conviction on torture charges.

22. See also Ellingwood (2011).

23. For a detailed analysis of these consequences on journalists in northern Mexico, see Relly and Bustamante (2014: 108–131).

24. Malone's paper, one of the most thorough analyses of this issue, examines other potential political consequences, noting that many of the causal linkages are not straightforward. She also concludes in the Mexican case that crime adversely affects casting valid ballots in elections (2010: 16).

25. For a clear-eyed evaluation, see Ingram, Rodríguez Ferreira, and Shirk (2011).

14

Counting the Costs
of Political Repression

Dolores Trevizo

Despite well-documented episodes of human rights violations and of corruption at the highest levels of military command, Mexico's armed forces have, on average, enjoyed high levels of trust. But a closer examination of public opinion suggests not only significant regional variation in such trust, but also change over time. I explore this variation by comparing trust in the military in the aftermath of Mexico's dirty war in the 1970s and 1980s, as the electoral system democratized after seventy-one years of one-party rule by the PRI (Partido Revolucionario Institucional, or Institutional Revolutionary Party), and then after the democratically elected president, Felipe Calderón, declared a war on drug cartels in December 2006.

This chapter not only establishes the existence of subnational legitimacy deficits not elsewhere documented, but I also show that such deficits both reflect and further contribute to a living memory of human rights violations. In particular, I show that the trace memory of past military abuses is mobilized by activists and others who frame the recent abuses resulting from the war on drug cartels as comparable to those that occurred during Mexico's dirty war; they do this even though the violations today are no longer politically motivated. My research thus not only supports the extant scholarship showing that military abuses degrade the quality of citizenship and democracy when they happen, but it further illuminates how—through the activation of collective memory—these abuses are corrosive to the legitimacy of the state even decades later.

To make my case, I first define the key concepts in the scholarship on legitimacy and collective memory before offering a brief history of military abuse in Mexico. With quantitative evidence, I then describe and explain when, how, and the extent to which trust in the military declined in some states. I follow this with a narrative to explain how these legitimacy deficits matter as living memory over time. To draw out the comparative implications of my empirical findings, I conclude the chapter with a brief secondary analysis of Colombia and Brazil. The comparisons indicate that the local legitimacy deficits that result from militarizing law enforcement create a collective memory that, over the long run, has the potential to undermine the legitimacy of the state itself.

The Literature on State Legitimacy and Legitimacy Deficits

Legitimacy, according to David Beetham (1991), is achieved when state power is not only legally valid, but morally justified from the standpoint of the citizens' beliefs, as demonstrated in their expressed consent. They manifest consent by participating in elections and pro-government rallies or, even symbolically, through oaths of allegiance. While armed revolutionary movements are the clearest examples of people withdrawing the right of those in power to rule, even nonviolent protests withdraw consent when they are massive and system challenging (Gilley 2009). But well short of such crises, legitimacy can be weakened along any dimension. Legitimacy deficits not only are dynamic, they even are reversible. Relations with people in civil society improve when state institutions deliver public goods in a competent, fair, universalistic, incorruptible, and transparent way.[1] Doing so further promotes cooperation and generalized trust among the citizenry, contributing not only to cultural and economic development, but also to the rich associational life linked to democratic pluralism.[2]

Centralized states especially earn the "right to rule" (Gilley 2009) by providing such essential public goods as welfare, justice, and especially physical security. Citizens not only distinguish between policies about which they simply disagree, they also discriminate between poor performance due to the lack of resources as opposed to incompetence, economic exploitation, or abuse of authority (Beetham 1991: 134). While different types of state malperformance may lead to the withdrawal of citizens' cooperation at faster or slower rates, the worst abuses range from entrenched rent-seeking corruption,[3] to the widespread violation of people's physical integrity human rights. Violations of the body are evident in cases of torture, arbitrary detention, political imprisonment, and extrajudicial killings. When committed by the state's security forces, such abuses degrade citizenship and contribute to collective insecurity in a way that undermines trust in the government. Diane Davis (2010) observes that such mistrust can create networks of allegiances and reciprocity to others, a situation she calls "fragmented sovereignties."

Further, since state violence creates collective traumas, and since such trauma affects families and collective bystanders, the delegitimizing effects of state repression can continue to register over time as more people learn about it. But this is just one way that collective trauma forms what Winifred

Tate (2007) calls the "living memory." As Maurice Halbwachs (1992) argues, over time, certain events become a trace memory at the collective level, and collective memories inform the political culture of various groups, including those operating in radically different contexts of the original events. This is because collective memory is reconstructed by communities in their ongoing social dynamics. As such, "the past is not preserved but is reconstructed on the basis of the present" (Halbwachs 1992: 40). Indeed, sometimes that reconstruction results in the radicalization of some people and even the institutionalization of the memory through the creation of new organizations (Trevizo 2014; Tate 2007). Drawing on the collective memory literature, I expand on the history of military abuse in Mexico before discussing how it may have created long-term legitimacy deficits.

Brief History of Military Abuse in Mexico

Of the many potential types of military abuse, those that occur in counterinsurgency operations are among the most memorable because armed conflict tends to result in the loss of many lives. Such was the case in Mexico as the armed forces developed a bad reputation in many communities in the second part of the twentieth century when they were deployed to put down armed insurgents. The military did so in Guerrero state beginning in the late 1960s, most dramatically in the 1970s, and on a smaller scale even through the 1990s; in Chiapas quickly, but quite dramatically, in January 1994; and, on a considerably smaller scale, in Oaxaca in the 1990s.

But the military also regularly engaged unarmed peasant protestors and sometimes violated their human rights in the process. This was especially so in the 1970s and 1980s when soldiers regularly evicted peasants who illegally squatted on private land in the hopes of forcing land reform (Trevizo 2011). Many such peasants, especially those in the south of the country who spoke an indigenous language, were first evicted and then jailed on trumped-up criminal charges frequently based on confessions extracted through torture (Trevizo 2014). In 1982, Amnesty International reported an estimated 600 peasant political prisoners as of 1981 (Amnesty International 1982). It was in this context that the rural poor and their leftist and urban allies fought state repression. Their so doing constituted the emergence of an incipient human rights movement, and the development of this movement succeeded in putting the issue of political repression squarely on the national agenda (Trevizo 2014).

Most recently, when President Calderón militarized law enforcement, the armed forces again stood accused of many human rights violations. As noted, on assuming power in December 2006, Calderón ordered the military and federal police to jointly stop the cartels. Although the use of the military in drug interdiction was not new, soldiers had previously been deployed only to the rural drug production zones. Calderón ordered the military to lead federal police forces because the law enforcement agencies ordinarily responsible for crime were outmatched by the cartels insofar as they were understaffed, poorly armed, locally disorganized, regionally uncoordinated, and ill-trained. Worse still, many corrupt police were employed by the cartels (Grayson 2011; Benítez Manaut 2013). By 2009, Calderón "deployed 45,000 soldiers and thousands of federal police in nearly a dozen of Mexico's states" (Beittel 2009: 1). But while Calderón's domestic war secured support and billions of dollars from the US government, it quickly turned into a crisis in Mexico.

In sum, in the past several decades, there have been various kinds of military interventions in Mexico. Since the type and extent of political struggles, cartel violence, and other events involving the military (e.g., natural disasters) vary at the subnational level, it follows that their interventions and thus their performances also vary by state. I therefore hypothesized that the level of discipline and professionalism of military personnel, as well as how haphazardly or abusively they engage citizens, likely affects where, why, how much, and for how long people trust them. Although the data do not permit a more granular analysis by ethnicity or other social variables, I offer an ecological analysis of the variation of trust in the military over time during periods of extraordinary state violence because human rights violations affect entire communities. This is so even though the vast majority of victims are young men.

Findings of This Study

Table 14.1 shows the subnational variation in trust in Mexico's armed forces, per the 2004–2010 Latin American Public Opinion Project survey data. This table indicates that the public's trust in the armed forces was, as an average, moderately lower shortly after the transition to democracy in 2004, than it was in 2010 when the drug war was well under way. But the subnational variation did not range as widely in 2004 as in 2010. It is possible that the lower average score for 2004 can be explained in part by the relatively low profile of the armed forces that year, with the notable exception of some states—as revealed in Table 14.2. This relatively low profile probably reflects the smaller scale of military efforts at drug interdiction prior to 2006, which were concentrated in rural production areas and never a priority for the federal executive (Daly, Heinle, and Shirk 2012). However, the fact that the states of Chiapas, Guerrero, and Oaxaca—not only among the

Table 14.1 Average Levels of Trust in Mexico's Armed Forces by State

State	2004	2008	2010
Aguascalientes	5.71	4.71	5.91
Baja California	5.40	6.79	6.48
Coahuila	5.33	5.53	5.44
Chiapas	4.98	5.68	4.75
Chihuahua	5.28	4.47	5.25
Distrito Federal	4.58	4.71	5.16
Durango	5.21	6.33	4.70
Guanajuato	4.95	5.99	5.10
Guerrero	4.72	5.48	5.04
Hidalgo	5.76	4.31	5.73
Jalisco	5.02	5.43	5.89
Estado de México	4.85	5.05	5.21
Michoacán	5.15	5.47	4.71
Morelos	4.64	5.17	4.84
Nayarit	5.54	5.54	5.75
Nuevo León	5.41	5.52	6.17
Oaxaca	4.49	5.75	5.07
Puebla	5.04	4.58	4.83
Querétaro	5.50	6.00	5.28
Quintana Roo	5.50	5.00	6.17
San Luis Potosí	5.00	5.56	5.82
Sinaloa	5.33	5.53	5.60
Sonora	4.88	5.33	5.37
Tabasco	5.09	4.75	5.63
Tamaulipas	5.19	5.78	5.21
Tlaxcala	5.38	5.17	5.09
Veracruz	5.28	5.32	5.26
Yucatán	5.24	6.19	5.46
Zacatecas	5.78	5.92	5.41
Mean	5.18	5.42	5.39
Median	5.21	5.48	5.27
Standard deviation	0.34	0.58	0.47
N	1,556	1,560	1,562

Notes: Based on a 7-point scale with 7 indicating the highest level of trust.

Every two years since 2004, the Latin American Public Opinion Project (LAPOP) collects face-to-face interviews in twenty-nine of thirty-two states on the basis of a random sample stratified by region and by urban-rural areas (comparable margin of error +/− 2.48). I ignored the 2006 survey as it was conducted in the last month of a highly contested presidential election that resulted in a loss of legitimacy of virtually all state and party institutions. I compared to the 2010 survey results because sufficient time had passed since December 2006, when the war on drug cartels began.

poorest, most rural, and most indigenous of the states, but also those that had experienced armed struggle through the 1990s—are well represented among those registering lower levels of trust in the armed forces begins to suggest that the military's counterinsurgency operations described above indeed hurt their image. In fact, simple bivariate correlations indicate that

Table 14.2 Physical Integrity Human Rights Violations Involving Army or Navy, per State, 1990–2010

State	1990–2006	2007–2010
Aguascalientes	0	0
Baja California	1	1
Baja California Sur	1	0
Campeche	0	0
Coahuila	0	2
Colima	1	0
Chiapas	1	0
Chihuahua	0	22
Distrito Federal	1	0
Durango	1	4
Guanajuato	0	1
Guerrero	8	2
Hidalgo	0	0
Jalisco	3	0
Estado de México	2	0
Michoacán	0	12
Morelos	0	2
Nayarit	0	1
Nuevo León	0	1
Oaxaca	1	3
Puebla	0	0
Querétaro	0	0
Quintana Roo	0	0
San Luis Potosí	0	0
Sinaloa	2	4
Sonora	1	4
Tabasco	0	3
Tamaulipas	0	4
Tlaxcala	0	0
Veracruz	0	1
Yucatán	0	0
Zacatecas	0	0

Source: National Human Rights Commission (CNDH) recommendations.

the states where there had earlier been higher than average numbers of anti-repression protests during the dirty war were also those in which people registered the lowest levels of trust in the armed forces as late as 2004 and even 2010.

Given these observations on state-level legitimacy deficits, it makes sense to delve further into the causes of distrust. To do so, I deployed a statistical analysis to explore the impact of both past and recent instances of military abuse on trust in the armed forces as measured first for 2004 (see Table 14.4) and second for 2010 (see Table 14.5). The dependent variable in both tables comprises three categories of states with high, average, or low levels of trust. Both sets of analysis model the relationship of abuse on trust by looking specifically at the impact of a measure of antire-pression protests from the late 1970s and early 1980s on the one hand, and a measure of the organizational density of human rights NGOs in the 1990s on the other. The second independent variable counts those NGOs linked to a national network of seventy-four organizations affiliated with Todos los Derechos para Todas y Todos. So, while the first independent variable reflects the immediate response to the dirty war by those most directly affected, the second independent variable captures the profession-al and institutional initiatives that emerged to monitor and publicize abus-es a decade later.

I also introduced a variable that counts the number of times that the military was found by the official National Human Rights Commission (CNDH) to have violated the physical integrity of citizens through arbitrary detentions, torture, or enforced disappearances, distinguishing between those abuses that occurred between 1991 and 2006 (prior to the declaration of war on the drug cartels) and those occurring during the height of this war from 2007 to 2010. Finally, the models include controls for both the size of each state's population and its level of organized crime. The latter has previ-ously been found to decrease the levels of satisfaction with democracy and to lower the trust in state institutions, including the armed forces (Blanco

Table 14.3 Means and Standard Deviations of Variables in the Analysis

Variable per State	Mean	SD	N
State's total population aged 17 years and older, 2000 census	1,804,856	1,640,418	32
State's total population 12 years of age and older, 2010 census	2,653,983	2,278,461	32
Intentional homicides per 100,000 per state, 2005	10.56	7.902	32
Organized crime homicides per state, 2011	513	669	32
Antirepression protests 1977–1983 per state	18.09	24.6	32
Number of local NGOs associated with Todos los Derechos para Todas y Todos	2.31	3.364	32
Number of CNDH documented human rights violations between 1999 and 2003	0.66	1.382	32
Number of CNDH documented human rights violations between 2007 and 2010	2.09	4.350	32
Average level of trust in the armed forces LAPOP data 2004	5.18	0.34	29
Average level of trust in the armed forces LAPOP data 2010	5.38	0.47	28

Note: NGO is nongovernmental organization; CNDC is National Human Rights Commission; LAPOP is Latin American Public Opinion Project.

Table 14.4 Trust in the Mexican Armed Forces, 2004[a]

	Average Level[b] of Trust in the Military, B/SE	Odds Ratio	High Level[b] of Trust in the Military, B/SE	Odds Ratio
State's population[c]	.000 (.000)	1	.000 (.000)	1
Intentional homicides as of 2005[d]	.030 (.132)	1.031	.065 (.168)	1.068
Density of human rights organizations per state (RedTDT)[e] post-1990	−.476** (.288)	.621	−1.418*** (.577)	.242
Antirepression peasant protests from 1977 to 1983[f]	−4.838* (3.716)	.008	−6.243* (3.977)	.002
National Human Rights Commission (CNDH) finds military violated physical integrity rights, 1990–2003	−.984 (1.318)	.374	−3.389* (2.267)	.034
Intercept	5.548* (4.094)		8.478** (4.498)	
−2 log likelihood intercept only	63.650			
−2 log likelihood final	32.7438	Chi-Square 31.211 (10 df)	$p < .001$	
Pseudo R-square: Nagelkerke = .74 McFadden's = .49				
N of states	10		9	

Notes: Given that the Latin American Public Opinion Project (LAPOP) data reported twenty-eight or twenty-nine states (out of a possible thirty-two Mexican states), my sample size is small. As even strong effects appear insignificant at the conventional levels when working with small samples, I evaluated the impact of variables at the $p < .10$ level, one-tailed tests (because my hypotheses are unidirectional). Finally, given the lack of consensus about the meaning of pseudo R-square, I reported but did not interpret these results. Standard errors are in parentheses.

a. An MLR regression is preferable to logit regressions because the dependent variable, average trust in the military by state, was reported as means by state.

b. The reference category is low level of trust in the military ($N = 10$).

c. The measure is the population older than seventeen years of age per the 2000 census.

d. Cartel violence is measured as intentional homicides (per 100,000) as of 2005 as reported by Blanco (2011: table 1, year 2005).

e. The variable is the number of local NGOs per state that are associated with the national network Todos los Derechos para Todas y Todos.

f. These data were collected and reported by Blanca Rubio (1987) on the basis of a news clipping archive, Información Sistematica. Because the news outlets offered few details beyond protest activity per state, these data cannot be disaggregated.

* $p < .10$, ** $p < .05$, *** $p < .01$ (one-tailed test).

Table 14.5 Trust in the Mexican Armed Forces, 2010[a]

	Average Level[b] of Trust in the Military, B/SE	Odds Ratio	High Level[b] of Trust in the Military, B/SE	Odds Ratio
State's population[c]	.000 (.000)	1	.000 (.000)	1
Organized crime as of 2011[d]	.883* (.619)	2.417	1.088* (.749)	2.970
Density of human rights organizations per state (RedTDT)[e] post-1990	−.107 (.200)	.898	−.192 (.239)	.826
Antirepression peasant protests from 1977 to 1983[f]	−1.507 (1.255)	.222	−2.096** (1.299)	.123
National Human Rights Commission (CNDH) finds military violated human rights between 2007 and 2010	−.041 (.115)	.959	−.998** (.556)	.369
Intercept	−1.930 (1.864)		.341 (1.559)	
−2 log likelihood intercept only	61.452			
−2 log likelihood final	45.246	Chi-Square 16.206 (10 df)	$p < .094$	
Pseudo *R*-square: Nagelkerke = .49 McFadden's = .26				
N of states	10		9	

Note: Standard errors are in parentheses.

a. Four states—Baja California Sur, Campeche, Colima, and Yucatan—were excluded from the Latin American Public Opinion Project (LAPOP) annual survey in 2010.

b. The reference category is low level of trust in the military ($N = 9$).

c. Per the 2010 census, the population per state variable is the number of people older than twelve years of age. The measure changes from the 2004 models because I could not find the same measure for the 2010 census. The two variables are highly correlated (.80).

d. For 2010, as the war on drugs was under way, I used a dummy variable for the most violent states (coded 1) due to drug cartel activity between 2007 and 2010 (as reported by Blanco 2011).

e. The variable is the number of local NGOs per state that are associated with the national network Todos los Derechos para Todas y Todos.

f. As noted, these data were collected and reported by Blanca Rubio (1987) on the basis of a news clipping archive, Información Sistematica.

* $p < .10$, ** $p < .05$, *** $p < .01$ (one-tailed test).

2011; Booth and Seligson 2009); though some studies—in contrast—found that high crime rates lead to increased support for hard-line law enforcement that can entail increased support for the military. Table 14.3 describes each of the variables in the analysis and reports their means and standard deviations.

Table 14.4, which reports only the findings for the baseline year of 2004, shows results that are generally consistent with my hypothesis, all else equal. Any increase in military abuses over the period 1990–2003 reduced the likelihood of citizens reporting a high level of trust in the armed forces. What is more, those states with a higher average number of protests against the repression of the dirty war years were less trusting of the armed forces as late as 2004. This noteworthy finding holds up even in the presence of the far more statistically significant measure of the presence of human rights NGOs in the immediately preceding years. Taken together, the results provide support for Davis's claim (2010) that trust networks between the military and the citizenry have weakened, though it does not add up to the categorical "destruction" of such trust as described by Davis. Rather it suggests that current distrust often has deep historical roots and so carries traces of the memory of past abuses into the present. The question then arises as to whether and in what degree such traces are reconstructed as collective memory for the purposes of contesting recent military violations in the context of Calderón's war on the drug cartels.

Trace Memory in the Delegitimizing Efforts of Anti–Drug War Activists

The decision to deploy the military to battle drug cartels in 2006 initially raised few protests because many people demanded public safety and assumed, in the abstract, that state violence could accomplish that. In highly publicized actions that at first gave the appearance of the restoration of law and order, soldiers captured cartel leaders, established checkpoints on roads, burned marijuana fields, and seized other drugs. But these actions led to even greater violence because the drug lords fought to protect their per annum $19 billion to $29 billion business. Further, the arrests or extradition (to the United States) of fifteen notable drug leaders in January 2007 created a power vacuum in the underworld, and opportunistic underlings fought to take their place by escalating violence. They did so to gain control over larger shares of the markets in drug and human trafficking (Grayson 2011). While the bloodbath that ensued responded to Calderón's war, it became a new business model (Lacey 2008). From 2008 on, there were assassinations of high-level police, military officers, and local mayors; there also were increasing reports of beheadings, massacres, extortion of small businesses, threats to elementary schools, criminal blockades of major highways, and a sharp rise in *sequestros* (kidnapping for ransom) (*Los Angeles Times* 2013; Beittel 2009).[4] And these were just the high-profile cases. Homicides linked to drug traffickers grew by 440 percent between 2007 and 2010 (Blanco 2011: 2).

By October 2011, more Mexicans (35 percent) considered insecurity/delinquency worse problems than that country's ongoing economic crisis, or its high levels of unemployment (ICESI 2011). Like their counterparts in Ciudad Juárez, many people in Tijuana and even Monterrey opted to not go out for dinner or shop past dusk, for fear of getting in the cross-fire between the criminals or between criminals and the state's security forces. They had good reason: by 2012, the cumulative death toll linked to Calderón's drug war was estimated to have topped 70,000, with an additional 10,000–20,000 people missing. According to Viridiana Rios Contreras (2014), hundreds of thousands of people were displaced by this war.

The magnitude of the death toll and the fact of bearing direct or mediated witness to public displays of beheadings or tortured or melted bodies, or of learning about mass graves, constitute a new collective trauma. It is not surprising, then, that as early as 2009 fully 40 percent of those polled disapproved of Calderón's war,[5] and several mass movements had organized to express moral outrage at his policy. Protestors insisted that the government locate the tens of thousands of people missing, or demanded justice for an even greater number of people killed. The largest such movement was led by Javier Sicilia, a poet who founded the Movement for Peace with Justice and Dignity after his son was murdered by a criminal. In still another expression of collective outrage, 23,000 people signed a petition organized by Natzai Sandoval, who filed a complaint with the International Criminal Court to investigate whether President Calderón and his top officials could be charged for war crimes and crimes against humanity.

Calderón was not the only one to be rebuked for this war. The military also lost the trust of some citizens between 2007 and 2010 because, as Table 14.2 suggests, it was not sufficiently trained to engage in local-level policing. Human Rights Watch, for example, documented not only 37,000 cases of arbitrary detentions (2011: 63), but also 74 "credible cases" of torture, with some of these torture cases resulting in about two dozen deaths (Human Rights Watch 2011). It also documented other instances of unjustified deadly force such as those that occur at military checkpoints when vehicles fail to stop, or during shoot-outs with criminals. It classified the latter as extrajudicial killings because soldiers or police manipulated the crime scene after the shoot-outs in attempted cover-ups (Human Rights Watch 2011: 6). The 2013 report by Human Rights Watch also argues that they have credible evidence of 149 cases of enforced disappearances committed by "public security forces." This measure is less damning of the military since it includes cases of local police officers who, as noted above, are easily corrupted by the cartels. Their evidence, however, clearly points to twenty abductions committed by the navy (Human Rights Watch 2013: 4).

Table 14.5, which reports the statistical findings for 2010, suggests that the armed forces lost the trust of many citizens as a result of the human rights violations that spiked during the war on drug cartels. This was so despite the fact that the rising levels of cartel violence simultaneously increased calls for law and order, including by strong-armed tactics. Consistent with other scholarship about how rising crime increases insecurity, Table 14.5 shows that every increase in organized crime in a given state nearly tripled the odds that people in that state would be among the most trusting of the armed forces. While consistent with the research showing that rising levels of insecurity lead to support for the forceful imposition of law and order, this finding might also be interpreted as a pragmatic assessment that the Mexican armed forces are simply more capable than the police. This is because the LAPOP survey asked, "¿Hasta qué punto tiene confianza usted en las Fuerzas Armadas?" The word *confianza* could be translated either to confidence or trust since idiomatic Spanish blurs the distinction in English between "trust" and "confidence." Seen in this light, the bifurcation of views about the armed forces makes more sense.

Table 14.5, in short, shows that the rising levels of cartel violence increased the average trust in the military net of all else, yet lowered the odds that there would be high levels of trust in the military in those states where the military was found to have violated the physical integrity rights of civilians during Calderón's war on the cartels. Specifically, the violations that occurred since the drug war began lowered otherwise high levels of trust in the military where the abuses happened most. Since this finding was more statistically significant than the increase in trust in states with high crime, it points to the inherent limits of, and thus the potential electoral costs associated with, military solutions to insecurity. As we have seen, the apparent benefit of exchanging civil liberties for *mano dura* law enforcement becomes a lot less clear to those abused by military personnel, or to those in close enough proximity to learn about it. This is so despite the fact that most people who live in extremely violent states see no alternative to the military since, from a realistic point of view, the armed forces are better than the local police forces in every possible way.

Importantly, neither the effects of rising crime nor of the drug war erased my findings about the legitimacy deficits created in the predemocracy period. Per Table 14.5, military abuse during the 1970s and 1980s continued to reduce the odds that civilians would in 2010 reside in those states with the highest levels of trust in the armed forces, all else being equal. We thus continue to see that trust in the armed forces was lowered not only because of the recent spike in human rights abuses, but also as a result of old dirty war grievances that, though barely observable, continue to matter to civil-military relations.

Beyond the numbers suggesting the trace memory of prior abuses, qualitative evidence captures the cognitive associations that people make of past and present violations. A phone interview with Senator Rosario Ibarra from the left-of-center party, the PRD, illustrates. Ibarra was interviewed in her role as the founder of ¡Eureka!, one of the oldest human rights organizations in Mexico. Like other family members in this group, Ibarra organized ¡Eureka! to search for her son who had been disappeared by the Mexican state in the late 1970s. Thirty years later, Senator Ibarra scarcely distinguished the abuses of the war on drugs and the dirty war when she argued that "the largest share [of the current disappearances] involves the army." In her view, the government continues to disappear people but "hide[s] behind organized crime."[6] The evidence, however, is too murky for that kind of conclusion. Just two years after her interview, Human Rights Watch (2013: 4) reported about twenty cases (or about 0.1 percent of the total missing since the drug war began) of enforced disappearances that can be attributed to the navy for the year 2011.

Despite the difference in contexts, actors, and policy, the perception that the current crisis is an uninterrupted extension of the dirty war is fairly widespread. The director of México Evalúa, an organization that focuses on security and public policy, similarly observed that the 2014 disappearances of forty-three students in Guerrero state, along with the mass graves that were discovered when officials searched for them, "take us to the past brutal images" (Wilkinson 2014). According to the *Los Angeles Times* reporter who interviewed Edna Jaime, México Evalúa's general director, many people "in Mexico say the latest incidents remind them of one of the country's darkest chapters, the so-called dirty war of the 1960s and '70s, a period of lawlessness and extreme repression of dissidents" (see Wilkinson 2014).

Since many human rights activists from the dirty war period ally themselves with the current human rights movement, they are among the key agents who frame the present as an extension of the past. Indeed, it is partly through their efforts that at least one of the mass slogans expressed by grassroots activists in the new human rights movement is recycled from the past. The slogan from the 1970s−1980s, "Vivos se los Llevaron! Vivos los Queremos!" has recently resurfaced in demonstrations organized to protest the drug war, criminal violence, and police corruption. It serves as an audible example of the past speaking as the present. Beyond contesting Calderón's definition of the situation, these frameworks of interpretation both provide content for and illustrate what is behind the polarization of attitudes toward the military observed in Tables 14.1 and 14.5.

The collective memory of the old dirty war in reference to the new drug war is clear evidence of deep legitimacy deficits precisely because the recent spike in human rights abuses is not a simple return to the worst of Mexico's authoritarian past. Notwithstanding President Calderón's initial failure to demand a public accounting of allegations of military misconduct, the abuses themselves are neither a matter of presidential policy nor military strategy, as they had been during the dirty war. Rather, in the absence of adequate police, insufficiently trained military recruits were sent to engage cartels and their inexperience and poor training cost many lives. But unlike in the predemocracy period, these abuses have been covered by the media and investigated by the CNDH in a way that matters. A recent report published by the Trans-Border Institute (see Daly, Heinle, and Shirk 2012) suggests a decline in complaints against the military since 2009. Most importantly, Calderón's right-of-center party, the PAN (Partido Acción Nacional, or National Action Party), was punished in the presidential elections of 2012 for his unpopular policies.

But though the most recent human rights violations reflect poor training as well as the lack of state capacity, ongoing military abuses contribute not only to Mexico's insecurity but also to the legitimacy crisis of the state. The very rise in crime as well as the emergence of various vigilante movements are three-dimensional manifestations of significant legitimacy deficits. Rising crime rates not only reflect the mass withdrawal of obedience, but the fact that cartels have geographic strongholds reflects complex allegiances—even the fragmentation of sovereignties in some areas (Davis 2010). This fragmentation is in evidence when people tacitly accept the security or other public services offered by the cartels or, most clearly, when they work for them. It is also evidenced in the fact that still other citizens join vigilante movements precisely to protect their communities from organized crime. Thus, Guerrero, the state with the worst of the dirty war violence of the 1970s, saw an early rise of some antistate vigilantes who resist deputization on the grounds that they are more afraid of the central state than they are of criminals (see also Wilkinson 2013b).

But in addition to this fragmentation of loyalties, recently various groups in civil society have come together in multiple mass demonstrations to demand governmental accountability and human rights. In so doing, various forces in civil society are mobilizing by the tens of thousands to strengthen democracy in Mexico.

Discussion of Comparative Implications:
Colombia and Brazil

My findings have parallels in other Latin American countries where a sharp rise in violence related to drug trafficking has also led to the militarization of law enforcement, the rise of vigilantes, private security forces, and armed body guards, along with the burgeoning of security technology. Like Mexico, the people in Colombia and Brazil also register high average levels of trust in the armed forces and such trust, as in Mexico, is also inversely related to their low confidence in their local police forces. Perhaps for this reason, law enforcement has been militarized in these two countries during decades-long efforts to fight large and socially powerful drug-trafficking organizations. About Brazil, Teresa P. R. Caldeira argues that "the popular support of police abuse suggests the existence not of a simple institutional dysfunction but of a pervasive and unchallenged cultural pattern that identifies order and authority with the use of violence" (2000: 139). In the case of Mexico, I offer a more complicated variant of this claim by showing that although widespread insecurity creates support for militarized law enforcement, doing so also creates legitimacy deficits among those abused by state forces. The inevitable abuse that arises when soldiers attempt to police communities erodes trust in the military among the very people whose real and extreme insecurity predisposes them to trust the military in the first place. When this happens, the legitimacy deficits form deep reservoirs of distrust that, in the right circumstance, loom large in subsequent social protests.

Developments in Colombia bring this out clearly since the military there has always been deployed for domestic order and national security—whether in response to interparty violence, insurgent guerrillas like the FARC (Revolutionary Armed Forces of Colombia) and others, or drug-trafficking organizations. The Colombian state created multiple flexible forces to respond to domestic problems and some such forces, such as the Cuerpo Èlite (Elite Corps), engage in civic policing roles (Vargas Velásquez 2014). Despite a history of human rights abuses as well as recent scandals involving the military during Álvaro Uribe Vélez's presidency (2002–2010), Colombia's army has high national average trust scores as of the 2010 LAPOP data. But as with Mexico, beneath the national average indicating much trust in the Colombian armed forces, there exist significant legitimacy deficits, deep wells of discontent caused by the sense of moral outrage by those who bear the brunt of human rights abuses, or who witness them.

To illustrate, Colombia's human rights movement began as it had in Mexico: as political resistance to the military's detentions and mass incarceration of leftists during the late 1970s and 1980s (Tate 2007).[7] As in

Mexico, the first wave of human rights activists in Colombia was comprised of either the direct victims of military violence or their family members. Like Mexico's, Colombia's human rights movement professionalized during the 1990s and succeeded in making the tens of thousands of people killed in the conflict there actually "count" (Tate 2007: 75). But it was also in the 1990s that national security policies increased the size and power of the Colombian armed forces and this resulted in more human rights violations. For example, army units staged faux combat with innocent civilians to raise the number of guerrillas supposedly killed in combat. This practice increased during Uribe's administration, not as a matter of policy but because of the pressure to show that the president's Democratic Security policies were effective. The "false positives" (*falsos positivos*) scandal implicated "a large number of military units" in premeditated murder for no other reason than to inflate their "kill counts," according to a UN special rapporteur (see "Summary" by Alston 2010). Soldiers inflated their kill counts by luring and then murdering civilians, who postmortem were dressed and staged to look as if they had been killed in combat. Partly in response to these scandals, the head of the army resigned and there have been large peace demonstrations in which tens of thousands of people have marched in Bogotá and other cities in favor of a negotiated peace settlement with the FARC guerillas (*The Guardian* 2013).[8] Other organizations have marched to denounce the enforced disappearances carried out by state agents (Tate 2007: 69). Indeed, well into the twenty-first century, various kinds of human rights or peace groups in Colombia denounced the mass detentions or the killing of innocent civilians that result from various *mano dura* national security strategies.

The polarization of attitudes about the military and *mano dura* policies is also evident in Brazil, a place where violence is the third leading cause of death among young men. Twenty-five years into democracy, many Brazilians accept *mano dura* as a viable way to deal with insecurity. Some Brazilians even support death squads—the unofficial killing operatives comprised of retired and off-duty police officers (sometimes they are called *justiceiros* or, more recently, *milicías*) (Caldeira 2002). The paradox is that, as on-duty officers, police are hated by many citizens who see them as corrupt, inept, ignorant, animalistic, and violent (Caldeira 2002: 248–249). But as off-duty or retired police who illegally operate in death squads, or in paramilitary *milicías*, they are tolerated because they are seen as offering protection via direct and immediate justice, if by torture or summary executions. Since the extrajudicial executions befall young men, especially the poorest and darkest among them, vigilante justice has widespread support among the many who fear violent crime and have no faith in the police or the criminal justice system (Caldeira 2000, 2002: 235–236).

A similar contradiction is evident in the fact that the favela pacification program, in which the military occupied favelas since 2008, has since been criticized by activists in massive street demonstrations. While at first deemed a success for having chased out the drug lords, the pacification of the favelas is now defined as an injustice by those who in 2013 and 2014 protested the human rights violations committed by the military police (not soldiers). These mass demonstrations were at first sparked by the police repression of those protesting bus fare hikes. An important reason why the political protests grew so massively in 2013 and 2014 is the widespread resentment about the abuse during the pacification campaigns years earlier. According to the *Los Angeles Times,* Brazilians "routinely complain of police abuse in *favelas,* often saying the state has done little more than bring in military presence, rather than providing much-needed infrastructure, safety, health and education services" (2014). The *New York Times* reporters put it this way: "The persistence of brutal police tactics, involving the abduction and torture of some residents, contributes to the anger against the police in some communities" (Romero and Barnes 2014). While the military police abuse has been documented by scholars, local human rights activists, and a UN special rapporteur, the deep grievances about them were broadcast to the world in the signs held by hundreds of thousands of protestors in some of the largest demonstrations Brazil had seen since the 1980s. The world watched as Brazil prepared for the World Cup (2014) and Summer Olympics (2016) in part by pacifying the favelas.

Together, these various protest movements against the excesses of militarized law enforcement suggest that, beneath the simplicity of national statistical averages and stable electoral procedures, there is good evidence of deep legitimacy deficits caused by military abuse. The citizens of these three countries clearly demand that their democratically elected leaders provide real security, but that they do so by protecting their human rights.

Conclusion

Democracy is under threat in Mexico, Colombia, and even Brazil where many, but certainly not all, people tolerate the exchange of civil liberties for militarized policing because of the insecurity caused by rising crime. Since soldiers are trained to kill enemy combatants rather than to engage in community-based policing, human rights abuses are frequently the unintended outcome. The kinds of violations that I documented in this chapter— arbitrary detentions, torture, and extrajudicial executions—are comparable in kind, but neither scale nor motive, to those committed during various dirty wars. But even though state violence is no longer politically motivated, the quality of citizenship as lived experience is degraded and degrading where abuses of authority remain high. Caldeira (2002) concurs, arguing that democracy is "disjunctive" where the right to vote has expanded political citizenship, but where civil citizenship remains weak or eroded.

I go further by arguing that ongoing human rights violations build on old legitimacy deficits and compound in ways that cannot be dismissed as insignificant, national statistical averages about trust in the military notwithstanding. I demonstrated that the parallels between the old dirty wars and the new wars against the drug cartels do not escape the current human rights activists who draw on the collective memory of prior state violence to understand the present abuses despite the differences in contexts. The living memory of past abuses is made relevant by activists and nonactivists who can frame and even experience recent military abuses as comparable to those in the past because the effects on individuals and collective bodies remain the same, whether or not intended by policy. As such military abuse not only degrades the quality of citizenship, and thus democracy, but the corrosive effects on the legitimacy of the state are long-lasting.

As I showed, the seriously aggrieved find alternative trust and security networks with gangs, cartels, armed vigilantes, or even, as in Mexico and Colombia, revolutionary groups. While not exactly evidence of fragmented sovereignty, the generalized distrust that has resulted challenges governability in some locations. When the state appears not only incapable of solving law and order problems but is seen as a major source of insecurity due to the excessive violence of the armed forces or the police, the social fabric begins to disintegrate. In this context, the number, inclusiveness, and quality of civic associations, and thus democracy, are further degraded.

But despite the violence from above and below that is so clearly observable, I conclude with a somewhat hopeful assessment insofar as I have also documented that the tolerance for authoritarian, *mano dura* interventions has its counterpoint. Just as significant legitimacy deficits create the conditions for the emergence of irregular armed forces, it is also the case that citizens can harness their grievances about military excesses and general insecurity to demand change from the central state. I observed that mass protest movements have challenged presidential decisions to militarily confront the drug cartels (Mexico and Colombia) and the gangs in the favelas (Brazil). What is more, the ability to protest has been greatly enhanced in the postauthoritarian period and elections have helped citizens hold officials accountable. Since the substance and quality of democracy are reflected in the strength of citizenship rights, the degree to which people have mobilized to demand change and also to express policy preferences through elections suggests that there is hope.

Notes

1. See Gilley (2009), Booth and Seligson (2009), Levi and Stoker (2000: 476), and Beetham (1991).

2. See Gilley (2009), Fukuyama (1992), and Putnam (1993).

3. See Booth and Seligson (2009).

4. See Human Rights Watch (2013), Grayson (2011), and Beittel (2009).

5. See Starr (2009).

6. Telephone interview with Senator Rosario Ibarra from Mexico City to Monterrey by Maria Santoyo-Borjas, January 2011.

7. Many of Colombia's political prisoners had been involved with left organizations, unions, and student organizations as well as with radical liberation theology. Some (not all) such groups were guerrillas.

8. The guerrillas are distrusted according to CNN (2012).

15

Lessons from the Democratic Record to Date

Dolores Trevizo

The preceding chapters offer a comprehensive assessment of the current state of democracy in (most of) Latin America by examining the progress of and challenges to democratic transformation over the course of the past two or three decades. This is a timely and important exercise given that the discontent with democracy documented in this volume calls out for analysis that moves beyond the common observation that electoral democracy cannot address all tangible evils. In response to the perception that electoral democracy should have accomplished more than it has since third-wave transitions began in the 1980s, the contribution of this book is to explain why the tempo of change has been slower than expected. To do so, the authors looked at the specificity of actually existing democracies in the region, rather than using a yardstick derived from the North American and European cases.

Without losing sight of the historical and political significance of the electoral reforms and constitutional amendments, the chapters here document why the elected leaders in the region have struggled to solve some of their most pressing social problems. Read collectively, a central theme that emerges is that the pace of democratic consolidation is slow because of the weight of the region's authoritarian past(s). Specifically, weak institutions are hampered by long-standing (predemocracy) organizational arrangements, informal pacts, and even cultural legacies and these, in turn, inhibit the development of better forms of accountability. Weak mechanisms of accountability make it difficult to implement the impartial rule of law or for government to respond to citizen demands, even for basic public goods. Still, democracy continues to be institutionalized, however slowly, in small but significant steps due to the demand for change from an increasingly organized and mobilized civil society. As such, this volume concludes that the glass is half full because social movements in the region continue to contest injustices, to insist on new rights, and, when they succeed, to have the latter enshrined in their respective constitutions.

In Chapter 6, Gerardo Munck addresses the question about the tempo of change not only by looking at the models of democracy that Latin Americans debate and experiment with, but also by focusing on the institutional and political constraints of the early post-transition period. He reminds us that, even after allowing elections, the military did not give elected officials the degree of freedom necessary to institute wholesale reforms, and the fear of military coups in the early post-transition period slowed the speed and depth of democratic transformation. For his part, in Chapter 2 Joe Foweraker goes further back in time and widens the analytic lens. He holds that the tempo of democratic transformation has also been set by another contradiction, one inherent in the expectation that the very state institutions impaired by the region's pattern of patrimonial state formation would deliver the full package of democracy and do so all at once. No democracy anywhere was born with all systems of checks and balances already in place, fully functional, and the history of patrimonial state formation in Latin American impedes the pace and direction of their development. Consequently, the informal rules and pacts that characterize this history remain a part of the political process in the democratic era. This means that elected officials not only contend with their elected opponents, but must often compromise the political agendas they were elected to implement to tend to the interests of oligarchic and, increasingly, corporate elites (see also Barndt, Chapter 12). Politically compromised and bureaucratically weak, officials struggle to respond to electorates, to tax effectively, to redistribute wealth progressively, and to provide goods and services to all.

Several authors in this book point to other institutional weaknesses that are carried over from Latin America's authoritarian past(s), as these continue to impede the pace and extent of democratic transformation. Most of our contributors emphasize that, with the exception of electoral courts and processes, there are few state institutions in place that as yet work well enough to hold elected officials accountable. Consequently, the power vested in the formal voting rights of the people—large percentages of whom were made even poorer by the neoliberal reforms and austerity measures that coincided with third-wave transitions—pale in comparison to the informal power of oligarchic and corporate interests (see also Doyle, Chapter 3; Rogers, Chapter 4; Barndt, Chapter 12).

The authors in this volume thus tend to agree that weak states make for weak democracies not only because they are more easily captured by oligarchic and corporate interests, but also because they do not have the bureaucratic capacity, or institutional power, to reach broadly across their national jurisdictions or deeply across all social strata to implement the impartial rule of law. Guillermo O'Donnell (2004) describes lawless, or near lawless, zones as brown areas and, in some countries in the region, brown areas are not confined to small hamlets on the periphery. Rather, they dot the map of large administrative units such as local states (e.g., Chihuahua in northern Mexico), or can comprise large, densely populated, urban centers. Further, there are some brown areas in which the bureaucratic institutions of the state, including law enforcement, are not even nominally present; this situation renders most residents of those areas outside of the law's protection and, thus, subject to the whims of nonelected local power brokers. In such countries brown areas can seriously challenge the governability in fragile democracies and, hence, their legitimacy.

But even areas with some institutional capacity to implement policy and enforce some laws are seriously compromised if the state's institutions for horizontal accountability are weak. Without strong or independent judiciaries, national legislatures, or ombudsmen, informal rules and flagrantly corrupt practices will tend to multiply. Whether informal rules are justified as compromises necessary to the public good or, as in the case of rent-seeking corruption, exploit public offices for private gain, the lack of accountability threatens democracy when officials individually decide when or even whether they uphold the rule of law. As Roderic Ai Camp argues in Chapter 13 about Mexico and many of its Central American neighbors, exceptions and special favors can pervade entire political systems such that well-meaning officials and citizens alike resign themselves to corruption as a way of interacting with officials.

Although horizontal accountability is not a criterion in the standard definition of democracy's procedural minimum, Daniel H. Levine and Jose E. Molina argue that it is "a central feature of the quality of democracy" (2011: 2). Beyond the possibility of formally (or informally) sanctioning public officials for wrongdoing, the chapters in this book emphasize that the lack of horizontal accountability affects the quality of democracy on multiple levels. Even before the act of voting, clientelism, cronyism, and nepotism undermine the very development of a robust public sphere (Foweraker, Chapter 2). There can be no real public debate based on assumptions of universal citizenship rights if people know that "vertical and particular claims of patronage, fealty, and power" are more effective in shaping the policy agenda or in exercising de jure rights (see Foweraker, Chapter 2; Camp, Chapter 13).

Accountability deficits also directly impinge on the quality of political representation, policy, and, thus, the legitimacy and viability of democracy. Several authors in this collection show that citizens are disaffected with both old and new political parties as these tend to be seen as representing the narrow interests of oligarchs, corporations, or corrupt local power brokers (Foweraker, Chapter 2; Barndt, Chapter 12; Doyle, Chapter 3; Munck, Chapter 6; Corrales, Chapter 7; Harvey, Chapter 11). David Doyle, for example, demonstrates in Chapter 3 that legislators from brown areas invade the central state and undermine democratic representation and policy effectiveness by working to capture pork for their home districts rather than on legislation that might serve the public good more broadly. Comparatively speaking, Doyle argues, weak states with many brown areas produce narrow, unstable, and rent-seeking policies. High-capacity states, in contrast, produce effective policy and citizen satisfaction as well as legitimacy for and stability of the political system.

Whereas Doyle's chapter explains the predominance of brown areas in some Latin American countries as compared to others, in Chapter 4 Melissa Ziegler Rogers looks at the subnational variation within a given country's regions to explain the degree of social spending. Like Doyle, Rogers focuses on the noxious policy effects of pork barrel politics by local power brokers. She adds that the electoral rules of a given country interact with the degree of subnational interregional inequality to determine whether or not redistributive policies will be passed. Unlike interpersonal inequality, interregional inequality drives down government spending in countries where electoral rules cultivate geographically based electoral constituencies (or simply, territorialize politics). Thus, beyond the strength or weakness of the state's administrative and institutional capacity, Rogers argues that interregional inequality and electoral rules also determine the quality of policy and of democracy. Combined, Doyle's and Rogers's analyses suggest that the chasm between strong and weak Latin American states as well as the gulf between rich and poor regions within countries are likely to widen precisely because state capacity, economic inequality, electoral rules, and public policy are endogenous; their interdependence reproduces the economic inequalities that sustain weak states and poor policy over time.

Many Latin Americans, and especially some indigenous communities, have responded to their frustrated expectations for change by rejecting traditional parties. While the crises of representation in the region may slowly create incentives to improve the quality of political representation and policy, thus far it has contributed to the rise of electoralist organizations that focus on winning specific campaigns rather than on the long-term work of party building and creating policy platforms. This new type of party requires an infusion of capital above and beyond membership dues, and this creates a dependency on large business owners or wealthy individuals. Competition results among economic elites and some capitalists respond by building their own parties by utilizing their business assets to create what in Chapter 12 Will Barndt calls corporation-based parties.

These new types of political parties are problematic for many reasons, not least of which is that they inadvertently contribute to widespread corruption. Barndt argues, for example, that left parties wishing to remain competitive against the electoral conservatism of corporate-backed parties have few options by which to obtain resources. The fact that they compete on such an unequal footing explains the number of corruption scandals implicating left parties that engage in state-based kickback schemes. Together, electoral conservatism and corruption threaten the legitimacy of the party system in general and contribute to various kinds of populism in the region. But as compared to ethno- or left-rentier-party populisms, corporation-based populism is more organized and better resourced to capture and hold state power. According to Barndt, in Panama, Guatemala, Honduras, El Salvador, Bolivia, Ecuador, and Peru, "oligopoly in the marketplace may come to be closely paralleled in the electoral sphere."

But if, as Barndt stresses, corporate money undermines the accountability and legitimacy of electoral democracy, so did the left's experiments with participatory democracy. Several such governments were elected in societies where neoliberal reforms had been most traumatic (Corrales, Chapter 7; Harvey, Chapter 11). Buoyed by the commodities boom (2003–2013), the most radical of these pink tide governments reduced poverty and empowered nontraditional groups with new constitutional rights. But according to Javier Corrales in Chapter 7, they also weakened democracy where discredited political parties were too weak to check the power of presidents. Corrales explains that this failure of horizontal accountability within national legislatures played out with alarming consequences in those countries engaged in the rentier-populist model of governance. Some of these governments engaged in clear efforts to concentrate power through hyperpresidentialism, clientelism, sectarianism, and attempts at expanding presidential term limits (see also Munck, Chapter 6). In addition to limiting political participation (and thus also weakening vertical accountability), Nicaragua, Venezuela, and Ecuador encroached on the autonomy of the Supreme Court.

Camp argues in Chapter 13 that accountability deficits clearly undermine the impartial rule of law and make it difficult for government to be responsive to citizens, whether their demands are for social justice or even basic security. While the commodities boom helped to reduce poverty, including in the liberal democracies, Todd Landman notes in Chapter 8 that poverty reduction still fell short of what Latin American governments might have been expected to achieve given the capacities of their national economies. Moreover, as Camp suggests, poverty reduction might work better when it is part of a larger package of policies that also target unemployment and educational reform.

Although poverty and income inequality in the region are hardly new, their negative effects are now exacerbated by the dramatic growth and violence of drug- and human-trafficking organizations in ways that also adversely affect the legitimacy and viability of democracy. This perfect storm was made possible by the systematic failures of accountability in the region, the outright corruption of various police forces, and the fact that drug-trafficking organizations offer employment and access to consumer goods, according to Camp. Grinding poverty and unemployment in the context of gross income inequality, lucrative drug trades, and weak and corrupt criminal justice systems collectively produce a generalized climate of insecurity. Such insecurity, in turn, undermines investment and economic growth. As Camp emphasizes, these interrelated problems create a vicious cycle that might only be broken with a full package of interrelated policy initiatives. Such a package would include policy aimed at simultaneously improving the educational and criminal justice systems, creating opportunities for investment, and reducing poverty and unemployment while also "bearing down on corruption, especially in federal and state police forces and in the administration of government." Clearly, these are the kinds of reforms that take time to implement and yield results, which, again, speaks to the slow process of change.

Finally, as Landman in Chapter 8 and I in Chapter 14 point out, the rise in human rights abuses related to various government efforts to combat transnational criminal organizations undermines the legitimacy of many Latin American states. Poverty, income inequality, criminality, and generalized violence not only damage interpersonal trust but they contribute to the growing sense that electoral democracy is a flawed political system, one among possible others (Camp, Chapter 13; Corrales, Chapter 7; Munck, Chapter 6). In Mexico, Colombia, and some countries in Central America, these problems seriously imperil governability and, thus, the legitimacy of democracy. But the prestige and legitimacy of the liberal democratic model among Latin Americans is not to be taken for granted. As Corrales and Munck show, many post-transition countries have experienced crises affecting their status as electoral democracies.

But despite the significant setbacks documented in this volume, there continues to be incremental forward movement toward the institutionalization of democracy. The authors of these chapters emphasize that this progress is due to the fact that Latin Americans are both unrelenting and collectively militant about their demands for justice vis-à-vis their pasts, their present, and their futures. As Landman has documented, just as democracy and human rights are intertwined, social movement demands for justice and democratic reforms are also mutually constitutive. The domestic prosecutions in Latin America that Kathryn Sikkink (2011) called "the justice cascade" registered an average improvement in the subsequent protection of human rights as well as a marginal improvement in democracy precisely in those countries where trials resulted in convictions (Landman, Chapter 8).

By virtue of their public shaming, domestic trials also indicated the proper role and place of the armed forces. And although organizational restructuring happens slowly, as David Pion-Berlin demonstrates in Chapter

5, the military has been put in its proper institutional place. This is no small achievement considering, as Munck observes in Chapter 6, that the military remained a de facto power in many Latin American countries shortly after they transitioned to electoral democracy. To be sure, transitional justice efforts continue to develop. Brazil's National Truth Commission Report was only recently released (December 2014) and the outcome of the attempt to prosecute Guatemala's former dictator, General Efraín Ríos Montt, on the grounds of genocide is uncertain, with a new trial scheduled for 2016. But in light of the region's history of military impunity, the significance of the transitional justice movements is clearer: in submitting to domestic trials, the armed forces have given up considerable power, accepted nonpolitical roles, and agreed to reorganization in the name of democracy.

Thus, despite the many regressive tendencies documented in this volume, progressive cultural and institutional changes are evident even if they are regularly obscured by persistent crises. As emphasized throughout the chapters, the routinization of electoral competition over time has not only endured, it has resulted in the greater representation of women and indigenous people (whose new rights are enshrined in various constitutions). As Jennifer M. Piscopo's analysis in Chapter 9 demonstrates, states are now required to enforce women's political rights, both to vote and be elected, through gender quotas and, increasingly, parity laws. Such laws force states to act in proactive, progressive ways and this official gender activism has resulted in women's greater representation in government at all levels. But it was prior women's activism that helped to construct these legal regimes, and their decades of struggle in civil society also contributed to the kind of cultural change whereby national electorates would eventually vote for, and in some cases reelect, female presidents. They voted for Violeta Chamorro (1990) and did so twice for Michelle Bachelet (2006–2010; 2014–), Dilma Rousseff (Brazil 2011–), and Cristina Fernández de Kirchner (2007–2015). Considering the recent history of military dictatorships in Chile, Brazil, and Argentina and given the fact that the first wave of gender quota laws in the 1990s was largely symbolic, these democratic gains are real.

And there are other indications of cultural change. In Chapter 11, Neil Harvey documents the organized efforts at developing women's political leadership of indigenous movements in the autonomous regions of Chiapas where Zapatistas are committed to equal representation in local leadership positions. However, as Jane S. Jaquette observes in her analysis in Chapter 10, change remains incomplete and, in her view, this is especially so in many indigenous communities in South America. Thus, like other scholars in this volume, Jaquette emphasizes that legal as well as everyday norms, state capacity, and broader institutional arrangements combine to affect the pace and depth of change.

Still, the evidence of slow progress remains undeniable and, to stress a point emphasized in this volume, the headway is due to the militancy of various forces in civil society. Whether via an armed uprising in Chiapas, Mexico (1994), Bolivia's water and gas wars, or Argentina's riots at the turn of the twenty-first century (Munck, Chapter 6), Latin Americans first protested the economic insecurity brought about by austerity and market reforms as their countries transitioned to democracy. And although the early antiausterity protests of the neoliberal era of the 1980s and 1990s reignited old right versus left (pro vs. antineoliberal) debates, Latin Americans have gone well beyond the ideological frameworks of the twentieth century. They continuously debate the models of democracy they want (Munck) and do so in ways that both build on as well as move beyond twentieth-century ideological paradigms. To illustrate, Harvey in Chapter 11 and others (e.g., Yashar 2005) have documented that indigenous movements forced a public recognition that various *indigenismos* (in the plural) form a part of multicultural national identities. Many of these indigenous movements critique capitalism, especially the encroachment on their lands, not on the basis of older notions of socialism and communism but with ideas about community, environmental stewardship, and the sanctity of land. In their efforts to protect territory, water, and communal practices, as well as to preserve their language and culture, some indigenous movements have also fought for local political autonomy rather than for state power as such. Where they have won, they practice community governance in a way that stresses balance and consensus rather than competition and debate between individuals (Harvey).

Not only do indigenous demands go beyond the standard social rights program of the traditional left but, according to Harvey, "The construction of indigenous autonomy is a more effective way to produce deeper-rooted political organization and achieve greater accountability of elected authorities." Even if this particular point is open to debate, indigenous movements, like the women's movements for gender equality, have clearly played an important role in determining the specific forms of democracy that emerged in the region.

And there are a multitude of other social actors who continue to engage in disruptive political action in an effort to influence political parties, the national policy agenda, state institutions, and the very model of democracy. They do so when they demand national security along with a broad spectrum of human rights, including LGBT rights; and they do so when they demand more accountable judiciaries, criminal justice systems, or professional police. They also forcefully demand less corruption. Just recently (September 2015) mass demonstrations in Guatemala forced President Otto Pérez Molina to resign and he, along with many in his administration, will now face criminal charges for their alleged roles in the La Línea corruption scandal. Also in 2015 hundreds of thousands of Brazilians protested the Petrobras corruption scandal. Throughout the country demonstrators demanded the impeachment of President Rousseff and expressed a sense of betrayal and a loss of faith in the Workers' Party, which allegedly received over $200 million "to finance political campaigns" (see Segal 2015).

The more radical participatory democracies of the region have not escaped highly disruptive mass contention. Corrales describes in Chapter 7 how environmentalists and indigenous groups continue to protest the ecological damage done by neoextractivist policies in Ecuador, Bolivia, and Nicaragua. Corrales observes that by 2015 many citizens of these countries, perhaps especially in Venezuela, were protesting the arbitrary style of government of the left. Importantly, this reinvigoration of civil society was both propelled by and reflects constitutional reforms, according to Foweraker in Chapter 2. This suggests, as Munck argues in Chapter 6, that the "nature and value of democracy" remain the key themes of political debate and mobilization.

Thus, in spite of the weight of the past and without minimizing the difficulties that the region has faced in its attempts to strengthen and deepen the quality of democracy, democratization in Latin America inches forward. If the formal mechanisms of horizontal accountability are weak, the authors assembled in this volume emphasize that noninstitutional and socially disruptive protests have responded in ways that contribute to change. We thus concur with Levine and Molina (2011) that social movements are potent, if informal, mechanisms for what they call "societal accountability."

As in the United States and the United Kingdom, democratization is a gradual yet dynamic and certainly an ongoing process. Collective actors who successfully demand rights through political contention are engaged in the slow process of making democracy (Foweraker, Chapter 2; Landman, Chapter 8; Trevizo, Chapter 14; Harvey, Chapter 11; Piscopo, Chapter 9). But since movements do not operate in a vacuum, their transformative potential may be checked by countermovements with alternative views about which model of democracy is best, or how it is to develop (Munck, Chapter 6). Alternatively, movements may be repressed by state forces or uncivil actors. Thus, the main lesson to be drawn from this volume is that Latin America's democratic projects are works in progress precisely because democratization is a long-term process contingent on the outcome of various social struggles.

Finally, although this book is a fairly comprehensive assessment of the current condition and nature of democracy in Latin America, it is not possible for a single volume to give proper consideration to all dimensions of democracy, whether national, subnational, or international. Consequently, these chapters can make only passing reference to a number of important topics, including executive-legislative relations; the judiciary and the criminal justice and penal systems; party systems, electoral politics, and political campaigning; varieties of political protest and movement outcomes; the political economy of democracy; and how women's presidencies in the region matter. Clearly, all of these topics are deserving of more detailed attention and treatment. But what this volume does try to do is bring these distinct elements together in a systemic perspective, where it is not the individual elements but their interconnectedness that matters for the analysis. In this way, it may move beyond the surface appearance of things to discern some of the core relationships—the inner workings—of Latin America's political systems overall.

Appendixes

Appendix 1 Summary Statistics and Variable Descriptions in Latin American Sample

Variable	Description	Mean	Min	Max	SD	Sources
Dependent variables						
Central government spending	Central government final consumption expenditure, calculated by economic function. Measured as share of GDP.	21.5	10.4	33.8	5.1	International Monetary Fund (IMF) Government Finance Statistics (GFS)
General government spending	General government final consumption expenditures including all government current expenditures for purchase of goods and services, compensation of employees as well as national defense and security. Measured as share of GDP.	12.8	2.9	22.7	3.7	World Bank, World Development Indicators
Independent variables						
Regional income inequality	Measure of regional income disparity using the country's average GDP per capita, the GDP per capita of subnational regions. Formulas from Lessmann (2009).					
Coefficient of variation, weighted (COVW)	The population-weighted coefficient of variation of regional GDP per capita. Units are proportions (rescaled to percentage points).	.47	.20	.85	.14	Calculated by author using national accounts
Gini coefficient	Estimates of the Gini index of household market (pretax, pretransfer) income inequality. Units are scales of 0 to 100 (the most unequal).	50.5	40.7	71.3	4.2	Standardized World Income Inequality Database (SWIID), Solt (2009)

Control variables						
Population (logged)	Log of Population (in millions).	3.1	.67	5.3	1.2	Penn World Table 8.0
GDP per capita (logged)	Log of GDP per capita (constant 2005 US$) adjusted for purchasing power parity.	8.8	7.9	9.6	.36	World Development Indicators
Trade (% GDP)	Sum of imports and exports divided by nominal GDP.	52.6	11.5	198	39.5	World Development Indicators
% Population > 65	Population age 65 years and older (% of total population).	5.5	3.5	10.7	1.8	World Development Indicators
Ethnic fractionalization		.53	.19	.74	.18	Alesina et al. (1999)
Federal system	2 if both subnational legislature and executive are elected; 1 if legislature is elected; 0 otherwise.	1	0	2	.9	Database of Political Institutions
Personal vote index	Ranking on 13 components (ballot structure, pool structure, ballot type, district magnitude, tier system, proportionality) of personal vote based on Carey and Shugart (1995).	5	1	13	3.3	Johnson and Wallack (2006)

Sources: Solt (2009); Penn World Table 8.0; Alesina et al. (2003); Database of Political Institutions; and Johnson and Wallack (2006).

Appendix 2 Personal Vote Rank in Latin American Sample

Country	Minimum Rank	Maximum Rank
Argentina	1	1
Bolivia	1	10
Brazil	7	7
Chile	5	5
Colombia	12	12
Ecuador	1	3
Mexico	6	6
Panama	6	6
Peru	5	5

Appendix 3 Change in Regional Inequality, 1990–2010

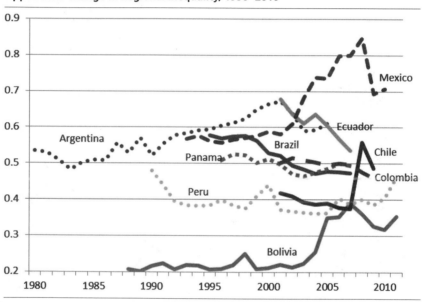

Appendix 4 Regional Inequality Dynamics in Latin American Sample

Country	SD	Min	Max	% Difference Min to Max
Argentina	0.053	0.483	0.672	0.392
Bolivia	0.064	0.201	0.390	0.935
Brazil	0.045	0.471	0.578	0.226
Chile	0.062	0.375	0.558	0.490
Colombia	0.032	0.362	0.480	0.326
Ecuador	0.047	0.536	0.678	0.264
Mexico	0.097	0.557	0.847	0.520
Panama	0.020	0.464	0.526	0.133
Peru	0.017	0.461	0.516	0.119

References

Abbott, Jeff. 2014. "Indigenous Women in Guatemala Demand End to State of Prevention." Upside Down World, November 7. http://Upsidedownworld.org /main/Guatemala-archives-33/5113-indigenous.

Abranches, Sérgio. 1988. "Presidencialismo de Coalizão: O Dilema Institucional Brasileiro." Dados 31(1): 5–38.

Acemoglu, Daron, Simon Johnson, and James A. Robinson. 2001. "The Colonial Origins of Comparative Development: An Empirical Investigation." American Economic Review 91(5): 1369–1401.

Acemoglu, Daron, and James A. Robinson. 2006. Economic Origins of Dictatorship and Democracy. Cambridge: Cambridge University Press.

Achtenberg, Emily. 2013. "Contested Development: The Geopolitics of Bolivia's TIPNIS Conflict." NACLA Report on the Americas 46(2): 6–11.

———. 2015. "Morales Greenlights TIPNIS Road, Oil and Gas Extraction in Bolivia's National Parks." North American Congress on Latin America (NACLA), December 15. https://nacla.org/blog/2015/06/15/morales-green lights-tipnis-road-oil-and-gas-extraction-bolivia's-national-parks.

Agosto, Gabriela, and Francisco Cueto Villamán. 2001. "República Dominicana." In Partidos Políticos de América Latina: Centroamérica, México, y República Dominicana, edited by Manuel Alcántara Sáez and Flavia Friedenberg, 615–698. Salamanca: Ediciones Universidad de Salamanca.

Agüero, Felipe. 1995. Soldiers, Civilians and Democracy: Post Franco Spain in Comparative Perspective. Baltimore: Johns Hopkins University Press.

Aguilar, Eva. 1996. "Ricardo Martinelli Renuncio Cansado De La Burocracia." La Prensa, July 20.

Ajenjo Fresno, Natalia. 2001. "Honduras." In Partidos Políticos de América Latina: Centroamérica, México, y República Dominicana, edited by Manuel Alcántara Sáez and Flavia Freidenberg, 179–273. Salamanca: Ediciones Universidad de Salamanca.

Al Jazeera. 2014. "Protest Against Nicaragua Canal Turns Violent." December 25. www.aljazeera.com/news/americas/2014/12/nicaragua-canal-protest -201412251303629570.html.

Alcántara, Manuel, and Elena M. Barahona. 2003. Política, Dinero y Institucionalización Partidista en América Latina. Mexico City: Universidad Iberoamericana.

Alcántara Sáez, Manuel, and Flavia Freidenberg, eds. 2001. Partidos Políticos de América Latina: Centroamérica, México, y República Dominicana, 3 vols. Salamanca: Ediciones Universidad de Salamanca.

Alcocer, Jorge, ed. 2013. *Cuota de género: Una sentencia histórica.* Mexico City: Nuevo Horizonte Editores.

Alesina, Alberto, Reza Baqir, and William Easterly. 1999. "Public Goods and Ethnic Divisions." *Quarterly Journal of Economics* 114(4): 1243–1284.

Alesina, Alberto, and Edward L. Glaeser. 2004. *Fighting Poverty in the US and Europe: A World of Difference.* New York: Oxford University Press.

Alesina, Alberto, Ricardo Hausmann, Rudolf Hommes, and Ernesto Stein. 1999. "Budget Institutions and Fiscal Performance in Latin America." *Journal of Development Economics* 59(2): 253–273.

Almond, Gabriel A., and Sidney Verba. 1965. *The Civic Culture: Political Attitudes and Democracy in Five Nations.* Boston: Little, Brown.

Alston, Philip. 2010. "Report of the Special Rapporteur on Extrajudicial, Summary or Arbitrary Executions." *Addendum. United Nations General Assembly Report. Human Rights Council, Fourteenth Session, Agenda item 3, Promotion and protection of all human rights, civil, political, economic, social and cultural rights, including the right to development.* New York: UN General Assembly.

Ames, Barry. 2002. *The Deadlock of Democracy in Brazil.* Ann Arbor: University of Michigan Press.

Amnesty International. 1982. *Yearly Report on Mexico.* London: Amnesty International.

Amorim Neto, Octávio, and Gary Cox. 1997. "Electoral Institutions, Cleavage Structures and the Number of Parties." *American Journal of Political Science* 41(1): 149–174.

Angell, Alan, Maria D'Alva Kinzo, and Diego Urbaneja. 1992. "Latin America." In *Electioneering: A Comparative Study of Continuity and Change,* edited by David Butler and Austin Ranney, 43–68. New York: Oxford University Press.

Ansell, Ben, and David Samuels. 2010. "Inequality and Democratization: A Contractarian Approach." *Comparative Political Studies* 43(12): 1543–1574.

Araújo, Clara. 2003. "Quotas for Women in the Brazilian Legislative System." Paper presented at the Implementation of Quotas: Latin American Experiences conference, Lima, Peru, February 23–24.

Archenti, Nélida. 2011. "La paridad política en América Latina y el Caribe: Percepciones y opiniones de los líderes de la región." Santiago, Chile: CEPAL (Comisión Económica par América Latina y el Caribe), División de Asuntos de Género.

Ardanaz, Martin, and Carlos Scartascini. 2013. "Inequality and Personal Income Taxation the Origins and Effects of Legislative Malapportionment." *Comparative Political Studies* 46(12): 1636–1663.

Argentina. 1983. Decree 15. In "Legislación Argentina." Tomo B. Ediciones Jurisprudencia, 1926–1927.

———. 2007. Decreto 1729. "Ciclo de Planeamiento de la Defensa Nacional." November 27. Ministerio de Defensa.

———. 2009. Decreto 1714. "Directiva de Política de Defensa Nacional." November 10. Ministerio de Defensa.

———. 2010. Ministerio de Defensa. 2010. *Libro Blanco de la Defensa,* 209.

Arias, Enrique Desmond, and Daniel M. Goldstein, eds. 2010. *Violent Democracies in Latin America.* Durham: Duke University Press.

Aristotle. 1969. *The Politics,* translated and edited by T. A. Sinclair. Harmondsworth: Penguin Books.

Artiga González, Álvaro. 2001. "El Salvador." In *Partidos Políticos de América Latina: Centroamérica, México, y República Dominicana,* edited by Manuel

Alcántara Sáez and Flavia Freidenberg, 135–178. Salamanca: Ediciones Universidad de Salamanca.

Atlas Comparativo de la Defensa en América Latina. 2007. "Argentina." Buenos Aires: RESDAL (Red de Seguridad y Defensa de América Latina), 110.

Austin, Reginald, and Maja Tjernstrom, eds. 2003. *Funding of Political Parties and Election Campaigns.* Stockholm: International Institute for Democracy and Electoral Assistance (IDEA).

Bacchi, Carol. 2006. "Arguing For and Against Quotas: Theoretical Issues." In *Women, Quotas, and Politics,* edited by Drude Dahlerup. New York: Routledge.

Bäck, Hanna, and Axel Hadenius. 2008. "Democracy and State Capacity: Exploring a J-Shaped Relationship. *Governance: An International Journal of Policy, Administration, and Institutions* 21(1): 1–24.

Baker, Andy. 2010. *The Market and the Masses in Latin America: Policy Reform and Consumption in Liberalizing Economies.* New York: Cambridge University Press.

Baker, Andy, and Kenneth F. Greene. 2011. "The Latin American Left's Mandate: Free-Market Policies and Issue Voting in New Democracies." *World Politics* 63(1): 43–77.

Baldez, Lisa. 2002. *Why Women Protest: Women's Movements in Chile.* Cambridge: Cambridge University Press.

———. 2004. "Elected Bodies: The Gender Quota Law for Legislative Candidates in Mexico." *Legislative Studies Quarterly* 24(2): 231–258.

———. 2007. "Primaries v. Quotas: Gender and Candidate Nominations in Mexico, 2003." *Latin American Politics and Society* 49(3): 69–96.

Baldez, Lisa, and John M. Carey. 2001. "Budget Procedure and Fiscal Strength in Post-Transition Chile." In *Presidents, Parliaments and Policies,* edited by Stephan Haggard and Matthew D. McCubbins. Cambridge: Cambridge University Press.

Bardallo Bandera, Joaquín. 2014. "A Tale of Two Latin American Countries Within the Same Region and a Very Different Democratic Rule of Law Experience." Ottawa, Canada: University of Ottawa.

Barndt, William T. 2014. "Corporation-Based Parties: The Present and Future of Business Politics in Latin America." *Latin American Politics and Society* 56(3): 1–22.

———. 2016. "Democracy for Sale: Corporation-Based Parties and the New Conservative Politics in the Americas." Unpublished manuscript, Pitzer College, Claremont, CA.

Baronnet, Bruno. 2011. "Entre el cargo comunitario y el compromiso Zapatista: Los promotores de la educación autónoma en la zona Selva Tzeltal." In *Luchas "muy otras": Zapatismo y autonomía en las comunidades indígenas de Chiapas,* edited by Bruno Baronnet, Mariana Mora Bayo, and Richard Stahler-Sholk, 195–235. Mexico City: Universidad Autónoma Metropolitana, Xochimilco; Centro de Investigaciones y Estudios Superiores en Antropología Social (CIESAS); and Universidad Autónoma de Chiapas (UNACH).

Barrig, Maruja. 2006. "What Is Justice? Indigenous Women in Development Projects." In *Women and Gender Equity in Development Theory and Practice,* edited by Jane S. Jaquette and Gale Summerfield, 107–133. Durham, NC: Duke University Press.

Barrueto, Felipe, and Patricio Navia. 2013. "Tipologías de democracia representativa en América Latina." *Política y Gobierno* 20(2): 265–307.

Battaglino, Jorge. 2013. "The Politics of Defense Revival in Argentina." *Defense and Security Analysis* 29(1): 11.

Bauer, Gretchen. 2014. "'A Lot of Headwraps': Innovations in a Second Wave of Electoral Gender Quotas in Sub-Saharan Africa." Working Paper No. 92. Fiesole, Italy: European University Institute, Robert Schuman Centre for Advanced Studies, Global Governance Programme.

Bautista Urbaneja, Diego, and Angel Eduardo Alvarez. 2005. "Financing Politics in Venezuela." In *The Financing of Politics: Latin American and European Perspectives,* edited by Carlos Malamud and Eduardo Posado-Carbó. London: Institute for the Study of the Americas.

Beck, Thorsten, George Clarke, Alberto Groff, Philip Keefer, and Patrick Walsh. 2001. "New Tools in Comparative Political Economy: The Database of Political Institutions." *The World Bank Economic Review* 15(1): 165–176.

Beckwith, Karen, and Kimberly Cowell-Meyers. 2007. "Sheer Numbers: Critical Representation Thresholds and Women's Political Representation." *Perspectives on Politics* 5(3): 553–565.

Beetham, David. 1991. *The Legitimation of Power.* Atlantic Heights, NJ: Humanities Press International.

Beetham, David, Edzia Carvalho, Todd Landman, and Stuart Weir. 2008. *Assessing the Quality of Democracy: A Practical Guide.* Stockholm: International IDEA.

Beittel, June S. 2009. "Mexico's Drug-Related Violence." Prepared for members and committees of Congress. Washington, DC: Congressional Research Service. www.fas.org/sgp/crs/row/R40582.pdf.

Benabou, Roland. 2000. "Unequal Societies: Income Distribution and the Social Contract." *American Economic Review* 96(1): 129.

Benítez Manaut, Raúl. 2013. "Organized Crime as the Highest Threat to Mexican National Security and Democracy." In *A War That Can't Be Won: Binational Perspectives on the War on Drugs,* edited by Tony Payan, Kathleen Staudt, and Z. Anthony Kruszewski. Tucson: University of Arizona Press.

Beramendi, Pablo. 2007. "Inequality and the Territorial Fragmentation of Solidarity." *International Organization* 61(4): 783.

———. 2012. *The Political Geography of Inequality: Regions and Redistribution.* Cambridge: Cambridge University Press.

Beramendi, Pablo, Melissa Rogers, and Alberto Diaz-Cayeros. Forthcoming. "Barriers to the Left Turn: Distributive Tensions in Latin American Federations." *Latin American Research Review.*

Beramendi, Pablo, and David Rueda. 2007. "Social Democracy Constrained: Indirect Taxation in Industrialized Democracies." *British Journal of Political Science* 37(4): 619–641.

Berens, Sarah. 2015. "Between Exclusion and Calculating Solidarity? Preferences for Private Versus Public Welfare Provision and the Size of the Informal Sector." *Socio-Economic Review* 13(4): 651–678.

Berkman, Heather, Carlos Scartascini, Ernesto Stein, and Mariano Tommasi. 2009. *Political Institutions, State Capabilities, and Public Policy: An International Dataset.* Washington, DC: Inter-American Development Bank.

Bimsa. 2006. "Encuesta Post-Electoral, Mexico 2006." July 21–24.

Blanco, Luisa. 2011. "The Impact of Insecurity on Democracy and Trust in Institutions in Mexico." Working Paper No. 25. Malibu, CA: Pepperdine University, School of Public Policy. http://digitalcommons.pepperdine.edu/spp workingpapers/25.

Boas, Taylor C. 2010. "Varieties of Electioneering: Presidential Campaigns in Latin America." *World Politics* 62(4): 636–675.

Bobbio, Norberto. 1996. *Right and Left: The Significance of a Political Distinction.* Chicago: University of Chicago Press.

Boesten, Jelke. 2010. *Intersecting Inequalities: Women and Social Policy in Peru, 1990–2000*. University Park: Pennsylvania State University Press.

Boix, Carles. 1999. "Setting the Rules of the Game: The Choice of Electoral Systems in Advanced Democracies." *American Political Science Review* 93(3): 609–624.

———. 2003. *Democracy and Redistribution*. New York: Cambridge University Press.

Boix, Carles, and Susan C. Stokes. 2003. "Endogenous Democratization." *World Politics* 55(4): 517–549.

Bolivia. 2010. Asamblea Legislativa Plurinacional. 2010. "Ley 26." Gaceta Oficial de Bolivia. June 30.

Bolton, Patrick, and Gerard Roland. 1997. "The Breakup of Nations: A Political Economy Analysis." *Quarterly Journal of Economics* 112(4): 1057–1090.

Booth, John A., and Mitchell A. Seligson. 2009. *The Legitimacy Puzzle in Latin America: Political Support and Democracy in Eight Nations*. New York: Cambridge University Press.

Boserup, Ester. 1970. *Woman's Role in Economic Development*. London: Allen and Unwin.

Bourque, Susan C., and Kay Barbara Warren. 1981. *Women of the Andes: Women and Patriarchy in Two Peruvian Towns*. Ann Arbor: University of Michigan Press.

Bowen, Sally. 2002. *The Fujimori File: Peru and Its President, 1990–2000*. Lima: Peru Monitor.

Brazil. 1999. Article 2 in Lei Complementar No. 97. June 9.

———. 2010a. Lei Complementar No. 136. August.

———. 2010b. Article 8 in Lei Complementar No. 7.364. November 23.

———. 2012. "Livro Branco." Livro Branco De Defesa Nacional. www.defesa.gov.br/arquivos/2012/mes07/lbdn.pdf.

Bresser Pereira, Luiz Carlos, José María Maravall, and Adam Przeworski. 1993. *Economic Reform in New Democracies: A Social-Democratic Approach*. New York: Cambridge University Press.

Brown Araúz, Harry. 2009. *Partidos políticos y elecciones en Panamá: Un enfoque institucionalista*. Panama City: Fundación Friedrich Ebert.

Bruneau, Tom C., and Richard B. Goetze Jr. 2006. "Ministries of Defense and Democratic Control." In *Who Guards the Guardians and How? Democratic Civil-Military Relations*, edited by Thomas C. Bruneau and Scott D. Tollefson. Austin: University of Texas Press.

Bruneau, Tom C., and Scott D. Tollefson, eds. 2006. *Who Guards the Guardians and How? Democratic Civil-Military Relations*. Austin: University of Texas Press.

———. 2014. "Civil-Military Relations in Brazil: A Reassessment." *Journal of Politics in Latin America* 6(2): 107–138.

Burchardt, Hans-Jürgen, and Kristina Dietz. 2014. "(Neo-)Extractivism—A New Challenge for Development Theory from Latin America." *Third World Quarterly* 35(3): 468–486.

Burnell, Peter J., and Alan Ware, eds. 2007. *Funding Democratization*. New Brunswick, NJ: Transaction.

Cain, Bruce E., John A. Ferejohn, and Morris P. Fiorina. 1987. *The Personal Vote: Constituency Service and Electoral Independence*. Cambridge: Harvard University Press.

Caldeira, Teresa P. R. 2000. *City of Walls: Crime, Segregation, and Citizenship in São Paulo*. Berkeley: University of California Press.

———. 2002. "The Paradox of Police Violence in Democratic Brazil." *Ethnography* 3(3): 235–263.

Cameron, Maxwell A. 2014. "The Myth of Competitive Authoritarianism in the Andes." Unpublished manuscript, University of British Columbia, Vancouver, BC.

Cameron, Maxwell A., and Kenneth E. Sharpe. 2010. "Andean Left Turns: Constituent Power and Constitution-Making." In *Latin America's Left Turns: Politics, Policies and Trajectories of Change,* edited by Maxwell A. Cameron and Eric Hershberg. Boulder: Lynne Rienner.

Camp, Roderic Ai. 2003. "Paseando por la línea democrática en México, ¿quién e democrático?" *Esté Pais,* November.

———. 2012. *The Oxford Handbook of Mexican Politics.* New York: Oxford University Press.

———. 2013a. "Peña Nieto's Cabinet, What Does It Tell Us About Mexican Leadership?" Democracy and Election Series. Washington, DC: Mexico Institute, Woodrow Wilson Center.

———. 2013b. "The 2012 Presidential Election in Mexico." *Journal of Latin American Studies* 45(3): 471.

Cantú, Francisco. 2014. "Identifying Irregularities in Mexican Local Elections." *American Journal of Political Science* 58(4): 13.

Caputo, Dante. 2011. "El desarrollo democrático en América Latina: Entre la crisis de legitimidad y la crisis de sustentabilidad." *Revista SAAP* 5(2): 437–452.

Carey, John M., and Matthew Soberg Shugart. 1995. "Incentives to Cultivate a Personal Vote: A Rank Ordering of Electoral Formulas." *Electoral Studies* 14(4): 417–439.

Carlin, Ryan E., et al. 2012. "Political Legitimacy and Democratic Values." In *The Political Culture of Democracy in the Americas,* edited by Mitchell A. Seligson, Amy Erica Smith, and Elizabeth J. Zechmeister, 199–211. Nashville: Vanderbilt University.

Carreras, Miguel. 2013. "The Impact of Criminal Violence on Regime Legitimacy in Latin America." *Latin American Research Review* 48(3): 100–102.

Carroll, Royce, and Matthew Shugart. 2007. "Neo-Madisonian Theory and Latin American Institutions." In *Regimes and Democracy in Latin America: Theories and Methods,* edited by Gerardo Munck. New York: Oxford University Press.

Carta Paramétrica. 2012. "Pierde aprecio la democracia en México." October.

———. 2013a. "Mexicanos estancados por la educación que se ofrece." February.

———. 2013b. "Mexicanos apoyan los puntos de la reforma educativa." April.

———. 2013c. "Tráfico de influencias: una práctica constant en el país." June.

———. 2013d. "La expropiación petrolera." August 22.

———. 2013e. "Apoyan desaparición de poderes por inseguridad." September.

———. 2013f. "Resultados Latinobarómetro 2013: El Caso de México," October.

———. 2014a. "La importancia de confiar en las instituciones, Las autodefensas en México." January.

———. 2014b. "La penetración del narcotráfico en la sociedad mexicana." February 28.

———. 2014c. "Mexicanos confían en el Código Nacional de Procedimientos Penales mejorará la impartición de justicia." March.

———. 2014d. "¿Por qué están a favor o en contra de la reforma energética?" June.

———. 2014e. "El saldo del proceso legislative." August 28.

———. 2014f. "Opiniones sobre los nuevos partidos en México." September.

———. 2014g. "Tlatlaya y los derechos humanos de los delincuentes." October 8.

Casar, María Amparo. 2010. "Executive-Legislative Relations: Continuity or Change?" In *Mexico's Democratic Challenges: Politics, Government, and*

Society, edited by Andrew Selee and Jacqueline Peschard, 117–120. Washington, DC: Woodrow Wilson Center Press.

Casas-Zamora, Kevin. 2005a. "State Funding and Campaign Finance Practices in Uruguay." In *The Financing of Politics: Latin American and European Perspectives,* edited by Carlos Malamud and Eduardo Posado-Carbó. London: Institute for the Study of the Americas.

———. 2005b. *Political Finance and State Funding for Parties.* Colchester: ECPR Press.

Castañeda-Angarita, Néstor, and David Doyle. 2015. "Redistribution and Taxation: How Business and Informal Labor Shape Partisan Tax Strategies." Unpublished manuscript, University College London (London) and University of Oxford (Oxford).

Cavarozzi, Marcelo. 1992. "Beyond Transitions to Democracy in Latin America." *Journal of Latin American Studies* 24(3): 665–684.

Centeno, Miguel. 2002. *Blood and Debt: War and the Nation-State in Latin America.* University Park: Pennsylvania State University Press.

Central America Data. 2012. "Venezuela and Nicaraguan Growth." May 8. http://m.centralamericadata.com/en/article/home/Venezuela_and_Nicaragua_Growth.

Cepeda Ulloa, Fernando. 2005. "Financing Politics in Colombia." In *The Financing of Politics: Latin American and European Perspectives,* edited by Carlos Malamud and Eduardo Posado-Carbó. London: Institute for the Study of the Americas.

Cervone, Emma. 2002. "Engendering Leadership: Indigenous Women Leaders in the Ecuadorian Andes." In *Gender's Place: Feminist Anthropologies of Latin America,* edited by Rosario Montoya, Leslie Jo Frazier, and Janice Hurtig, 179–196. New York: Palgrave Macmillan.

Cevallos, Juan. 2013. "Estalla protesta en la calle por el Yasuní." *La República,* August 15. www.larepublica.ec/blog/economia/2013/08/15/estalla-protesta-en-la-calle-por-el-yasuni/.

Cheibub, José Antonio, Adam Przeworski, and Sebastian Saiegh. 2004. "Government Coalition and Legislative Effectiveness Under Parliamentarism and Presidentialism." *British Journal of Political Science* 34(4): 565–587.

Chenault, Venida. 2011. *Weaving Strength, Weaving Power: Violence and Abuse Against Indigenous Women.* Durham: Carolina Academic Press.

Childs, Sarah, and Mona Lena Krook. 2006. "Should Feminists Give Up on Critical Mass? A Contingent 'Yes.'" *Politics and Gender* 2(4): 522–530.

Chile. 1990. Article 47 in Ley 18.948. "Ley Orgánica Constitucional de las Fuerzas Armadas." February 27.

———. 2010. Ley 20.424. *Estatuto Orgánico del Ministerio de Defensa Nacional.*

———. "Subsecretaría de Defensa." Ministerio de Defensa Nacional. www.defensa.cl/subsecretaria-de-defensa/.

Chile Constitution. 1980. Chapter XI: Articles 101 and 106, with amendments through 2012.

Chimienti, Adam, and Sebastian Matthes. 2013. "Ecuador: Extractivism for the Twenty-First Century?" *NACLA Report on the Americas* 46(4): 59–61.

Claessens, Stijn, Erik Feijen, and Luc Laeven. 2008. "Political Connections and Preferential Access to Finance: The Role of Campaign Contributions." *Journal of Financial Economics* 88(3): 554–580.

Cleary, Edward. 1997. *The Struggle for Human Rights in Latin America.* Westport, CT: Praeger.

————. 2007. *Mobilizing for Human Rights in Latin America.* Boulder: Kumarian Press.

CNN. 2011. "Bolivian President Asks for Forgiveness After Attacks on Indigenous Groups." September 29. www.cnn.com/2011/09/29/world/americas/bolivia protests.

————. 2012. "Time Is Right, but Past Failures Haunt Colombia Peace Talks." August 29. www.cnn.com/2012/08/28/world/americas/colombia-farc-peace-talks.

Cohen, Youssef. 1987. "Democracy from Above: The Origins of Military Dictatorship in Brazil." *World Politics* 40(1): 30–54.

————. 1994. *Radicals, Reformers, and Reactionaries: The Prisoner's Dilemma and the Collapse of Democracy in Latin America.* Chicago: University of Chicago Press.

Collier, David, and Steven Levitsky. 1997. "Democracy with Adjectives: Conceptual Innovation in Comparative Research." *World Politics* 49(3): 430–451.

Collier, Ruth B., and David Collier. 1991. *Shaping the Political Arena: Critical Junctures, the Labor Movement, and the Regime Dynamics in Latin America.* Princeton: Princeton University Press.

Colombia. 2000. Corte Constitucional de Colombia. Sentencia C-371/00. Bogotá. March 29.

————. 2009. Acto Legislativo Número 1 de 2009. Diario Oficial, No. 47, 410. July 14.

Conaghan, Catherine M. 2006. *Fujimori's Peru: Deception in the Public Sphere.* Pittsburgh: University of Pittsburgh Press.

————. 2011. "Ecuador: Rafael Correa and the People's Revolution." In *The Resurgence of the Latin American Left,* edited by Steven Levitsky and Kenneth M. Roberts. Baltimore: Johns Hopkins University Press.

Coneval. 2014. "Pobreza y derechos sociales de niñas: Niños y adolescentes en México, 2014." Mexico City: Coneval. www.coneval.gob.mx.

Consejo para la Consolidación de la Democracia. 1988. *Presidencialismo vs. parlamentarismo: Materiales para el estudio de la reforma constitucional.* Buenos Aires: Editorial Universitaria De Buenos Aires (EUDEBA).

Consulta Mitofsky. 2011. "Novena Encuesta nacional sobre percepción de inseguridad ciudadana en México." Mexico City: Consulta Mitofsky. www.mucd.org.mx/novenaencuestapercepcionciudadana1.pdf.

————. 2014. "Percepción del país: Economía, política, seguridad."Mexico City: Consulta Mitofsky. www.opinamexico.org/opinion/EvaGob.pdf.

Cooper, Michael J., Huseyin Gulen, and Alexei V. Ovtchinnikov. 2010. "Corporate Political Contributions and Stock Returns." *Journal of Finance* 65(2): 687–724.

Coppedge, Michael. 1998. "The Evolution of Latin American Party Systems." In *Politics, Society, and Democracy: Latin America*, edited by Scott Mainwaring and Arturo Valenzuela, 171–206. Boulder, CO: Westview.

————. 2000. "Venezuelan Parties and the Representation of Elite Interests." In *Conservative Parties, the Right, and Democracy in Latin America*, edited by Kevin J. Middlebrook. Baltimore: Johns Hopkins University Press.

————. 2012. *Democratization and Research Methods.* Cambridge: Cambridge University Press.

Coppedge, Michael, and John Gerring. 2011. "Conceptualizing and Measuring Democracy." *Perspectives on Politics* 9(2): 247–267.

Corrales, Javier. 2003. "Market Reforms." In *Constructing Democratic Governance,* edited by Jorge I. Domínguez and Michael Shifter. Baltimore: Johns Hopkins University Press.

———. 2010a. *The Politics of Sexuality in Latin America: A Reader on Lesbian, Gay, Bisexual, and Transgender Rights*. Pittsburgh: University of Pittsburgh Press.

———. 2010b. "The Repeating Revolution: Chávez's New Politics and Old Economics." In *Leftist Governments in Latin America: Successes and Shortcomings*, edited by Kurt Weyland, Raúl L. Madrid, and Wendy Hunter. Cambridge: Cambridge University Press.

———. 2011. "Why Polarize? Advantages and Disadvantages of a Rational-Choice Analysis of Government-Opposition Relations in Venezuela." In *Revolution in Venezuela*, edited by Jonathan Eastwood and Thomas Ponniah. New Haven: Harvard University.

———. 2013a. "Constitutional Rewrites in Latin America, 1987–2009." In *Constructing Democratic Governance in Latin America*, 4th ed., edited by Jorge I. Dominguez and Michael Shifter, 13–47. Baltimore: Johns Hopkins University Press.

———. 2013b. *The Promise of Participation: Experiments in Participatory Governance in Honduras and Guatemala*. London: Palgrave Macmillan.

Costa Rica. 2008. Sala Constitucional de la Corte Suprema de Justicia. Resolution 2008009582. San José. June 11.

———. 2010. Asamblea Legislativa de la República de Costa Rica. "Ley 8901." San José. November 3.

———. 2012. Sala Constitucional de la Corte Suprema de Justicia. Resolution 2012001966. San José.

———. 2014a. Sala Constitucional de la Corte Suprema de Justicia. Sentencia 2014-004630. San José.

———. 2014b. Comisión Permanente Especial de la Mujer. "Dictamen Afirmativo de Mayoría. Expediente 19.019." *La Gaceta* No. 58. San José. March 25.

———. 2014c. Departamento de Servicios Técnicos, Asamblea Legislativa de la República de Costa Rica. 2014. "Informe Jurídico." San José. May 28.

Cox, Gary, and Matthew McCubbins. 2001. "The Institutional Determinants of Economic Policy." In *Presidents, Parliaments and Policy: Political Economy of Institutions and Decisions*, edited by Stephan Haggard and Matthew McCubbins. Cambridge: Cambridge University Press.

Cox, Gary, and Scott Morgenstern. 2001. "Latin America's Reactive Assemblies and Proactive Presidents." *Comparative Politics* 33(2): 171–189.

Craske, Nikki. 1999. *Women in Politics in Latin America*. New Brunswick, NJ: Rutgers University Press.

Crisp, Brian F., Scott W. Desposato, and Kristin Kanthak. 2011. "Legislative Pivots, Presidential Powers, and Policy Stability." *Journal of Law, Economics, and Organization* 27(1): 1–27.

Crocker, Adriana, ed. 2011. *Diffusion of Gender Quotas in Latin America and Beyond*. New York: Peter Lang.

Cusack, Thomas R., Torben Iversen, and David Soskice. 2007. "Economic Interests and the Origins of Electoral Systems." *American Political Science Review* 101(3): 373–391.

Dagnino, Evelina. 2003. "Citizenship in Latin America: An Introduction." *Latin American Perspectives* 30(2): 3–17.

Dahl, Robert A. 1961. *Who Governs? Democracy and Power in an American City*. New Haven: Yale University Press.

———. 1971. *Polyarchy*. New Haven: Yale University Press.

———. 1989. *Democracy and Its Critics*. New Haven: Yale University Press.

————. 1998. *On Democracy.* New Haven: Yale University Press.

————. 2001. "Polyarchy." In *Encyclopedia of Democratic Thought,* edited by Joe Foweraker and Barry Clarke. London: Routledge.

Dahlerup, Drude. 2006. "The Story of the Theory of Critical Mass." *Politics and Gender* 2(4): 511–522.

Dahlerup, Drude, and Lenita Freidenvall. 2005. "Quotas as a 'Fast Track' to Equal Representation for Women." *International Feminist Journal of Politics* 7(1): 26–48.

Dahlerup, Drude, and Pippa Norris. 2014. "On the Fast Track: An Integrated Theory for the Global Spread of Electoral Gender Quotas." Paper presented at the annual meeting of the American Political Science Association, Washington, DC, August 28–31.

Daly, Catherine, Kimberly Heinle, and David A. Shirk. 2012. "Armed with Impunity: Curbing Military Human Rights Abuses in Mexico, a Special Report." San Diego: Trans-Border Institute at the University of San Diego.

Dammert, Lucía. 2013. "Security Challenges for Democratic Governance." In *Constructing Democratic Governance in Latin America,* 4th ed., edited by Jorge I. Dominguez and Michael Shifter, 78–101. Baltimore: Johns Hopkins University Press.

Davis, Diane E. 2006. "Undermining the Rule of Law: Democratization and the Dark Side of Police Reform in Mexico." *Latin American Politics and Society* 48(1): 55–86.

————. 2010. "Irregular Armed Forces, Shifting Patterns of Commitment, and Fragmented Sovereignty in the Developing World." *Theory Society* 39(3): 397–413.

De Jesus, Carolina Maria. 1963. *Child of the Dark: The Diaries of Carolina Maria de Jesus.* New York: Signet. Published in Brazil as *Quarto de despejo* (1960).

De la Cadena, Marisol. 2015. *Earth Beings: Ecology of Practice Across Andean Worlds.* Durham, NC: Duke University Press.

De la Torre, Carlos. 2000. *Populist Seduction in Latin America: The Ecuadorian Experience.* Athens: Ohio University Center for International Studies.

————. 2009. "El Populismo Radical en los Andes." *Journal of Democracy en Español* 1: 23–37.

————. 2013. "In the Name of the People: Democratization, Popular Organizations, and Populism in Venezuela, Bolivia, and Ecuador." *European Review of Latin American and Caribbean Studies* 95: 27–48.

De la Torre, Carlos, and Catherine M. Conaghan. 2009. "The Hybrid Campaign: Tradition and Modernity in Ecuador's 2006 Presidential Election." *International Journal of Press/Politics* 14(3): 333–352.

Debs, Alexandre, and Gretchen Helmke. 2010. "Inequality Under Democracy: Explaining the Left Decade in Latin America." *Quarterly Journal of Political Science* 5(3): 209–241.

Deere, Carmen Diana, and Magdalena León. 2001. *Empowering Women: Land and Property Rights in Latin America.* Pittsburgh: University of Pittsburgh Press.

Del Castillo, Pilar, and Daniel Zovatto, eds. 1998. *La Financiación de la Política en Iberoamérica.* San José, Costa Rica: Instituto InterAmericano de Derechos Humanos/Centro de Asesoria y Promocion Electoral.

Deveaux, Monique. 2006. *Gender and Justice in Multicultural Liberal States.* Oxford: Oxford University Press.

Diamond, Larry. 1999. *Democracy in Development.* Baltimore: Johns Hopkins University Press.

Dion, Michelle L., and Vicki Birchfield. 2010. "Economic Development, Income Inequality, and Preferences for Redistribution." *International Studies Quarterly* 54(2): 315–334.

Dominguez, Alejandro Diaz. 2004. "Reelection Issues in New Mexico's Electoral Reform." February 13. http://alejandrodiazd.wordpress.com/?s=reelection +issues.

Doorenspleet, R. 2005. *Democratic Transitions: Exploring the Structural Sources of the Fourth Wave.* Boulder: Lynne Rienner.

Doyle, David. 2014. "The Political Economy of Policy Volatility in Latin America." *Latin American Politics and Society* 56(4): 1–21.

———. 2015. "Remittances and Social Spending." *American Political Science Review* 109(4): 785–802.

Ecuador. 2002. El Tribunal Constitucional. Decisión 028-2002. Quito. November 15.

Edmonds, Martin. 1985. *Central Organizations of Defense.* Boulder, CO: Westview Press.

Edmonds-Poli, Emily. 2013. "The Effects of Drug-War Related Violence on Mexico's Press and Democracy." Working Paper Series on Civic Engagement and Public Security in Mexico. April. Washington, DC: Mexico Institute, Woodrow Wilson Center.

Edwards, Sebastian. 1995. *Crisis and Reform in Latin America: From Despair to Hope.* New York: Oxford University Press and World Bank.

———. 2010. *Left Behind: Latin America and the False Promise of Populism.* Chicago: University of Chicago Press.

El Salvador. 2013. "Cuotas de mujeres en Ley de Partidos no resuelve paridad."*ContraPunto*, February 21. www.contrapunto.com.sv/archivo2016 /politica/cuotas-de-mujeres-en-ley-de-partidos-no-resuelve-paridad.

Ellingwood, Ken. 2011. "Mexico News Companies Agree to Drug War Coverage Guidelines." *Los Angeles Times,* March 25.

Escaith, Hubert, and Igor Paunovic. 2004. "Reformas estructurales en América Latina y el Caribe en el período 1970–2000: Indices y notas metodológicas." Santiago, Chile: Economic Commission for Latin America and the Caribbean (ECLAC).

Etchemendy, Sebastián, and Candelaria Garay. 2011. "Argentina: Left Populism in Comparative Perspective, 2003–2009." In *The Resurgence of the Latin American Left,* edited by Steven Levitsky and Kenneth M. Roberts. Baltimore: Johns Hopkins University Press.

Evans, Peter B., and James E. Rauch. 1999. "Bureaucracy and Growth: A Cross National Analysis of the Effects of 'Weberian' State Structures on Economic Growth." *American Sociological Review* 64(5): 748–765.

EZLN (Ejército Zapatista de Liberación Nacional). 2013a. *Gobierno Autónomo I: Cuaderno de texto de primer grado del curso de "La libertad según l@s Zapatistas."* Mexico. http://kehuelga.net/archivos/zapatistas/escuelita/gobierno -autonomo-1.pdf.

———. 2013b. *Participación de las Mujeres en el Gobierno Autónomo, Cuaderno de texto de primer grado del curso de "La libertad según l@s Zapatistas."* Mexico.

Faccio, Mara. 2006. "Politically Connected Firms." *American Economic Review* 96(1): 369–386.

Farrell, David M., and Paul Webb. 2000. "Political Parties as Campaign Organizations." In *Parties Without Partisans: Political Change in Advanced*

Industrial Democracies, edited by Russell J. Dalton and Martin P. Wattenberg, 102–128. Oxford: Oxford University Press.

FBIS-LAT (Foreign Broadcast Information Service–Latin America). 1983. P. B5. December 8.

———. 1984. P. B7. February 8.

Ferreira, Francisco, Julian Messina, Jamele Rigolini, Luis-Felipe López-Calva, Maria Ana Lugo, and Renos Vakis. 2013. *Economic Mobility and the Rise of the Latin American Middle Class.* Washington, DC: World Bank.

Filho, João Roberto Martins. 2010. "Tensões Militares no Governo Lula (2003–2009): A pré-historia do acordo com a França." *Revista Brasileira de Ciencia Política* 4: 285–291.

Fitch, J. Samuel. 1977. *The Military Coup d'Etat as a Political Process: Ecuador 1948–1966.* Baltimore: Johns Hopkins University Press.

Flores-Macías, Gustavo A. 2012. *After Neoliberalism? The Left and Economic Reforms in Latin America.* Oxford: Oxford University Press.

Flynn, Peter. 2005. "Brazil and Lula, 2005: Crisis, Corruption and Change in Political Perspective" Third World Quarterly 26(8): 1221-1267.

Forbis, Melissa. 2011. Autonomía y un punado de hierbas: La disputa por las identidades de género y étnicas por medio del sanar. In *Luchas "muy otras": Zapatismo y autonomía en las comunidades indígenas de Chiapas,* edited by Bruno Baronnet, Mariana Mora Bayo, and Richard Stahler-Sholk, 371–403. Mexico City and San Cristóbal de Las Casas, Mexico: Universidad Autónoma Metropolitana, Xochimilco, CIESAS, and UNACH.

Foweraker, Joe. 1997. "Popular Mobilization and Political Culture in Mexico." In *Citizens of the Pyramid: Essays on Mexican Political Culture,* edited by Wil Pansters, 225–246. Amsterdam: Thela.

———. 1998. "Institutional Design, Party Systems and Governability— Differentiating the Presidential Regimes of Latin America." *British Journal of Political Science* 28(4): 651–676.

———. 2005. "Toward a Political Sociology of Social Mobilization in Latin America." In *Rethinking Development in Latin America,* edited by Charles Wood and Brian Roberts. University Park: Pennsylvania State University Press.

Foweraker, Joe, and Roman Krznaric. 2000. "Measuring Liberal Democratic Performance: An Empirical and Conceptual Critique." *Political Studies* 48(4): 759–787.

———. 2002. "The Uneven Performance of the Democracies of the 3rd Wave: Electoral Politics and the Imperfect Rule of Law in Latin America." *Latin American Politics and Society* 44(3): 29–60.

———. 2003. "Differentiating the Democratic Performance of the West." *European Journal of Political Research* 42(3): 313–340.

Foweraker, Joe, and Todd Landman. 1997. *Citizenship Rights and Social Movements: A Comparative and Statistical Analysis.* Oxford: Oxford University Press.

Foweraker, Joe, Todd Landman, and Neil Harvey. 2003. *Governing Latin America.* Cambridge: Polity Press.

Franceschet, Susan. 2005. *Women and Politics in Chile.* Boulder: Lynne Rienner.

Franceschet, Susan, and Jennifer M. Piscopo. 2008. "Quotas and Women's Substantive Representation: Lessons from Argentina." *Politics and Gender* 4(3): 393–425.

———. 2013. "Equality, Democracy, and the Broadening and Deepening of Gender Quotas." *Politics and Gender* 9(3): 310–316.

Franco, Jean. 2009. "The Crisis of Liberalism and the Case for Subalternity." *A Contracorriente: Una revista de historia social y literature de América Latina* 7(1): 495–501.

Franco, Rafael Pérez. 1979. In *Quiénes son el PAN*, 197–198. Mexico City: Imprenta Unión.

Freeman, M. 2002. *Human Rights: An Interdisciplinary Approach*. Cambridge, UK: Polity.

Freidenberg, Flavia. 2001. "Ecuador." In *Partidos Políticos de América Latina: Centroamérica, México, y República Dominicana,* edited by Manuel Alcántara Sáez and Flavia Freidenberg. Mexico City: Fondo de Cultura Economica.

Freidenberg, Flavia, and Steven Levitsky. 2007. "Informal Organization of Parties in Latin America." *Desarrollo Economico* 46(4): 539–568.

FTI Consulting. 2014. "Mexico Is the Fifth Most Dangerous Country in Latin America for Business." March 3. www.fticonsulting.com.

Fukuda-Parr, Sakiko, Terra Lawson-Remer, and Susan Randolph. 2015. *Fulfilling Social and Economic Rights*. Oxford: Oxford University Press.

Fukuyama, F. 1992. *The End of History and the Last Man*. New York: Avon Books.

Gallie, W. B. 1956. "Essentially Contested Concepts." *Proceedings of the Aristotelian Society* 56: 167–198.

García Canclini, Néstor. 2001. *Consumers and Citizens: Globalization and Multicultural Conflicts*. Minneapolis: University of Minnesota Press.

García Quesada, Ana Isabel. 2011. "From Temporary Measures to the Parity Principle: The Case of Costa Rica." In *Diffusion of Gender Quotas in Latin America and Beyond,* edited by Adriana Crocker, 114–129. New York: Peter Lang.

Gargarella, Roberto. 2010. *The Legal Foundations of Inequality: Constitutionalism in the Americas 1776–1860*. New York: Cambridge University Press.

———. 2013. *Latin American Constitutionalism (1810–2010): The Engine Room of the Constitution*. Oxford: Oxford University Press.

Garretón, Manuel Antonio. 2005. "Coping with Opacity: The Financing of Politics in Chile." In *The Financing of Politics: Latin American and European Perspectives,* edited by Carlos Malamud and Eduardo Posado-Carbó. London: Institute for the Study of the Americas.

———. 2007. *Del post-pinochetismo a la sociedad democrática: Globalización y política en el bicentenario*. Santiago, Chile: Random House Mondadori.

———. 2012. *Neoliberalismo corregido y progresismo limitado: Los gobiernos de la concertación en Chile, 1990–2010*. Santiago, Chile: Editorial Arcis and Consejo Latinoamericano de Ciencias Sociales (CLACSO).

Garretón, Manuel Antonio, Marcelo Cavarozzi, Peter Cleaves, Gary Gereffi, and Jonathan Hartlyn. 2003. *Latin America in the Twenty-First Century: Toward a New Sociopolitical Matrix*. Boulder: Lynne Rienner.

Gastañaduí, Santiago. 2004. "El JNE impulse Proyecto de paridad de género para las próximas elecciones." *Red Innovación*, November 12. www .redinnovacion.org/blog/posts/el-jne-impulsa-proyecto-de-paridad-de -generopara-las-proximas-elecciones-peru.

Gaventa, John. 1980. *Power and Powerlessness: Quiescence and Rebellion in an Appalachian Valley*. Urbana: University of Illinois Press.

Geddes, Barbara. 1994. *Politician's Dilemma: Building State Capacity in Latin America*. Berkeley: University of California Press.

Gerber, Elisabeth R., and Jeffrey B. Lewis. 2004. "Beyond the Median: Voter Preferences, District Heterogeneity, and Political Representation." *Journal of Political Economy* 112(6): 1364–1383.

Gerring, John, Strom C. Thacker, and Carola Moreno. 2005. "Centripetal Democratic Governance: A Theory and Global Inquiry." *American Political Science Review* 99(4): 567–581.

Gerschenkron, Alexander. 1962. *Economic Backwardness in Historical Perspective.* Cambridge: Harvard University Press.

Gervasoni, Carlos. 2010a. "A Rentier Theory of Subnational Regimes." *World Politics* 62(2): 302–340.

———. 2010b. "Measuring Variance in Subnational Regimes: Results from an Expert-Based Operationalization of Democracy in the Argentine Provinces." *Journal of Politics in Latin America* 2(2): 13–52.

Gibson, Edward L. 1996. *Class and Conservative Politics: Argentina in Comparative Perspective.* Baltimore: Johns Hopkins University Press.

———. 2005. "Boundary Control." *World Politics* 58(1): 101–132.

Gibson, Edward L., and Ernesto Calvo. 2000. "Federalism and Low-Maintenance Constituencies: Territorial Dimensions of Economic Reform in Argentina." *Studies in Comparative International Development* 35(3): 32–55.

Gilens, Martina, and Benjamin Page. 2014. "Testing Theories of American Politics: Elites, Interest Groups and Average Citizens." *Perspectives on Politics* 12(3): 564–581.

Gilley, Bruce. 2009. *The Right to Rule.* New York: Columbia University Press.

Giuranno, Michele G. 2009. "Regional Income Disparity and the Size of the Public Sector." *Journal of Public Economic Theory* 32(3): 321–346.

Godoy Arcaya, Oscar, ed. 1990. *Hacia una democracia moderna: La opción parlamentaria.* Santiago, Chile: Ediciones Universidad Católica de Chile.

Goldfrank, Benjamin. 2011. "The Left and Participatory Democracy: Brazil, Uruguay, and Venezuela." In *The Resurgence of the Latin American Left,* edited by Steven Levitsky and Kenneth M. Roberts. Baltimore: Johns Hopkins University Press.

González, Victoria, and Karen Kampwirth, eds. 2001. *Radical Women in Latin America: Left and Right.* University Park: Pennsylvania State University Press.

Goodale, Mark. 2009. *Dilemmas of Modernity: Bolivian Encounters with Law and Liberalism.* Stanford: Stanford University Press.

Gooren, Henri. 2010. "Ortega for President: The Religious Rebirth of Sandinismo in Nicaragua." *European Review of Latin American and Caribbean Studies* 89: 47–63.

Gouveia, Miguel, and Neal A. Masia. 1998. "Does the Median Voter Model Explain the Size of Government? Evidence from the States." *Public Choice* 97(1–2): 159–177.

Grayson, George W. 2011. *Mexico: Narco-Violence and a Failed State?* New Brunswick, NJ: Transaction.

Greene, Kenneth F. 2007. *Why Dominant Parties Lose: Mexico's Democratization in Comparative Perspective.* New York: Cambridge University Press.

Grimmer, Justin. 2013. "Appropriators Not Position Takers: The Distorting Effects of Electoral Incentives on Congressional Representation." *American Journal of Political Science* 57(3): 624–642.

Griner, Steven, and Daniel Zovatto. 2005. *Funding of Parties and Election Campaigns in the Americas.* San José, Costa Rica: OAS/IDEA.

The Guardian. 2013. "Colombia Peace Marches Draw Thousands." April 9. http://www.theguardian.com/world/2013/apr/10/colombia-farc.

Guatemala. 1999. Congreso de la República de Guatemala. Decreto Número 7–99. Guatemala City. March 9.

Guyer, Julián González, et al. 2007. "Analisis crítico de la estructura del Ministerio de Defensa Nacional." In *Defensa Nacional y FF.AA. Democracia e Integración Regional,* edited by Julián González Guyer et al. Montevideo: Programa de Investigación sobre Seguridad.

Habermas, Jurgen. 1985. *The Theory of Communicative Action,* vol. 1. Boston: Beacon Press.

————. 1991. *The Structural Transformation of the Public Sphere.* Boston: MIT Press.

Halbwachs, Maurice. 1992. *On Collective Memory.* Chicago: University of Chicago Press.

Harbers, Imke. 2009. "Decentralization and the Development of Nationalized Party Systems in New Democracies: Evidence from Latin America." *Comparative Political Studies* 43(5): 606–627.

Hardt, Michael, and Antonio Negri. 2000. *Empire.* Cambridge: Harvard University Press.

Harnecker, Marta. 2007. *Rebuilding the Left.* London: Zed Books.

Harris, Olivia. 1985. "Complementaridad y conflicto: Una vision andina del hombre y de la mujer." *Revista Allpanchis* 25: 17–39.

Hartsock, Nancy. 1983. *Money, Sex and Power: Toward a Feminist Historical Materialism.* Boston: Northeastern University Press.

Harvey, Neil. 2016. "Practicing Autonomy: Zapatismo and Decolonial Liberation." *Latin American and Caribbean Ethnic Studies* 11(1): 24.

Haugen, Gary, and Victor Boutros. 2010. "And Justice for All: Enforcing Human Rights for the World's Poor." *Foreign Affairs* 89(3): 51–62.

Hausmann, Ricardo, and Michael Gavin. 1996. "Securing Stability and Growth in a Shock Prone Region: The Policy Challenge for Latin America." Working Paper No. 315. Washington, DC: Inter-American Development Bank.

Hawkins, Darren. 2002. *International Human Rights and Authoritarian Rule in Chile.* Lincoln: University of Nebraska Press.

Hayner, Priscilla B. 1994. "Fifteen Truth Commissions—1974 to1994: A Comparative Study." *Human Rights Quarterly* 16(4): 597–655.

————. 2002. *Unspeakable Truths: Facing the Challenge of Truth Commissions.* London: Routledge.

Heath, Roseanna, Leslie Schwindt-Bayer, and Michelle Taylor-Robinson. 2005. "Women on the Sidelines: Women's Representation on Committees in Latin American Legislatures." *American Journal of Political Science* 49(2): 420–436.

Helmke, Gretchen, and Steven Levitsky. 2006. "Introduction." In *Informal Institutions and Democracy: Lessons from Latin America,* edited by Gretchen Helmke and Steven Levitsky, 1–30. Baltimore: Johns Hopkins University Press.

Hernandez, Daniel. 2010. "Evo Morales: 'Chicken Causes Baldness and Homosexuality.'" *Los Angeles Times,* April 23. http://latimesblogs.latimes.com/laplaza/2010/04/bolivia-president.html.

Hernández Sánchez, Ana Isabel. 2001. "Paraguay." In *Partidos Políticos de América Latina: Centroamérica, México, y República Dominicana,* edited by Manuel Alcántara Sáez and Flavia Freidenberg, 355–388. Salamanca: Ediciones Universidad de Salamanca.

Heston, Alan, Robert Summers, and Bettina Aten. 2012. Penn World Table Version 7.1. Center for International Comparisons of Production, Income and Prices at the University of Pennsylvania.

Hinojosa, Magda. 2012. *Selecting Women, Electing Women: Political Representation and Candidate Selection in Latin America.* Philadelphia: Temple University Press.

Hinojosa, Magda, and Jennifer M. Piscopo. 2013. "Promoción del derecho de las mujeres a ser elegidas." In *Cuotas de género: Vision comparada,* edited by José Alejandro Luna Ramos. Mexico City: Electoral Tribunal of the Federal Judicial Power.

Hirschman, Albert O. 1970. *Exit, Voice and Loyalty: Responses to Declines in Firms, Organizations and States.* Cambridge: Harvard University Press.

Hiskey, Jonathan, Mary Malone, and Diana Orcés. 2014. "Violence and Migration in Central America." *AmericasBarometer Insights* 101: 6.

Hochstetler, Kathryn. 2006. "Rethinking Presidentialism: Challenges and Presidential Falls in South America." *Comparative Politics* 38(4): 401–418.

Hogenboom, Barbara. 2012. "The New Politics of Mineral Extraction in Latin America." *Journal of Developing Societies* 28(2): 129–132.

Honduras. 2012. República de Honduras. Decreto No. 54-2012. *La Gaceta* No. 32,820. Tegucigalpa. May 15.

Horowitz, Donald. 1971. "Three Dimensions of Ethnic Politics." *World Politics* 23(2): 232–244.

Htun, Mala. 2004. "Is Gender Like Ethnicity? The Political Representation of Identity Groups." *Perspectives on Politics* 2(3): 439–458.

Htun, Mala, and Mark P. Jones. 2002. "Electoral Quotas and Women's Leadership in Latin America." In *Gender and the Politics of Rights and Democracy in Latin America,* edited by Nikki Craske and Maxine Molyneux. New York: Palgrave.

Huber, Evelyne, Jennifer Pribble, and J. D. Stephens. 2010. "The Chilean Left in Power: Achievement, Failures, and Omissions." In *Leftist Governments in Latin America: Successes and Shortcomings,* edited by Kurt Weyland, Raúl Madrid, and Wendy Hunter. New York: Cambridge University Press.

Huber, Evelyne, and John D. Stephens. 2012. *Democracy and the Left: Social Policy and Inequality in Latin America.* Chicago: University of Chicago Press.

Human Rights Watch. 2011. *Neither Rights nor Security: Killings, Torture, and Disappearances in Mexico's "War on Drugs."* New York: Human Rights Watch.

———. 2013. *Mexico's Disappeared: The Enduring Cost of a Crisis Ignored.* New York: Human Rights Watch.

———. 2014. *World Report, Mexico.* New York: Human Rights Watch.

Hunter, Wendy. 2010. *The Transformation of the Workers' Party in Brazil, 1989–2009.* New York: Cambridge University Press.

Huntington, Samuel. 1968. *Political Order in Changing Societies.* New Haven: Yale University Press.

———. 1991. *The Third Wave: Democratization in the Late Twentieth Century.* Norman: University of Oklahoma Press.

———. 1993. "The Clash of Civilizations?" *Foreign Affairs* 72(3): 22–49.

ICESI (Instituto Ciudadano de Estudios Sobre la Inseguridad). 2011. "Análisis de la Séptima Encuesta Nacional Sobre Inseguridad." www.icesi.org.mx/estadisticas/estadistcas_encuestasNacionales_ensi7.asp.

IDEA (International Institute for Democracy and Electoral Assistance) and CIM (Inter-American Commission on Women's Rights). 2013. *La apuesta por la paridad: Democatizando el sistema politico en América Latina.* Lima: Regional Andean Office.

Ingram, Matthew, Octavio Rodríguez Ferreira, and David Shirk. 2011. "Assessing Mexico's Judicial Reform, Views of Judges, Prosecutors, and Public Defenders." San Diego: Trans-Border Institute.

Institute for Economics and Peace. 2014. "Peace and Economic Growth at the Sub-national Level." In *Global Peace Index 2014,* 69. Oxford: Institute for Economics and Peace.

Instituto Tecnológico Autónomo de México and the Mexico Institute and the Woodrow Wilson International Center for Scholars. 2012. *A New Beginning for Mexican Oil*, November.

Insulza, José Miguel. 2014. "Sólo el diálogo puede cambiar la dinámica de confrontación." *El País*, February 26.

International Monetary Fund. Government Finance Statistics. Database.

Iversen, Torben, and David Soskice. 2006. "Electoral Institutions and the Politics of Coalitions: Why Some Democracies Redistribute More Than Others." *American Political Science Review* 100(2): 165.

Ivison, Duncan, Paul Patton, and Will Sanders, eds. 2000. *Political Theory and the Rights of Indigenous Peoples*. Cambridge: Cambridge University Press.

Jaggers, K., and T. R. Gurr. 1995. "Tracking Democracy's Third Wave with the Polity III Data." *Journal of Peace Research* 32(4): 469–482.

Jaquette, Jane, ed. 1989. *The Women's Movement in Latin America: Feminism and the Transition to Democracy*. Winchester, MA: Unwin Hyman.

———. 1994. *The Women's Movement in Latin America: Participation and Democracy*. Boulder: Westview Press.

———. 1997. "Women in Power: From Tokenism to Critical Mass." *Foreign Policy* 108: 23–37.

———. 2009. *Feminist Agendas and Democracy in Latin America*. Durham: Duke University Press.

Johnson, Gregg, and Brian Crisp. 2003. "Mandates, Powers, and Policies." *American Journal of Political Science* 47(1): 128–142.

Johnson, Joel W., and Jessica S. Wallack. 2006. "Electoral Systems and the Personal Vote." Unpublished manuscript, University of California at San Diego.

Jones, Mark P. 1995. *Electoral Laws and the Survival of Presidential Democracies*. Notre Dame: University of Notre Dame Press.

———. 1996. "Increasing Women's Representation via Gender Quotas: The Argentine Ley de Cupos." *Women and Politics* 16(4): 75–98.

———. 2008. "The Recruitment and Selection of Legislative Candidates in Argentina." In *Pathways to Power: Political Recruitment and Candidate Selection in Latin America*, edited by Gretchen Helmke and Steven Levitsky. University Park: Pennsylvania State University Press.

———. 2009. "Gender Quota Laws and the Election of Women: Evidence from the Latin American Vanguard." *Comparative Political Studies* 42(1): 56–81.

Jones, Mark P., Santiago Alles, and Carolina Tchintian. 2012. "Cuotas de género, leyes electorales, y elección de legisladoras en América Latina." *Revista de Ciecnia Política* 32 (2): 331–357.

Jones, Mark P., Sebasitain Saiegh, Pablo T. Spiller, and Mariano Tommasi. 2002. "Amateur Legislators—Professional Politicians: The Consequences of Party-Centered Electoral Rules in a Federal System." *American Journal of Political Science* 46(3): 656–669.

Kane, Gillian. 2013. "After Jailing Women, Bolivia Weighs Legalizing Abortion." *The Atlantic*, June 24. www.theatlantic.com/international/archive/2013/06/after -jailing-women-bolivia-weighs-legalizing-abortion/277147/.

Karl, Terry, and Philippe Schmitter. 1991. "Modes of Transition in Latin America and Eastern Europe." *International Social Science Journal* 128(2): 267–282.

Kaufman, Robert. 2009. "The Political Effects of Inequality in Latin America: Some Inconvenient Facts." *Comparative Politics* 41(3): 359–377.

———. 2010. "The Political Left, the Export Boom, and the Populist Temptation." In *Latin America's Left Turn*, edited by Steven Levitsky and Kenneth Roberts, 93–116. Cambridge: Cambridge University Press.

Kaufmann, Daniel, Aart Kraay, and Massimo Mastruzzi. 2010. "The Worldwide Governance Indicators: Methodology and Analytical Issues." Policy Research Working Paper No. 5430. Washington, DC: World Bank.

Kingstone, Peter R. 2011. *The Political Economy of Latin America: Reflections on Neoliberalism and Development.* New York: Routledge.

Kitschelt, Herbert, Kirk Hawkins, Juan Pablo Luna, Guillermo Rosas, and Elizabeth Zechmeister Levit. 2010. *Latin American Party Systems.* Cambridge: Cambridge University Press.

Krauze, Enrique. 1984. "Por una democracia sin adjetivos." *Vuelta* 9(86): 4–13.

Krech, Shepard, III. 2000. *The Ecological Indian: History and Myth.* New York: W. W. Norton.

Krook, Mona Lena, Joni Lovenduski, and Judith Squires. 2009. "Gender Quotas and Models of Political Citizenship." *British Journal of Political Science* 39(4): 781–803.

Kurtz, Marcus J. 2013. *Latin American State Building in Comparative Perspective: Social Foundation of Institutional Order.* Cambridge: Cambridge University Press.

Lacey, Marc. 2008. "Killings in Drug War in Mexico Double in '08." *New York Times,* December 9.

Laclau, Ernesto. 2005. *On Populist Reason.* London: Verso.

———. 2006. "La deriva populista y la centroizquierda latinoamericana." *Nueva Sociedad* 205: 56–61.

Landman, Todd. 1999. "Economic Development and Democracy: The View from Latin America." *Political Studies* 47(4): 607–626.

———. 2005a. *Protecting Human Rights: A Comparative Study.* Washington, DC: Georgetown University Press.

———. 2005b. "Review Article: The Political Science of Human Rights." *British Journal of Political Science* 35(3): 549–572.

———. 2006. "Development, Democracy, and Human Rights in Latin America." In *Capitalism and Human Rights,* edited by Janet Dine and Andrew Fagan, 330–357. Cheltenham: Edward Elgar.

———. 2008. *Issues and Methods in Comparative Politics: An Introduction,* 3rd ed. London: Routledge.

———. 2010. "Violence, Democracy, and Human Rights in Latin America." In *Violent Democracies in Latin America,* edited by Enrique Desmond Arias and Daniel M. Goldstein, 226–241. Durham: Duke University Press.

———. 2013. *Democracy and Human Rights: The Precarious Triumph of Ideals.* London: Bloomsbury.

Landman, Todd, and Edzia Carvalho. 2009. *Measuring Human Rights,* London: Routledge.

Landman, Todd, and Marco Larizza. 2009. "Inequality and Human Rights: Who Controls What, When, and How." *International Studies Quarterly* 53(3): 715–736.

Latin News. 2015. "Nicaragua: Long Awaited 'Gran Canal' Study Presented." June 11. www.latinnews.com/component/k2/item/65219.html?period=+&archive=33 &search=nicaragua+canal&cat_id=798260%3Anicaragua-long-awaited-gran -canal-study-presented.

Lavena, Cecilia F. 2013. "What Determines Permissiveness Toward Corruption? A Study of Attitudes in Latin America." *Public Integrity* 15(4): 361.

Lavrín, Asunción. 1995. *Women, Feminism, and Social Change in Argentina, Chile and Uruguay, 1890–1949.* Lincoln: University of Nebraska Press.

Lebon, Nathalie. 2010. "Women Building Plural Democracy in Latin America and the Caribbean." In *Women's Activism in Latin America and the Caribbean,* edited by Nathalie Lebon and Elizabeth Maier. New Brunswick, NJ: Rutgers University Press.

Lessmann, Christian. 2009. "Fiscal Decentralization and Regional Disparity: Evidence from Cross-Section and Panel Data." *Environment and Planning A* 41(10): 2455–2473.

Levi, Margaret, and Laura Stoker. 2000. "Political Trust and Trustworthiness." *Annual Review of Political Science* 3: 475–507.

Levine, Daniel H., and Jose E. Molina, eds. 2011. *The Quality of Democracy in Latin America.* Boulder, CO: Lynne Rienner.

Levitsky, Steven. 2001. "Inside the Black Box: Recent Studies of Latin American Party Organizations." *Studies in Comparative International Development* 36(2): 92–110.

———. 2003. *Transforming Labor-Based Parties in Latin America: Argentine Peronism in Comparative Perspective.* New York: Cambridge University Press.

Levitsky, Steven, and Katrina Burgess. 2003. "Explaining Populist Party Adaptation in Latin America: Environmental and Organizational Determinants of Party Change in Argentina, Mexico, Peru, and Venezuela." *Comparative Political Studies* 36(8): 859–880.

Levitsky, Steven, and Maxwell A. Cameron. 2003. "Democracy Without Parties? Political Parties and Regime Change in Peru." *Latin American Politics and Society* 45(3): 1–33.

Levitsky, Steven, Jorge Domínguez, Brendon Van Dyck, and James Loxton, eds. 2016. *The Challenge of Party Building in Latin America.* Manuscript submitted for publication.

Levitsky, Steven, and Gretchen Helmke, eds. 2006. *Informal Institutions and Democracy: Lessons from Latin America.* Baltimore: Johns Hopkins University Press.

Levitsky, Steven, and Kenneth M. Roberts. 2011. "Democracy, Development, and the Left." In *The Resurgence of the Latin American Left,* edited by Steven Levitsky and Kenneth M. Roberts. Baltimore: Johns Hopkins University Press.

Levitsky, Steven, and Lucan Way. 2010. *Competitive Authoritarianism: International Linkage, Organizational Power, and the Fate of Hybrid Regimes.* New York: Cambridge University Press.

Levy, Santiago, and Norbert Schady. 2013. "Latin America's Social Policy Challenge: Education, Social Insurance, Redistribution." *The Journal of Economic Perspectives* 27(2): 193–218.

Lichbach, Mark. 2013. *Democratic Theory and Causal Methodology in Comparative Politics.* Cambridge: Cambridge University Press.

Linz, Juan J. 1978. *The Breakdown of Democratic Regimes: Crisis, Breakdown, and Reequilibriation.* Baltimore: Johns Hopkins University Press.

———. 1990. "The Perils of Presidentialism." *Journal of Democracy* 1(1): 51–69.

Linz, Juan J., and Arturo Valenzuela, eds. 1994. *The Failure of Presidential Democracy.* Baltimore: Johns Hopkins University Press.

Lipset, Seymour M. 1959. "Some Social Requisites for Democracy: Economic Development and Political Legitimacy." *American Political Science Review* 53(1): 69–105.

———. 1960. *Political Man.* London: Heinemann.

———. 1994. "The Social Requisites of Democracy Revisited." *American Sociological Review* 59(1): 1–22.

Llanos, M., and L. Marsteintredet, eds. 2010. *Presidential Breakdowns in Latin America: Causes and Outcomes of Executive Instability in Developing Democracies.* London: Palgrave Macmillan.

Loayza, Norman, Luis Servén, and Naotaka Sugawara. 2009. "Informality in Latin America and the Caribbean." Bank Policy Research Working Paper Series. Washington, DC: World Bank.

López-Alves, Fernando. 2000. *State Formation and Democracy in Latin America, 1810–1900.* Durham: Duke University Press.

López Maya, Margarita. 2011. "Venezuela: Hugo Chávez and the Popular Left." In *The Resurgence of the Latin American Left,* edited by Steven Levitsky and Kenneth M. Roberts. Baltimore: Johns Hopkins University Press.

Los Angeles Times. 2013. "Mayor Who Spoke Out Against Cartels Found Dead." November 19.

———. 2014. "Dancer's Death in Rio Triggers Clashes Between Police, Residents." April 23.

Loveman, Brian. 1993. *The Constitution of Tyranny: Regimes of Exception in Spanish America.* Pittsburgh: University of Pittsburgh Press.

Lucero, José Antonio. 2013. "Ambivalent Multiculturalisms: Perversity, Futility and Jeopardy in Latin America." In *Latin America's Multicultural Movements: The Struggle Between Communitarianism, Autonomy and Human Rights,* edited by Todd A. Eisenstadt, Michael S. Danielson, Moisés Jaime Ballón Corres, and Carlos Sorroza Palo, 18–39. Oxford: Oxford University Press.

Luna, Juan Pablo. 2010. "Segmented Party-Voter Linkages in Latin America: The Case of the UDI." *Journal of Latin American Studies* 42(2): 325–356.

Luna, Juan Pablo, and David Altman. 2011. "Uprooted but Stable: Chilean Parties and the Concept of Party System Institutionalization." *Latin American Politics and Society* 53(2): 1–28.

Luna, Juan Pablo, and Cristóbal Rovira Kaltwasser, eds. 2014. *The Resilience of the Latin American Right.* Baltimore: Johns Hopkins University Press.

Lustig, Nora, Luis F. Lopez-Calva, and Eduardo Ortiz-Juarez. 2013. "Declining Inequality in Latin America in the 2000s: The Cases of Argentina, Brazil, and Mexico." *World Development* 44: 129–141.

Madrid, Raúl. 2008. "The Rise of Ethno-Populism in Latin America." *World Politics* 60(3): 475–508.

———. 2012. *The Rise of Ethnic Politics in Latin America.* Cambridge: Cambridge University Press.

———. 2014. *The Rise of Ethnic Politics in Latin America,* 2nd ed. New York: Cambridge University Press.

Madrid, Raúl L., Wendy Hunter, and Kurt Weyland. 2010. "The Policies and Performance of the Contestatory and Moderate Left." In *Leftist Governments in Latin America: Successes and Shortcomings,* edited by Kurt Weyland, Raúl Madrid, and Wendy Hunter. New York: Cambridge University Press.

Madriz Sotillo, Jhannett. 2012. "Visibilización de la mujer en la República Bolivariana de Venezuela." *Derecho Electoral* [revista del *Tribunal Suprema de Elecciones*] 13: 318–335.

Mainwaring, Scott P. 1999. *Rethinking Party Systems in the Third Wave of Democracy: The Case of Brazil.* Stanford: Stanford University Press.

Mainwaring, Scott, and Anibal Pérez-Liñán. 2003. "Level of Development and Democracy: Latin-American Exceptionalism, 1945–1966." *Comparative Political Studies* 36(9): 1031–1067.

————. 2013. *Democracy and Dictatorships in Latin America: Emergence, Survival, and Fall.* Cambridge: Cambridge University Press.

Mainwaring, Scott, and Timothy R. Scully. 2008. "Latin America: Eight Lessons for Governance." *Journal of Democracy* 19(3): 113–127.

Malamud, Carlos. 2015. "El 'fuera Correa, fuera' y la institucionalidad de Ecuador." *Infolatam.* www.infolatam.com/2015/08/03/el-fuera-correa-fuera-y -la-institucionalidad-de-ecuador/.

Malamud, Carlos, and Eduardo Posado-Carbó, eds. 2005. *The Financing of Politics: Latin American and European Perspectives.* London: Institute for the Study of the Americas.

Malone, Mary Fran R. 2010. "Does Crime Undermine Public Support for Democracy? Evidence from Central America and Mexico." Paper presented at the annual meeting of the American Political Science Association, Washington, DC, September 2–5.

Mancini, Paolo, and David L. Swanson. 1996. "Politics, Media, and Modern Democracy: An Introduction." In *Politics, Media, and Modern Democracy: An International Study of Innovations in Electoral Campaigning and Their Consequences,* edited by Paolo Mancini and David Swanson, 1–26. Westport, CT: Praeger.

Mansbridge, Jane. 1996. "Reconstructing Democracy." In *Revisioning the Political: Feminist Reconstructions of Traditional Concepts in Western Political Theory,* edited by Nancy Hirschmann and Christine de Stefano, 119–127. Boulder, CO: Westview Press.

Mantilla Falcón, Julissa. 2009. "Gender and Human Rights: Lessons from the Peruvian Truth and Reconciliation Commission." In *Feminist Agendas and Democracy in Latin America,* edited by Jane S. Jaquette, 129–144. Durham, NC: Duke University Press.

Manzetti, Luigi. 2014. "Accountability and Corruption in Argentina During the Kirchners' Era." *Latin American Research Review* 49(2): 193.

March, James G., and Johan P. Olsen. 1984. "The New Institutionalism: Organizational Factors in Political Life." *American Political Science Review* 78(3): 738.

Marimán, Pablo, and José Aylwin. 2008. "Las identidades territoriales mapuche y el Estado chileno: Conflicto interétnico en un contexto de globalización." In *Gobernar (en) la diversidad: Experiencias indígenas desde América Latina: Hacia la investigación co-labor,* edited by Xochitl Leyva, Araceli Burguete, and Shannon Speed, 111–150. CIESAS-Mexico City: CIESAS and Editorial Miguel Angel Porrúa.

Marsteintredet, Leiv, and Einar Berntzen. 2008. "Reducing the Perils of Presidentialism in Latin America Through Presidential Interruptions." *Comparative Politics* 41(1): 83–101.

Martínez-Gallardo, Cecilia, and Petra Schleiter. 2014. "Choosing Whom to Trust: Agency Risks and Cabinet Partisanship in Presidential Democracies." *Comparative Political Studies* 48(2): 231–264.

Marx, Jutta, Jutta Borner, and Mariana Caminotti. 2007. *Las legisladoras: Cupos de género y política en Argentina y Brasil* [Women legislators: Gender quotas and politics in Argentina and Brazil]. Buenos Aires: Siglo XXI.

Mazzuca, Sebastián L. 2010. "Access to Power Versus Exercise of Power: Reconceptualizing the Quality of Democracy in Latin America." *Studies in Comparative International Development* 45(3): 334–357.

————. 2013. "Lessons from Latin America: The Rise of Rentier Populism." *Journal of Democracy* 24(2): 108–122.

McMenamin, Iain. 2012. "If Money Talks, What Does It Say? Varieties of Capitalism and Business Financing of Parties." *World Politics* 64(1): 1–38.

Mejía Acosta, Andrés. 2006. "Crafting Legislative Ghost Coalitions in Ecuador: Informal Institutions and Economic Reform in an Unlikely Case." In *Informal Institutions and Democracy: Lessons from Latin America*, edited by Gretchen Helmke and Steven Levitsky. Baltimore: Johns Hopkins University Press.

Meltzer, Allan H., and Scott F. Richard. 1981. "A Rational Theory of the Size of Government." *Journal of Political Economy* 89(5): 914–927.

Menchú, Rigoberta. 1984. *I, Rigoberta Menchú: An Indian Woman in Guatemala*. New York: Verso.

Mendoza, Breny. 2014a. *Ensayos de crítica feminista en nuestra América*. Mexico City: Editorial Herder.

———. 2014b. "Coloniality of Gender and Power: From Postcoloniality to Decoloniality." In *The Oxford Handbook of Feminist Theory*, edited by Lisa Disch and Mary Hawkesworth. Oxford: Oxford University Press.

Merino, Mauricio. 2013. "The Second Democratic Transition in Mexico: Efforts, Obstacles and Challenges to Mexico in the Quest for a Comprehensive, Coordinated Form of Accountability." Washington, DC: Mexico Institute, Woodrow Wilson Center.

Merkel, Wolfgang. 1999. "Defective Democracies." Working Paper No. 132. Madrid: Institute Juan March.

Mexico. 2011. "Presidencia de la República." *Quinto informe de gobierno, anexo estadístico,* 127–128. September 1.

———. 2013. Presidencia de la República. "Primer informe de gobierno, anexo estadístico." September 1, 366.

———. 2014a. Tribunal Electoral del Poder Judicial de la Federación (Mexico). "Tésis IV." Mexico City. August 2.

———. 2014b. Tribunal Electoral del Poder Judicial de la Federación (Mexico). "Tésis VIII." Mexico City. March 26.

———. 2014c. Gobierno del Distrito Federal (Ciudad de México). "Decreto por el que se reforman diversas disposiciones de la Ley Orgánica de la Administración Pública del Distrito Federal." Gaceta Oficial Distrito Federal No. 1839. Mexico City, April 15.

Mezrahi, Yemile. 2003. *From Martyrdom to Power: The Partido Acción Nacional in Mexico*. Notre Dame, IN: University of Notre Dame Press.

Michels, Robert. 1959. *Political Parties: A Sociological Study of the Oligarchical Tendencies of Modern Democracy*. New York: Dover.

Middlebrook, Kevin J. 2000. In *Conservative Parties, the Right, and Democracy in Latin America*, edited by Kevin J. Middlebrook. Baltimore: Johns Hopkins University Press.

Miguel, Luis Felipe. 2012. "Policy Priorities and Women's Double Bind in Brazil." In *The Impact of Gender Quotas,* edited by Susan Franceschet, Mona Lena Krook, and Jennifer M. Piscopo. New York: Oxford University Press.

Milesi-Ferretti, Gian Maria, Roberto Perotti, and Massimo Rostagno. 2002. "Electoral Systems and Public Spending." *Quarterly Journal of Economics* 117(2): 609–657.

Miller, Francesca. 1991. *Latin American Women and the Search for Social Justice*. Hanover, NH: University Press of New England.

Miroff, Nick. 2014. "Ecuador's Popular, Powerful President Rafael Correa Is a Study in Contradictions." *Washington Post,* March 15. www.washingtonpost.com/world/ecuadors-popular-powerful-president-rafael-correa-is-a-study-in-contradictions/2014/03/15/452111fc-3eaa-401b-b2c8-cc4e85fccb40_story.html.

Molina, José E., Janeth Hernández Márquez, Ángel E. Álvarez, Margarita López Maya, Henry Vaivads, and Valia Pereira Almao. 2001. "Venezuela." In *Partidos Políticos de América Latina: Países Andinos,* edited by Manuel Alcántara Sáez and Flavia Freidenberg. Salamanca: Ediciones Universidad de Salamanca.

Molyneux, Maxine. 2000. "Gender and Twentieth Century State Formation in Latin America." In *Hidden Histories of Gender and the State in Latin America,* edited by Elizabeth Dore and Maxine Molyneux. Durham: Duke University Press.

———. 2003. *Women's Movements in International Perspective: Latin America and Beyond.* London: Institute for Latin American Studies.

———. 2006. "Mothers at the Service of the New Poverty Agenda: Progresa/Oportunidades, Mexico's Conditional Transfer Programme." *Social and Policy Administration* 40(4): 425–449.

Montenegro, Germán. 2013. "Mas vale pájaro en mano que cien volando." In *Organización de la Defensa y Control Civil de las Fuerzas Armadas en América Latina,* edited by David Pion-Berlin and José Manuel Ugarte, 210. Buenos Aires: Jorge Baudino Ediciones.

Moreno, E., B. Crisp, and M. Shugart. 2003. "The Accountability Deficit in Latin America." In *Democratic Accountability in Latin America,* edited by Scott Mainwaring and Christopher Welna. New York: Oxford University Press.

Morgan, Jana, and Rosario Espinal. 2010. *Political Culture of Democracy in the Dominican Republic 2010.* Nashville: Vanderbilt University.

Morley, Samuel A., Roberto Machado, and Stefano Pettinato. 1999. *Indexes of Structural Reform in Latin America.* Santiago, Chile: ECLAC.

Mosca, Gaetano. 1939. *The Ruling Class.* New York: McGraw-Hill.

Munck, Gerardo L. 2009. *Measuring Democracy: A Bridge Between Scholarship and Politics.* Baltimore: Johns Hopkins University Press.

Muñoz Ramírez, Gloria. 2003. *EZLN 20 y 10: El fuego y la palabra.* Mexico City: La Jornada Ediciones.

Murillo, María Victoria, Virginia Oliveros, and Milan Vaishnav. 2009. "Voting for the Left or Governing on the Left?" In *Latin America's Left Turn,* edited by Steven Levitsky and Kenneth Roberts. Cambridge: Cambridge University Press.

———. 2010. *Dataset on Political Ideology of Presidents and Parties in Latin America.* New York: Columbia University Press.

Murillo, Por Álvaro. 2014. "Diputadas impulsan proyectos de ley para garantizar paridad de sexo en el Congreso." *La Nación,* February 18.

Myrdal, Gunnar. 1944. *An American Dilemma: The Negro and Democracy.* New York: Harper Bros.

Nacif, Benito. 2012. "The Fall of the Dominant Presidency: Lawmaking Under Divided Government in Mexico." In *The Oxford Handbook of Mexican Politics,* edited by Roderic Ai Camp, 235–237. New York: Oxford University Press.

Negretto, Gabriel L. 2006. "Minority Presidents and Democratic Performance in Latin America." *Latin American Politics and Society* 48(3): 63–92.

———. 2014. *Making Constitutions.* Cambridge: Cambridge University Press.

Neto, Octavio Amorim. 2012. "Democracy, Civil-Military Relations, and Defense Policy in Brazil." Paper prepared for the annual meeting of the American Political Science Association, New Orleans, August 16–September 2.

———. 2014. "Democracy, Civil-Military Relations, and Defense Policy in Brazil." Paper prepared for the IX meeting of the Brazilian Political Science Association, Brasília, August 4–7.

Nicaragua. 2010. Presidente de la República. Decreto 29-2010 (June 16). La Gaceta, Diario Oficial No. 121. Managua. June 28.

Nolte, Detlef, and Almut Schilling-Vacaflor, eds. 2012. *New Constitutionalism in Latin America.* Farnham: Ashgate.

Norden, Deborah. 1996. *Military Rebellion in Argentina: Between Coups and Consolidation.* Lincoln: University of Nebraska Press.

North, Douglas, and Robert Thomas. 1973. *The Rise of the Western World.* New York: Cambridge University Press.

Notimex. 2014. "Buscan garantizar equidad de género en el Congreso de la Unión." April 22. www.20minutos.com.mx/noticia/b142110/buscan-garantizar equidad -de-genero-en-el-congreso-de-la-union/.

Nun, José. 2003. *Democracy: Government of the People or Government of the Politicians?* Lanham, MD: Rowman and Littlefield.

Nussbaum, Martha. 1999. *Women and Human Development: The Capabilities Approach.* New York: Cambridge University Press.

Oakeshott, Michael. 1977. *Rationalism in Politics and Other Essays.* London: Methuen.

O'Donnell, Guillermo. 1993a. *Transitions from Authoritarian Rule: Tentative Conclusions About Uncertain Democracies* Baltimore: Johns Hopkins University Press.

———. 1993b. "On the State, Democratization and Some Conceptual Problems (A Latin American View with Glances at Some Post-Communist Countries)." Kellogg Institute Working Paper No. 192. The Helen Kellogg Institute for International Studies Notre Dame, University of Notre Dame.

———. 1994. "Delegative Democracy." *Journal of Democracy* 5(1): 55–69.

———. 1996. "Poverty and Inequality in Latin America: Some Political Reflections." Kellogg Institute Working Paper No. 225.

———. 1998a. "Horizontal Accountability in New Democracies." *Journal of Democracy* 9(3): 112–126.

———. 1998b. "Polyarchies and the (Un)Rule of Law in Latin America." Kellogg Institute Working Paper No. 254.

———. 1999a. "Illusions About Consolidation." In *Counterpoints: Selected Essays on Authoritarianism and Democratization,* edited by Guillermo O'Donnell, 175–194. Notre Dame, IN: University of Notre Dame Press.

———. 1999b. "On the State, Democratization, and Some Conceptual Problems: A Latin American View with Glances at Some Post-Communist Countries." In *Counterpoints: Selected Essays on Authoritarianism and Democratization,* edited by Guillermo O'Donnell, 133–157. Notre Dame, IN: University of Notre Dame Press.

———. 1999c. "Horizontal Accountability in New Democracies." In *The Self-Restraining State: Power and Accountability in New Democracies,* edited by Andreas Schedler, Larry Diamond, and Marc F. Plattner. Boulder: Lynne Rienner.

———. 1999d. "Polyarchies and the (Un)Rule of Law in Latin America." In *The (Un)Rule of Law and the Underprivileged in Latin America,* edited by Juan E. Méndez, Guillermo O'Donnell, and Paulo Sérgio Pinheiro, 303–337. Notre Dame, IN: University of Notre Dame Press.

———. 2004. "The Quality of Democracy: Why the Rule of Law Matters." *Journal of Democracy* 15(4): 32–46.

———. 2007. *Dissonances: Democratic Critiques of Democracy.* Notre Dame: University of Notre Dame Press.

O'Donnell, Guillermo, Jorge Vargas Cullell, and Osvaldo Iazzetta, eds. 2004. *The Quality of Democracy Theory and Applications.* Notre Dame: University of Notre Dame Press.

O'Donnell, Guillermo and Philippe C. Schmitter. 1986. *Transitions from Authoritarian Rule: Tentative Conclusions about Uncertain Democracies* Baltimore: The Johns Hopkins University Press.

Okin, Susan M. 1999. "Is Multiculturalism Bad for Women?" In *Is Multiculturalism Bad for Women?* edited by Joshua Cohen, Matthew Howard, and Martha Nussbaum, 9–24. Princeton, NJ: Princeton University Press.

Olsen, Tricia D., Leigh A. Payne, and Andrew G. Reiter. 2010. *Transitional Justice in the Balance: Comparing Processes, Weighing Efficacy.* Washington, DC: United States Institute for Peace.

Otis, John, and Kejal Vyas. 2015. "Venezuela's Allies Break Oil Habit." *Wall Street Journal,* May 1. www.wsj.com/articles/venezuelas-allies-break-oil-habit -1430536886.

Pachamama Alliance. 2013. "Government of Ecuador Shuts Down Fundación Pachamama." December 4. www.pachamama.org/news/government-of -ecuador-shuts-down-fundacion-pachamama.

Pacto por México. 2013. "Pacto por Mexico, Acuerdos." www.pactopormexico.org. English version: http://mexcc.files.wordpress.com/2013/03/pacto-pormc 3a9xico.pdf.

Panama. 1999. República de Panama. Ley No. 4 de 1999. Panama City. January 29.

Panizza, Francisco. 2009. *Contemporary Latin America: Development and Democracy Beyond the Washington Consensus.* London: Zed Books.

Pareto, Vilfredo. 1991. *The Rise and Fall of Elites: An Application of Theoretical Sociology.* New Brunswick, NJ: Transaction.

Payne, L. 2000. *Uncivil Movements: The Armed Right Wing and Democracy in Latin America.* Baltimore: Johns Hopkins University Press.

Pereira, Carlos, Shane P. Singh, and Bernardo Mueller. 2011. "Political Institutions, Policymaking, and Policy Stability in Latin America." *Latin American Politics and Society* 53(1): 59–88.

Pérez-Liñán, Aníbal. 2007. *Presidential Impeachment and the New Political Instability in Latin America.* Cambridge: Cambridge University Press.

Persson, Torsten, Gerard Roland, and Guido Tabellini. 1997. "Separation of Powers and Political Accountability." *Quarterly Journal of Economics* 112(4): 1163−1202.

Peru. 2007. Congreso de la República de Peru. 2007. Ley No. 28983. Lima. March 12.

Philip, George, and Francisco Panizza. 2011. *The Triumph of Politics: The Return of the Left in Venezuela, Bolivia and Ecuador.* Cambridge, UK: Polity Press.

Picq, Manuela Lavinas. 2008. "Gender Within Ethnicity: Human Rights and Identity Politics in Ecuador." n *New Voices in the Study of Democracy in Latin America,* edited by Guillermo O'Donnell, Joseph Tulchin, and Augusto Varas, 273–307. Washington, DC: Woodrow Wilson International Center for Scholars.

Pion-Berlin, David. 2009. "Defense Organizations and Civil-Military Relations in Latin America." *Armed Forces and Society* 35(3): 562−586.

Pisarello, Gerardo. 2012. *Un largo Termidor: Historia y crítica del constitucionalismo antidemocrático.* Quito: Corte Constitucional para el Período de Transición.

Piscopo, Jennifer M. 2016. "Democracy as Gender Balance: The Shift from Quotas to Parity in Latin America." *Politics, Groups, and Identities* 4(2): 214–230.

Piscopo, Jennifer M., and Gwynn Thomas. 2016. "Challenging Gender Inequality Within the State: Policy Agencies and Quota Laws in Latin America." In *Women, Politics, and Democracy in Latin America,* edited by Tomáš Došek, Flavia Freidenberg, Mariana Caminotti, and Betilde Muñoz-Pogossian. New York: Palgrave Macmillan.

Plasser, Fritz, with Gunda Plasser. 2002. *Global Political Campaigning: A Worldwide Analysis of Campaign Professionals and Their Practices.* Westport, CT: Praeger.

"Platform for Action." 1995. *Women in Power and Decisionmaking Diagnosis.* September, Beijing. Available at www.un.org/womenwatch/daw/beijing/platform/decision.htm.

Poe, Steven C., and C. Neal Tate. 1994. "Repression of Human Rights to Personal Integrity in the 1980s: A Global Analysis." *American Political Science Review* 88(4): 853–872.

Poe, Steven C., C. Neal Tate, and Linda Camp Keith. 1999. "Repression of the Human Right to Personal Integrity Revisited: A Global Cross-National Study Covering the Years 1976–1993." *International Studies Quarterly* 43(2): 291–313.

Politzer, Patricia. 2011. *Bachelet en tierra de hombres.* Barcelona: Editorial Debate.

Postero, Nancy Grey. 2007. *Now We Are Citizens: Indigenous Politics in Postmulticultural Bolivia.* Stanford: Stanford University Press.

Przeworski, Adam. 1991. *Democracy and the Market: Political and Economic Reforms in Eastern Europe and Latin America.* New York: Cambridge University Press.

Przeworski, Adam, and Fernando Limongi. 1997. "Modernization: Theories and Facts." *World Politics* 49(2): 155–183.

Przeworski, Adam, Michael E. Alvarez, Jose Antonio Cheibub, and Fernando Limongi. 2000. *Democracy and Development: Political Institutions and Well-Being in the World, 1950–1990.* Cambridge: Cambridge University Press.

Putnam, Robert. 1993. *Making Democracy Work: Civic Traditions in Modern Italy.* Princeton, NJ: Princeton University Press.

Queirolo, Rosario. 2013. *The Success of the Left in Latin America: Untainted Parties, Market Reforms, and Voting Behavior.* Notre Dame, IN: University of Notre Dame Press.

Quispe Ponce, María Candelaria. 2014. "Cuotas electorales de género en Puno." *Los Andes,* November.

Radcliffe, Sarah A., Nina Laurie, and Robert Andolina. 2009. In *Indigenous Development in the Andes: Culture, Power, and Transnationalism,* edited by Robert Andolina, Nina Laurie, and Sarah A. Radcliffe, 195–222. Durham, NC: Duke University Press.

Raile, Eric D., Carlos Pereira, and Timothy J. Power. 2011. "The Executive Toolbox: Building Legislative Support in a Multiparty Presidential Regime." *Political Research Quarterly* 64(2): 323–334.

Randall, Vicky, and Georgina Waylen, eds. 1998. *Gender, Politics, and the State.* New York: Routledge.

Ratha, Dilip, and Ana Silwal. 2012. "Remittance Flows in 2011—An Update." Migration and Development Brief No. 18. Washington, DC: World Bank.

Rauch, James E., and Peter B. Evans. 2000. "Bureaucratic Structure and Bureaucratic Performance in Less Developed Countries." *Journal of Public Economics* 75(1): 49–71.

Ray, Sarah Jaquette. 2013. *The Ecological Other: Environmental Exclusion in American Culture.* Tucson: University of Arizona Press.

Rehfeld, Andrew. 2005. *The Concept of Constituency: Political Representation, Democratic Legitimacy, and Institutional Design.* Cambridge: Cambridge University Press.

Reiff, David. 1999. "The Precarious Triumph of Human Rights." *New York Times,*

August 8. www.nytimes.com/1999/08/08/magazine/the-precarious-triumph-of
-human-rights.html.

Relly, Jeannine E., and Celeste González de Bustamante. 2014. "Silencing Mexico:
A Study of Influences on Journalists in the Northern States." *International
Journal of Press/Politics* 19(1): 108–131.

Renique, Gerardo. 2013. "Peru: Humala Submits to the United States and the
Mining Industry." *NACLA Report on the Americas* 46(3): 12–17.

Report of the World Conference of the International Women's Year. 1975. Paragraphs
57–66. Mexico City, June 19–July 2. www.un.org/womenwatch
/daw/beijing/otherconferences/Mexico/Mexico%20conference%20report%20op
timized.pdf.

Rial, Juan. 1992. *Estructura legal de las fuerzas armadas del Uruguay: Un análisis
político.* Montevideo: Centro de Informaciones y Estudios del Uruguay (CIESU).

Rios Contreras, Viridiana. 2014. "The Role of Drug-Related Violence and Extortion
in Promoting Mexican Migration: Unexpected Consequences of a Drug War."
Latin American Research Review 49(3): 199–217.

Risse, Thomas, S. C. Ropp, and Kathryn Sikkink, eds. 1999. *The Power of Human
Rights: International Norms and Domestic Change.* Cambridge: Cambridge
University Press.

Roberts, Kenneth M. 1995. "Neoliberalism and the Transformation of Populism in
Latin America: The Peruvian Case." *World Politics* 48(1): 82–116.

———. 1998. *Deepening Democracy? The Modern Left and Social Movements in
Chile and Peru.* Stanford: Stanford University Press.

———. 2002. "Social Inequalities Without Class Cleavages: Party Systems and
Labor Movements in Latin America's Neoliberal Era." *Studies in Comparative
International Development* 36(4): 3–33.

———. 2003. "Social Correlates of Party System Demise and Populist Resurgence
in Venezuela." *Latin American Politics and Society* 45(3): 35–57.

———. 2006. "Do Parties Matter? Lessons from the Fujimori Experience." In *The
Fujimori Legacy: The Rise of Electoral Authoritarianism,* edited by Julio F.
Carrión. University Park: Pennsylvania State University Press.

———. 2007. "The Crisis of Labor Politics in Latin America: Parties and Labor
Movements During the Transition to Neoliberalism." *International Labor and
Working-Class History* 72(1): 116–133.

———. 2013. "Market Reform, Programmatic (De)Alignment and Party System
Stability in Latin America." *Comparative Political Studies* 46(11): 1422–1452.

———. 2015. *Changing Course: Party Systems in Latin America's Neoliberal Era.*
New York: Cambridge University Press.

Robledo, Marcos. 2013. "Más allá de las reformas de la defensa." In *Organización
de la Defensa y Control Civil de las Fuerzas Armadas en América Latina,* edited
by David Pion-Berlin and José Manuel Ugarte, 160–161. Buenos Aires: Jorge
Baudino Ediciones.

Rogers, Melissa. 2016. *The Politics of Place and the Limits to Redistribution.* New
York: Routledge.

Rogers, Tim. 2009. "Nicaragua's Newest Tycoon? 'Socialist' President Daniel
Ortega." *Christian Science Monitor,* October 14. www.csmonitor.com
/World/Americas/2009/1014/p06s01-woam.html.

———. 2011. "Venezuela's Chávez Bankrolled Nicaragua with $1.6 Billion Since
2007." *Christian Science Monitor,* April 7. www.csmonitor.com/World
/Americas/2011/0407/Venezuela-s-Chavez-bankrolled-Nicaragua-with-1.6
-billion-since-2007.

302   *References*

Roig-Franzia, Manuel. 2008. "Mexican Drug Cartels Making Audacious Pitch for Recruits." *Washington Post,* May 7.

Romer, Thomas. 1975. "Individual Welfare, Majority Voting, and the Properties of a Linear Income Tax." *Journal of Public Economics* 4(2): 163–185.

Romero, Simon, and Taylor Barnes. 2014. "Rio Grapples with Violence Against Police Officers as World Cup Nears. *New York Times,* May 30.

Rubio, Blanca V. 1987. *Resistencia Campesina y Explotación Rural en Mexico.* Mexico City: Ediciones Era.

Russo, José Luis, and Felisa Ceña, Delgado. 2000. "Evolución de la convergencia y disparidades provinciales en Argentina." *Revista de Estudios Regionales* 57: 151–173.

Rustow, Dankwart. 1970. "Democratic Transition: Toward a Dynamic Model." *Comparative Politics* 2(3): 337–363.

Sagot, Montserrat. 2010. "Does the Political Participation of Women Matter? Democratic Representation, Affirmative Action, and Quotas in Costa Rica." *IDS Bulletin* 41(5): 25–34.

Saint-Pierre, Hector. 2008. "Metodología para el análisis de los ministerios de defensa: El caso Brasil." Buenos Aires: RESDAL.

Salas Alfaro, Sergio Iván. 2001. "Costa Rica." In *Partidos Políticos de América Latina: Centroamérica, México, y República Dominicana,* edited by Manuel Alcántara Sáez and Flavia Freidenberg, 31–134. Mexico City: Fondo de Cultura Económica.

Samuels, David. 2001. "Money, Elections, and Democracy in Brazil." *Latin American Politics and Society* 43(2): 27–48.

———. 2002. "Progressive Ambition, Federalism, and Pork-Barreling in Brazil." In *Legislative Politics in Latin America,* edited by Scott Morgenstern and Benito Nacif. Cambridge: Cambridge University Press.

———. 2008. "Brazilian Democracy Under Lula and the PT." In *Constructing Democratic Governance in Latin America,* 3rd ed., edited by Jorge Domínguez and Michael J. Shifter, 152–176. Baltimore: Johns Hopkins University Press.

Samuels, David, and Richard Snyder. 2001. "The Value of a Vote: Malapportionment in Comparative Perspective." *British Journal of Political Science* 31(4): 651–671.

Sanchez, Omar. 2009. "Party Non-Systems: A Conceptual Innovation." *Party Politics* 15(4): 487–520.

Santiuste Cué, Salvador. 2001. "Nicaragua." In *Partidos Políticos de América Latina: Centroamérica, México, y República Dominicana,* edited by Manuel Alcántara Sáez and Flavia Freidenberg, 479–452. Salamanca: Ediciones Universidad de Salamanca.

Sawers, Larry. 1996. *The Other Argentina: The Interior and National Development.* Boulder, CO: Westview Press.

Saxonhouse, Arlene. 1985. *Women in the History of Political Thought: Ancient Greece to Machiavelli.* New York: Praeger.

Scarrow, Susan. 2007. "Political Finance in Comparative Perspective." *Annual Review of Political Science* 10: 193–210.

Scartascini, Carlos, Ernesto Stein, and Mariano Tommasi. 2009. "Political Institutions, Intertemporal Cooperation, and the Quality of Policies." Working Paper No. 676. Washington, DC: Inter-American Development Bank.

Schedler, Andreas. 2013. *The Politics of Uncertainty: Sustaining and Subverting Electoral Authoritarianism.* Oxford: Oxford University Press.

Schmidt, Gregory. 2011. "Gender Quotas in Peru: Origins, Interactions with Electoral

Rules, and Re-Election." In *Diffusion of Gender Quotas in Latin America and Beyond,* edited by Adriana Crocker, 98–113. New York: Peter Lang.

Schmitter, Philippe C., and Terry L. Karl. 1991. "What Democracy Is . . . and Is Not." *Journal of Democracy* 2(3): 75–88.

Schumpeter, Joseph. 1943. *Capitalism, Socialism, Democracy.* London: Allen and Unwin.

Schwindt-Bayer, Leslie. 2009. "Making Quotas Work: The Effect of Gender Quota Laws on the Election of Women." *Legislative Studies Quarterly* 24(1): 5–28.

———. 2010. *Political Power and Women's Representation in Latin America.* New York: Oxford University Press.

Seelke, Clare Ribando. 2013. *Supporting Criminal Justice Reform in Mexico, the U.S. Role.* Washington, DC: Congressional Research Service.

Segal, David. 2015. "Petrobras Oil Scandal Leaves Brazilians Lamenting a Lost Dream." *New York Times,* August 7. www.nytimes.com/2015/08/09/business /international/effects-of-petrobras-scandal-leave-brazilians-lamenting-a-lost -dream.html?_r=0.

Selee, Andrew. 2011. *Decentralization, Democratization, and Informal Power in Mexico.* University Park: Pennsylvania State University Press.

Seligson, Mitchell A., Amy Erica Smith, and Elizabeth J. Zechmeister, eds. 2012. *The Political Culture of Democracy in the Americas, 2012: Towards Equality of Opportunity.* Nashville: Latin American Public Opinion Project (LAPOP), Vanderbilt University.

The Sentencing Project. 2014. *Race and Punishment: Racial Perceptions of Crime and Support for Punitive Policies.* Washington, DC: The Sentencing Project.

Serra, Narcís. 2010. *The Military Transition: Democratic Reform of the Armed Forces.* Cambridge: Cambridge University Press.

Serrano, Alfonso. 2015. "Titanic Canal Project Divides Nicaragua." Al Jazeera America, April 6. http://projects.aljazeera.com/2015/04/nicaragua-canal/.

Shirk, David. 2011. *The Drug War in Mexico Confronting a Shared Threat.* New York: Council on Foreign Relations.

Shugart, Matthew Soberg, and John M. Carey, eds. 1992. *Presidents and Assemblies: Constitutional Design and Electoral Dynamics.* Cambridge: Cambridge University Press.

Shugart, Matthew, and Stephan Haggard. 2001. "Institutions and Public Policy in Presidential Systems." In *Presidents, Parliaments and Policies,* edited by Stephan Haggard and Matthew D. McCubbins, 73. Cambridge: Cambridge University Press.

Siavelis, Peter. 2006. "Accommodating Informal Institutions and Chilean Democracy." In *Informal Institutions and Democracy: Lessons from Latin America,* edited by Gretchen Helmke and Steven Levitsky. Baltimore: Johns Hopkins University Press.

Sieder, Rachel, ed. 2002. *Multiculturalism in Latin America: Indigenous Rights, Diversity and Democracy.* London: Palgrave Macmillan.

Sikkink, Kathryn. 2011. *The Justice Cascade.* New York: Norton.

Simmons, Beth. 2009. *Mobilizing for Human Rights: International Law in Domestic Politics.* Cambridge: Cambridge University Press.

Smith-Cannoy, Heather. 2012. *Insincere Commitments: Human Rights Treaties, Abusive States and Citizen Activism.* Washington, DC: Georgetown University Press.

Sohnen, Eleanor. 2012. "Paying for Crime: A Review of the Relationships Between Insecurity and Development in Mexico and Central America." Washington, DC:

Regional Migration Study Group, Woodrow Wilson Center for International Scholars.

Soifer, Hillel. 2006. "Authority over Distance: Explaining Variations in State Infrastructural Power in Latin America." PhD diss. Harvard University.

———. 2009. "The Sources of Infrastructural Power: Evidence from Nineteenth Century Chilean Education." *Latin American Research Review* 44(2): 58–80.

Solt, Frederick. 2009. "Standardizing the World Income Inequality Database." *Social Science Quarterly* 90(2): 231–242.

Speed, Shannon. 2008. *Rights in Rebellion: Indigenous Struggle for Human Rights in Chiapas.* Stanford: Stanford University Press.

Spiller, Pablo T., Ernesto Stein, and Mariano Tommasi. 2008. "Political Institutions, Policy-Making and Policy: An Introduction." In *Policy-Making in Latin America: How Politics Shapes Policies,* edited by Ernesto Stein and Pablo Spiller. Washington, DC: Inter-American Development Bank.

Stahler-Sholk, Richard. 2011. "Autonomía y economía política de resistencia en las Cañadas de Ocosingo." In *Luchas "muy otras": Zapatismo y autonomía en las comunidades indígenas de Chiapas,* edited by Bruno Baronnet, Mariana Mora Bayo, and Richard Stahler-Sholk, 409–445. Mexico City and San Cristóbal de Las Casas: Universidad Autónoma Metropolitana, UAM-Xochimilco CIESAS, and UNACH.

Stanig, Piero. 2014. "Regulation of Speech and Media Coverage of Corruption: An Empirical Analysis of the Mexican Press." *American Journal of Political Science* 59(1): 175–193.

Starr, Pamela. 2009. "PAN Mid-Term Election Loss Could Cripple Calderón." *Focal Point,* online newsletter of the Canadian Foundation for the Americas, April. http://www.focal.ca/pdf/focalpoint_april2009.pdf.

———. 2014. "Mexico's Problematic Reforms." *Current History* 113(760): 54.

Steinmo, Sven, Kathleen Thelen, and Frank Longstreth, eds. 1992. *Structuring Politics: Historical Institutionalism in Comparative Analysis.* Cambridge: Cambridge University Press.

Stepan, Alfred. 2004. "Toward a New Comparative Politics of Federalism, Multinationalism, and Democracy: Beyond Rikerian Federalism." In *Federalism and Democracy in Latin America,* edited by Edward Gibson, 29–84. Baltimore: Johns Hopkins University Press.

Stokes, Susan C. 2001. *Mandates and Democracy: Neoliberalism by Surprise in Latin America.* Cambridge: Cambridge University Press.

———. 2007. "Political Clientelism." In *The Oxford Handbook of Comparative Politics,* edited by Carles Boix and Susan C. Stokes. Oxford: Oxford University Press.

Stratmann, Thomas. 2005. "Some Talk: Money in Politics. A (Partial) Review of the Literature." *Public Choice* 124(1): 135–156.

Strøm, Kaare. 2006. "Parliamentary Design and Delegation." In *Delegation and Accountability in Parliamentary Democracies,* edited by Kaare Strøm, Wolfgang C. Müller, and Torbjörn Bergman. Oxford: Oxford University Press.

Subcomandante Marcos. 2003. *Chiapas: la Treceava Estela.* Chiapas, Mexico: Ediciones del Frente Zapatista de Liberación Nacional.

Sullivan, John P. 2014. "Mexican Cartel Op-Ed No. 7: Mexico: Crucible of State Change." *Small Wars Journal,* January 13.

Tate, Winifred. 2007. *Counting the Dead: The Culture and Politics of Human Rights Activism in Colombia.* Berkeley: University of California Press.

Tella, Rafael Di, and Ignacio Franceschelli. 2009. "Government Advertising and

Media Coverage of Corruption Scandals." National Bureau of Economic Research, Working Paper No. 15420, Cambridge, MA.

Thies, Cameron. 2005. "War, Rivalry and State Building in Latin America." *American Journal of Political Science* 48(1): 53–72.

Tilly, Charles. 1990. *Coercion, Capital and European States, AD 990–1990.* Cambridge: Cambridge University Press.

Tommasi, Mariano. 2011. "Latin America: How State Capacity Determines Policy Success." *Governance* 24(2): 199–203.

Touraine, Alain. 1989. *América Latina: Política y sociedad.* Madrid: Espasa-Calpe.

Towns, Ann. 2012. "Norms and Social Hierarchies: Understanding International Policy Diffusion 'From Below.'" *International Organization* 66(2): 179–209.

Trevizo, Dolores. 2011. *Rural Protest in the Making of Democracy in Mexico, 1968–2000.* University Park: Pennsylvania State University Press.

———. 2014. "Political Repression and the Struggles for Human Rights in Mexico: 1968–1990s." *Social Science History* 38(3–4): 483–511.

Tsebelis, George. 2002. *Veto Players: How Political Institutions Work.* Princeton: Princeton University Press.

Tucker, Duncan. 2013. "Mexico's New Level of Transparency." Al Jazeera, December 22.

Unger, Roberto Mangabeira. 1987. *False Necessity: Anti-Necessitarian Social Theory in the Service of Radical Democracy.* Cambridge: Cambridge University Press.

———. 1990. *A Alternativa Transformadora: Como Democratizar o Brasil.* Rio de Janeiro: Editora Guanabara Koogan.

———. 1998. *Democracy Realized: The Progressive Alternative.* London: Verso.

UNODC (United Nations Office on Drugs and Crime). 2013. *World Drug Report.* Vienna: United Nations Office on Drugs and Crime.

Uruguay. 1941a. Article 11 in Ley 10.050. "Ley Orgánica Militar." September 10.

———. 1941b. Article 16 in "Ley Orgánica Militar."

———. 2007. Article 12.5 in Ley No. 18.172. "Rendición de cuentas y balance de ejecución presupuestal, al ejercicio 2006." August. Contaduría General de la Nación.

———. 2010. Decreto 215/010. "Reglamento Orgánico-Funcional de la Administración Superior del Ministerio de Defensa Nacional." July 14. Ministerio de Defensa Nacional.

———. 2015. "Taller Pre-despiegue en OMP: Formación en Derechos Humanos y DIH." Dirección General de Política de Defensa. Ministerio de Defensa Nacional.

———. 1974. Article 76 in Ley 14.157. "Ley Orgánica de las fuerzas armadas."

Van Cott, Donna Lee. 2001. "Explaining Ethnic Autonomy Regimes in Latin America." *Studies in Comparative International Development* 35(4): 30–58.

———. 2003. "From Exclusion to Inclusion: Bolivia's 2002 Elections." *Journal of Latin American Studies* 35(4): 751–775.

———. 2005. *From Movements to Parties in Latin America: The Evolution of Ethnic Politics.* Cambridge: Cambridge University Press.

———. 2008. *Radical Democracy in the Andes.* Cambridge: Cambridge University Press.

Van der Haar, Gemma. 2001. *Gaining Ground: Land Reform and the Constitution of Community in the Tojolabal Highlands of Chiapas.* Amsterdam: Rosenberg.

Vargas Llosa, Mario. 2009. *Sables y Utopías: Visiones de América Latina.* Madrid: Aguilar.

Vargas Velásquez, Alejo. 2014. "The Profile of the Colombian Armed Forces: A Result of the Struggle Against Guerrillas, Drug-Trafficking and Terrorism." In *Debating Civil-Military Relations in Latin America,* edited by David R. Mares and Rafael Martínez. Brighton: Sussex Academic Press.

Wade, Peter. 2010. *Race and Ethnicity in Latin America,* 2nd ed. London: Pluto Press.

Waisbord, Silvio R. 1996. "Secular Politics: The Modernization of Argentine Electioneering." In *Politics, Media, and Modern Democracy: An International Study of Innovations in Electoral Campaigning and Their Consequences,* edited by David L. Swanson and Paolo Mancini. Westport, CT: Praeger.

Walker, Ignacio. 2013. *Democracy in Latin America: Between Hope and Despair.* Notre Dame: University of Notre Dame Press.

Walsh, Catherine. 2010. "Shifting the Geopolitics of Critical Knowledge: Decolonial Thought and Cultural Studies 'Others' in the Andes." In *Globalization and the Decolonial Option,* edited by Walter D. Mignolo and Arturo Escobar. New York: Routledge.

Warren, Kay B., and Jean E. Jackson. 2002. "Introduction." In *Indigenous Movements, Self-Representation, and the State in Latin America,* edited by Kay B. Warren and Jean E. Jackson, 1–46. Princeton: Princeton University Press.

Waylen, Georgina. 1994. "Women and Democratization: Conceptualizing Gender Relations in Transition Politics." *World Politics* 46(3): 327–354.

———. 2007. *Engendering Transitions: Women's Mobilization, Institutions, and Gender Outcomes.* New York: Oxford University Press.

Weber, Max. (1922) 1978. *Economy and Society: An Outline of Interpretive Sociology.* Berkeley: University of California Press.

Weffort, Francisco C. 1992. "New Democracies, Which Democracies?" Working Paper No. 198. Washington, DC: Latin American Program, Woodrow Wilson Center.

Weismantel, Mary J. 1998. *Food, Gender and Poverty in the Ecuadorian Andes.* Prospect Heights, IL: Waveland Press.

Weyland, Kurt. 1996. "Neopopulism and Neoliberalism in Latin America: Unexpected Affinities." *Studies in Comparative International Development* 31(3): 3–32.

———. 1999. "Populism in the Age of Neoliberalism." In *Populism in Latin America,* edited by Michael Conniff. Tuscaloosa: University of Alabama Press.

———. 2001. "Clarifying a Contested Concept: Populism in the Study of Latin American Politics." *Comparative Politics* 34(1): 1–22.

Whitehead, Laurence. 1992. "State Organization in Latin America Since 1930." In *Cambridge History of Latin America,* edited by Leslie Bethell, 3–98. Cambridge: Cambridge University Press.

———. 1994. "State Development in Latin America Since 1930." Vol. 6, Part 2 in *The Cambridge History of Latin America,* edited by Leslie Bethell. Cambridge: Cambridge University Press.

Wibbels, Erik, and Moises Arce. 2003. "Globalization, Taxation, and Burden-Shifting in Latin America." *International Organization* 57(1): 111–136.

Wiesehomeier, Nina, and David Doyle. 2014. "Profiling the Electorate: Ideology and Attitudes of Right-Wing Voters." In *The Resilience of the Latin American Right,* edited by Juan Pablo Luna and Cristóbal Rovira-Kaltwasser. Baltimore: Johns Hopkins University Press.

Wilkinson, Tracy. 2013a. "Mexico President Wins Key Party Vote on Reform of National Oil Company." *Los Angeles Times,* March 4.

———. 2013b. "After Return to Mexico, She Fights Crime, Runs Afoul of Law." *Los Angeles Times,* September 25.

———. 2014. "Exit of Guerrero State Governor Seen as Too Little in Mexico." *Los Angeles Times,* October 25.

Women Suffrage and Beyond: Confronting the Democratic Deficit. http://womensuffrage .org/?page_id=69.

Wood, Duncan. 2012. "A New Beginning for Mexican Oil." Washington, DC: Woodrow Wilson International Center for Scholars. www.wilsoncenter.org /publication/new-beginning-for-mexican-oil.

World Bank. 2006. "Decentralized Service Delivery for the Poor." Washington, DC: World Bank.

———. 2011. *Migration and Remittances Factbook,* 2nd ed. Washington, DC: World Bank.

World Justice Project. 2014. "Rule of Law Index 2014." March. www .worldjusticeproject.org/rule-of-law-index.

Xie, Selena, and Javier Corrales. 2010. "LGBT Rights in Ecuador's 2008 Constitution." In *The Politics of Sexuality in Latin America: A Reader on Lesbian, Gay, Bisexual, and Transgender Rights,* edited by Javier Corrales and Mario Pecheny. Pittsburgh: University of Pittsburgh Press.

Yashar, Deborah. 2005. *Contesting Citizenship in Latin America: The Rise of Indigenous Movements and the Postliberal Challenge.* Cambridge: Cambridge University Press.

Zakaria, Fareed. 1997. "The Rise of Illiberal Democracy." *Foreign Affairs* 76(6): 22–43.

Zanger, Sabine C. 2000. "A Global Analysis of the Effect of Regime Changes on Life Integrity Violations, 1977–1993." *Journal of Peace Research* 37(2): 217–233.

Zechmeister, Elizabeth. 2006. "What's Left and Who's Right? A Q-Method Study of Individual and Contextual Influences on the Meaning of Ideological Labels." *Political Behavior* 28(2): 151–173.

Zetterberg, Pär. 2008. "The Downside of Gender Quotas? Institutional Constraints on Women in Mexican State Legislatures." *Parliamentary Affairs* 61(3): 442–460.

Zibechi, Raúl. 2012. "Colombia: Militarism and Social Movement." In *Territories in Resistance: A Cartography of Latin American Social Movements,* edited by Raúl Zibechi, 159–169. Oakland, CA: AK Press.

Zovatto, Daniel. 2001. "América Latina." In *Dinero y Contienda Político-Electoral: Reto de la Democracia,* edited by Manuel Carrillo, Alonso Lujambio, Carlos Navarro, and Daniel Zovatto, 33–45. Mexico City: Fondo de Cultura Económica.

Zylberberg Panebianco, Violeta. 2006. "We Can No Longer Be Like Hens with Our Heads Bowed, We Must Raise Our Heads and Look Ahead: A Consideration of the Daily Life of Zapatista Women." In *Dissident Women: Gender and Cultural Politics in Chiapas,* edited by Shannon Speed, Rosalva Aída Hernández Castillo, and Lynn Stephen, 222–237. Austin: University of Texas Press.

The Contributors

Will Barndt is assistant professor of political studies at Pitzer College in Claremont, California.

Roderic Ai Camp is Philip McKenna Professor of the Pacific Rim at Claremont McKenna College.

Javier Corrales is Dwight W. Morrow 1895 Professor of Political Science at Amherst College.

David Doyle is associate professor of comparative politics in the Department of Politics and International Relations at the University of Oxford, where he is also a fellow of St. Hugh's College and a fellow of the Latin American Centre.

Joe Foweraker is emeritus fellow and professor of Latin American politics at St. Antony's College, University of Oxford, and also honorary professor at the University of Exeter.

Neil Harvey is professor in the Department of Government at New Mexico State University.

Jane S. Jaquette is emeritus professor of politics and of diplomacy and world affairs at Occidental College.

Todd Landman is professor of political science and pro vice chancellor of the Faculty of Social Sciences at the University of Nottingham.

Gerardo L. Munck is professor in the School of International Relations at the University of Southern California.

David Pion-Berlin is professor of political science at the University of California, Riverside.

Jennifer M. Piscopo is assistant professor of politics at Occidental College.

Melissa Ziegler Rogers is assistant professor in the Department of Politics and Policy at Claremont Graduate University.

Dolores Trevizo is professor of sociology at Occidental College.

Index

Abortion, 129

Accountability, 1, 31n14; corporate interests and, 7, 8, 262; democracy and, 19–20; ethnic parties and, 198; horizontal, 10, 20, 31n18, 127, 263; human rights and, 134–135; journalists and, 231; oligarchy and, 7, 8, 23, 31n19; participatory democracy and, 119–120; populism and, 26; public policy and, 8; rule of law and, 261; vertical, 20, 119–120, 127, 198; of Zapatistas, 203–204

Achievement possibilities frontier (APF), 142

African Americans: equality of, 182; identity politics of, 181

Agency loss, 34, 38

Alemán, Arnoldo, 98n, 121

Alfonsín, Raúl, 79–80

ALN. See Nicaraguan Liberal Alliance

Alternation, 109

An American Dilemma (Myrdal), 181

Andean societies, 173–174

Antineoliberalism protests, 105

APF. See Achievement possibilities frontier

Argentina: Alfonsín as president of, 79, 80; free-market protests in, 97; gender quota laws in, 149, 153; Kirchner, Cristina, as president of, 2, 90, 109; Kirchner, Néstor, as president of, 2, 80, 90; Menem as president of, 27, 80; Perón as president of, 79

Argentine Defense Ministry, 90; Defense Law and, 80–81; Defense

ministers of, 79, 80, 81; funding of, 81–82; structure of, 79

Aristotle, 29n2; politeia defined by, 32n32

Assembly for the Sovereignty of the Peoples (ASP), 193

Authoritarianism, 137, 138; electoral weakness from, 262

Autonomy: of indigenous communities, 179–180, 189, 268; military, 6; Zapatistas and, 13, 177–178, 198–199

Bachelet, Michelle, 135

Beetham, David, 242

Beijing Platform for Action (1995), 151–152

Berkman, Heather, 43

Bicameralism, 64

Black power movement, 181

Bobbio, Norberto, 110, 112n3

Bolivarian revolution, 146

Bolivia, 2, 118tab; free-market protests in, 97; indigenous communities and, 172; Law on Popular Participation in, 193; majority-female lower house in, 166; March for Territory and Dignity in, 189–190; MAS in, 193; MIP in, 195; Morales as president of, 2, 27, 109, 113n11; neoextractivism in, 122–127; parity in, 165; Supreme Decree 2366 in, 126; TIPNIS in, 126–127; water and gas wars in, 185n13

Boutros, Victor, 182–183

Brazil: brown areas and, 35–36; coalition

311

About the Book

Why is there so much discontent with democracy across Latin America? Are regimes being judged by unrealistic standards of success—or is there legitimate cause for criticism in light of widespread failures to deliver either transparency or effective public policies? Addressing these questions across a variety of dimensions, the authors explore the diverse ways in which the specific nature of Latin American democracy explains the current performance of the region's democratic governments.

Joe Foweraker is honorary professor of politics at the University of Exeter, as well as emeritus fellow of St Antony's College at the University of Oxford, where he previously was professor of Latin American politics. **Dolores Trevizo** is professor of sociology at Occidental College. She is author of *Rural Protest and the Making of Democracy in Mexico, 1968–2000*.